50% OFF Online Social Work ASWB Clinical Prep Course!

Dear Customer,

We consider it an honor and a privilege that you chose our LCSW Study Guide. As a way of showing our appreciation and to help us better serve you, we have partnered with Mometrix Test Preparation to offer you **50% off their online Social Work ASWB Clinical Prep Course**. Many LCSW courses are needlessly expensive and don't deliver enough value. With their course, you get access to the best LCSW prep material, and **you only pay half price**.

Mometrix has structured their online course to perfectly complement your printed study guide. The LCSW Prep Course contains **in-depth lessons** that cover all the most important topics, **30+ video reviews** that explain difficult concepts, **over 1,000 practice questions** to ensure you feel prepared, and more than **400 digital flashcards**, so you can study while you're on the go.

Online NCE Prep Course

Topics Covered:	*Course Features:*
• Human Development, Diversity, and Behavior in the Environment	• LCSW Study Guide o Get content that complements our best-selling study guide.
• Assessment, Diagnosis, and Treatment Planning	• Full-Length Practice Tests o With over 1,000 practice questions, you can test yourself again and again.
• Psychotherapy, Clinical Interventions, and Case Management	• Mobile Friendly o If you need to study on the go, the course is easily accessible from your mobile device.
• Professional Values and Ethics	• LCSW Flashcards o Their course includes a flashcard mode with over 400 content cards to help you study.

To receive this discount, visit www.mometrix.com/university/aswbc or scan the QR code with your phone. At the checkout page, enter the discount code: **LCSW50TPB**

If you have any questions or concerns, please contact Mometrix at support@mometrix.com.

Sincerely,

 in partnership with

FREE Test Taking Tips Video/DVD Offer

To better serve you, we created videos covering test taking tips that we want to give you for FREE. **These videos cover world-class tips that will help you succeed on your test.**

We just ask that you send us feedback about this product. Please let us know what you thought about it—whether good, bad, or indifferent.

To get your **FREE videos**, you can use the QR code below or email freevideos@studyguideteam.com with "Free Videos" in the subject line and the following information in the body of the email:

    a. The title of your product

    b. Your product rating on a scale of 1-5, with 5 being the highest

    c. Your feedback about the product

If you have any questions or concerns, please don't hesitate to contact us at info@studyguideteam.com.

Thank you!

LCSW Study Guide 2024-2025

3 Practice Tests and ASWB Clinical Exam Prep
for Social Work Licensing
[5th Edition]

Lydia Morrison

Interested in buying more than 10 copies of our product? Contact us about bulk discounts:
bulkorders@studyguideteam.com

ISBN 13: 9781637759462

Table of Contents

Welcome

Dear Reader,

Welcome to your new Test Prep Books study guide! We are pleased that you chose us to help you prepare for your exam. There are many study options to choose from, and we appreciate you choosing us. Studying can be a daunting task, but we have designed a smart, effective study guide to help prepare you for what lies ahead.

Whether you're a parent helping your child learn and grow, a high school student working hard to get into your dream college, or a nursing student studying for a complex exam, we want to help give you the tools you need to succeed. We hope this study guide gives you the skills and the confidence to thrive, and we can't thank you enough for allowing us to be part of your journey.

In an effort to continue to improve our products, we welcome feedback from our customers. We look forward to hearing from you. Suggestions, success stories, and criticisms can all be communicated by emailing us at info@studyguideteam.com.

Sincerely,
Test Prep Books Team

FREE Videos/DVD OFFER

Doing well on your exam requires both knowing the test content and understanding how to use that knowledge to do well on the test. We offer completely FREE test taking tip videos. **These videos cover world-class tips that you can use to succeed on your test.**

To get your **FREE videos**, you can use the QR code below or email freevideos@studyguideteam.com with "Free Videos" in the subject line and the following information in the body of the email:

  a. The title of your product
  b. Your product rating on a scale of 1-5, with 5 being the highest
  c. Your feedback about the product

If you have any questions or concerns, please don't hesitate to contact us at info@studyguideteam.com.

1

Quick Overview

As you draw closer to taking your exam, effective preparation becomes more and more important. Thankfully, you have this study guide to help you get ready. Use this guide to help keep your studying on track and refer to it often.

This study guide contains several key sections that will help you be successful on your exam. The guide contains tips for what you should do the night before and the day of the test. Also included are test-taking tips. Knowing the right information is not always enough. Many well-prepared test takers struggle with exams. These tips will help equip you to accurately read, assess, and answer test questions.

A large part of the guide is devoted to showing you what content to expect on the exam and to helping you better understand that content. In this guide are practice test questions so that you can see how well you have grasped the content. Then, answer explanations are provided so that you can understand why you missed certain questions.

Don't try to cram the night before you take your exam. This is not a wise strategy for a few reasons. First, your retention of the information will be low. Your time would be better used by reviewing information you already know rather than trying to learn a lot of new information. Second, you will likely become stressed as you try to gain a large amount of knowledge in a short amount of time. Third, you will be depriving yourself of sleep. So be sure to go to bed at a reasonable time the night before. Being well-rested helps you focus and remain calm.

Be sure to eat a substantial breakfast the morning of the exam. If you are taking the exam in the afternoon, be sure to have a good lunch as well. Being hungry is distracting and can make it difficult to focus. You have hopefully spent lots of time preparing for the exam. Don't let an empty stomach get in the way of success!

When travelling to the testing center, leave earlier than needed. That way, you have a buffer in case you experience any delays. This will help you remain calm and will keep you from missing your appointment time at the testing center.

Be sure to pace yourself during the exam. Don't try to rush through the exam. There is no need to risk performing poorly on the exam just so you can leave the testing center early. Allow yourself to use all of the allotted time if needed.

Remain positive while taking the exam even if you feel like you are performing poorly. Thinking about the content you should have mastered will not help you perform better on the exam.

Once the exam is complete, take some time to relax. Even if you feel that you need to take the exam again, you will be well served by some down time before you begin studying again. It's often easier to convince yourself to study if you know that it will come with a reward!

Test-Taking Strategies

1. Predicting the Answer

When you feel confident in your preparation for a multiple-choice test, try predicting the answer before reading the answer choices. This is especially useful on questions that test objective factual knowledge. By predicting the answer before reading the available choices, you eliminate the possibility that you will be distracted or led astray by an incorrect answer choice. You will feel more confident in your selection if you read the question, predict the answer, and then find your prediction among the answer choices. After using this strategy, be sure to still read all of the answer choices carefully and completely. If you feel unprepared, you should not attempt to predict the answers. This would be a waste of time and an opportunity for your mind to wander in the wrong direction.

2. Reading the Whole Question

Too often, test takers scan a multiple-choice question, recognize a few familiar words, and immediately jump to the answer choices. Test authors are aware of this common impatience, and they will sometimes prey upon it. For instance, a test author might subtly turn the question into a negative, or he or she might redirect the focus of the question right at the end. The only way to avoid falling into these traps is to read the entirety of the question carefully before reading the answer choices.

3. Looking for Wrong Answers

Long and complicated multiple-choice questions can be intimidating. One way to simplify a difficult multiple-choice question is to eliminate all of the answer choices that are clearly wrong. In most sets of answers, there will be at least one selection that can be dismissed right away. If the test is administered on paper, the test taker could draw a line through it to indicate that it may be ignored; otherwise, the test taker will have to perform this operation mentally or on scratch paper. In either case, once the obviously incorrect answers have been eliminated, the remaining choices may be considered. Sometimes identifying the clearly wrong answers will give the test taker some information about the correct answer. For instance, if one of the remaining answer choices is a direct opposite of one of the eliminated answer choices, it may well be the correct answer. The opposite of obviously wrong is obviously right! Of course, this is not always the case. Some answers are obviously incorrect simply because they are irrelevant to the question being asked. Still, identifying and eliminating some incorrect answer choices is a good way to simplify a multiple-choice question.

4. Don't Overanalyze

Anxious test takers often overanalyze questions. When you are nervous, your brain will often run wild, causing you to make associations and discover clues that don't actually exist. If you feel that this may be a problem for you, do whatever you can to slow down during the test. Try taking a deep breath or counting to ten. As you read and consider the question, restrict yourself to the particular words used by the author. Avoid thought tangents about what the author *really* meant, or what he or she was *trying* to say. The only things that matter on a multiple-choice test are the words that are actually in the question. You must avoid reading too much into a multiple-choice question, or supposing that the writer meant something other than what he or she wrote.

5. No Need for Panic

It is wise to learn as many strategies as possible before taking a multiple-choice test, but it is likely that you will come across a few questions for which you simply don't know the answer. In this situation, avoid panicking. Because most multiple-choice tests include dozens of questions, the relative value of a single wrong answer is small. As much

3

as possible, you should compartmentalize each question on a multiple-choice test. In other words, you should not allow your feelings about one question to affect your success on the others. When you find a question that you either don't understand or don't know how to answer, just take a deep breath and do your best. Read the entire question slowly and carefully. Try rephrasing the question a couple of different ways. Then, read all of the answer choices carefully. After eliminating obviously wrong answers, make a selection and move on to the next question.

6. Confusing Answer Choices

When working on a difficult multiple-choice question, there may be a tendency to focus on the answer choices that are the easiest to understand. Many people, whether consciously or not, gravitate to the answer choices that require the least concentration, knowledge, and memory. This is a mistake. When you come across an answer choice that is confusing, you should give it extra attention. A question might be confusing because you do not know  the subject matter to which it refers. If this is the case, don't eliminate the answer before you have affirmatively settled on another. When you come across an answer choice of this type, set it aside as you look at the remaining choices. If you can confidently assert that one of the other choices is correct, you can leave the confusing answer aside. Otherwise, you will need to take a moment to try to better understand the confusing answer choice. Rephrasing is one way to tease out the sense of a confusing answer choice.

7. Your First Instinct

Many people struggle with multiple-choice tests because they overthink the questions. If you have studied sufficiently for the test, you should be prepared to trust your first instinct once you have carefully and completely read the question and all of the answer choices. There is a great deal of research suggesting that the mind can come to the correct conclusion very quickly once it has obtained all of the relevant information. At times, it may seem to you as if your intuition is working faster even than your reasoning mind. This may in fact be true. The knowledge you obtain while studying may be retrieved from your subconscious before you have a chance to work out the associations that support it. Verify your instinct by working out the reasons that it should be trusted.

8. Key Words

Many test takers struggle with multiple-choice questions because they have poor reading comprehension skills. Quickly reading and understanding a multiple-choice question requires a mixture of skill and experience. To help with this, try jotting down a few key words and phrases on a piece of scrap paper. Doing this concentrates the process of reading and forces the mind to weigh the relative importance of the question's parts. In selecting words and phrases to write down, the test taker thinks about the question more deeply and carefully. This is especially true for multiple-choice questions that are preceded by a long prompt.

4

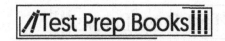

9. Subtle Negatives

One of the oldest tricks in the multiple-choice test writer's book is to subtly reverse the meaning of a question with a word like *not* or *except*. If you are not paying attention to each word in the question, you can easily be led astray by this trick. For instance, a common question format is, "Which of the following is...?" Obviously, if the question instead is, "Which of the following is not...?," then the answer will be quite different. Even worse, the test makers are aware of the potential for this mistake and will include one answer choice that would be correct if the question were not negated or reversed. A test taker who misses the reversal will find what he or she believes to be a correct answer and will be so confident that he or she will fail to reread the question and discover the original error. The only way to avoid this is to practice a wide variety of multiple-choice questions and to pay close attention to each and every word.

10. Reading Every Answer Choice

It may seem obvious, but you should always read every one of the answer choices! Too many test takers fall into the habit of scanning the question and assuming that they understand the question because they recognize a few key words. From there, they pick the first answer choice that answers the question they believe they have read. Test takers who read all of the answer choices might discover that one of the latter answer choices is actually *more* correct. Moreover, reading all of the answer choices can remind you of facts related to the question that can help you arrive at the correct answer. Sometimes, a misstatement or incorrect detail in one of the latter answer choices will trigger your memory of the subject and will enable you to find the right answer. Failing to read all of the answer choices is like not reading all of the items on a restaurant menu: you might miss out on the perfect choice.

11. Spot the Hedges

One of the keys to success on multiple-choice tests is paying close attention to every word. This is never truer than with words like *almost*, *most*, *some*, and *sometimes*. These words are called "hedges" because they indicate that a statement is not totally true or not true in every place and time. An absolute statement will contain no hedges, but

in many subjects, the answers are not always straightforward or absolute. There are always exceptions to the rules in these subjects. For this reason, you should favor those multiple-choice questions that contain hedging language. The presence of qualifying words indicates that the author is taking special care with his or her words, which is certainly important when composing the right answer. After all, there are many ways to be wrong, but there is only one way to be right! For this reason, it is wise to avoid answers that are absolute when taking a multiple-choice test. An absolute answer is one that says things are either all one way or all another. They often include words like *every*, *always*, *best*, and *never*. If you are taking a multiple-choice test in a subject that doesn't lend itself to absolute answers, be on your guard if you see any of these words.

12. Long Answers

In many subject areas, the answers are not simple. As already mentioned, the right answer often requires hedges. Another common feature of the answers to a complex or subjective question are qualifying clauses, which are groups of words that subtly modify the meaning of the sentence. If the question or answer choice describes a rule to which there are exceptions or the subject matter is complicated, ambiguous, or confusing, the correct answer will require many words in order to be expressed clearly and accurately. In essence, you should not be deterred by answer choices that seem excessively long. Oftentimes, the author of the text will not be able to write the correct answer without offering some qualifications and

modifications. Your job is to read the answer choices thoroughly and completely and to select the one that most accurately and precisely answers the question.

13. Restating to Understand

Sometimes, a question on a multiple-choice test is difficult not because of what it asks but because of how it is written. If this is the case, restate the question or answer choice in different words. This process serves a couple of important purposes. First, it forces you to concentrate on the core of the question. In order to rephrase the question accurately, you have to understand it well. Rephrasing the question will concentrate your mind on the key words and ideas. Second, it will present the information to your mind in a fresh way. This process may trigger your memory and render some useful scrap of information picked up while studying.

14. True Statements

Sometimes an answer choice will be true in itself, but it does not answer the question. This is one of the main reasons why it is essential to read the question carefully and completely before proceeding to the answer choices. Too often, test takers skip ahead to the answer choices and look for true statements. Having found one of these, they are content to select it without reference to the question above. The savvy test taker will always read the entire question before turning to the answer choices. Then, having settled on a correct answer choice, he or she will refer to the original question and ensure that the selected answer is relevant. The mistake of choosing a correct-but-irrelevant answer choice is especially common on questions related to specific pieces of objective knowledge.

15. No Patterns

One of the more dangerous ideas that circulates about multiple-choice tests is that the correct answers tend to fall into patterns. These erroneous ideas range from a belief that B and C are the most common right answers, to the idea that an unprepared test-taker should answer "A-B-A-C-A-D-A-B-A." It cannot be emphasized enough that pattern-seeking of this type is exactly the WRONG way to approach a multiple-choice test. To begin with, it is highly unlikely that the test maker will plot the correct answers according to some predetermined pattern. The questions are scrambled and delivered in a random order. Furthermore, even if the test maker was following a pattern in the assignation of correct answers, there is no reason why the test taker would know which pattern he or she was using. Any attempt to discern a pattern in the answer choices is a waste of time and a distraction from the real work of taking the test. A test taker would be much better served by extra preparation before the test than by reliance on a pattern in the answers.

Introduction to the ASWB Clinical Exam

Function of the Test

The ASWB Clinical Exam is one of five social work licensing exams given by the Association of Social Work Boards. The others are: Associate, Bachelors, Masters, and Advanced Generalist. Each is intended to determine entry-level proficiency for particular social work education and experience levels. These exams are utilized by the social work regulatory bodies throughout the United States and the Canadian provinces of Alberta and British Columbia, as one of the components to determine whether a social worker has the competency and knowledge to safely practice professionally. The total number of ASWB Clinical Exams attempted across all jurisdictions in 2016 was 13,958, with a pass rate of 78.2 percent.

There are several steps that need to be followed prior to registering for the ASWB Clinical Exam. It is first necessary to contact the social work regulatory board in the prospective test taker's region to request a license application. Once this is received, the application needs to be submitted to the appropriate social work board. The social work board will then alert the examinee with its approval to register for the ASWB Clinical examination.

Test Administration

The ASWB Clinical Exam is administered electronically by appointment at <u>Pearson Professional Centers</u>, with locations around the world. Registered candidates can arrange a day and time to take the test via <u>Pearson VUE's website</u>. There are no pre-scheduled dates for this exam. Examinees are given four hours to take the test, which is taken on a networked computer.

If an applicant receives a failing score, he or she must wait a period of ninety days prior to taking the exam again. Some regions place restrictions on the number of times a candidate may retake an ASWB examination. In order to take a retest, it is required to re-register and once again pay the examination fee in full.

Accommodations are available for candidates with disabilities. To make these arrangements, approval of the accommodation request must first be given by the appropriate social work board and ASWB. Most boards include the pertinent form in their application packet.

Some jurisdictions permit special arrangements for candidates for whom English is not a first language. It is necessary to contact the appropriate board to see whether such arrangements are permitted. ESL arrangements must be pre-approved by the board and ASWB prior to registering.

Test Format

Each ASWB Clinical test contains 170 selected response questions intended to gauge the candidate's proficiencies in the following clinical practice areas: Human Development, Diversity, and Behavior in the Environment; Assessment, Diagnosis, and Treatment Planning; Psychotherapy, Clinical Interventions, and Case Management; and Professional Values and Ethics

Questions are organized into content areas, competencies, knowledge, skills, and abilities statements (KSAs). Content areas gauge broad areas of topic proficiency. Competencies measure the knowledge, skills, and abilities within each subject area that is crucial to a social worker's job. The KSAs provide additional specifics about the exam content included in the competencies. Each KSA features a distinct knowledge element that may be tested anywhere in the exam and forms the foundation for the individual test questions.

Content Area	Percent of Test	Subtopics
Human Development, Diversity and Behavior in the Environment	24%	<ul><li>Human Growth and Development</li><li>Human Behavior in the Social Environment</li><li>Diversity and Discrimination</li></ul>
Assessment, Diagnosis, and Treatment Planning	30%	<ul><li>Biopsychosocial History and Collateral Data</li><li>Assessment and Diagnosis</li><li>Treatment Planning</li></ul>
Psychotherapy, Clinical Interventions, and Case Management	27%	<ul><li>Therapeutic Relationship</li><li>The Intervention Process</li><li>Service Delivery and Management of Cases</li><li>Consultation and Interdisciplinary Collaboration</li></ul>
Professional Values and Ethics	19%	<ul><li>Professional Values and Ethical Issues</li><li>Confidentiality</li><li>Professional Development and Use of Self</li></ul>

Scoring

Of the 170 test questions on the ASWB Clinical exam, only 150 are included in the score; the remaining twenty are sample pretest questions to determine whether they should be included in future exams. They are randomly spread throughout the examination.

Like the other ASWB social work licensing exams, the Clinical test is scored on a pass/fail basis. All jurisdictions utilizing the ASWB exams recognize the same pass point (number of questions a candidate must answer correctly in order to pass the exam), but this number can vary, depending on the exam version and category. Typically, pass points range from 93 to 107 correct questions out of the 150 that are scored.

Each score report outlines the number of questions correctly answered and the number needed to pass the version of the exam that was taken. Each jurisdiction has different ways of listing a passing score: it can be depicted as a 70, a 75, or a pass. The 70 used in one region and the 75 used in another, are both used to depict the same pass point. The exams are NOT easier or more difficult to pass in one state or province versus another. The methods are just two different ways to report the same outcome.

Recent/Future Developments

Starting in January 2016, California's Board of Behavioral Sciences (BBS) replaced the Clinical Vignette Exam with the ASWB Clinical Exam to issue clinical social work licenses. However, according to state regulations, candidates for social work licenses are still required to take a law and ethics exam (formerly the Standard Written Exam). As a result, it is now necessary for applicants in California to take both the ASWB Clinical Exam and the California Law and Ethics Exam. The state of California also now accepts transfers from candidates who received a passing score on the ASWB exam in the past. Therefore, candidates who are from other U.S. states may request California clinical social work licenses without going through the retesting process. Additionally, licensed California social workers receiving passing grades on the ASWB Clinical Exam can transfer test scores to other states where the exam is accepted.

Bonus Content

We host multiple bonus items online, including all three practice tests in digital format. Scan the QR code or go to this link to access this content:

testprepbooks.com/bonus/aswbclinical

The first time you access the page, you will need to register as a "new user" and verify your email address.

Study Prep Plan for the ASWB Clinical Exam

1 **Schedule -** Use one of our study schedules below or come up with one of your own.

2 **Relax -** Test anxiety can hurt even the best students. There are many ways to reduce stress. Find the one that works best for you.

3 **Execute -** Once you have a good plan in place, be sure to stick to it.

One Week Study Schedule		
Day 1	Human Development, Diversity, and Behav...	
Day 2	Assessment, Diagnosis, and Treatment...	
Day 3	Psychotherapy, Clinical Interventions, and...	
Day 4	Professional Values and Ethics	
Day 5	Practice Tests #1 & #2	
Day 6	Practice Test #3	
Day 7	Take Your Exam!	

Two Week Study Schedule			
Day 1	Human Development, Diversity, and Behav...	Day 8	Psychotherapy, Clinical Interventions, and...
Day 2	Sexual Development Throughout the Lifespan	Day 9	Service Delivery and Management of Cases
Day 3	Human Behavior in the Social Environment	Day 10	Professional Values and Ethics
Day 4	Co-Occurring Disorders and Conditions	Day 11	Practice Test #1
Day 5	Assessment, Diagnosis, and Treatment Planning	Day 12	Practice Test #2
Day 6	Assessing Motivation, Resistance, and...	Day 13	Practice Test #3
Day 7	Treatment Planning	Day 14	Take Your Exam!

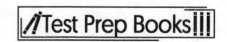

One Month Study Schedule							
Day 1	Human Development, Diversity, and Behav...	Day 11	Client's Danger to Self and Others	Day 21	Professional Values and Ethics
Day 2	Sexual Development Throughout the...	Day 12	Mental and Emotional Illness Throughout...	Day 22	Professional Development and Use of Self
Day 3	Factors Influencing Self-Image	Day 13	Treatment Planning	Day 23	Practice Questions
Day 4	Human Behavior in the Social Environment	Day 14	Practice Questions	Day 24	Practice Test #1
Day 5	Crisis Intervention Theories	Day 15	Psychotherapy, Clinical Interventions, and Case Management	Day 25	Answer Explanations
Day 6	Co-Occurring Disorders and...	Day 16	The Intervention Process	Day 26	Practice Test #2
Day 7	Diversity and Discrimination	Day 17	Psychoanalytic and Psychodynamic...	Day 27	Answer Explanations
Day 8	Practice Questions	Day 18	Service Delivery and Management of Cases	Day 28	Practice Test #3
Day 9	Assessment, Diagnosis, and Treatment Planning	Day 19	Consultation and Interdisciplinary Collaboration	Day 29	Answer Explanations
Day 10	Assessment and Diagnosis	Day 20	Practice Questions	Day 30	Take Your Exam!

Build your own prep plan by visiting:
testprepbooks.com/prep

11

As you study for your test, we'd like to take the opportunity to remind you that you are capable of great things! With the right tools and dedication, you truly can do anything you set your mind to. The fact that you are holding this book right now shows how committed you are. In case no one has told you lately, you've got this! Our intention behind including this coloring page is to give you the chance to take some time to engage your creative side when you need a little brain-break from studying. As a company, we want to encourage people like you to achieve their dreams by providing good quality study materials for the tests and certifications that improve careers and change lives. As individuals, many of us have taken such tests in our careers, and we know how challenging this process can be. While we can't come alongside you and cheer you on personally, we can offer you the space to recall your purpose, reconnect with your passion, and refresh your brain through an artistic practice. We wish you every success, and happy studying!

Human Development, Diversity, and Behavior in the Environment

Human Growth and Development

Human Development Throughout the Lifespan

There are a number of theories on human growth and development. The most important theories are addressed in this section.

<u>Freud's Model of Development</u>
Freud is known for his research on stages of human development and his assertion that there were five stages of psychosexual development:

Oral Stage (birth to 18 months)

- An infant's focus of gratification involves the mouth.
- The primary need is security.
- Security needs are met when caretakers provide baby with essentials, such as food, shelter, warmth, and cleanliness.

Anal Stage (18 months to age 3)

- A child's focus of gratification involves the anus and the bladder.
- These organs represent sensual satisfaction.
- Internal conflict arises when the child begins the process of toilet training.

Phallic Stage (age 3 to age 6)

- The child engages in exploration of their body with greater interest in genitals.
- Oedipus and Electra complexes may occur.
- There is a pseudo-sexual attraction to the parent of the opposite gender.
- Conflict arises when the child realizes he/she has failed to win control over the parents' bond with one another.

Latent Stage (age 6 to puberty)

- The child's sexual interests become subdued or dormant.
- Energy is focused on school, hobbies, athletics, and mastering social skills.

Genital stage (puberty until death)

- The teen becomes aware of physical changes and onset of sexual feelings.
- The individual is less egocentric and more compassionate.
- There's a motivation to seek relationships that are emotionally and sexually satisfying.
- Success in this stage lays groundwork for future relationships that are healthy and long lasting.

15

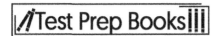

Erikson's Model of Development

Erikson devised eight stages of psychosocial development. He emphasized the importance of social context, asserting that family and environment are major contributors to child development.

Trust vs. Mistrust (birth to 18 months)

- The primary goal is to learn to trust others.
- Trust occurs when a caretaker appropriately responds to a need in a timely, caring manner.
- Mistrust occurs when caretakers fail to meet the infant's basic needs.

Autonomy vs. Shame and Doubt (18 months to age 3)

- The primary goal is the development of self-control without loss of self-esteem.
- The toddler develops cooperation and self-expression skills.
- Failure to reach this goal leads to defiance, anger, and social problems.

Initiative vs. Guilt (age 3 to age 6)

- Initiative means confidently devising a plan and following it through to completion.
- Guilt is generated by fear that actions taken will result in disapproval.
- Failure to achieve initiative can lead to anxiety and fearfulness in new situations.

Industry vs. Inferiority (age 6 to age 11)

- Industry refers to purposeful, meaningful behavior.
- Inferiority refers to having a sense of unworthiness or uselessness.
- The child focuses on learning skills, such as making friends and self-care activities—e.g., dressing or bathing.
- Failure in this stage could lead to negative social or academic performance and the lack of self-confidence.

Identity vs. Role Confusion (age 12 to age 18)

- This stage involves the desire to fit in and to figure out one's own unique identity.
- Self-assessment of sexual identity, talents, and vocational direction occurs.
- Role confusion is the result of juggling multiple physical changes, increased responsibility, academic demands, and a need to understand how one fits into the greater picture.

Intimacy vs. Isolation (age 18 to age 40)

- This stage pertains to an ability to take risks by entering the workforce, finding a long term relation, and possibly becoming a parent.
- Failure to navigate this stage leads to isolation, loneliness, and depression.

Generativity vs. Stagnation (age 40 to age 60)

- This stage involves developing stability in areas of finance, career, and relationships, as well as a sense that one is contributing something valuable to society.
- Failure to achieve these objectives leads to unhappiness with one's status and feeling unimportant.

Ego integrity vs. Despair (mid-sixties to death)

- Important life tasks, such as child rearing and career, are being completed.
- Reviewing and evaluating how one's life was spent occurs.

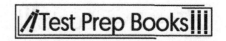

- Success in this stage provides a sense of fulfillment.
- Failure emerges if one is dissatisfied with accomplishments, which leads to depression or despair.

Piaget's Model of Development

Piaget is best known for his concept that children's minds are not just smaller versions of adult minds, but that they also grow and develop in different ways. His work has been influential within academic settings and has helped educators better determine what and how children can learn at various stages of their educational process. The

Erikson's Psychosocial Stages of Development

Stage	Age	Psychosocial Crisis	Basic Virtue
1	Infancy (0 to 1½)	Trust vs. mistrust	Hope
2	Early Childhood (1½ to 3)	Autonomy vs. shame	Will
3	Play Age (3 to 5)	Initiative vs. guilt	Purpose
4	School Age (5 to 12)	Industry vs. inferiority	Competency
5	Adolescence (12 to 18)	Ego identity vs. role confusion	Fidelity
6	Young Adult (18 to 40)	Intimacy vs. isolation	Love
7	Adult hood (40 to 65)	Generativity vs. stagnation	Care
8	Maturity (65+)	Ego integrity vs. despair	Wisdom

following are the key ideas related to his research into the way cognition develops in children:

- **Assimilation**: A process by which a person accepts and organizes information then incorporates new material into existing knowledge
- **Accommodation**: A process by which old ideas must be changed or replaced due to obtaining new information from the environment
- **Schemas**: A set of thoughts, ideas, or perceptions that fit together and are constantly challenged by gaining new information and creating change through knowledge

Piaget also recognized and defined the following *four stages of cognitive development*:

Stage 1: Sensorimotor Stage (birth to age 2)

- The infant becomes aware of being an entity separate from the environment.
- Object permanence occurs as the baby realizes that people or objects still exist, even if they are out of sight.
- Object permanence builds a sense of security as the baby learns that though mommy has left the room, she will still return.
- This reduces fear of abandonment and increases their confidence about the environment.

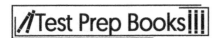
Stage 2: Pre-operational Stage (age 2 to age 7)

- The child moves from being barely verbal to using language to describe people, places, and things.
- The child remains egocentric and unable to clearly understand the viewpoint of others.

The process of quantifying and qualifying emerges, and the child can sort, categorize, and analyze in a rough, unpolished form.

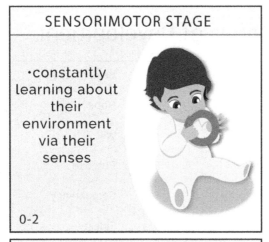
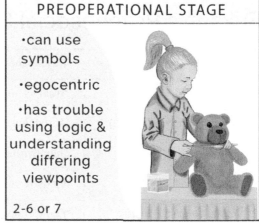
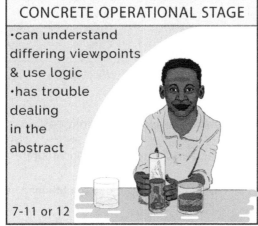

Stage 3: Concrete Operational Stage (age 7 to age 11)

- The ability to problem-solve and reach logical conclusions evolves.
- By age 10 or 11, children begin to doubt magical stories, such as the Tooth Fairy or the Easter Bunny.
- Previously-held beliefs are questioned.

Stage 4: Formal Operational Stage (age 12 through remaining lifetime)

- More complex processes can now be assimilated.
- Egocentrism diminishes.
- One assimilates and accommodates beliefs that others have needs and feelings too.
- New schemas are created.
- The individual seeks their niche in life in terms of talents, goals, and preferences.

Ivan Pavlov (Classical Conditioning)

Another important concept of development has to do with learning and the way in which humans learn new behaviors. A famous psychologist, **Ivan Pavlov**, conducted research with dogs that proved to be ground-breaking in the field of classical conditioning. In his experiment, a ringing bell was paired with the presentation of food, which produced salivation in the dog. The ringing sound eventually produced salivation from the dog even in the absence of food. Salivation then became the conditioned response to hearing a bell, and thus, the theory of classical conditioning was developed. The important finding of this research is that we learn by association.

B.F. Skinner (Operant Conditioning)

Skinner also did important research in the field of learning, specifically operant conditioning. **Operant conditioning theory** focuses on behavioral changes that can be seen or measured. The basic concept is that behavior that is reinforced will increase and behavior that is punished will decrease. There are several key concepts integral to an understanding of this form of learning:

- **Positive Reinforcement**: Anything that serves as a form of reward, including food, money, praise, or attention
- **Negative reinforcement**: An unpleasant stimulus that is removed when behavior is elicited, such as a man finally cutting the grass to stop his wife from nagging him about it
- **Punishment**: An unpleasant response from the environment—e.g., a slap, an unkind word, or a speeding ticket—that when encountered, increases the likelihood that a behavior will cease. Two problems arise with using punishment. Once the negative stimulus is removed, the behavior is likely to continue. Punishment can also cause humiliation, anger, resentment, and aggression.
- **Superstition**: An incorrect perception that one stimulus is connected to another. Skinner found that when teaching a rat to press a lever for food, if the rat chases its tail before pressing the lever, it will mistakenly believe that the tail chase is required and will do both behaviors each time it wants food.
- **Shaping**: The process of changing behavior gradually by rewarding approximations of the desired behavior, e.g., first rewarding a rat for moving closer to the lever

Skinner found that there are different schedules of reinforcement and that some work better than others. These include the following:

- **Continuous rate**: Person or animal is rewarded every time a behavior is demonstrated
- **Fixed ratio**: Reward is given after a fixed number of attempts
- **Variable ratio**: Reward is forthcoming at unpredictable rates, like a slot machine
- **Fixed interval**: Reward is given only after a specific amount of time has passed
- **Variable interval**: Reward is given after an unpredictable amount of time has passed
- **Extinction**: Occurs when a behavior disappears or is extinguished because it is no longer being reinforced. To stop tantrum behavior in toddlers, ignoring the behavior will decrease or stop the tantrum if the desired reward is parental attention or parental aggravation.

Seasons of Life Theory (Levinson)

This theory of adult development is classified by development stages, with each stage defined by different, yet meaningful and developmentally necessary, tasks. There are transition periods where stages overlap.

The **pre-adulthood stage** ends at age twenty-two. Beginning at birth, this is the stage when a person develops and prepares for adulthood. It is a time of major growth and transition as the individual develops a state of independence.

The **early adulthood transition** occurs roughly from the age of seventeen to the age of twenty-two. Pre-adulthood is ending and early adulthood is beginning, but the time of transition is actually part of both periods. Physical development is completed, but this time of transition can be compared to the infancy of a new period of

development. During this stage, adolescence ends and the individual begins to make decisions about adult life. He or she further develops independence and separates from the family of origin.

Early adulthood stage is roughly age seventeen to forty-five. This stage begins with the early adult transition. From a biological perspective, an individual's twenties and thirties are at the peak of the life cycle. This stage can be the time during which individuals have their greatest energy but are also experiencing the greatest amount of stress as they try to establish families and careers simultaneously.

Midlife transition is roughly age forty to forty-five. This is a time of transition that bridges the end of early adulthood and the beginning of middle adulthood. At this time of life, people tend to become more reflective and compassionate and less concerned with external demands. Values may change, and it is possibly a time where crisis is experienced due to limited time to reach goals. Individuals become aware of death and leaving a legacy.

Middle adulthood stage is roughly age forty to sixty-five. There is a diminishment of biological capacities, but only minimally. Most individuals are able to continue to lead fulfilling and relatively energetic lives. Many take on a mentoring role and responsibility for the further development of young adults. Choices must be made about livelihood and retirement.

Late adulthood is at roughly age sixty. A transition period occurs from around sixty to sixty-five. Late adulthood is a time of reflection on other stages and on accomplishments. During this stage, retirement takes place and the individual gives up their role in the workplace. Crisis occurs at this stage due to declining power and less accolades of work performed.

Social Clock Theory (Bernice Neugarten)

Neugarten proposed that every society has a **social clock**: an understood expectation for when certain life events should happen (e.g., getting married, buying a home, having children). When individuals do not adhere to this timeframe, they often experience stress, the sense of disappointing others, or the experience of an internal "clock ticking" and reminding them that time is running out.

Normal and Abnormal Physical, Cognitive Emotional, and Sexual Development

Typical and Atypical Physical Growth and Development

It is important to understand normal developmental milestones. Not all children progress at the same rate, but there are some guidelines that help determine whether the child has any developmental delays that might prevent them from reaching goals by a certain age.

Infancy Through Age Five

During the first year of life, abundant changes occur. The child learns basic, but important, skills. The child is learning to manipulate objects, hold their head without support, crawl, and pull up into a standing position. The toddler should be able to walk without assistance by eighteen months. By age two, the child should be running and able to climb steps one stair at a time. By age three, the child should be curious and full of questions about how the world works or why people behave in certain ways. The child should have the balance and coordination to climb stairs using only one foot per stair. By age four, the child is increasingly independent, demonstrating skills like attending to toilet needs and dressing with some adult assistance.

School Age to Adolescence

By age five, speech is becoming more fluent, and the ability to draw simple figures improves. Dressing without help is achieved. By age six, speech should be fluent and motor skills are strengthened The youth is now able to navigate playground equipment and kick or throw a ball. Social skills, such as teamwork or friendship development, are evolving. The child must learn to deal with failure or frustration and find ways to be accepted by peers. They

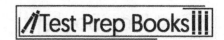

become more proficient in reading, math, and writing skills. Towards the end of this phase, around age twelve, secondary sexual characteristics, such as darker body hair or breast development, may occur.

Adolescence

This is a period of extraordinary change. The process of **individuation** is occurring. The teen views themself as someone who will someday live independently of parents. More time is spent with peers and less with family. Identity formation arises, and the teen experiments with different kinds of clothing, music, and hairstyles to see what feels comfortable and what supports their view of the world. Sexuality is explored, and determinations are being made about sexual preferences and orientation. Sexual experimentation is common, and some teens actually form long-term intimate relationships, although others are satisfied to make shorter-term intimate connections. There is often a period of experimentation with drugs or alcohol. As the thinking process matures, there may be a questioning of rules and expectations of those in authority. Moodiness is common, and troubled teens are likely to "act out" their emotions, sometimes in harmful ways.

Typical and Atypical Cognitive Growth and Development

Cognitive development refers to development of a child's capacity for perception, thought, learning, information processing, and other mental processes. The *nature vs. nurture* debate questions whether cognitive development is primarily influenced by genetics or upbringing. Evidence indicates that the interaction between nature and nurture determines the path of development.

Some commonly recognized milestones in early cognitive development:

- One to three months: focuses on faces and moving objects, differentiates between different types of tastes, sees all colors in the spectrum

- Three to six months: recognizes familiar faces and sounds, imitates expressions

- Six to twelve months: begins to determine how far away something is, understands that things still exist when they are not seen (object permanence)

- One to two years: recognizes similar objects, understands and responds to some words

- Two to three years: sorts objects into appropriate categories, responds to directions, names objects

- Three to four years: Demonstrates increased attention span of five to fifteen minutes, shows curiosity and seeks answers to questions, organizes objects by characteristics

- Four to five years: Draws human shapes, counts to five or higher, uses rhyming words

The **zone of proximal development** is the range of tasks that a child can carry out with assistance, but not independently. Parents and educators can advance a child's learning by providing opportunities within the zone of proximal development, allowing the child to develop the ability to accomplish those actions gradually without assistance.

Typical and Atypical Social Growth, Development, and the Socialization Process

Social development refers to the development of the skills that allow individuals to have effective interpersonal relationships and to contribute in a positive manner to the world around them.

Social learning is taught directly by caregivers and educators, but it is also learned indirectly by the experience of various social relationships.

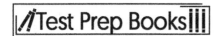

Social development is commonly influenced by extended family, communities, religious institutions, schools, and sports teams or social groups. Positive social development is supported when caregivers do the following:

- Attune to a child's needs and feelings
- Demonstrate respect for others
- Teach children how to handle conflict and solve problems encountered during social experiences
- Help children learn to take the perspective of another person and develop empathy
- Encourage discussion of morals and values and listen to the child's opinions on those topics
- Explain rules and encourage fair treatment of others
- Encourage cooperation, rather than competition

Social development begins from birth as a child learns to attach to their mother and other caregivers. During adolescence, social development focuses on peer relationships and self-identity. In adulthood, social relationships are also important, but the goal is to establish secure and long-term relationships with family and friends.

Other important contributors to social development are **social institutions**, such as family, church, and school, which assist people in realizing their full potential. **Lev Vygotsky** was a pioneer in this field with his concept of cultural mediation. This theory emphasizes that one's feelings, thoughts, and behaviors are significantly influenced by others in their environment.

Typical and Atypical Emotional Growth and Development

Emotional development encompasses the development of the following abilities:

- Identifying and understanding the feelings that one experiences
- Identifying and understanding the feelings of others
- Emotional and behavioral regulation
- Empathy
- Establishing relationships with others

Caregivers who are nurturing and responsive enable children to learn to regulate emotions and feel safe in the environment around them.

- By age two to three months, infants express delight and distress, begin smiling, and may be able to be soothed by rocking.

- By three to four months, infants communicate via crying and begin to express interest and surprise.

- Between four to nine months, infants respond differently to strangers in comparison to known individuals, solicit attention, show a particular attachment for a primary caregiver, and have an expanded range of expressed emotions that include anger, fear, and shyness.

- At ten to twelve months, babies show an increase in exploration and curiosity, demonstrate affection, and display a sense of humor.

- Children at age twelve to twenty-four months often demonstrate anger via aggression, laugh in social situations, recognize themselves in a mirror, engage in symbolic play, and have a complete range of emotional expression.

- Around age two, children begin using different facial expressions to show their emotions, begin to play cooperatively, and may transition from being calm and affectionate to temperamental and easily frustrated.

- At age three, children engage in more social and imaginative play, show interest in the feelings of others, begin to learn to manage frustration, and are often inconsistent and stubborn.

- Children at age four show improved cooperation, express sympathy, and may exhibit lying and/or guilty behavior.

- At age five, children can play rule-based games, often want to do what is expected of them, express emotion easily, and choose friends for themselves.

- Children at age six typically describe themselves in terms of their external attributes, have a difficult time coping with challenges and criticism, prefer routines, and show inconsistent self-control.

- Around age seven, children can typically describe causes and outcomes of emotions and show better regulation of emotions in most situations.

- From ages eight to ten, children have an increased need for independence, want to be viewed as intelligent, experience and better understand emotional subtleties, and may be defiant.

- During adolescence, children begin to master emotional skills to manage stress, increase self-awareness, develop identity, show increased ability for empathy, and learn to manage conflict.

Normal versus abnormal behavior is difficult to distinguish because each person is unique, so creating a standard of normal can be challenging. Though labeling behaviors as normal or abnormal can be problematic, it is important to have some standard by which it is possible to identify those behaviors that are indicative of an underlying psychological condition. Notwithstanding the challenges, it is possible and helpful to have general definitions of normal and abnormal behavior.

Normal behaviors are those that are common to the majority of the population, as related to emotional functioning, social interactions, and mental capacity. **Abnormal behavior** is generally considered that which is maladaptive, dysfunctional, and disruptive to life. These behaviors may be an exaggeration of a normal behavior or even an absence of a typical response. They do not conform to the accepted patterns or common behaviors of society. Sadness over the death of a loved one is considered normal, but disabling depression that interferes with school and work responsibilities is not. The **DSM-5-TR** is the current standard for determining the diagnostic criteria that distinguishes abnormal behavior from normal.

Typical and Atypical Sexual Growth and Development

While not everyone develops sexually on exactly the same timeline, there are certain expectations that define healthy and unhealthy sexual development. These expectations differ based on age. During the early stage of life, from birth until age two, the child is focused on developing a relationship of trust with caregivers. Eventually, children become aware of their genitals and explore these through self-touch. By ages two to five, they begin to develop the ability to name and describe genitalia. They understand that male and female bodies are different. They have little inhibition about nudity.

As children enter middle childhood (ages six to eight or nine), they begin to understand the concept of puberty and what to expect about future body changes. They have a more sophisticated knowledge of reproduction, and may become more inhibited about nudity.

By the age of nine or ten, some children show signs of puberty, although the typical age of onset is eleven for girls and thirteen for boys. During puberty, there is a dramatic development in both primary and secondary sex characteristics. Children at this age show an increased interest in sex and may have questions about sexual orientation, sexual practices, or how the opposite sex behaves. By age twelve or thirteen, they begin to understand the consequences of sexual behavior, such as pregnancy or STDs. As they enter later adolescence, they may form longer relationships with their love interests, but many prefer casual dating. They are beginning to form an identity in terms of sexual orientation, preferences, and values.

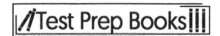
It is important to understand red flags that may be signs of unhealthy sexual development. These may be brought on by abuse or by exposure to sexually explicit scenes. Children who are preoccupied with sexuality at an early age and whose behaviors differ from peers their own age may be at risk. Other indicators include attempting adult-like sexual interactions. These behaviors may include oral to genital contact or some form of penetration of another person's body.

These issues should raise concerns:

- A child overly preoccupied with sexual thoughts, language, or behaviors, rather than in more age-appropriate play
- A child engaging in sex play with children who are much older or much younger
- A child using sexual behavior to harm others
- A child involved in sexual play with animals
- A child uses explicit sexual language that is not age appropriate

A **sexually-reactive child** refers to one who is exposed to sexual stimuli prior to being sexually mature enough to understand the implications. The child becomes overly preoccupied with sexual matters and often acts out what they witnessed or experienced.

Sexual Development Throughout the Lifespan

Sigmund Freud's Psychosexual Stages of Development

Sigmund Freud was an Austrian neurologist who is considered the father of psychoanalysis. Freud developed important concepts in Western psychology such as the id, ego, and superego. He wrote literature focusing on what he called the *unconscious* and the repression and expression that stems from it.

Freud also focused on human development, especially relating to sexuality. Freud theorized that each stage of human development is characterized by a sexual focus on a different bodily area (**erogenous zone**), which can serve as a source of either pleasure or frustration. He believed that **libido** (psychosexual energy) is the determinant of behavior during each of five fixed stages, and that if a developing child experiences frustration during one of these stages, a resulting fixation (or lingering focus) on that stage will occur.

To understand Freud's developmental stages fully, one must also understand his conceptualization of the human personality.

Freud describes three levels of the mind as follows:

- **Consciousness**: the part of the mind that holds accessible and current thoughts
- **Pre-consciousness**: the area that holds thoughts that can be accessed by memory
- **Unconscious**: where the mind motivates behavior and contains thoughts, feelings, and impulses that are not easily accessible

Freud believed that the personality, or psyche, consists of three parts called the Psychic Apparatus, each of which develops at a different time.

Id

The **id** is the most basic and primitive part of the human psyche, based on instincts and all of the biological aspects of a person's being. An infant's personality consists only of the id, as the other aspects have not yet developed. The id is entirely unconscious and operates on the pleasure principle, seeking immediate gratification of every urge. It has two instincts: a death instinct called **thanatos** and a survival instinct called **eros**. The energy from eros is called the **libido**.

Ego

The **ego** is the second personality component that begins to develop over the first few years of life. The ego is responsible for meeting the needs of id in a socially acceptable, realistic manner. Unlike the id, the ego operates on the reality principle, which allows it to consider pros and cons, to have awareness that other people have feelings, and to delay gratification when necessary.

Super Ego

The **super ego** is the final personality component, developed by about age five. The superego is essentially a person's internal moral system or sense of right and wrong. The super ego suppresses the instincts and urges of the id, but also attempts to convince the ego to act idealistically, rather than realistically.

In a healthy personality, there is balance between the three personality components. The individual has **ego strength**—the ability to function well in the world despite the conflicting pressures that the id and superego place upon the ego.

Five Stages of Psychosexual Development

Oral Stage (Birth to Eighteen Months)

The infant satisfies its libido by feeding and by exploring the environment, primarily by putting objects in its mouth. The id dominates the oral stage of development, and every action an infant undertakes is guided by the pleasure principle. The key task of this phase is weaning from the breast, which also results in the infant's first experience of loss. Too much or too little focus on oral gratification at this stage was theorized to lead to an oral fixation and an immature personality. Examples of an oral fixation were believed to be excessive eating, drinking, or smoking.

Anal Stage (Eighteen Months to Three Years)

The key task of this stage is toilet training, which causes a conflict between the id (which wants immediate gratification of the urge to eliminate waste) and the ego (which requires delay of gratification necessary to use the toilet). A positive experience with toilet training was believed to lead to a sense of competence that continues into adulthood. Anal-retentive personality results from overly-strict toilet training, characterized by rigid and obsessive thinking. Likewise, anal-expulsive personality results from a lax approach to toilet training, characterized by disorganization and messiness.

Phallic Stage (Three to Six Years)

The libidinal focus during this stage is on the genital area, and it is during this stage that children learn to differentiate between males and females. The Oedipus Complex develops during this stage; Freud believed that a young boy views his father as a rival for his mother's attention and wants to eliminate his father in order to take his place. Similar to the Oedipus Complex, the Electra Complex says that a young girl may view her mother as her rival. Freud also believed that girls experience penis envy. The key task of this stage is identification with the same-sex parent.

Latency (Six years to Puberty)

During this period, libidinal energy is still present, but the child is able to direct that energy toward school, friendships, and activities.

Genital Stage (Puberty to Adulthood)

The libidinal focus is once again on the genital area (as it is during the phallic stage), but at this point, the psyche is more developed. During the genital stage, an individual achieves sexual maturation, becomes independent of their parents, resolves any remaining conflict from the earlier stages, and is able to function as a responsible adult in terms of both work and relationships.

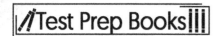

Spiritual Development Throughout the Lifespan

Spiritual development refers to the way a person grows and changes spiritually, particularly regarding the purpose for their existence, over the course of their life. This process may have conscious or unconscious origins, and it may be affected by other growth and development factors. Spiritual development is often linked to the stages of cognitive development, but evidence-based research pertaining strictly to spiritual development is limited. Theories often focus on the influence of psychosocial constructs (such as morality), cognitive beliefs, and religious or faith-based influences.

Jean Piaget (1896–1980) is renowned for his work in the field of cognitive development. He examined social, biological, and psychological constructs that influence cognitive development and intellect. He theorized four stages of cognitive development, from birth through adulthood. He believed that a multitude of constructs influences a person's moral beliefs and values, and this leads to their ultimate perspective on themselves and the environment.

Lawrence Kohlberg (1927–1987) studied moral psychology and development, and he developed a theory of the stages of moral reasoning. He theorized that individuals model behavior and behavior patterns around them to develop concepts of right and wrong as they progress through life. The more aware a person becomes of the effects of their thoughts, actions, and decisions, the more capacity they have for moral decision-making. This may be connected to shaping an individual's spiritual beliefs.

James Fowler (1940–2015), a theologian and university professor, contributed his "**stages of faith**" development, which breaks spiritual evolution down into six stages. He believed in the importance of safety and nurturing in the early years, which leads individuals to feel they are in touch with a greater good. Comparatively, individuals who feel unsafe or do not feel nurtured in their younger years are less likely to focus on spiritual aspects of life. Fowler made connections between his stages of faith and the developmental stages of Piaget and Kohlberg.

Racial, Ethnic, and Cultural Development Throughout the Lifespan

Racial, ethnic, and cultural identities are developed over the course of a lifespan and influenced by a number of factors. Atkinson, Morten, and Sue's **racial and cultural identity development model** is accepted as one of the fundamental theories. This theory states that most individuals try to conform to the primary culture with which they're surrounded or which they believe is considered superior by peers. However, as the individual develops, they begin to seek out and reflect upon any underlying differences. Ideally, the developed individual ultimately becomes comfortable identifying in the way that feels best to him or her while respecting others' differences. Theorists have also focused on how specific minority groups develop racial, ethnic, and cultural identities.

For example, **Jean Kim**'s **theory of Asian racial identity development** focuses on Eastern populations. Minorities from Asian countries such as India, China, or Japan who grow up in the United States may act in traditional ways at home with their family unit, but they may struggle immensely to identify and assimilate with peers at school. This may be due to the fact that Asian culture is largely rooted in a collective, community identity (as opposed to the more individualistic Western culture). Additionally, Eastern and Western languages, traditions, and foods are different. While younger individuals may try to assimilate, older Asian individuals may tend to group together as they age. **Bernardo Ferdman** and **Placida Gallegos**'s model of **Latino identity development** states that for Latino groups, ethnicity plays a larger role than race in self-identification. Finally, a number of researchers have theorized constructs and influences of white and black racial identity and culture. Often, these two racial identities are interrelated. Researchers have focused on how the two races co-exist, based on historical interactions and contemporary narratives.

Physical, Mental, and Cognitive Disabilities Throughout the Lifespan

Approximately 7 percent of U.S. children have some type of disability. The most common physical disabilities that impact development are cerebral palsy, hearing issues, and visual issues. Learning disabilities are also common—these could be Down's syndrome or other developmental delays. Common psychiatric disabilities are ADHD and autism spectrum disorders. Others include mood disorders, oppositional disorders, anxiety disorders, and, in rare cases, schizophrenia. The impact upon the child and family corresponds to the family's ability to adapt to the condition and their ability to connect to community resources.

How the individual develops and copes with the disability depends greatly upon the social context and the child's own personal attributes. Raising a disabled child puts tremendous stress on parents and siblings. There are issues of stigma, financial burden, missed days of work for parents, and the time and energy needed to seek useful resources. Siblings may be called upon to take roles of parenting to help out. These siblings may be bullied by peers who make fun of their disabled family member. They may feel neglected by their parents. Additionally, there may be a need for special housing and special schools. Low-income families may face barriers to accessing services such as transportation, medical specialists, or assistance with childcare.

The impact of disabilities on development depends largely on (1) the extent of the disability and (2) whether that disability is experienced across the lifespan or for a limited amount of time. Positive coping skills and sufficient social support may lessen the impact of a disability. Although the tendency is to focus on negative impact, disabilities may also leave a positive impact in terms of the strengthening of relationships or the development of skills that an individual may not have otherwise acquired.

Interplay of Biological, Psychological, Social, and Spiritual Factors

The interplay of an individual's biological, psychological, social, and spiritual factors is an indicator of overall health and happiness. If one or more of these factors are imbalanced, the individual is unlikely to feel as though they are at their highest level of well-being or personal fulfillment (even if a clinically diagnosed disease is not present). This framework is often utilized in social-work settings where mental or emotional health appears to be compromised. Practitioners address the issue in the client's life by examining their physical and physiological health, medical history, personal history, moods, reactions to events, environment, family life, home life, cultural beliefs, personal relationships, faith or belief system, spirituality, personal desires, and other factors to provide holistic drivers for any necessary interventions.

A number of these factors strongly influence each other. For example, a client who feels tremendous stress daily at work may find themselves constantly falling sick with colds, as stress negatively affects the immune system's ability to perform. Clients with clinically diagnosed mood disorders may have a more difficult time coping with major stressors, such as a divorce. Clients who report having some level of faith or spiritual belief system often appear to have higher levels of positivity and healthier coping mechanisms in the face of adverse personal events. As practitioners intervene in such scenarios, they must address not only the individual client, but all the systems in which the client exists and interacts. Practitioners may also need to work with the client's families, in communities, or in other group settings in order to effectively create balance between biological, psychological, social, and spiritual factors.

Basic Human Needs

Abraham Maslow is the most notable researcher in the area of basic human needs. Maslow theorized that human needs could be described in the form of a pyramid, with the base of the pyramid representing the most basic needs and the higher layers representing loftier goals and needs. Unless the basic needs are met, a person cannot move on to higher needs. For example, a homeless woman living under a bridge will need food, shelter, and safety before

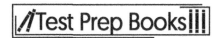
she can consider dealing with her alcoholism. The foundational layer in Maslow's hierarchy is physiological needs, and the final layer at the pinnacle of the pyramid is self-transcendence.

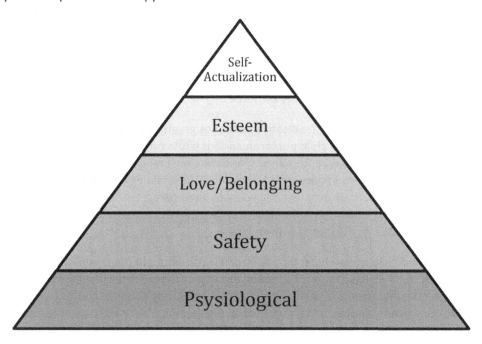

Maslow's Hierarchy of Needs

Physiological Needs: These needs, which pertain to what humans need to survive, must be met first. These needs include the basics, such as food, water, clothing, and housing.

Safety Needs: Once primary needs are met, the person may now focus on safety issues. This would include safety from abuse and neglect, natural disaster, or war.

Love and Belonging: Once the first levels of need have been satisfied, people are next driven to find a sense of acceptance and belonging within social groups, such as family, community, or religious organizations. Maslow suggests that humans have a basic need for love, affection, and sexual intimacy. Failure to achieve this level can lead to difficulty in forming and maintaining close relationships with others.

Esteem: The need for esteem is driven by a desire for recognition, respect, and acceptance within a social context.

Self-Actualization: The U.S. Army slogan, "Be All You Can Be," expresses this layer of need. Reaching one's highest potential is the focus. According to Maslow, this cannot be achieved until all the others are mastered.

Self-Transcendence: Devised by Maslow in his later years, he felt self-actualization did not completely satisfy his image of a person reaching their highest potential. To achieve self-transcendence, one must commit to a goal that is outside of one's self, such as practicing altruism or finding a deeper level of spirituality.

Attachment and Bonding

It has become more important than ever to understand attachment and bonding, especially in relation to changes within the U.S. culture's attitudes about child welfare over the last fifty years. Child Protective Service Teams have become more active in every city. The medical profession, the educational system, and the mental health profession are more informed about children at risk. As a result, more children are being taken from parents, sometimes as early as the day of birth. An older child victim may travel from relative to relative, back to the mother, then into

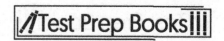

foster or group homes. These children do not have an opportunity to form attachments with their caregivers, nor do caregivers have the opportunity to bond with the children.

Bonding refers to a mother's initial connection to her baby. This generally occurs within the first hours or days of the birth. Mothers who are able and willing to hold their child close to them shortly after birth generally have more positive relationships with the child. When a mother fails to bond, the child is at greater risk for having behavioral problems.

Attachment, on the other hand, refers to a more gradual development of the baby's relationship with their caretaker. A secure attachment naturally grows out of a positive, loving relationship in which there is soothing physical contact, emotional and physical safety, and responsiveness to the child's needs. The baby who has a secure attachment will venture out from their safe base, but immediately seek their mother when fearful or anxious, having learned that mommy will be there to protect him or her. This type of secure relationship becomes impossible if the child is moved from home to home or has experienced abuse or neglect.

A child whose needs have not been met or who has learned through mistreatment that the world is unfriendly and hostile may develop an avoidant attachment or ambivalent attachment. An **avoidant attachment** is characterized by a detached relationship in which the child does not seek out the caregiver when distressed, but acts independently. A child with **ambivalent attachment** shows inconsistency toward the caregiver; sometimes the child clings to him or her, but at other times, the child resists their comfort. Establishing a secure, positive attachment with a caregiver is crucial to a child's life-long emotional and social success. The development of attachment disorder is often present in foster children or those adopted later in life and can create much frustration and heartache as more stable parents step in and attempt to bond with them.

Effect of Aging on Biopsychosocial Functioning

Biological Aging
Biological aging is based on physical changes that have an impact on the performance of the body's organs and systems.

Psychological Aging
Psychological aging is based on changes in personality, cognitive ability, adaptive ability, and perception. Basic personality traits appear to be relatively stable through the lifespan, as does an individual's self-image. One aspect that does tend to change, however, is the tendency to become more inwardly focused, which may also result in reduced impulsivity and increased caution.

Studies have shown that a pattern of age-related changes in intelligence can typically be observed after age sixty, although changes vary widely across individuals. Furthermore, the somewhat poorer testing results are reflected in fluid intelligence (i.e., reasoning, problem-solving, and abstract thinking unrelated to experience or learned information), but not in crystallized intelligence (i.e., knowledge based on skills, learning, and experience). Normal age-related changes in memory typically involve acquisition of new information and retrieval of information from memory storage. **Sensory decline** is also a common experience for aging individuals.

Social Aging
Social aging is based on changes in one's relationships with family, friends, acquaintances, systems, and organizations. Most older persons experience a narrowing of their social networks. However, they are more likely to have more positive interactions within those networks, and they are more likely to experience more positive feelings about family members than younger persons do.

Disengagement theory states that it is natural and inevitable for older adults to withdraw from their social systems and to reduce interactions with others. This theory has been highly criticized and is incompatible with other well-

known psychosocial aging theories. **Activity theory** proposes that social activity serves as a buffer to aging; successful aging occurs among those who maintain their social connections and activity levels. **Continuity theory** proposes that with age, individuals attempt to maintain activities and relationships that were typical for them as younger adults.

Gerontology

Gerontology is the study of biological, cognitive, and psychological features of the aging process. It includes the study of the impact of an aging population on social and economic trends. **Gerontologists** practice in the fields of medicine, psychology, physical and occupational therapy, as well as social work. **Geriatric social work** practice refers to a range of services provided to the population of those over age 60. Geriatric social workers are found in nursing homes, counseling programs, advocacy centers, and other programs serving seniors. Aging adults must deal with the very real issues of palliative care, hospice, and other end of life issues. The job of social workers is to support them through difficult decision-making processes and to counsel them as they deal with the complicated emotional and spiritual concerns of aging.

Personality Theories

There are several noted theories as to how personality is formed. In 400 B.C.E., **Hippocrates** attempted to identify personalities based on four temperaments. He called these **humors,** and these were associated with body fluid presence, such as phlegm or bile.

In the 1940s, **William Sheldon** came up with his body type theories that include the **endomorph**, an overweight individual with an easy-going personality; the **mesomorph**, a muscular person with an aggressive personality; and the **ectomorph**, a thin individual with an artistic or intellectual personality.

Gordon Allport developed the trait theory of personality development. He believed that certain personalities were comprised of clusters of traits and that these traits could be categorized into cardinal, central, and secondary traits.

Freud believed the personality was composed of the id, the ego and superego. The **id** refers to a person's unconscious, with its suppressed desires and unresolved conflicts, whereas the **ego** and **superego** are more influenced by the conscious mind. He believed that these three components were often in conflict with one another and that how one resolved these conflicts determined personality. He also stressed the importance of childhood experience in personality development.

Carl Rogers was a proponent of the humanistic theory of personality development. This approach emphasized self-perception and a desire for striving to become the best person one can become. His theory was based on the basic goodness and potential of each person.

The behavioral theories of B.F. Skinner and others related to personality development imply that one's persona is developed as a result of classical or operant conditioning. Reinforcement and punishment guide behavioral choices.

Factors Influencing Self-Image

Self-image has to do with how people view themselves. This concept includes **self-esteem**, whether a person has feelings of high or low worth. The concept of self evolves throughout the lifespan, but it always plays a significant role in how a person functions in life.

Impact of Cultural Heritage on Self-Image

Although personal factors play a large role, self-esteem is also based on how closely a person matches the dominant values of their culture. For example, Western society tends to value assertiveness, independence, and individuality.

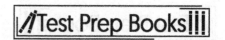

Living up to these values is seen as an important accomplishment, and thus, children receive messages about their personal competence and success based on whether or not they are living up to these ideals.

Children are more likely to develop a positive self-concept when they are able to exhibit behaviors that are valued in their family, home, and culture.

One study suggests that across cultures, self-esteem is based on one's control of life and choices, living up to one's "duties," benefiting others or society, and one's achievements. However, the degree to which one's culture values each of those factors has an impact on how the individual derives their self-esteem.

A widely cited example of the way that a culture can affect a person's self-image is in the portrayal of women's bodies in the media. In the United States, young women are exposed to underweight models and unrealistically drawn cartoon "heroines," which can lead to the development of unachievable expectations and significant negative perceptions about their bodies.

Impact of Race and Ethnicity on Self-Image

Culture, race, and ethnicity can greatly impact one's self-image, whether one is part of a majority population or a minority population. One's ethnic and racial background provides a sense of belonging and identity. Depending on a country's treatment of a particular group, self-image can be negatively impacted through racism and discrimination. Racial jokes and racial slurs are common. Stereotypes abound, and some people judge entire racial groups based on the behavior of a few. Such treatment consistently impacts the self-esteem of minority groups. Non-white Americans who grew up in the fifties or earlier were denied access to restaurants, theaters, high schools, professions, universities, and recreational activities. Even within the last fifty to sixty years, African Americans who had achieved great status in the fields of music, sports, and entertainment were still denied access to certain clubs, hotels, or restaurants.

Every person must explore and come to terms with their own culture, ethnicity, and race. Sometimes, this even means rejecting cultural aspects with which he or she disagrees and embracing new and evolving cultural norms. This is a significant part of self-identity development among teenagers and young adults as they are part of a new generation that may be culturally different from their parents. Those who have more exposure to other cultures and backgrounds will have a more open perspective and are better able to evaluate their own culture and ethnicity objectively.

Effects of Spirituality

Spirituality is sometimes mistaken for religion, but in fact, they are quite different terms. **Religion** is an organized system of beliefs that generally contain a code of conduct and often involve specific devotional or ritual observations. **Spirituality** is more abstract and includes participation in spiritual activities such as meditation, chanting, or prayer. A spiritual person may or may not belong to a religious organization. Spirituality places emphasis on the growth and well-being of the mind, body, and spirit.

Studies have shown that persons who embrace spirituality tend to live both longer and happier lives. Several benefits of being a spiritual person include the following:

- Individuals are encouraged to strive towards being a better person.
- There is an increased likelihood of connections with others.
- It offers hope to the hopeless through strong faith
- It provides a path to heal from emotional pain.
- It helps reduce anxiety through meditation and other spiritual activities.
- It leads to greater life commitment via the optimism spiritual persons tend to have.

31

Impact of Age on Self-Image

Aging is an inevitable phase of human development, and the impact is physical, psychological, social, and economic. **Self-image** is the perception of oneself, but the perception is influenced by societal values. Some cultures revere the elderly and look to them for wisdom and strength. These cultures include the Native Americans, Chinese, Koreans, and Indians. In the United States, there is a different perception of aging. Many elderly Americans feel less valuable or important once they enter retirement. At the same time, they are coping with undesirable body changes and learning to accept that, physically, they can no longer do what they once did. In the U.S., youth and physical attractiveness are highly valued. The elderly are seldom seen as important social figures. They are also less connected with families today, with only 3.7% of homes reporting multigenerational households, per Census Bureau reports. Currently, family support and family contact are less available. However, for some segments of the population, technology has allowed relatives to visit regularly with grandchildren and even participate in family meals or get-togethers.

Infancy: The ego is in charge. The baby thinks primarily of basic needs, such as food or warmth.

Childhood: In early to middle childhood, children tend to rate themselves higher than peers in terms of talents and intellect. As middle school approaches, there is a decline in self-evaluations. This could be related to feeling unattractive due to physical changes or being teased or bullied by peers in that age group.

Adolescence: In the early stage of adolescence (ages 9 to 13), another drop in self-esteem occurs. This is thought to be related to the need to let go of childish pleasures, such as a beloved toy or previous interests and step up to the plate of becoming a more responsible person. This can be a painful sacrifice for some youth. The next drop in self-worth occurs at the end of adolescence and beginning of young adulthood (ages 18 to 23). It is during this period that young adults realize that they truly are responsible for their own lives, yet they have not yet achieved a sense of mastery in the academic or vocational world. They are fearful and full of doubt about the ability to be successful as an independent adult.

Adulthood: Studies indicate a small but steady increase in self-image by mid-twenties. In general, during this period, men tend to have higher self-esteem than women. Persons who live in poor socioeconomic conditions tend to have lower self-esteem than their more financially stable peers. As later adulthood nears (the 70s), women tend to catch up with men in terms of how they evaluate themselves. Women in their eighties tend to have a more positive self-image than male counterparts. As a general rule, for both genders, there is a gradual increase in one's sense of self-worth throughout the life span until late middle age. Research shows that most adults' self-image peaks at around age 60.

Impacts of Disability on Self-Image

Disabilities impact self-image regardless of age; however, an individual who is born with a disability tends to fare better than one who acquires one later in life. Responses vary based upon severity of impairments. Some later-life medical conditions cause the individual to give up independence as the person is forced to retire the car keys or move to an institutional setting. Less severe acquired disabilities that still allow the person to maintain much of their previous lifestyle are painful but easier to accept. An individual's personality make-up and resilience to coping with change are also important factors. It is not uncommon for older adults to lapse into depression. This is often generated by a combination of losses. As one enters the later stages of life, loss of friends and family members is common. There may be declines in status, earning capacity, or physical abilities, all of which contribute to depression and negatively impact self-image.

Effects of Trauma on Self-image

Trauma can have a significant impact on self-image as a person's entire identity becomes intertwined with the traumatic event and the subsequent emotions. Some victims of trauma report a sense of isolation from others, feeling that they are not good enough or that they are less competent or less attractive than their peers. This

generates feelings of shame and unworthiness, which, in turn, can lead to depression or anxiety. Some trauma survivors—especially victims of child or domestic abuse—feel a deep sense of betrayal and label the world and people as unsafe. They have trouble trusting others, and they may perform poorly in major areas of functioning, such as work or relationships. Some abuse survivors describe themselves as "damaged goods." Some individuals may engage in self-harm behaviors or may feel so depressed that suicide is seen as the only solution. These persons are prone to substance use as a means to numb the emotional pain. Addictive behavior can also negatively impact one's self-esteem. The more resilient will use their painful experiences as a tool for self-growth and may eventually learn to help others who have been through similar experiences.

Body Image

Body image refers to the thoughts and feelings about the appearance of one's body as well as thoughts and feelings about how one's body is perceived by others. Body image is shaped by the messages that we receive from the people around us, the culture we live in, and the media.

Persistent negative body image can be associated with these factors:

- Low self-esteem
- Depression and/or anxiety
- Sexual risk-taking
- Impaired relationship satisfaction
- Withdrawal from activities where one's body may be visible to others (e.g., exercise, sexual activity, swimming, seeking medical care)
- Development of eating disorders

Parenting Skills and Capacities

Good parenting practices are essential for raising emotionally healthy children. Child psychologists vary on what types of parenting styles are most effective, but there are four generally recognized styles of parenting.

Authoritarian parenting style: This style of parenting reinforces the role of parent as controller and decision maker. Children are rarely given input into decisions impacting their lives, and the parent takes on a dictatorial role. Children raised by this kind of parent are often obedient and tend to be proficient. The drawback is that they do not rank high on the happiness scale.

Authoritative parenting style: This style of parenting allows for a greater sense of democracy in which children are given some degree of input into issues that impact their lives. There is a healthy balance between firmness and affection. Children raised in this environment tend to be capable, successful, and happy individuals.

Permissive parenting style: This type of parenting allows children to be more expressive and freer with both feelings and actions; they are allowed to behave in whatever manner they please. There are very few rules, and no consequences will be given, even if a rule is violated. These children are more likely to experience problems in school and relationships with others. In the long run, they are often unhappy with their lives.

Uninvolved parenting style: This form of parenting often occurs in dysfunctional families in which parents are emotionally or physically unavailable. They may be remiss in setting clear expectations, yet they may overreact when the child misbehaves or fails to understand what is expected. This is often seen in families where poverty is extreme or addictions or mental illnesses are present.

The authoritative style of parenting is considered to be the most effective form of parenting, yet much depends on the individual child or parent and the economic situation or cultural setting. One rule of thumb is that whatever style one chooses, it is helpful to remain consistent. A parent who is permissive one day and authoritarian the next

sends mixed and confusing messages to the child. It is also important that the child is completely aware of rules, expectations, and consequences that may follow if the rules are broken. Communicating a sense that children are loved, wanted, and accepted is one of the most important parts of parenting.

Basic Principles of Human Genetics

Social workers will begin to see more work done in the area of human genetics in the coming years. Since social workers are often the first individuals to diagnose mental disorders, it's imperative for workers to understand the ethical and legal implications behind a genetic diagnosis. The following is a list of social work *practice skills* related to genetics:

- Biopsychosocial assessment of clients who may have genetic disorders
- Providing assistance to clients with genetic disorders by identifying and/or developing programs for them
- Providing risks-benefits counseling before a client undergoes genetic testing
- Providing post-test counseling following diagnosis of a disorder
- Providing counseling related to family planning
- Providing adoption-related counseling pertaining to implications of an adoptee's genetic information

The following is a list of social work values related to genetics:

- **Accessibility**: availability of genetic screening to those who need it
- **Self-determination**: protection of rights when individuals are asked to take part in population screening
- **Autonomy**: the right and ability for an individual to choose whether or not to undergo genetic testing
- **Confidentiality**: assurance and maintenance of the privacy of genetic testing results
- Research: data from screening used for the purpose of developing services that may benefit others

Ethical dilemmas may arise as the result of genetic testing. Social workers should refer to the NASW Code of Ethics (1996) for guidance, paying particular attention to the ethical standards of self-determination, informed consent, and social and political action.

Family Life Cycle

Family life cycle theories assume that, as members of a family unit, individuals pass through different stages of life. Although various theories will break down the stages somewhat differently, the following is a common conceptualization of the stages:

Unattached Young Adult
The primary tasks for this stage are selecting a lifestyle and a life partner. Focus is on establishing independence as an adult and independence from one's family of origin.

Newly-Married Couple
The focus in this stage is on establishing the marital system. Two families are joined together, and relationships must be realigned.

Family with Young Children
The focus in this stage is on accepting new family members and transitioning from a marital system to a family system. The couple takes on a parenting role. Relationships must again be realigned with the extended family (e.g., grandparents).

Family with Adolescents

The focus here is on accommodating the emerging independence of the adolescents in the family. The parent-child relationship experiences changes, and the parents may also begin to take on caregiving roles with regard to their own parents.

Launching Family

The focus in this stage is on accepting the new independent role of an adult child and transitioning through the separation. Parents also must face their own transition into middle or older age.

Family in Later Years

In this stage, spousal roles must be re-examined and re-defined. One focus may be the development of interests and activities outside of work and family. Another focus is on navigation of the aging process and losses that may occur.

The basic family life cycle can vary significantly as a result of cultural influences, expectations, and particular family circumstances (e.g., single-parent family, blended family, multi-generational family).

Family Life Education in Social Work Practice

Family life education is an important aspect of social work practice in the psychoeducational realm of treatment. Families sometimes need to be educated concerning their biopsychosocial structure and other kinds of family structures. Family life models have changed in recent years and continue to change at a rapid pace with the advent of the legalization of gay marriage and the increase in extended and blended families. Family life has become very diverse, and social workers need to be educated on these models so they can further educate clients.

Aging Parents on Adult Children

There are about 10 million Americans over the age of fifty who are caring for aging parents. In the last fifteen years, thanks to modern medicine, the adult population has begun living longer. As a result, the number of adult children between the ages of fifty and seventy who provide care to aging parents has tripled. This amounts to about 25 percent of adult children who provide either personal or economic assistance.

Research indicates that becoming a personal caregiver to a parent increases the rates of depression, substance use, and heart disease. These adult children sometimes take significant financial blows in the form of lost income, earlier than planned retirement, and reduced pension plans, due to leaving the workforce earlier. At the same time, these adult children are assisting their own children as they move towards independence. Those in the youngest generation may still be in college or in the early stages of starting a career and still look to parents for some financial assistance. From a different perspective, the positives of this situation are that children are able to form deeper bonds with grandparents, and the longevity of life in loved ones can have a very positive impact on all involved.

Systems and Ecological Perspectives and Theories

Systems Theory in social work refers to the view that human behavior is explained by the influences of the various systems to which individuals belong. When evaluating and conceptualizing an individual's behavior, that behavior must be considered in the context of the individual's family, society, and other systems.

All systems are seen as possessing interrelated parts and exerting influence on each other. There are many iterations of the premise of the basic systems theory. In practice, systems theory allows a social worker to better understand the dynamics of a client's systems while also creating an appropriate intervention approach. The originator of systems theory in social work was **Ludwig von Bertalanffy**, a biologist who was influenced by sociologists **Max Weber** and **Emile Durkheim**.

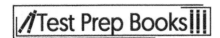

Talcott Parsons expanded on earlier work with his framework of structural functionalism, which proposes that a system is defined by its function in its social environment.

The **four states of social systems** are adaptation to the social environment, goal attainment, integration with other systems, and latency or homeostasis (social patterns and norms are maintained). It's also important to note the designations of social systems in social work. **Microsystems** are small systems, like an individual or a couple. **Mezzosystems** are medium-sized systems made up of extended families or groups to which the individual belongs. **Macrosystems** are large systems made up of organizations or communities.

The **ecological systems perspective** is concerned with the transactions between systems. It says that people and families must be considered within cultural and societal contexts, which also necessitates examining the events that have occurred in an individual's life. Changes made by the individual that cause the entire system to shift must also be considered.

The following are common interventions based on systems theory:

- o Strengthening a part of the system in order to improve the whole system

- o Creating a genogram: a family tree constructed with a client in order to improve understanding of the familial relationships and to identify recurring patterns

- o Connecting clients to organizations or individuals who can help them to function better within and between their systems

- o Developing an ecomap: an illustration of client's systems, such as family and community and how it changes over time

Strengths-Based and Resilience Theories

Rather than focusing on problems and pathology, the **strengths perspective** (or **strengths-based approach**) in social work encourages social workers to focus on a client's strengths or assets and to build upon the client's inherent resiliency and positive characteristics. Outcome studies regarding use of the "strengths" perspective are limited; however, it is posited that a strengths-based approach could help to remove some of the stigma attached to groups or conditions (e.g., mental illness, poverty).

Resilience theories account for risk factors that may threaten an individual's ability to cope with adverse events. **Risk factors** include lack of support, diagnosis of mental health disorders, and resource constraints. **Protective factors** support high levels of resiliency and can include the ability to think positively about situations, the ability to feel hope, strong confidence in one's self-reliance, problem-solving abilities, and competence. Developing resilience should be treated as a preventative approach, rather than a reactive approach.

Strengths- and resilience-based approaches allow individuals to feel empowered and maintain a sense of self-efficacy, both of which are crucial components for lasting behavior change and resolution. Additionally, they minimize client's self-identification with a problem or issue, which can cause the client to fall into a self-fulfilling prophecy. It is important to note that clients can build the capacity to be resilient as a healthy method of coping. This type of skill building can often serve as a crucial component of an intervention. Exercises may include reframing perspectives, journaling, learning new abilities (such as problem-solving skills), practicing flexibility when unexpected changes arise, and examining public stories of strength and resiliency with the client. Finally, practitioners can support clients by providing positive reinforcement and feedback when the client displays strong and resilient behaviors.

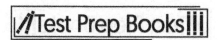

Loss, Separation, and Grief

The **concept of loss** is at the root of many depressive episodes. Losses can include anything one holds dearly. Losing a loved one, a pet, a job, housing, or financial or social status can all bring emotional pain. Other losses include the loss of physical or mental health. **Separation** is a form of loss that can occur in many forms, including divorce, military deployment, a job that requires one to move far away, or the loss of custody of a child. **Grief** is the emotional response to loss. Grief includes the main emotion of sadness, but other strong emotions may be present as well. Other feelings include confusion, anger, frustration, anxiety, or guilt.

The **Five Stages of Grief** is a concept developed by **Elisabeth Kubler-Ross** in her book *On Death and Dying* in 1969. The five stages model originally pertained to those experiencing the dying process as the result of a terminal illness, but the model has been widely used to understand the grief reactions that people have in response to a number of situations, including loss of a loved one. The stages were first posited to be linear, but Kubler-Ross later stated that they are five common experiences that may or may not be experienced during grieving.

Denial
This is the first stage. It occurs when a person becomes aware that they have lost someone or something dear but refuses to accept the truth. This stage is generally brief as the person begins to process irrefutable evidence.

Anger
This is a period of venting anger at anyone who the person feels contributed to the loss occurring. It may be towards God, the drunk driver who caused an accident, or the CPS worker who takes a child from the home. In the case of a suicide, there could be anger at the deceased for choosing to leave.

Bargaining
This stage is almost a form of magical thinking. A person may think that if they promise to do better, work harder, or pray harder, the loss process can be reversed. This is generally a short-lived phase as one realizes that promises made will still not bring back that which has been lost.

Depression
During the fourth stage, a person allows themself to feel the sadness, and they may experience an even deeper emotional pain while learning to accept the loss and move forward. It may be a time of crying, despondency, and anguish. It must be experienced in order to move to the next stage.

Acceptance
The last stage is the point at which the grieving person recognizes that, while the pain is tremendous, they will be able to handle it. Those at this stage understand that time will ease some of the suffering. They are learning to make peace with the experience and move forward with their lives.

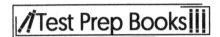
Human Behavior in the Social Environment

Person-In-Environment (PIE) Theory

Carel Germain described person-in-environment interaction based upon earlier work in systems theory. This perspective takes into consideration an individual's environmental and systemic influences. It is specific to social work, which differentiates it from other like professions.

- **Life stress**: the normal tension that occurs as the result of both external demands and internal experiences
    - What is experienced as stressful varies across people and their perceptions. For example, two people placed in the same environment may have completely different experiences due to the ways in which they experience and perceive the situation.
- **Adaptation**: when the environment and the individual change in response to the interaction with each other
- **Coping**: individual use of one's own strengths and problem-solving abilities to navigate life stress and develop self-esteem and hope
- **Power:** can be a source of stress to individuals as well as the larger system when misused by certain groups
- **Human Relatedness**: the ability of individuals to cultivate relationships
- Three related concepts are *self-direction*, *competence*, and *self-esteem*. These attributes are interdependent and occur cross-culturally.

Family Dynamics and Functioning

Family dynamics are the interactions between family members in a family system. As discussed previously, under "Family Theories," each family is a unique system; however, there are some common patterns of family dynamics.

Common influences on family dynamics:

- The type and quality of relationship that the parents have
- An absent parent
- A parent who is either extremely strict or extremely lenient
- The mix of personalities in the family
- A sick or disabled family member
- External events, particularly traumatic ones that have affected family members
- Family dynamics in previous generations or the current extended family

Common roles in the family that may result from particular family dynamics:

- **The problem child**: child with problematic behavior, which may serve as a distraction from other problems that the family, particularly the parents, do not want to face
- Scapegoat: the family member to whom others unjustly attribute problems, often viewed as "bad," while other family members are viewed as "good"
- Peacekeeper: a family member who serves to mediate relationships and reduce family stress

The Effects of Family Dynamics on Individuals

There are many ways in which the family influences the individual socially, emotionally, and psychologically. All family systems have their own unique characteristics, with both good and bad functional tendencies. The family interactions are among the earliest and most formative relationships that a person has, so they define the relational

patterns that the individual develops and utilizes with all subsequent relationships. Parenting styles, conflict resolution methods, beliefs and values, and coping mechanisms are just a few things that a person learns from their family of origin. It is also within the family that a person first develops an image of self and identity, often having to do with the role that they are given within the family system and the messages communicated by parents. If a child has a secure and healthy relationship with the family members, this will likely lead to overall well-being and emotional stability as an adult.

When it comes to physical or mental illness, the role that the family plays is critical in lowering risk factors and minimizing symptoms. A strongly supportive family will help a person function at the highest level possible. Oftentimes, family members can serve as caregivers or play less formal—but still critical—roles in supporting a person's health.

Dynamics of Interpersonal Relationships

Interpersonal relationships refer to interactions (often of a close, friendly, romantic, or intimate nature) between people. They can form due to shared personal, professional, social, charitable, or political interests. Strong interpersonal relationships are built over time as participants are willing to honestly communicate on a regular basis, support one another's well-being, and develop a shared history. Psychological, evolutionary, and anthropological contexts suggest that humans are an inherently altruistic, community-oriented species that relies on interpersonal relationships to survive and thrive. These types of relationships (when healthy) provide security, a sense of belonging, an exchange of benefits and rewards, and a sense of self-esteem. Healthy interpersonal relationships are characterized by mutual respect, care, and consideration between members. Almost all groups assemble into a power structure of some kind, with natural leaders taking over decision-making, resource sharing, and other tasks that affect the group as a whole. **Dysfunctional interpersonal relationships** may be characterized by an extreme power imbalance and dominance by one or more involved members, often leading to submissiveness, learned helplessness, and feelings of low self-esteem in the relationship's less powerful members. Submissive members of a group may find themselves without material resources or respect from the rest of the group.

Abuse and Neglect Throughout the Lifespan

Indicators and Dynamics of Sexual Abuse

Sexual abuse is forced or coerced sexual contact or exposure, usually by someone older or in a position of authority over the victim. Sexual abuse can also include forcing someone to watch sexual acts or receive messages involving unwanted sexual content. The impact of sexual abuse is complex, and the emotional and psychological response to the trauma may evolve as the victim gets older and understands more fully what happened to them. Children who suffer sexual abuse may struggle from confusion about the abuse, especially if they are told by the perpetrator that it is right and good and if that person is someone with whom they have a relationship of trust. They may be blamed by the perpetrator for the abuse, which leads to further feelings of confusion and guilt. If they report the abuse to someone who does not believe it, the long-term effects of the abuse may be even greater, as well as the guilt, self-doubt, and shame. A history of sexual abuse will normally impact a person's relationships with others throughout life, and there may be issues of trust as well as confused feelings toward sex.

Indicators of Sexual Abuse (Child)

- The statement that one has been sexually assaulted
- Mistrust or fear of those who bear resemblance to the abuser, potentially due to gender or size (children may be mistrustful of all adults)
- Changes in behavior
- Depression
- Anxiety with presenting symptoms (hair loss, fluctuations in weight)

- Increased fearfulness (possible night terrors and enuresis/bed wetting from children)
- Withdrawal from preferred activities/social isolation
- Compulsive masturbation
- Substance use
- Overly-sexualized behavior
- Parent, spouse, or caregiver demonstrating inappropriate behaviors
- Role confusion, distortion of child's role in the family
- Jealousness or over-protection of the victim
- Excessive, abnormal alone time with the child
- Lack of appropriate social and emotional contacts outside the home
- Substance and/or alcohol abuse
- Parent or caregiver reports being sexually abused previously (possible normalization or continuation of the cyclic behavior)

Indicators and Dynamics of Psychological Abuse and Neglect

Psychological abuse—or **emotional abuse**—is more difficult to define than sexual or physical abuse, but it can be just as damaging to the victim. **Psychological neglect**, especially as a child, involves withholding the love, affection, and emotional security that a child needs in order to grow and thrive. **Psychological abuse** involves emotional manipulation that uses strategies of shame, fear, and guilt to control someone's behaviors. Another aspect of psychological abuse can be **verbal abuse** which takes the form of yelling, constant criticisms or belittling, threats, or name-calling.

Alternatively, the child may be ignored, be made the witness of violence, or isolated as a punishment. These are all forms of psychological abuse and neglect. Because of the often vague or indefinable aspects of psychological abuse, it may be difficult for victims to understand or believe that they are being mistreated. Even if they do, they may be convinced that no one will believe them because of the manipulation of the perpetrator, who may either threaten or undermine the victim to such an extent that they are unwilling to take any action. Long term, a victim of psychological abuse is more likely to be fearful and withdrawn as a result of the many insecurities that have developed because of the abuse.

Indicators and Dynamics of Physical Abuse and Neglect

Physical abuse can be defined as bodily mistreatment, including hitting, slapping, kicking, burning, unnecessary constraints, strangling, or other acts of physical violence. Physical abuse is often perpetrated out of anger or frustration, as is the case with parents who use physical abuse to inappropriately discipline their children. In cases where there is a higher level of family stress or conflict or when parents have not received adequate training in parenting strategies, the levels of physical abuse may be higher. Physical abuse can also take place in adult relationships, most usually in an intimate relationship where one person struggles with anger management. Victims of physical abuse may show obvious signs of the abuse, such as injuries or multiple trips to the emergency room. However, there are other less obvious signs of physical abuse, such as fearful withdrawal, aggression, or other forms of misbehavior.

Physical neglect is withholding anything that is necessary for physical health and safety, as well as educational and medical needs. If a parent, for example, does not provide a child with enough food or with warm clothes in the winter, this would be considered neglect. This type of neglect can sometimes be deliberate, but may also be the result of ignorance or a lack of resources.

Effects of Physical, Sexual, and Psychological Abuse

People may experience abuse at the hands of strangers, caretakers, or close friends and family. The effects of abuse are traumatic, pervasive, and long lasting. Beyond affecting the abused parties, abuse often impacts those who are

close to the victims. Physical, sexual, and psychological child abuse can lead to impaired intellect, learning disabilities, deficits in trust and language skills, long-term inappropriate behaviors, or lack of coping mechanisms. As abused children grow, they may be unable to make healthy friendships or lack the ability to desire or maintain intimate relationships. They may have failed marriages, or they may perpetuate the cycle of abuse when they become parents. They may often feel unworthy or that they did something to cause the abuse. This often has an impact on their attachment styles and how they relate to others.

In adults, abuse may cause permanent or temporary physical damage, low self-esteem, shame, despair, or feelings of helplessness. Victims of abuse as an adult may experience mental health disorders such anxiety and depression. If children witness their loved ones experiencing abuse, it may be traumatic for them, or they may normalize the behavior and perpetuate abuse themselves. Elder abuse, especially in nursing homes, often goes undetected as victims may be weak or losing mental faculties. Elders are especially vulnerable to physical and financial abuse. Effects may include rapid physical or mental deterioration, submissiveness, bedsores, increased rate of illness, or premature death.

In traumatic cases, both children and adults may become severely depressed or anxious. They may abuse substances or commit suicide.

Perpetrators of Abuse, Neglect, and Exploitation

Abuse perpetrators are individuals who cause or allow mistreatment of a child or other dependent. Common characteristics of abuse perpetrators are having experienced or witnessed abuse during childhood; lack of coping skills to manage anger and frustration; isolation or lack of a substantial support system; immaturity with poor regulation of emotions; abuse of alcohol or other substances; inappropriate expectations for the behavior of others; and poor social skills.

Effects of Life Events, Stressors, and Crises

Life events are experienced by all families and can be both positive and negative—everything from marriage or childbirth to death or divorce. If the life event is more negative and sudden, it may be considered a crisis, such as the unexpected loss of a family member, diagnosis of a major illness, a car crash, financial trouble, or something even more intense like a natural disaster or terrorist attack. Even positive life events can become crises for families if they have difficulty adjusting to the changes. Crises often involve both hard decisions and emotional turmoil.

The **ABCX Model**, introduced by **Reuben Hill**, seeks to explain how families deal with stressful situations that arise. **A** is the event that occurs, **B** is the family resources, **C** is the family perception, and **X** stands for a crisis. It claims that the event, plus the family resources and plus the family's perception, all combine to determine whether the event is viewed as a crisis and whether the family is able to cope with it. Depending on the family's ability to adapt their normal functioning patterns, a life event or crisis can either strengthen their relationships and the family unit or tear them apart. A family can effectively deal with the crisis if they utilize **positive coping mechanisms**, such as pursuing practical solutions to deal with the issues that arise, seeking counseling from a therapist or clergy, engaging social supports, and communicating openly with each other. **Negative coping strategies** could involve drug or alcohol use, isolation, or displacement of anger and frustration onto family members. Though all families will face a period of disordered chaos in trying to deal with a crisis, the families that are successful are those that can engage in new and positive coping methods.

Impact of Stress, Trauma, and Violence

Trauma affects everyone differently. The reaction depends on the person's emotional resiliency, history of past trauma, and other factors. Some trauma survivors exhibit symptoms that clearly meet the criteria for PTSD, while

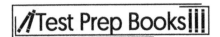

others exhibit smaller clusters of symptoms, such as anxiety or depression. Others show little or no symptoms. Below is an overview of common responses:

- **Foreshortened future**: This refers to the sense that one's life is shortened or forever altered and that a normal life may never be experienced again.

- **Emotional responses**: These may be fear, sadness, shame, anger, guilt, and/or anxiety.

- **Physical reactions**: Survivors of trauma often have multiple somatic issues, including gastrointestinal complaints, neurological problems, poor sleep, and muscle pain.

- **Hyperarousal**: Trauma survivors often become hypervigilant. They are frightened by neutral stimuli, such as a dog barking or a child screaming. They may experience a continual feeling that something terrible is going to happen.

- **Intrusive thoughts**: Survivors can become flooded with unwanted thoughts and memories about the trauma.

- **Trigger/flashbacks**: Triggers are stimuli that set off memories and provide a sensory reminder of the traumatic event.

- **Dissociation**: This coping mechanism allows the person to "check out" temporarily. This process severs connections to the painful memories.

- **Self-harm**: Some survivors use self-harm as a means of distraction from emotional pain. This could transition into more serious self-harm and can result in suicidal behaviors if not treated.

- **Substance use**: Many survivors use substances to medicate unpleasant emotions, such as fear or shame.

Common Effects of Stress, Trauma, and Violence

Many people equate stress with an emotional experience, but stress can actually have a profound effect on the body, cognition, and behavior as well.

Common Effects of Stress		
Body	**Mood**	**Behavior**
Headache	Anxiety	Overeating or undereating
Muscle tension or pain	Restlessness	Angry outbursts
Chest pain	Lack of motivation or focus	Drug or alcohol abuse
Fatigue	Irritability or anger	Tobacco use
Change in sex drive	Sadness or depression	Social withdrawal
Stomach upset		
Sleep problems		

Although everyone experiences some degree of stress, stress becomes trauma when the intensity of the stress causes a person to feel helpless and seriously threatened, either physically or psychologically. Unfortunately, trauma and violence are common experiences for both adults and children, and the risk for traumatic and/or violent events is particularly high for individuals suffering from mental illness. Some people will experience a trauma with little to no lasting impact, while others may struggle with the aftermath of the trauma for the rest of their lives.

Many variables can either exacerbate or ameliorate the impact of trauma:

- Whether the event occurred once or was ongoing
- Whether the event occurred during childhood or adulthood
- Intensity of the traumatic event

- Personal experience vs. observation
- Ability to access supportive resources
- The way in which people and systems respond to the individual who has been traumatized

Potential effects of trauma and violence:

- Substance use and abuse
- Mental health problems
- Risk-taking behavior
- Self-injurious behavior
- Increased likelihood or exacerbation of chronic illnesses, including cardiovascular disease
- Difficulties with daily functioning, including navigating careers and relationships

Post-Traumatic Stress Disorder (PTSD)

Some people who have experienced trauma or violence will experience an impact significant enough to be diagnosed with PTSD. Symptoms must last for more than one month before the diagnosis of PTSD is considered and must include the following:

- One or more **re-experiencing symptoms** (flashbacks, disturbing dreams, frightening thoughts)

- One or more **avoidance symptoms** (avoiding reminders of the trauma, experiencing emotional "numbing," losing interest in activities that one previously enjoyed)

- Two or more **arousal and reactivity symptoms** (startling easily, experiencing tension, hypervigilance, difficulty falling or staying asleep, eruptions of anger)

- Two or more **cognition and mood symptoms** (difficulty remembering the traumatic event, persistent negative thoughts, excessive feelings of blame or guilt)

Crisis Intervention Theories

Crisis intervention is typically a short-term treatment usually lasting four to six weeks and is implemented when a client enters treatment following some type of traumatic event that causes significant distress. This event causes a state of disequilibrium when a client is out of balance and can no longer function effectively.

Gerald Caplan's Stages of Crises

Caplan theorized that individuals need to maintain homeostasis or remain in balance with their environment. A crisis is caused by an individual's reaction to a situation, not by an actual incident. Following a crisis event, an individual experiences the following stages:

Stage 1

Increase in feelings of stress immediately following the event. Client may experience denial and typically tries to resolve the stressful reactions using past problem-solving and coping skills.

Stage 2

Client experiences higher levels of stress as the usual coping mechanisms fail. Client may employ higher-level coping skills to alleviate the increasing stress levels.

Stage 3

As stressful feelings continue to escalate, client experiences major emotional turmoil, possible feelings of hopelessness, depression, and anxiety.

43

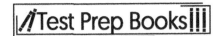
Stage 4

The final stage is marked by complete psychological and emotional collapse, or the individual finds a method to resolve the situation; however, there may be remaining emotional and psychological dysfunction or impairment if the coping mechanisms used were maladaptive.

Social workers can either use generic crisis intervention models for varied types of crises or can create an individualized plan for assisting the client. The main goal of crisis intervention should be to help clients develop and use adaptive coping skills to return to the level of functioning prior to the crisis.

The Crisis Intervention Process

Engage and Assess

Social workers participate in client engagement by helping to de-escalate volatile emotional states through establishing rapport, using empathy, employing emotional management techniques, and accessing outside systems (family, friends, and support groups). Additionally, the social worker assesses the crisis situation to determine the level of care required (general triage may include intensities ranging from one to three) and how the client has been impacted.

Set Goals and Implement Treatment

Goal setting should occur in collaboration with a client's treatment plan. Intervention strategies, tasks, and timeframes should correspond with the desired goal and objectives. The primary goal should be to assist clients in returning to pre-crisis functioning. However, there will likely be additional and related goals and tasks as the plan of action is implemented.

Evaluate and Terminate

At the end of the process, the worker concludes treatment and evaluates the completion of goals. It is important to discuss with the client the coping skills that they have developed, including how they might be able to use those skills for future crises and challenges.

Effect of Poverty

Poverty is often the foundation of a number of other socioeconomic and health problems faced by individuals, families, and communities. Without resources such as money, transportation, or housing, it becomes difficult to buy healthy food, access medical care, drive to work, have quality childcare, or live in a safe area. For adults in poverty, the extreme level of stress that arises from trying to pay bills, provide basic necessities for themselves and their families, and manage multiple jobs often leads to a number of mental, physical, and emotional problems.

These can include substance use, domestic violence, inability to maintain family units and romantic relationships, hopelessness, depression, and desperation. Children who live and grow up in poverty are prone to traumatic and catastrophic health risk factors, such as experiencing or witnessing violence, chronic malnutrition, higher rates of illness, and mood disorders. Experiencing such adverse events in childhood is associated with high levels of stress, impaired functioning, and impaired cognitive ability that can be irreparable. Individuals experiencing poverty are more likely to visit the emergency room for health problems (and often be unable to pay), require government assistance, and commit crimes (often in order to obtain necessary resources). These outcomes create a financial burden on the community and local economy.

Impact of the Environment

The Impact of the Physical Environment on Client Systems

The ecological perspective focuses on the **person in environment**, or the interaction between the individual and the environment around them (including physical environment and family). Privilege, or lack thereof, may also have a large impact on the development of individuals.

As mentioned, the **person-in-environment (PIE) theory** emphasizes the importance of viewing and treating a person within the context of their environment, rather than as a completely independent entity. In order to understand and effectively treat a person, it is critical to evaluate the environment they are in and the physical, emotional, and psychological impact that it has had regarding individual strengths and needs. The environment includes the dynamics of family, school, work place, culture, and social relationships. Rather than being exclusively person-focused or environment-focused, the PIE theory looks at the interplay between the two. If a person is displaying anxiety or depression, for example, the goal would be to determine what cultural, social, or familial factors may be playing a role. PIE seeks to have a holistic view, which then leads to broader and more comprehensive treatment options.

The importance of the PIE theory can be seen working with children. Often children with behavioral or emotional issues are identified as the primary problem. However, when the situation is explored more closely, there are almost always other factors that are contributing to the child's behaviors, including parental conflict, abuse and neglect, or some traumatic experience. If the child's environment is not evaluated and their behaviors are the only focus, it is impossible to determine the root cause of the presenting problem or the most appropriate steps to take. Similarly, it would be futile to merely change or address the child's environment without also dealing directly with the child's emotional and behavioral needs. The person, their emotions and behaviors, and their environment and the circumstances in which they live are all significant when it comes to planning treatment.

The Impact of the Political Environment on Policy-Making and Client Systems

Social welfare legislation can have a dramatic effect on social work practice. Some legislation may help solve social problems that social workers encounter and other legislation may create more problems, challenges, and barriers through which social workers must help clients navigate. To be effective, social workers must be knowledgeable about legislative measures that affect clients. Social workers can also take on the role of legislative advocate by working to change, modify, or create legislation that can benefit groups of people.

Significant Social Welfare Legislation:

- Civil Rights Act of 1964
- Older Americans Act of 1965
- The Child Abuse and Prevention Act of 1974
- Adoption Assistance and Child Welfare Act of 1980
- Americans with Disabilities Act of 1990
- The Family Medical Leave Act of 1993
- The Health Insurance Portability and Accountability Act of 1996 (HIPAA)
- The Patient Protection and Affordable Care Act of 2010

Impact of Social Environment on Client Systems

Social institutions exist to meet the needs of individuals, promote prosocial behavior, define social norms, and create order.

There are five major social institutions:

Family

- Regulates sexual behavior (monogamy)
- Creates and provides for new society members
- Socializes new society members

Religion

- Provides explanations for the unexplainable
- Supports societal norms and values
- Provides a means of coping with life situations

Government

- Institutionalizes norms (by creating laws)
- Enforces laws
- Protects members of society
- Provides a means of resolving conflict

Education

- Prepares society members to contribute to the society in specified roles
- Teaches skills necessary to function within the society

Economics

- Produces and distributes goods needed by society members
- Provides services necessary to the society

Impact of Economic Changes on Client Systems

Economic changes, particularly negative ones, can have a substantial impact on client systems.

- In times of economic turmoil, people tend to cut back on spending and stop seeking services in order to conserve money. Over time, this can lead to a backlog of individuals with major problems that need to be addressed, burdening many components of society.

- A poor economic climate can also exacerbate pre-existing problems, such as depression or substance use, and can create significantly more stress on the family unit, which may spill over into work or school.

- Unemployment has been linked to a withdrawal from social activity, low self-esteem, an increased sense of hopelessness, poorer mental health, and an increase in substance use.

- Such change has an impact within a family, and when enough families are affected, entire communities can experience shifts in attitude and behaviors.

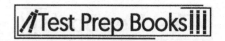

- The experience of living in poverty for many years or at crucial points in time is linked to certain individual outcomes. Children living at the poverty level during preschool and elementary school years are less likely to finish their schooling than are those who experience poverty during later childhood or adolescence only.

- When economic factors are at play with regard to a client's well-being, social workers must be prepared to assist with the development of appropriate coping skills and identification of resources for the client and family system.

The Impact of the Cultural Environment on Client Systems

As mentioned, it is important not to use information about culture, race, and ethnicity in a stereotypical or overgeneralized manner. There are vast differences within groups. For example, group members holding a traditional viewpoint are likely to identify very strongly with their group and to reject the practices of other groups. In contrast, other individuals may be acculturated into a dominant group culture and may not identify with their culture of origin.

Race refers to biologically distinct populations within the human species. *Ethnicity* is a cultural term referring to the common customs, language, and heritage of a category of people. *Ethnic identity* is the identification with a particular group of people who share one's culture and heritage.

William Cross's Stages of Identity Development

William Cross is a theorist and researcher in the field of ethnicity identity development. He is known for his **Nigrescence model** and for his novel *Shades of Black*. The following depicts William Cross's Stages of Identity Development for people of color:

- **Pre-encounter**: Unless prompted to do so, children do not critically evaluate the race-related messages that they receive from the world around them.

- **Encounter**: Often experienced in early adolescence, the individual has one or more experiences that are related to race. Though it is possible for the experiences to be positive, this is often when an individual first experiences racism or discrimination and begins to understand the personal impact of their race.

- **Immersion-Emersion**: After experiencing a race-related incident, the individual strongly identifies with their racial group and may seek out information about history and culture.

- **Internalization**: Racial identity is solidified, and the individual experiences a sense of security in identifying with their race.

- **Internalization-Commitment**: Racial identity is taken one step further into activism pertaining to issues related to the experiences of the individual's racial group.

Sue & Sue's Stages of Racial/Cultural Identity Development

Derald Sue and David Sue developed **Stages of Racial/Cultural Identity Development**. **Derald Sue** is a professor of counseling psychology at Columbia University. **David Sue** is a professor emeritus of psychology at Western Washington University. Their works revolve around multicultural issues in counseling and multicultural therapy. The following are the stages of racial-cultural identity development:

- **Conformity**: The individual displays a distinct preference for the dominant culture and holds negative views of their own racial and/or cultural groups. They may also experience shame or embarrassment.

- **Dissonance**: The individual undergoes a period of re-thinking or challenging their beliefs. For the first time, the individual examines and appreciates positive aspects of their own racial/cultural group.

- **Resistance and Immersion**: The individual shows preference for minority views and actively rejects the views of the dominant culture, experiencing pride about and connection to their racial or cultural group.

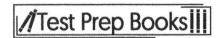

- **Introspection**: The individual becomes aware of the negative impact of the resistance and immersion stage and may realize that they do not actually disagree with all majority views or endorse all minority views.

- **Integrative Awareness**: The individual is able to appreciate both their own culture and differing cultures.

Social and Economic Justice

Professional Commitment to Promoting Social Justice

Social justice is defined as equal rights, opportunities, and privileges for all members of society. The **Code of Ethics of the National Association of Social Workers** (revised 2008) specifically lists social justice as a core value. The **NASW Code of Ethics** states, "Social workers pursue social change, particularly with and on behalf of vulnerable and oppressed individuals and groups of people. Social workers' social change efforts are focused primarily on issues of poverty, unemployment, discrimination, and other forms of social injustice. These activities seek to promote sensitivity to and knowledge about oppression and cultural and ethnic diversity. Social workers strive to ensure access to needed information, services, and resources; equality of opportunity; and meaningful participation in decision-making for all people."

Social Change and Community Development

Community development theory focuses on oppressed people who are in the process of overcoming social problems that were imposed upon them by external forces. In the process of community development, members of a community learn how to improve that community and gain control of their local environment. **Community-level change** brings people together and demonstrates the power of solidarity. This theory also acknowledges the reality that many problems are at the social, rather than individual, level. An implication of the theory is that therapy addresses only the symptoms of a problem and not the underlying causes.

Impact of Globalization on Clients

Globalization, or the process of working and operating in a hyper-connected, international capacity, has affected nearly every industry, including social work. Social workers are no longer limited to working with clients who are in close geographical proximity. They now have the ability to connect with audiences and clients all over the world through social media, email, virtual consultation, and web platforms. This expanded level of outreach can be positive, in that mental health and behavioral interventions, support, and awareness are more easily accessible. However, connecting online with clients can sometimes hinder the quality of personal interaction that practitioners cultivate with their clients. Additionally, it can be tricky to navigate the financial, legal, and security aspects of working with clients online, as these standards vary by geographical location.

Globalization has also opened new topics of interest for social workers. Globalization has led to increased working time, increased use of technology, and increased interactions across cultural, socioeconomic, and gender lines. In many ways, these changes have been associated with higher levels of work-related stress, health problems such as poor sleep, increased rates of mood disorders such as depression and anxiety, and higher awareness of harassment against women and subordinate employees. These are all issues that social workers may not have typically handled with clients in previous decades. They must now become skilled in addressing these issues. Finally, the use of technology, screens, and social media in children has been potentially linked with addictive behaviors, cyberbullying, and increased depression and anxiety rates. This is yet another avenue in which social workers must develop interventions that work in a relatively new context with variables about which research is still emerging.

Criminal Justice Systems

Social workers can have an important role in the criminal justice system. Prison and jail systems are full, and less than a third of incarcerated individuals who are released remain free. Most end up back in the criminal justice

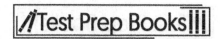

system. Additionally, a number of incarcerated individuals have mental and emotional disorders that often contribute to unlawful behavior. These can include substance use problems or high levels of personal stress. Social workers are trained to understand these contexts, and therefore they can provide valuable insight and counsel before, during, and after legal cases. Therefore, social workers can intervene and offer support during all phases of the justice system. Social workers can work with individuals who were the victims of criminal activities. They are also able to work with perpetrators who have been released, thereby helping to prevent re-incarceration.

Social workers can also provide support to the families of both victims and perpetrators, assist with the transition of having a family member in jail, assist with the transition of having a family member released, and support in educational and professional activities after release. Finally, social workers can have a meaningful impact in the lives of children who may be at risk of ending up in the criminal justice system. By focusing interventions on vulnerable youth, such as education, positive recreational activities, mentoring programs, support for parents, and so on, social workers potentially have the ability to prevent youth and families from ever entering the criminal justice system. This is a much more powerful approach for positive behavior and social change, rather than addressing individual, family, and community issues after crimes have already been committed. Social workers will need to remember to show compassion and withhold judgment when working with criminal offenders; however, they must also be mindful to protect their personal safety in these situations.

Impact of Out-of-Home Placement

Children and elderly or disabled persons are sometimes legally removed from homes when it is determined there is a safety concern such as abuse or neglect. In these situations, the goal of removal is to secure the health, safety, and well-being of the displaced individual. It is likely that many other interventions have been attempted and have not worked, with removal being a last resort. These individuals, particularly children, who have lived in chaotic, dysfunctional environments will already have psychological and behavioral problems, including anxiety, depression, acting out, and displays of aggression. Following removal, these behaviors will likely escalate. Additionally, the parents or other caregivers who have had dependents taken away will also experience anger, confusion, guilt, and an assortment of challenges. Social workers can assume many roles in out-of-home placement, including working with the family of origin, the individual who has been displaced, or the respite caregivers.

Couples Development

Many couples enter treatment after experiencing long-standing problems and may seek help because all other options have failed. One of the goals of couples' therapy is to help clients develop effective communication and problem-solving skills so they can solve problems throughout and after treatment. Other goals include helping the couple form a more objective view of their relationship, modifying dysfunctional behavior/patterns, increasing emotional expression, and recognizing strengths. Workers should create an environment to help the couple understand treatment goals, feel safe in expressing their feelings, and reconnect by developing trust in each other. Interventions for couples are often centered on goals geared toward preventing conflicting verbal communication and improving empathy, respect, and intimacy in a relationship. Therapeutic interventions, along with exercises, are designed to help couples learn to treat each other as partners and not rivals. Cognitive Behavioral Therapy is also used when working with couples. It uses cognitive restructuring techniques to help change distorted thinking and modify behavior.

Impact of Physical and Mental Illness on Family Dynamics

In some ways, physical illness is easier for a family to understand and deal with than mental illness because the symptoms and diagnosis are usually more obvious. When a person is diagnosed with a mental illness, the family may have a hard time accepting its reality. They may deny the diagnosis or try to find alternative explanations. There may be feelings of confusion or embarrassment, especially when those outside the family become aware of the illness. Because of the stigma that comes with mental illness, family members may become judgmental toward

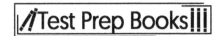

the individual who has been diagnosed. Since symptoms of mental illness often manifest themselves as emotional or behavioral responses, the family members can be tempted to blame the person with the mental illness and become frustrated with the perceived lack of responsibility and willingness to change.

As with physical illness, mental illness may impact the responsibility structure of the family as well as the financial situation, since all family members must adjust to caring for the mentally ill person. Beyond this, there may be irritation or bitterness toward the person suffering, which may be exacerbated by every episode of anxiety, anger, depression, or psychosis on the part of the mentally ill individual. It may be helpful for the social worker to provide the family with education about the illness, as well as involve them in treatment, when possible. It also helps to engage the family in counseling. Support groups or services for the family are also critical in helping them deal with the stressors they face. While families need to acknowledge the reality and seriousness of the mental illness, they also must recognize that, with their help and support, the ill person can thrive and successfully cope with the illness.

Co-Occurring Disorders and Conditions

Co-occurring disorders may also be known as **dual disorders** or **dual diagnoses**. Co-occurring disorders are more prevalent in clients who have substance use history (or presently use substances). Substance use is diagnosed when the use of the substance interferes with normal functioning at work, school, home, in relationships, or exacerbates a medical condition. A substance use diagnosis is often made in conjunction with a mood or anxiety related disorder, resulting in a dual diagnosis.

Co-occurring disorders or dual diagnoses may be difficult to diagnose due to the nature of symptom presentation. Some symptoms of addiction or substance use may appear to be related to another mental health disorder; conversely, some symptoms of mental health disorders may appear to be related to substance use. On the contrary, there are some signs that a co-occurring disorder is present:

Mental health symptoms worsening while undergoing treatment: For example, a client suffering from depression may be prescribed anti-depressants to address depressive symptoms. However, if the client is using substances, he or she may mix other medications with anti-depressants. This can be dangerous in itself, but it may also create a prolonged false sense of well-being while under the influence. Once this feeling fades, it can be confusing for the client to realize whether the prescribed medications are working. Even worse, the client may increase recreational substance use, leading to worse overall mental health symptoms over time.

Persistent substance use problems with treatment: There are some substance use treatment centers that transition clients off of one medication and place them on another, for example, methadone. This may result in a transfer of dependence and ongoing substance use while the client is receiving treatment for mental health disorders.

Another scenario is that a client may seek treatment from a substance use treatment center with clinicians that are not equipped to provide adequate mental health treatment for the client. As the mental health problems persist or worsen while undergoing withdrawal, the client may continue to engage in substance use as a coping skill, therefore making the substance use problem appear resistant to treatment.

It is important for co-occurring disorders or dual diagnoses to be treated together because they occur simultaneously. This may be done utilizing a multidisciplinary team approach in an outpatient or inpatient setting. Treatment of dual diagnoses or co-occurring disorders at the same time in the same setting by the same treatment team is also known as an **integrated treatment** approach.

Psychological Defense Mechanisms

Sigmund Freud's **psychoanalytic theory** focused on the conflicts, drives, and unacceptable desires in the unconscious mind and how they affect a person. One method of dealing with unconscious conflicts is through

defense mechanisms, which are the mind's way of protecting a person from unacceptable thoughts. Here are some of the most common defense mechanisms:

- **Repression** is when a person suppresses thoughts or memories that are too difficult to handle. They are pushed out of the conscious mind, and a person may experience memory loss or have psychogenic amnesia related to those memories.

- **Displacement** takes place when someone displaces the feelings that they have toward one person, such as anger, and puts it on another person who may be less threatening. For example, someone may express anger toward a spouse, but the person that they are truly angry at is their boss.

- **Sublimation** is when the socially unacceptable thought is transformed into healthy, acceptable behavior in another direction. Pain may become poetry, for example.

- **Rationalization** is when unacceptable feelings or thoughts are rationally and logically explained and defended.

- **Reaction formation** occurs when the negative feeling is covered up by a false or exaggerated version of its opposite. In such a case, a person may display strong feelings of affection toward someone, though internally and unconsciously hate that person.

- **Denial** is refusing to accept painful facts or situations and instead acting as if they are not true or have not happened.

- **Projection** is putting one's own feelings onto someone else and acting as if they are the one who feels that way instead of oneself.

Addiction Theories

Addiction is a complex process involving biological, social, cultural, and genetic factors. There is some disagreement in the addiction treatment community about the causes and best treatments for substance use disorders. There are several models of addiction.

The earliest theory of addiction is called the **Moral Model**. This model implies that the person abuses substances because they are morally weak. The addict is viewed as a sinner or criminal and one who does not have the intestinal fortitude to change negative behaviors, therefore choosing to wallow in the misery of their sins.

The **disease model** or **medical model** of addiction, upon which the twelve-step program of Alcoholics Anonymous (AA) is based, specifies that the addict suffers from an illness that will never be cured and is progressive in its development. Even if the individual ceases alcohol intake, the disease remains. AA literature indicates that when one relapses, even after years of sobriety, the addict picks up, not where he left off, but where the disease would have taken him if the drinking had continued. It is seen as a medical disorder and, at times, referred to in the Big Book of AA as having an allergy, with alcohol as the identified allergen. This theory is accepted and understood by many successful AA participants who have maintained sobriety throughout this program for years and who have shared their experience of strength and hope to help others struggling with addiction.

The **bio-psychosocial model** of addiction focuses on the role of the environment. Cultural and social factors influence one's beliefs and attitudes about substance use. In certain religions, it is unacceptable to use alcohol. In others, it may be encouraged—such as the huge sale and consumption of beer at Catholic picnics and fish fries. An addict's observation of others and their patterns of alcohol ingestion influences their attraction to drug or alcohol use as a means for tension relief or a form of celebration. Exposure to family or community members who use large quantities of intoxicants may serve to normalize dysfunctional patterns of use. Some youth observe their parents drink a quart of vodka each night and believe that their family members are just normal drinkers whereas other youth are raised in environments where alcohol is unacceptable or served only on rare occasions.

The **learning theory** of addiction is based on concepts related to positive reinforcement. The assumption underpinning this model is that addiction is a behavior learned through operant conditioning, classical conditioning, and social learning. Social learning takes place through observation. Learning theory posits that the interplay between these three factors contribute to the initiation, maintenance, and relapse of addictive behaviors. The intoxicant serves as an immediate reinforcement in the form of increased euphoria or relaxation. In some cases, it also deters withdrawal symptoms. Both of these forms of reinforcement increase the likelihood that the behavior will be repeated in an effort to recreate the sensation of feeling better.

Genetic theory is based on research indicating that biological children of parents who struggle with addiction are more prone to addiction than children of non-addicts. According to genetic therapy, this genetic predisposition towards addiction accounts for about half of one's susceptibility to becoming an addict. Theorists of this model agree that other factors, such as social experiences, have an impact upon the formation of an addiction.

Effects of Addiction and Substance Use

The repercussions of the addict's behavior can affect many significant aspects of life. The impact of addictions is felt not only by the addict, but also by everyone in that person's family and circle of social support. Those most powerfully affected are the immediate family members—particularly those who live under the same roof as the addict. Friends, extended family, co-workers, and employers also experience fallout from the addict's behaviors.

The spouses or partners of people who struggle with addiction often feel depressed, anxious, and angry. Persons in the throes of addiction often lie and steal to maintain their habit. It is not uncommon for people who struggle with addiction to steal from friends, family, or employers. Families must deal with the anxiety of not knowing when their loved one will come home or what mood or condition the person may demonstrate upon arriving home. Some families must deal with the shame of seeing their loved one arrested or knowing that this person harmed others while under the influence. Others simply become embarrassed by behaviors that loved ones exhibit in public or their failure to show up for an important event, such as a graduation.

Children of parents who struggle with addiction experience embarrassment, fear, anxiety, and sadness. They are more likely to be abused or neglected, especially in single parent homes. Children may suffer when money intended for basic needs is spent on drugs or alcohol instead. When abuse and/or neglect are reported to CPS, these children may be taken from parents and placed in a series of group or foster homes. In some cases, custody is completely severed. Such experiences may lead to deep psychological scars for those closest to the addict.

Indicators of Addiction and Substance Use

Substance use and addiction problems come in many forms. These problems are often undetected or incorrectly attributed to other causes. Indicators include:

- Problems at work or school
- Friction with romantic partners, friends, or colleagues
- Neglect of household responsibilities, self-care, or hygiene
- Reckless behavior leading to legal trouble or financial problems
- Violence
- Tolerance of the substance/behavior over time
- Inability to stop using the substance/engaging in the behavior
- No longer engaging in normal activities in order to spend time/resources on the substance or behavior

Role Theories

Different role theories have culminated in the social role theory, which emphasizes that people's behaviors are motivated by the roles they are given within society. These roles can include aspects of race, gender, employment, position in the family, etc. When a person assumes a particular role, they tend to adopt the expectations of that role as governed by social norms and conventions. Some roles, such as gender, may affect many domains of life, while others—like being a student—may be confined to a particular situation or environment. The roles that a person adopts can strongly impact self-image and behaviors.

Social roles can both negatively and positively impact the individual. While the smooth functioning of society is dependent on different people fulfilling different roles and responsibilities, certain role expectations can limit a person's individuality and self-determination. For example, typical gender roles may cause a woman to feel that her role in society is restricted by the expectations placed upon her.

Feminist Theory

Feminist theory is the study of relations between the sexes, especially in the context of inequality. Discussions often include the topics of gender roles, gender in work-life contexts, societal norms for the genders, and cultural perceptions of gender. Feminist theory also focuses on gender relations and certain power relationships. Feminist pioneers have fought for equal political and social rights for men and women (such as the right to vote or the ability to work outside the home), for making previously male-oriented terms gender neutral (such as using "firefighter" instead of "fireman), for female body positivity and acceptance, for sexual and reproductive rights and protection, and for encouraging supportive relationships between the genders. Feminist theories also support equality for men in such areas as paternity leave, stay at home parenting for fathers, and a redefined masculinity that includes heightened emotional intelligence, awareness, and expression. Feminist theory researchers have been striving to reinvigorate feminist studies, believing that prior theories formed by primarily male researchers should be reexamined.

Influential Feminist Theorists

A number of American female psychologists, psychiatrists, and psychoanalysts have been influential in shaping psychological research that pertains to development in women and in serving as leaders in feminist theory.

Anna Freud (1895–1982) made significant contributions to the field of psychoanalysis, especially regarding the ego and child development. She was the youngest daughter of Sigmund Freud. Some of her works include *Introduction to Psychoanalysis: Lectures for Child Analysts and Teachers* and *Ego and the Mechanisms of Defense.*

Jean Baker Miller (1927–2006) is best known for authoring the revered text *Toward a New Psychology of Women* (1976). She is also known for her work with **relational-cultural theory**, which focuses on how culture affects relationships and how healthy connections with others are an integral part of psychological health and personal growth. These ideas often played a role in diagnosing and treating depression in women.

Carol Tavris (1944–) promotes critical thinking and evidence-based research in psychology, focusing on cognitive dissonance. She believes many of women's so-called psychological issues are actually social beliefs about women's limitations, and that these social beliefs are not backed by science.

Nancy Chodorow (1944–) authored the renowned text *Psychoanalysis and the Sociology of Gender* (1978). Her research focuses on mothering, gender systems, how the family influences female roles in society, and gender identity formation.

Harriet Lerner (1944–) is best known for her work regarding gender roles in marriage, cultural gender norms, and how women can balance self-care with other competing priorities in their lives.

Carol Gilligan (1936–) was a research assistant to **Lawrence Kohlberg**. She argues that his theories of moral development are male-focused and do not apply to women. Her research focuses on the development of morals and ethics in women. She initially published her findings as *In a Different Voice* in 1982.

Gail Sheehy (1937–2020) was an author and journalist who wrote Passages (1976), which supports many of the beliefs and ideas of feminist psychologists. This book covers the different periods of life that women progress through and the emotions they experience in each one. The Library of Congress honored *Passages* as one of the top ten most influential books of its time.

Group Development and Functioning

Some aspects of planning interventions for a group will be similar to planning for an individual. Other aspects are unique to groups. Methods for planning interventions with a group may include:

- Conducting a needs assessment for the group to determine issues
- Ensuring that key stakeholders are involved in data collection and planning
- Continuously involving and updating all stakeholders
- Delegating components of the intervention appropriately by individuals' strengths and resources
- Establishing SMART objectives for changes (specific, measurable, achievable, relevant, time-based)
- Setting goals
- Developing an evaluation plan to assess progress

Techniques for Managing Group Process and Maintaining Group Functioning

Before working on issues, the process of group therapy begins with members becoming familiar with each other. There should be group rules that the entire group agrees upon before entering therapy. The social worker acts as a guide and mediator, and sometimes an instructor, for the group. There are phases of group and may also act as an instructor for the group. There are phases of group therapy process and functioning that include forming, norming, and storming elements. Groups may be open and allow members in at any time, or they may be closed, which means that a group is specifically formed and only select participants are allowed entrance. Both the social worker and the group members are responsible for managing group dynamics.

The group and the social worker are involved in managing group process and maintaining group functioning. Group participants may be invested in maintaining group coherence and functioning, and someone may take the role of gatekeeper in maintaining the group. The social worker may assume the role of leader concerning group process and functioning and may be responsible for group growth and termination. Sometimes group members take specific roles within the group, such as helper, peacemaker, or gatekeeper. At times, group members may also assume negative roles within the group setting. The social worker should recognize when negative roles are assumed and facilitate the members in changing their tendency to take on those negative roles.

Communication Theories and Styles

One of the main names associated with communication theory is **Niklas Luhmann**, a sociologist and systems theorist. In **Luhmann's theory**, it is the communication *between* people and not the people themselves that makes up a social system.

Luhmann used the term **autopoiesis** to define social systems as self-creating, meaning that a social system has the ability to produce itself and maintain itself. Luhmann believed that communications make up the system as well as create other communications. The meaning of a communication is the response it generates.

The **Shannon and Weaver model of communication**, though its origins are mathematical and technical, is cited as one of the primary communication models. This model was the first to conceptualize the activity of the sender and

the receiver. For communication to occur in this model, the sending entity has to prepare and actively deliver information, and the receiver has to wait and actively accept information. The **Berlo model of communication** added that all communication also needed a channel over which to travel.

There are four primary communication styles. **Passive communication** refers to senders who avoid full, direct, and clear verbal or written expression to send a message. Rather, their body language and behaviors may provide a large chunk of the intended message. **Passive communicators** tend to avoid direct communication; they are unassertive, quiet, and anxious. **Aggressive communicators** are overly direct senders, so much so that their communications may harm those who are listening to them. Aggressive communicators are characterized as dominating, impulsive, and critical. **Passive-aggressive communication** refers to senders who outwardly show mildly expressive communication but inwardly feel aggression that is manifested in body language or behavior. **Passive-aggressive communicators** often have a difficult time with confrontation, expressing powerful feelings, and understanding anger. **Assertive communication** refers to senders who are clear and firm yet considerate when stating their message. Assertive communicators tend to speak clearly, feel in control, and respect themselves and others.

Theories of Conflict

Conflict theories center on the premise that all human interactions involve some degree of power struggle, and this struggle may be exacerbated by differences in ideologies, acquisition of resources, culture and class differences, or other variables. Eventually, some groups end up controlling resources and decision-making, therefore limiting opportunities for more submissive or resource-constrained groups. These dynamics eventually shape the culture and interpersonal relationships of a group, whether it is a small team or a country's entire society.

Karl Marx (1818–1883) contributed one of the most widely recognized social conflict theories, **Marxism**, which sees conflict between socio-economic classes as the driver of history. Marx saw capitalist societies as necessarily entangled in conflicts between the working class and the ruling class over resources and opportunities. As privileged groups leave wealth and other resources to their descendants, those descendants have more opportunities, compared to groups who possess lesser quantities and quality of resources. Marx also believed these class conflicts would eventually unseat the ruling class.

Ludwig Gumplowicz (1838–1909) focused on conflicts that arise between different cultures. They arise as one group's desired way of living is threatened by a group with vastly different ideals, especially if one group tries to force its cultural and ethnic norms, beliefs, and systems on another group. These norms may encompass religious views, social views, financial views, family views, and racial views.

C. Wright Mills (1916–1952) developed conflict theories that focus on class structures and political parties. Inspired by Karl Marx, Mills focused his theories on ruling classes in societies and how their behaviors influence the larger group. He states that those in authority shape a society's culture and beliefs; however, the majority of the society does not have the same resources to uphold these behaviors. This is likely to eventually lead to conflict.

Diversity and Discrimination

Biopsychosocial Functioning Throughout the Lifespan

Disability can be a difficult adjustment, especially when it comes on acutely. People may experience disability from a traumatic incident, or it may come on gradually from a chronic disease. Some individuals are born with disabilities; they and their families and caregivers must adjust traditional ways of living. The **biopsychosocial model** is a view that accounts for biological factors, psychological factors, social factors, and their interplay within certain contexts. With regard to disability, an individual who experiences a disability is likely to go through biological changes, psychological adjustments, and social issues. From a biological perspective, an individual with a disability may have a

body part that does not function typically. This in turn may affect adjacent body parts or other biological functions. For example, a patient with a heart disability is also likely to have certain vascular dysfunctions. From a psychological standpoint, an individual with a disability may have trouble adjusting if the disability is sudden (e.g., an unanticipated amputation).

This individual may struggle with feelings of depression or low self-worth, or they may simply feel a general sense of limitation. Socially, people with disabilities may feel it is more difficult for them to do things that other people can do easily. They may worry about making friends or finding romantic partners, or they may worry that they will be unfairly discriminated against in public or in the workplace. Children, especially, may experience teasing or exclusion from peers who are not developmentally mature enough to regularly exhibit sensitivity and compassion. Adults and elders with disabilities may mourn losses of freedom or changes in their lifestyles more than children who were born with disabilities and therefore have not experienced any other way of living. Practitioners who work with individuals experiencing disability should use strengths-based approaches to empower the client to live as well as they can with a disability. Acceptance, positive reinforcement, positive perspective and mindsets, and fostering a sense of community among individuals who are facing similar struggles are ways to support individuals with disabilities.

Effect of Culture, Race, and Ethnicity on Behaviors, Attitudes, and Identity

It is important not to use information about culture, race, and ethnicity in a stereotypical or overgeneralized manner. There are vast differences within groups. For example, group members holding a traditional viewpoint are likely to identify very strongly with their group and to reject the practices of other groups. In contrast, other individuals may be acculturated into a dominant group culture and may not identify with their culture of origin. With that caution in mind, some broad statements may be made to help social workers gain a better understanding of the ways in which race, culture, and/or ethnicity can influence behavior and attitude:

Native Americans
Core values include sharing, honor, respect, interdependence, obligation to family, group cohesion, and co-existence with nature.

Latinos
There is enormous variability among the various Latino groups due to the in their histories and cultural experiences. Values include family, avoidance of conflict, respect for others, religiosity, and patriarchy.

Asian Americans
Great diversity among groups should be noted, as this is a very broad category. Typically, shared values across Asian cultures include family honor, deference to authority and to elders, humility, and avoidance of confrontation.

White Americans
Personal preferences or desires frequently supersede those of the family unit. Values may include capitalism, individuality, and freedom.

African-Americans
Extended family is held as very important; women are viewed as the center and strength of the family unit. Church and the extended church community may play a large role in an individual or family's life. There is a distrust of government and authority figures.

Pacific Islanders and Native Hawaiians
Values include the interconnectedness between all people, not just family, that is related by blood, community, and sharing. They are often polytheistic, with a belief that spirits exist in animals and in objects.

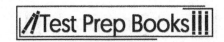

Effects of Discrimination and Stereotypes on Behaviors, Attitudes, and Identity

Discrimination is the unfair or unequal treatment of a person or group that is based on a characteristic, such as race, ethnicity, religion, age, sex, or sexual orientation.

Direct discrimination refers to unfair treatment based on someone's characteristics. An example would be refusing to hire someone because of their ethnicity.

Indirect discrimination refers to situations in which a policy applies the same to everyone, but a person or group of people are negatively impacted due to certain characteristics. For example, a company might require that everyone help unload shipments that come to the office. The policy is the same for everyone, but it's discriminatory towards any disabled employees. In a workplace environment, indirect discrimination can sometimes be allowed if there's a compelling reason for the requirement. For example, firefighters have to meet certain physical criteria due to the nature of their work.

Another form of discrimination is **harassment**. This involves unwanted bullying or humiliation intentionally directed to another person. **Secondary victimization** refers to the unfair treatment received when a person reports discrimination and is not supported by authorities.

Effects of discrimination on an individual may include depression, anxiety, and other mental health issues as well as medical/health-related problems caused by lack of access to health resources. Effects of discrimination on society include diminished resources (e.g., employment, educational opportunities, healthcare) and a culture characterized by fear, anger, or apathy.

Influence of Sexual Orientation on Behaviors, Attitudes, and Identity

Even with today's advances in technology, medicine, and genetics, scientists have not clearly established how sexual orientation develops. It is believed that sexual orientation is a complex interplay of environmental, hormonal, and genetic influences. According to the American Psychological Association, **sexual orientation** refers to an innate attraction to either or both sexes, as well as the person's identity in relation to their attraction. As such, the Association opposes psychiatric treatments such as **conversion therapy**—a form of treatment designed to help homosexuals become heterosexuals through therapy and, sometimes, medical interventions.

Research indicates that family composition may play a role in sexual orientation. For example, homosexual males are more likely to have older male siblings than homosexual women. For men, other factors include being the youngest child or having older mothers, absent fathers, or divorced parents. In women, examples include being an only child, being the youngest child, being the only girl in the sibling group, or experiencing the death of a mother during adolescence. Setting and culture also influence homosexual behavior, e.g., urban areas vs. rural areas.

Impact of Transgender and Transitioning Process on Behaviors, Attitudes, Identity, and Relationships

Being **transgender** can be defined as identifying as a gender other than the gender one was born with. Publicly sharing that one is transgender can be difficult for some individuals. Transgender individuals may live in a community where their identity is not positively accepted or is misunderstood, and they may feel shamed or ridiculed. It may be a difficult experience for close family members to understand the perspective of a transgender individual, which can affect the cohesiveness of family relationships and the family unit. Transgender individuals may also feel a lack of acknowledgement when others fail to use the correct pronouns or respect other identity wishes.

Some transgender individuals choose to medically transition to the gender they identify as. This is a procedure that requires physical, emotional, and psychological support. Individuals not receiving support during their transition can experience extreme feelings of sadness, isolation, and lack of belonging. Medically transitioning individuals also undergo hormonal changes in addition to surgical procedures, and these can cause unexpected feelings and reactions in the individual. There are also medical risks that go along with both the surgical and hormonal procedures of transitioning that the individual has to be aware of and manage. Finally, after the transition is complete, individuals may struggle with living as someone who is relatively unfamiliar to their friends, family members, and colleagues. The transgender person may or may not experience support and acceptance in these groups and relationships, and some group members may even act aggressively toward the transgender person. If this is the case, it may be helpful to find support groups where transgender individuals can find not only friendship and community, but also guidance on how to navigate their new life, society, friends and relationships, and medical recovery.

Systemic Discrimination

Systemic (institutionalized) discrimination refers to discrimination taking place within a society or other institution (e.g., a religion or educational system). Such discrimination can be either intentional or unintentional and results from the majority of people within the institution holding stereotypical beliefs and engaging in discriminatory practices.

Systemic discrimination is often reflected in the laws, policies, or practices of the institution. Systemic discrimination creates or maintains a disadvantage to a group of people by way of patterns of behavior; it can have wide-reaching effects within a region, profession, or specific institution.

The following are example of systemic discrimination:

- Hiring practices that create barriers or result in lower wages for certain groups
- U.S. Supreme Court case, *Plessy vs. Ferguson* (1896) – "separate but equal" public facilities for African-Americans
- Oppression of women in certain countries (e.g., being unable to vote, obtain education, or hold jobs)

Culturally Competent Social Work Practice

Social workers must be culturally competent to meet the needs of all clients. One way to do this is to have the staff demographics reflective of the community served. Workers must also recognize the differences in individuals of the same culture and not use a cookie-cutter approach to deal with people of the same demographic group. Social workers must also work to create agency policies that encourage culturally sensitive treatment and do not allow discriminatory practices. When choosing interventions, treatment methods, and evaluation techniques, workers must also consider the appropriateness of the selection for the client's cultural background.

According to the NASW Code of Ethics, social workers must:

- Understand and be knowledgeable of their clients' culture and demonstrate sensitivity in providing services.
- Become educated as it relates to oppression and diversity regarding race, ethnicity, nationality, gender, disability, sexual orientation, age, and religion.
- Be aware of their own biases and prejudices and use culturally sensitive language in communications with clients.

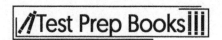

Gender, Gender Identity, and Sexual Orientation Concepts

The term **gender** refers to a range of physical, behavioral, psychological, or cultural characteristics that create the difference between masculinity and femininity. **Gender identity** is a person's understanding of their own gender, especially as it relates to being male or female. **Sexual orientation** is a more complex concept as it refers to the type of sexual attraction one feels for others and how they identify sexually. This is not to be confused with **sexual preference**, which refers to the specific types of sexual stimulation one most enjoys.

Types of Sexual Orientation

- **Heterosexual**: An individual who is sexually and emotionally attracted to members of the opposite gender, also known as "straight"
- **Homosexual**: An individual who is sexually and emotionally attracted to members of the same gender, sometimes referred to as "gay" or "lesbian"
- **Bisexual**: A male or female who is sexually attracted to both same and opposite gender sex partners
- **Asexual**: An individual who has a low level of interest in sexual interactions with others

Types of Gender Identity

- **Bi-gender**: An individual who fluctuates between the self-image of traditionally male and female stereotypes and identifies with both genders
- **Transgender**: A generalized term referring to a variety of sexual identities that do not fit under more traditional categories, a person who feels to be of a different gender than the one he or she is born with
- **Transsexual**: A person who identifies emotionally and psychologically with the gender other than that assigned at birth, lives as a person of the opposite gender

Those who are transgender or transsexual may be homosexual, heterosexual, or asexual.

Practice Quiz

1. What is the last stage of Freud's model of the five stages of human development?
    a. Latent stage
    b. Adult stage
    c. Genital stage
    d. Self-actualization stage

2. In Erikson's eight stages of development, identity vs. role confusion begins at age 12 and contains all but which of the following challenges?
    a. Working through and understanding multiple changes and demands placed upon the child as he or she moves toward adulthood
    b. Increasing understanding of sexual, hormonal, and other physical changes that are occurring
    c. Finding a long-term partner and starting a family
    d. Assessment of one's talents, sexual preferences, and vocational interests

3. According to Piaget, what is the process by which old ideas or beliefs must be replaced with new ones due to obtaining new and more factual information?
    a. Schemas
    b. Assimilation
    c. Object permanence
    d. Accommodation

4. Ivan Pavlov is best known in the field of psychology for his concepts regarding which of the following?
    a. Classical conditioning
    b. Training dogs to behave obediently
    c. Development of sexual identity and orientation
    d. How positive reinforcement affects behavior in children

5. According to B.F. Skinner, providing positive reinforcement increases the likelihood that a desired behavior will be repeated. Which of the following is NOT a form of positive reinforcement when working with children?
    a. A trip to the park with Mom following a week of good behavior
    b. Praise in response to a task well done
    c. Taking away TV and computer privileges for a week
    d. Putting a colorful sticker on a poster each time the child goes to bed on time

See answers on the next page.

Answer Explanations

1. C: The Genital stage starts in adolescence and lays the groundwork for future life relationships. As one enters adolescence, sexual identity and orientation begin to develop. Values regarding sexuality, views about the opposite sex, and the process of interacting with others on a more intimate level occur. These more mature elements of relationship-building lay the foundation for future relationships, but not only from a sexual standpoint. Choice A, the Latent stage, occurs from age 6 to puberty, and it is a time when the child's sexual energy becomes somewhat dormant. Choices B and D are not included in Freud's model of human development.

2. C: Developing a long-term relationship and starting a family are concepts more closely associated with stage six of Erikson's model. This is intimacy vs. isolation, occurring from age 18 through age 40. During this period, one is faced with the challenge of coming to terms with sexual preference, choosing a career path, and determining where, with whom, and how one plans to live. Long-term, future-oriented thinking is required. This phase is important because if it is not successfully mastered, the following phases—generativity vs. stagnation and ego integrity vs. despair— could lead to emotional pain and anxiety in later life.

3. D: Accommodation occurs when one recognizes that previous beliefs were incorrect or no longer beneficial, based upon learning and integrating new information. Accommodation should occur throughout one's life as new information enters the consciousness and the process of assimilation occurs. If one is unable to accommodate new ideas, then it is difficult to grow emotionally and intellectually. If an individual continues to insist that a yellow legal pad and an encyclopedia are just as efficient as using a computer to complete a complex research project, accommodation has failed to occur. This forces the person to work at a snail's pace in comparison to using technology to more quickly and accurately complete the task. Choice *A* is incorrect in that schemas are a set of thoughts and ideas that fit together and present the person with a belief, or even a script, for life. Choice *B* is incorrect because assimilation refers to the process of integrating the new information gained through accommodation. Choice *C* refers to object permanence, a process in which an infant learns that even though a person or object leaves the room, that person still exists, and this understanding reduces anxiety and fear of abandonment.

4. A: Pavlov developed the theory of classical conditioning in which it has been demonstrated that pairing one stimulus with another produces specific responses in animals and humans. In his famous experiment, he noted that when feeding a dog and simultaneously pairing that feeding with the sound of a bell, the ringing of the bell eventually became associated with feeding time. Soon, a behavioral change was noted. The dog salivated to the sound of the bell, even when no food was provided. This demonstrated that people and animals can learn things through pairing one stimulus with another. Although dog training was part of his research, Choice *B* is wrong as it was not the focus of his research. Choice *C* reflects one of Erikson's stages of development, and *D* relates more to the function of behavioral theory devised by B.F. Skinner.

5. C: Taking away privileges for a week is a form of punishment for negative behavior, not a reward for positive behavior. While punishment can be an effective means for changing behavior, research indicates it is less desirable than positive reinforcement. Choices *A*, *B*, and *D* are all forms of positive reinforcement in which a person is rewarded for performing a specific behavior.

Assessment, Diagnosis, and Treatment Planning

Biopsychosocial History and Collateral Data

Biopsychosocial Assessment

In order for an assessment to be comprehensive, the practitioner must gather information and assess the individual **holistically**, which includes examining systems related to the biological, psychological, and social or sociocultural factors of functioning. In some cases, a spiritual component may be included. This process is based on the **biopsychosocial framework** that describes the interaction between biological, psychological, and social factors. The key components of the biopsychosocial assessment can be broken down into five parts: Identification, Chief Complaint, Social/Environmental Issues, History, and Mental Status Exam.

Identification
Identification consists of the details or demographic information about the client that can be seen with the eye and documented accordingly. Some examples of identification information are age, gender, height, weight, and clothing.

Chief Complaint
The chief complaint is the client's version of what the overarching problem is, in their own words. The client's description of the chief complaint may include factors from the past that the client views as an obstacle to optimal functioning. It could also be an issue that was previously resolved but reoccurs, thus requiring the client to develop additional coping skills.

Social/Environmental Issues
The social and environmental issue component evaluates social development and physical settings. **Social development** is critical to understanding the types of support systems the client has and includes information about the client's primary family group, including parents, siblings, and extended family members.

The client's peers and social networks should also be examined. There should be a clear distinction between peers available *online* (such as through online social networks) and peers the client interacts with *face-to-face,* as online systems may provide different forms of support than in-person systems.

The client's work environment and school or vocational settings should also be noted in this portion of the assessment. The client's current housing situation and view of financial status are also included to determine the type of resources the client has. Legal issues may also be included.

History
History includes all of the events in the client's past. Clients may need to be interviewed several times in order to get a thorough picture of their history. Some information in a client's history, such as events that occurred during the stages of infancy and early childhood, may need to be gathered from collateral sources. Collateral sources are persons outside of the client, e.g., family members, police officers, friends, or other medical providers who can provide information related to the client's levels of functioning, life events, and other potential areas of significance in the client's treatment. Obtaining the client's historical information is usually a multi-stage process and can involve the following methods of data collection:

Presenting Problem
Clients should be asked to describe what brings them in for treatment. Although a client may attempt to delve into information that is well in the past, the practitioner should redirect the client to emphasize the past week or two. Emphasis is placed on the client's current situation when assessing the presenting problem.

Past Personal

When reviewing a client's history, noting biological development, may determine whether or not the client hit milestones and the ensuing impact it had on their health. In reviewing biological development, other physical factors should also be assessed for impact on current emotional well-being, including those that may no longer persist, like a childhood illness. As much information as possible regarding the client's entire lifespan (birth to present) should be gathered, with attention paid to sexual development.

Medical

During the medical component of the assessment process, information should be obtained on the client's previous or current physiological diagnoses. These diagnoses can contribute to the client's current situation.

For example, a client with frequent headaches and back pain may be unable to sleep well and therefore be experiencing the physical and psychosocial effects of sleep deprivation. Additional information on other conditions, such as pregnancy, surgeries, or disabilities, should also be explored during this time.

Mental Health

Previous mental health diagnoses, symptoms, and/or evaluations should be discussed. If a client discloses prior diagnoses or evaluations, the practitioner should determine the following:

- Whether the client has been hospitalized (inpatient)
- Whether the client has received supervised treatment in an outpatient setting (to include psychotherapeutic intervention)
- Whether the client has been prescribed medications
- Whether the client has undertaken other treatments related to mental health diagnoses

The client's psychological development should also be reviewed. It is important to gather details on how clients view their emotional development, including their general affect.

The client's cognitive development, in relation to information previously obtained regarding the biological development, should also be reviewed.

Substance Use

Without demonstrating judgment, practitioners should encourage clients to disclose whether or not they have used controlled substances. It is important that thorough information is gathered and symptoms related to substance use are assessed BEFORE rendering a primary mental health disorder diagnosis.

Should a client disclose that he or she has engaged in the use of substances, information as to the type of substance, frequency of use, and duration of exposure to the lifestyle, should be gathered. Additionally, information on what the client perceives as the positive and negative aspects of substance use should be gathered, noting whether or not the client perceives any consequences of substance use, such as job loss, decreased contact with family and friends, and physical appearance.

Techniques and Instruments Used to Assess Clients/Client Systems

Many psychometric instruments exist to assess and diagnose psychological functioning. Some of the most common tests include:

Beck Depression Inventory-II (BDI-II)

BDI-II is a twenty-one-question inventory used to measure presence and severity of depression symptoms in individuals aged thirteen years and older.

Bricklin Perceptual Scales (BPS)

BPS is a thirty-two-question inventory designed for children who are at least six years old. It examines the perception the child has of each parent or caregiver and is often used in custody cases.

Millon Instruments

- **Millon Clinical Multiaxial Inventory III (MCMI-III)**: This 175-question inventory is used to determine indicators of specific psychiatric disorders in adults aged eighteen years and older.
- **Millon Adolescent Clinical Inventory (MACI)**: This 160-question inventory is used to determine indicators of specific psychiatric disorders in adolescents aged thirteen to nineteen years.
- **Millon Adolescent Personality Inventory (MAPI)**: This 150-question inventory is used to determine specific personality indicators in adolescents aged thirteen to eighteen years.
- **Millon Behavioral Health Inventory (MBHI)**: This 165-question inventory is used to determine psychosocial factors that may help or hinder medical intervention in adults aged eighteen years and older.

Minnesota Multiphasic Personality Inventory (MMPI-2)

MMPI-2 is a 567-item inventory. It is one of the most widely administered objective personality tests. It is used to determine indicators of psychopathology in adults aged eighteen years and older.

Myers-Briggs Type Indicator

Myers-Briggs is a 93-question inventory widely used to help people aged fourteen years or older determine what personality traits influence their perception of the world and decision-making processes. A preference is identified within each of four different dimensions: extraverted (E) or introverted (I); sensing (S) or intuitive (I); thinking (T) or feeling (F); and judging (J) or perceiving (P).

Quality of Life Inventory (QOLI)

QOLI is a 32-question inventory that determines the perception of personal happiness and satisfaction in individuals aged seventeen years and older.

Thematic Apperception Test (TAT)

TAT is a narrative and visual test that typically requires the individual to create a story and allows the practitioner insight into the individual's underlying emotional state, desires, behavioral motives, and needs. It's used for individuals aged five years and older.

Rorschach Test

Rorschach test is a visual test that records an individual's perception and description of various inkblots. It's used to determine underlying personality or thought disorders in individuals aged five years and older.

Wechsler Adult Intelligence Scale–Fourth Edition (WAIS-IV)

WAIS-IV is a series of subtests that assesses cognitive ability in individuals aged sixteen years and older.

Information Available from Other Sources

When working with clients, social workers need to compile a complete and accurate assessment of the client's background. Assessments may include information from a variety of sources. **Primary sources of information** are those provided directly by the client. This may include the intake form they complete, direct responses to questions asked by the social worker (such as during an interview or counseling session), documented medical history provided straight from the client, journal entries or other personal communications of the client, or body language exhibited in person. **Secondary sources of information** are taken from a source other than the client.

A medical history provided by the client's doctor, rather than by the client, is considered a secondary source. Records from the client's place of employment, schools, and public data such as home ownership or jail information are also examples of secondary sources of information. Social workers may choose to interview or provide group services to a client's family and friends. Any information that is shared about the client by people close to him or her is considered secondary information. Additionally, if the social worker chooses to conduct literature reviews or searches of evidence-based research to shape an intervention, they are seeking secondary sources.

When requesting or seeking secondary information, such as from employment records or from interviews with family members, social workers must carefully consider the legal, ethical, and moral consequences of their actions. Whenever applicable, consent to seek and use secondary source information should be provided by the client. When this is not possible, such as with a client who is physically or mentally unable to provide valid consent, social workers should use empathy, compassion, a high standard of ethics, and discretion when searching for information about the client. The client should be treated with dignity and respect during this process. All information should be gathered with the sole intention of providing help and support in the client's best interest.

Obtaining Sensitive Information

Interviews are a critical component of social work practice wherein clients provide verbal reports, accounts, or narratives that serve as the main source of information and data collected during the assessment process.

The basis of the interview is a verbal report that involves introductions between the practitioner and client. In some practice settings, the verbal report may be supplemented by an **information sheet** that provides client demographics and a brief overview of the *presenting problem*. **Presenting problems** are prevailing circumstances, symptoms, or difficulties that the client believes is a problem requiring psychotherapeutic assistance.

Principle: Practitioners Need to Establish Rapport with the Client

Providing a description of the services provided and what the client can expect during sessions is the practitioner's first opportunity to build rapport with the client. Rapport development impacts the thoroughness of the information provided from the client. If the level of rapport is limited, the client may not feel comfortable enough to provide sufficient information. The level of rapport also affects the type of impression the client wishes to make on the practitioner. Consequently, it is linked to the client's perception of self-awareness. Some key points to remember are as follows:

- The social worker's own personal characteristics (gender, race, age, etc.) may affect the level of client interaction, based on the client's cultural background.

- Clients may adjust their responses to questions based on how they perceive the social worker's characteristics.

- The social worker's demographics may also have an impact on how the client feels about disclosing sensitive information, such as domestic violence, sexual conduct, or child abuse.

Principle: The Basics of Social Work Practice Should be Used When an Interview is Conducted

Once the introductions have been made and an overview of services and interview processes provided, the client should be asked to explain why they came in for treatment.

Empowering clients to share their concerns and emphasizing the point of hearing things from their perspective provides the practitioner with an opportunity to gauge a client and start "where the client is" in the initial phases of the assessment process.

Technique

The use of encouraging, neutral phrases will help move the conversation forward and encourage the client to share, e.g., "What brings you in to see me today?"

While being encouraging to the client, it is important that practitioners are genuine and not phony. Practitioners should avoid overly complimentary statements, such as "I'm so glad you came in today!" If the client senses the interest is insincere, they may not wish to share.

Principle: The Practitioner Should Start Where the Client Is

After engaging the client, they should be allowed to open up, "vent," or speak freely for approximately fifteen minutes.

Technique

While the client is delving into any emotions, the practitioner should utilize active listening to keep the client engaged. Additionally, it is important to observe the client's **non-verbal cues** (posture, gestures, voice tone and pitch, and facial expressions) that lend to the emotional state. Once the client shares primary concerns, the practitioner can focus on what is important to the client.

The practitioner should observe the client's emotional state, allowing them to feel those emotions freely while providing the account of the problem. Demonstrating empathy is important when responding to the client's emotions. The emotion observed should be acknowledged. For example, if a client is crying, the practitioner can state, "You seem saddened about this," to demonstrate empathy. This practice can also hone in on an important area of the client's life that may be addressed later.

Once the client has been allowed to speak freely, the practitioner should utilize exploratory interviewing skills to delve into the specifics of topics that seemed particularly troubling for the client during the disclosure of the presenting problem.

After the client has revealed the presenting problem and the emotional state has been observed, the client should be asked to delve further into details about current life circumstances. This will provide an opportunity for the practitioner to gain additional information related to the context of the client's problem. It also allows the practitioner to uncover particularly troubling areas that can be explored later. Moreover, it may reveal certain boundaries for the client who is unwilling or unready to discuss certain details of their life.

Principle: It is Important to Engage the Client Verbally While Simultaneously Observing Non-Verbal Cues

The practitioner should ask questions to provide clarification and deeper insight into the client's problems and level of functioning.

Question Techniques

Open-ended questions may provide more detail and allow the client to expand into other areas that can be explored later.

Closed-ended questions are ideal for fact-finding from a client.

Clarification questions should be asked whenever necessary. This may be done through active listening and reflective sharing on the social worker's part to foster comprehensive communication and further build rapport.

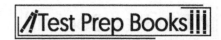

Note Taking Techniques

If the client has questions as to why notes are taken, the reasoning behind it should be explained, and a copy should be offered to the client to make them feel more comfortable and involved in the interview process.

Observation of client behaviors during the interview may be indicative of how the client behaves or reacts in settings outside of the session. Conversely, clients may act outside of their norm, due to the perceived pressure from the interview process. The aforementioned questions and non-verbal observations are essential to determine factors of the client's personality and the context of presenting issues.

Practitioners should also be aware that their interactions affect client behaviors and responses during the interview process. For example, the client may mimic **rigid body language** (folded arms, crossed legs, minimal eye contact) from the practitioner and become defensive in speech pattern, pitch, or tone.

Active Listening and Observation

Active listening is crucial to the relationship and rapport building stage with clients. Social workers must be fully engaged in the listening process and not be distracted by thoughts of what will come next or intervention planning. The worker must not only hear the audible language the client is offering but must also look at the non-verbal behaviors and the underlying meaning in the words and expressions of the client. Nonverbal behaviors include body language, facial expressions, voice quality, and physical reactions of the client. Other aspects of active listening include head nodding, eye contact, and using phrases that show understanding and provide clarity (e.g., "What I hear you saying is…" and "You (may) wish to…"). Workers may verify that they understand the client's message by paraphrasing and asking for validation that it is correct (e.g., "What I hear you saying is…").

Indicators of Sexual Dysfunction

Sexual dysfunction can be related to physical or psychological causes and symptoms—or both. A medical examination can determine if the cause is physical and can usually provide treatment options that include medication or lifestyle changes. If the cause is psychological, such as a result of abuse, depression, or stress, then psychotherapeutic intervention may also be needed. Indicators of sexual dysfunction include:

- Erectile dysfunction in men
- Vaginal dryness or pain in women
- Pain during intercourse or arousal
- Lack of interest in sexual behavior (physically, mentally, or emotionally)
- Fear of sexual interaction
- Inability or difficulty reaching orgasm
- Inability to become aroused or difficulty maintaining arousal
- Negative emotions associated with sexual behavior (e.g., guilt, fear, shame, regret)

Symptoms of Neurologic and Organic Disorders

Neurological and organic processes control the nervous system, and, consequently, all of the physical sensations, muscle contractions, perceptions, sensory experiences, and other biological mechanisms. Therefore, if something goes wrong in these processes, the symptoms that present can vary vastly. These symptoms include:

- **Pain**: muscle pain, joint pain, nerve pain, tingling or burning in an area
- Physical dysfunction: muscle paralysis, muscle tremors, muscle spasms, involuntary muscle tics, imbalance, fainting, vertigo, slurred speech, loss of tongue control

- Abnormal sensations: tingling, burning, hot or cold bursts on the skin, inability to feel cold or heat, incorrect indicators for cold and heat (e.g., touching something warm only to have it feel cool, numbness, "creepy-crawly" feelings on the skin

- Sensory dysfunction: sudden partial or complete blindness, abnormal smell and taste perception, hallucination, ringing in the ears

- Cognitive changes: loss of memory, difficulty in comprehending language or speech, inability to form sentences, difficulty recognizing familiar objects or faces

Assessment and Diagnosis

Problem Formulation

The **problem system** refers to factors that are relevant to the client's presenting problem, which may include other people or environmental elements the client deems relevant to the situation. It is important that questions be asked to determine what the client's perception of the presenting problem is.

Additionally, the practitioner should determine if there are other legal, medical, or physical issues related to the problem. For a comprehensive assessment, the client should also be asked how long the problem has been present and if there are any triggers that he/she believes contribute to the problem. Identification of external supports and access to resources is also key when examining and discussing the problem system.

The presenting problem is generally revealed in the client's statement about why he or she has come in for treatment. If collateral sources are used, information can also be gathered from one or more of the collateral sources who have insight as to why the client is in need of assistance.

Disclosure of the presenting problem allows the social worker to determine the prevailing concerns deemed important by the client.

Social workers can gain a sense of how distressed the client is about the problem or situation and what client expectations are for treatment.

The manner in which the client describes the presenting problem can also provide insight as to how emotionally tied the client is to the problem and whether or not the client came in under their own volition.

It is important to determine the true root causes of the presenting problem. Although a client may come in and voice a concern, it may not be the root cause of the issue. Rather, this concern may simply be an item the client feels comfortable discussing. For example, a client who is experiencing sexual issues may initially speak about anxiety before disclosing the actual problem. This may require an investment of time to allow the client to become comfortable trusting the practitioner.

The history of the problem is important to address because it clarifies any factors contributing to the presenting problem, as well as any deeper underlying issues. Gathering background information on the problem history is also helpful for developing interventions. There are three key areas to address when reviewing the problem history: onset, progression, and severity:

Onset
Problem onset addresses when the problem started. It usually includes triggers or events that led up to the start of the problem; these events may also be contributing factors.

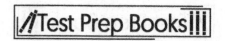

Progression

Assessment of the progression of the problem requires determining the frequency of the problem. The practitioner should ask questions to determine if the problem is intermittent (how often and for how long), if it is acute or chronic, and if there are multiple problems that may or may not appear in a pattern or recurring cluster.

Severity

Practitioners should determine how severe the client feels the problem is, what factors contribute to making the problem more severe, and how the situation impacts the client's adaptive functioning. This may be determined by addressing the following questions:

- Does the problem affect the client at work?

- Is there difficulty performing personal care because of the problem?

- The practitioner should ascertain whether or not the client has access to resources that can provide adequate care (running water, shelter, and clothing).

- The client's living situation should be explored if there are difficulties with personal care activities.

- The practitioner should also ask if there are others for whom the client is responsible, like children or elderly parents/relatives.

- Has the problem caused the client to withdraw from preferred activities?

- Has the client used alcohol or other controlled substances to alleviate or escape the problem? If so, for how long and to what degree?

Psychosocial Stressors

Psychosocial stressors related to the problem should also be addressed by examining what the stressors are and addressing how they may influence the presenting problem.

A **Likert Scale** can be designed to assess the client's perception of how certain stressors are influential.

A **Life Events Scale** can also be utilized to assess the impact of psychosocial stressors. This scale has more than 40 life changes including divorce, death of immediate family members, marriage, work termination, and retirement, and it provides a quantitative level of stress associated with such major events.

Problem ABCs

The **ABCs of a problem** refer to the Antecedent, Behavior, and Consequences linked to a client's perceived problem. The discovery of these items allows the client to define the problem specifically and examine factors affecting emotional well-being.

Antecedents to a problem may be prefaced by the involvement of certain individuals in the client's life. It is important to gather understanding on how the client was involved with these individuals and how the client felt affected. Environmental antecedents may also be present.

The client may disclose interactions that lead to problematic **behaviors**, based on the aforementioned information in the evaluation of the antecedent. When addressing the behavior, it is important that practitioners gather information on what is said before, during, and after the maladaptive behavior takes place.

The **consequences** to a presenting problem are comprised of both cognitive—or personal (internal)—and environmental (external) interactions or reactions to the behavior. The client and other identified participants linked to the problem will reveal their belief sets and values based on the role played in either sustaining the behavior or attempting to decrease it.

The client's coping skills should be evaluated to determine the type of mechanism that he or she implements when the problem is present and whether or not it is an appropriate coping mechanism for the situation.

If the client presents with a heightened emotional reaction as a consequence to the problem, it could progress into another problem and create more complex issues for the client.

At this juncture, the information previously gathered on the client's legal and medical history should be incorporated into the assessment process as it may have a significant impact on the factors shaping the client's problem and the resulting consequences..

Involving Clients/Client Systems in Problem Identification

Accurately identifying an individual's problem helps the practitioner tailor an appropriate intervention. This process includes defining the issue and why it's an issue in the individual's life. It's important to note that the problem is separate from the individual in order to allow the individual to look at the issue objectively without directing blame or shame. Problem identification can be accomplished by administering written or verbal assessments, interviewing the individual's social system or support, and holistically examining the individual's personal situation.

Mental Status Examination

A **mental status exam** is a concise, complete evaluation of the client's current mental functioning level regarding cognitive and behavioral aspects (rapport-building, mood, thought content, hygiene). There are mini-mental status examinations available that allow practitioners to provide a snapshot of the client's overall level of functioning with limited resources and time available. Mental status examinations are usually conducted regularly and discreetly through questioning and noting non-verbal indicators (such as appearance) in order for the practitioner to best guide the session.

Practitioners should document a mental status examination as part of the individual's personal file in order to complete an accurate assessment with all client information. This examination also serves as a baseline for the development and implementation of ensuing therapies, treatments, and interventions. The **mental status** typically includes details about the individual, such as appearance, grooming, facial expressions and general body language, cognition, orientation, manner of speech, indicators of the influence of any controlled substances, mood, impulse control, judgment, thinking style, memory, intellectual functioning, perception of reality, presence of hallucinations or delusions, and interest in the session.

Incorporating Psychological and Educational Tests into Assessment

Psychological and educational tests play a critical role in understanding client backgrounds, belief systems, and perspectives as part of the overall assessment. They also indicate any current or potential psychological, social, or physical needs that the client may have. These pieces of information shape the way social workers develop and tailor interventions for a specific client; they also allow social workers to maintain the highest level of safety for the patient as well as themselves. **Psychological testing** usually includes an interview component, in which the social worker may conduct the initial intake assessment, ask the client personal and family-related questions, and notice body language and other physical behaviors.

Answers to interview questions and body language observations are incorporated into assessments by indicating potential risk or protective factors, individual capacity to accept and receive services, and strengths and challenges that the social worker can incorporate into the client's treatment plan. Clients are also often tested for their communication, comprehension, reasoning, and logic skills in order to determine which methods of intervention will be best received. For example, a client who is unable to communicate verbally may not benefit from simply listening to the social worker providing counseling; a non-verbal, interactive approach will need to be developed for

70

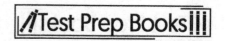

such a client. Clients may also take personality and behavior tests, which allow the social worker to incorporate aspects of the client's beliefs, attitudes, perspectives, and reactions into the assessment.

Psychosocial Stress

Psychosocial stress occurs when an individual perceives a real or imagined threat and feels unable to cope with it. Unchecked, stress can lead to physiological and mental health problems such as heart disease, depression, and anxiety. Indicators of psychosocial stress include:

- High blood pressure
- Regular feelings of sadness, irritability, or anxiousness
- Withdrawal from social events
- Sweating
- Feeling faint or dizzy
- Feeling jittery or antsy
- Muscle and joint pain and stiffness
- Teeth clenching and grinding; chronic jaw pain
- Headaches
- Feeling constantly overwhelmed or unable to complete routine tasks
- Chronic fatigue or sleep problems
- Inability to concentrate

Exploitation Across the Lifespan

Exploitation is taking advantage of someone in a vulnerable position for personal gain.

Financial exploitation of older adults occurs when caretakers, family members, or other individuals take advantage of the elderly member's finances. Indicators of financial exploitation are missing identification, money, credit cards, documents, or valuable possessions; large or frequent checks made out to cash; frequent or expensive gifts for caregiver; older adult's unawareness of income or bills; and blank checks, cash withdrawals, or money wires/transfers.

Sexual exploitation of children occurs when an individual takes advantage of a minor by trading sexual acts or pornography for basic needs. Indications of sexual exploitation are spending time with older individuals or an older "boyfriend" or "girlfriend"; spending time in inappropriate locations such as hotels or bars; signs of emotional or physical abuse or neglect; uncertainty of where one's self is (as they have moved around to various geographic locations); being missing from home or not attending school; acting fearful or anxious around others; and signs of being groomed (someone building a connection with the child, either online or in-person, in order to gain trust and ultimately abuse and/or exploit the child). Individuals who are being groomed might be secretive about their behavior, might possess unexplained money or items, and may have access to alcohol and/or drugs.

Girls are disproportionately affected by sexual exploitation and trafficking. The majority of children and adolescents are exploited by someone they know.

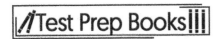

Traumatic Stress and Violence

In normal circumstances, an individual is typically able to return to a calm state after a stressor passes. Traumatic stress and violence, however, cause long-term effects, and the patient may not be able to recover to a normal state. Indicators of traumatic stress and violence include:

- Unexplained anger or outbursts
- Substance use and abuse
- Uncontrolled behaviors such as binge eating, compulsive shopping, gambling, hoarding, or sex addiction
- Attachment issues
- Chronic and intense feelings of shame, regret, guilt, and/or fear
- Obsessive thoughts or behaviors related to the traumatic event
- Eating disorders
- Self-harm, self-injury, or other self-destructive behaviors
- Sleep problems such as insomnia or sleeping too much
- Intense anxiety, especially in social or crowded situations
- fear, clinginess, aggression, withdrawal, or regression in developmental behavior in children

Methods Used to Assess Trauma

Trauma occurs when a client experiences a deeply disturbing experience that yields an intense emotional response. Traumatic events may interfere with a client's baseline level of functioning. It is important for the social work practitioner to have an understanding of the detrimental effects, both visible and invisible, that traumatization can have on a client.

The practitioner should have an understanding of the client's baseline level of functioning. This information may be gathered first-hand from the client or through collateral sources if the client is unable or unwilling to provide that information.

The practitioner should have an understanding of how to guide the client gently through describing the traumatic experience and the emotions related to it. In doing so, the practitioner should have an understanding of the widespread, lasting, effects that trauma can have, as well as the multiple recovery and treatment options. This knowledge also helps prevent re-traumatizing the client.

An adult client may present with traumatic stressors due to one or more events that occurred during childhood. Symptoms of anxiety, depression, or other mood disorders that are actually related to the traumatic event(s) may present in session and daily functioning. A practitioner should be aware that symptoms of trauma could manifest in places and interactions outside of the client, such as within the family system, with peers, and at work.

Risk Assessment Methods

The practitioner conducts **risk assessments** to determine any influence that could result in harm or increased risk of harm to the individual. Assessing risk can be an ongoing process, as it's important to always have updated, accurate information. Risk-assessment methods will also vary depending on the circumstance (i.e., criminal justice, child abuse or neglect, community care). Some common methodology themes in risk assessment include the following:

Universal Risk Screening

This is a general screening for certain risky behaviors (e.g., violent behavior, substance use problems, self-harm) that may result in additional screenings, referral for treatment, or stronger outcomes such as institutionalization (in the instance of high suicide risk, for example). This screening often takes place in initial consultations or as part of the individual's intake forms and may be administered on an ongoing basis (e.g., at every session) to remain current.

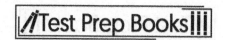

Unstructured Methods

These typically include clinical assessments without any specific, prepared structure. While high-level professionals often make judgments during this process, outcomes can sometimes be considered biased and unreliable.

Actuarial Methods

These include highly logical, regimented tests and scales used to predict the likelihood of certain behavior patterns in a specified time frame. While scientific and evaluative in nature, some argue that these methods may place undue blame on individuals or be too inflexible to allow for the likely interplay of many influencing factors in an individual's presenting issue.

Structured Professional Judgment

This combination of the previous two methods is generally the most accepted. It uses structured tools appropriate for the scope of the case but allows for the judgment and flexibility of the practitioner to decide what information is useful and to note any external information that may not be caught by standardized assessments.

Client's Danger to Self and Others

Practitioners should always be alert to indicators that individuals may pose a threat to themselves or others. These indicators may be obvious or discreet and may include:

- Substance use and abuse
- Sudden apathy towards others or society
- Sudden lack of personal care or grooming
- Isolation
- Apparent personality change
- Drastic mood shifts
- Marked change in mood. Both depressed mood and a positive change in mood can be associated with suicidal thoughts or plans. A sudden positive change may indicate that the individual has made a decision and is no longer experiencing personal turmoil.
- Verbalization of feelings such as extreme self-loathing, desire to be dead, being a burden to others, or volatility toward others.

Risk Factors for Danger to Self and Others

A client who presents as a danger to self or others should be assessed through a biopsychosocial lens. In addition, tailoring crisis management techniques to the immediate problem can help de-escalate the situation. Open-ended questions should be used to gather as much information from the client as possible. It is also important to consult collateral information from any nearby family members to document other pertinent information about the client.

- The client should be asked if there are plans to harm anyone. If the client states yes, the practitioner should determine what the plan entails.

- Any and all threats made should be taken seriously and reported to the proper authorities. Colleagues may be consulted to determine the validity of a threat if the practitioner is unclear on the client's intent.

- Identifying the critical event and antecedent that preceded it is important. The client should be asked to provide as much information on this as they are willing in order for the practitioner to to gain a better perspective of the client's point of view.

- Determining whether or not the client has engaged in self-injurious behaviors (SIB) is also important. Here are a few examples of SIB:

  o Excessive use of alcohol or other substances

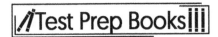
- o   Cutting

- o   Banging one's head against a hard object

- o   Ignoring necessary medical advice (not taking prescribed pills, leaving a hospital against medical advice)

- The practitioner should also evaluate the social and cultural factors that contribute to how the client reacts to stressful situations, including the following:

  - o   History of violence

  - o   Stability of relationships (school, work, and home)

  - o   Social isolation or withdrawal from others

  - o   Limited access to social resources

- Any recent life stressors that would lead to the client carrying through with a plan to harm self or others

- Assessing the client's current thought process is important. Do they present with confusion, clarity of the situation, or irrational thinking?

- If the client has a clear, concrete plan of action, then the risk for harm to self or others should be considered high.

Risk Factors Related to Suicide

- Previous attempts at committing suicide
- History of cutting
- Multiple hospitalizations related to self-injurious or reckless behavior, such as those noted below:
- Drug overdose
- Alcohol poisoning
- Inhalation of carbon monoxide
- Statement of a plan to commit suicide/suicidal ideations and access to the means to complete it
- Ownership or access to a lethal firearm
- Stated plan to cut one's wrists "the right way"
- Warnings or statements that suicide is planned
- Other factors related to suicide risk
- Age—middle-aged adults present highest suicide risk over other age groups
- Gender—males more likely to commit suicide than females
- Adolescents—high suicide risk, especially those heavily-entrenched in social media groups as a means of support and socialization
- Presence of a mental health disorder
- Life stressors from work or school
- Family history of suicide
- Family discord or other relationship trauma (divorce, break-up, widowed)
- Excessive drug or alcohol use
- Chronic illness
- Job loss

Assessing the Client's/Client System's Strengths, Resources, and Challenges

Once the client has identified the existing problem and systems, the client's **internal support systems** should be assessed, which includes examining the client's strengths and coping abilities. As with other facets of the

74

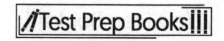

assessment process, the client can provide a verbal report answering an open-ended question about what they view as current strengths and weaknesses.

Additionally, the social work practitioner can ask the client to provide a narrative related to a recent experience (it does not necessarily have to be linked to the presenting problem), in order to showcase strengths and weaknesses. Using finding questions can guide the client to describe their reaction to events comprehensively, to identify what favorable actions were taken, and to research what alternative actions could be taken. The social work practitioner may then summarize back to the client the strengths they heard in the narrative. This ensures that the client feels heard and understood.

The social work practitioner may also use scales to assess the client's strengths and weaknesses. A **dual perspective worksheet** may be utilized to identify the supports and obstacles perceived by the client in current social interactions. The worksheet helps create a visual map of the areas of strength the client can rely on as a means of improving areas of functioning, while simultaneously allowing the client to see areas that could use additional improvement. The social work practitioner can create a treatment plan with the client to develop or enhance coping skills, focusing on strengthening weaker areas and utilizing stronger ones.

Indicators of Motivation, Resistance, and Readiness to Change

Motivation and resistance impact a client's readiness to change behavior. These are two crucial components to examine when developing an intervention plan. **High motivation** is indicated by self-confidence and self-efficacy, as the client believes they are capable of change. High motivation is also characterized by a client's desire to correct an identified problem, work toward a goal, and reliably show up for sessions. High motivation also shows in the client's belief that implementing a change will improve their overall quality of life.

Resistance can refer to any behavior that indicates the client does not want to work with the social worker or improve their personal situation. Resistance may be indicated by a client's refusal to show up on time, or at all, for sessions. A client involuntarily coming to sessions (such as by a court order) may state that there is no tangible problem to work on, or the client may state they feel no changes are occurring. Social workers should examine resistance holistically to ensure they are not contributing to it. For example, clients may exhibit resistance to counseling sessions if they do not feel comfortable with the social worker, if they do not understand the social worker, or if they are expected to work on issues that they do not yet feel ready to address.

Readiness to change occurs in six stages: **pre-contemplation** (where an individual does not believe a need for change exists or is not self-aware), **contemplation** (where an individual recognizes a problem but is not ready to address it), **preparation** (where an individual recognizes a problem and sets the stage for change), **action** (where an individual takes active, involved steps to stop a problem), **maintenance** (where the individual commits to the desired behaviors), and **termination** (where the individual is able to regularly sustain the desired behaviors without relapse).

Assessing Motivation, Resistance, and Readiness to Change

Motivation and resistance pertain to the individual's readiness to acknowledge and change behaviors. Motivation is higher and resistance is lower when an individual feels ready to make a change. Some indicators of high motivation and low resistance include:

- Awareness and open acknowledgment of the presenting issue
- Willingness to list pros and cons of behavior change
- Willingness to make small steps toward and document outcomes of behavior change
- Acknowledgment that changing behavior is in the individual's best interest

Some indicators of low motivation and high resistance include:

75

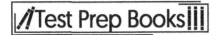

- Lack of recognition of a present problem
- Hostility or apathy towards the practitioner (which may be revealed by skipping sessions)
- Discussion of a presenting issue without openness to changing associated behaviors

Practitioners can increase the client's motivation by discussing changes positively in terms that demonstrate benefit to the client's life, allowing the client to set their own goals and providing assistance only for those specific goals, highlighting the tools the client possesses to make changes, and acknowledging and respecting the client's fears about change.

Assessing the Client's/Client System's Communication Skills

An individual can communicate verbally and non-verbally through body language or silence. Interviews, two-way casual conversations, and written or verbal standardized assessments can help the practitioner determine the individual's communication skills. Role-playing a specific situation can help the practitioner determine how an individual communicates in certain contexts. Assessing the individual's personal, family, social, or cultural context can also provide valuable insight to communication skills and help validate an assessment.

Assessing the Client's/Client System's Coping Abilities

Ego strength is the ability of the individual to be resilient in the face of stressors. Generally, individuals with high ego strength will be able to return to a normal emotional state after experiencing crisis. They will be able to appropriately process it and cope with the demand of doing so. Positive or high ego strength is marked by:

- The ability to acknowledge mood shifts without getting overwhelmed
- The ability to cope positively with loss and setbacks
- Realizing painful or sad feelings will decrease in intensity over time
- Taking personal responsibility for actions and reactions
- Self-discipline in the face of temptation or addictive urges
- Setting and respecting firm limits and boundaries
- Avoiding people who are negative influences
- Learning from mistakes rather than blaming oneself or someone else

Consequently, the absence of these indicators may reveal areas around which to tailor intervention or treatment. These indicators may be determined through verbal discussion or standardized assessments.

Strengths and Challenges of the Client

A **client's personal and system strengths** are aspects that support and promote an effective intervention and recovery. Individual client strengths may include a desire for positive change, willingness to collaborate with the social worker in developing an intervention, an interest in personal growth, resiliency, the presence of positive coping mechanisms, reliable transportation to and from counseling sessions, a way to pay for services, and any other physical, psychological, emotional, or financial behavior that promotes a continuous journey toward a positive resolution for the client. The client's system refers to their personal support system (such as family, friends, and professional colleagues) and the environment in which the client lives and works. Strengths in the client's system include aspects like close friends and family who support intervention procedures, employers that allow time off or sponsored insurance for receiving care, and colleagues that support the client's goals during the work day.

Client challenges include any personal aspect that may be a barrier to an effective intervention. Challenges may include a client who does not desire to change, who is not willingly attending social services, who feels their situation is hopeless, or who does not have the means to reliably attend intervention services (whether due to financial reasons, lack of child care, lack of transportation, and so on). Challenges in the client's system may include

76

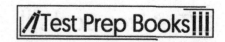

a non-supportive family unit (one that does not support receiving social services or that is unwilling to examine the family's role in the client's issues), a lack of close friendships or relationships, the inability to leave work for sessions, or cultural norms or beliefs that stigmatize receiving counseling services.

Diagnostic and Statistical Manual of the American Psychiatric Association

The current American Psychiatric Association manual for the classification of mental disorders is the *Diagnostic and Statistical Manual of Mental Disorders, Fifth Edition, Text Revision*, or the **DSM-5-TR**. It is an updated and revised version of the APA's previous classification and diagnostic tool from 2013, the **DSM-5**. The **DSM-5-TR** serves as an authority for mental health diagnosis and functions as a tool for counselors to make treatment recommendations. The *DSM-5-TR* is organized in accordance with the developmental lifespan. In addition to guiding diagnosis, the updated framework of the *DSM-5-TR* is designed to help researchers and clinicians better understand how disorders relate to one another and ultimately improve treatment outcomes for patients.

There are several notable changes to the *DSM-5-TR* as of 2022:

- the addition of scientific knowledge accumulated since the 2013 update
- the recognition of the role of culture in psychiatric diagnosis
- the revision of language used regarding race, gender, and gender identity
- the description of a Cultural Formulation Interview for use in the counseling intake process
- the correction of ICD codes for mental health disorders
- the addition of more precise criteria for childhood conditions
- the addition of a new mental disorder, Prolonged Grief Disorder, to the category of Trauma- and Stressor-Related Disorders
- the addition of new conditions of clinical attention
- the updated names of two disorders, Functional Neurological Symptom Disorder and Intellectual Development Disorder
- the addition and removal of diagnosis specifiers, including those for Bipolar I, Bipolar II, Obsessive-Compulsive Related Disorder, Persistent Depressive Disorder, and Gender Dysphoria

Complete Listing of *DSM-5-TR* Diagnostic Criteria Chapters
- Neurodevelopmental Disorders
- Schizophrenia Spectrum and other Psychotic Disorders
- Bipolar and Related Disorders
- Depressive Disorders
- Anxiety Disorders
- Elimination Disorders
- Other Mental Disorders and Additional Codes
- Obsessive-Compulsive and Related Disorders
- Trauma- and Stressor-Related Disorders
- Dissociative Disorders
- Somatic Symptom and Related Disorders
- Feeding and Eating Disorders
- Sleep-Wake Disorders
- Sexual Dysfunctions
- Gender Dysphoria
- Disruptive, Impulse-Control and Conduct Disorders
- Substance-Related and Addictive Disorders
- Neurocognitive Disorders

- Personality Disorders
- Paraphilic Disorders
- Medication-Induced Movement Disorders and Other Adverse Effects of Medication
- Other Conditions That May Be a Focus of Clinical Attention

Mental and Emotional Illness Throughout the Lifespan

Mental and emotional illness can present in a number of ways and vary depending on the illness, the person, and the circumstances. Some symptoms of mental and emotional illness include:

- Chronic feelings of sadness
- Inability to focus
- Extreme mood variation
- Loss of interest in activities one used to enjoy
- Lack of sexual interest or desire
- Intense, and sometimes unexplainable, feelings of guilt, shame, regret, fear, or worry
- Chronic fatigue
- Sleep problems, such as insomnia or sleeping too much
- Feeling overwhelmed by daily routines or tasks
- Substance use
- Compulsive or obsessive thoughts or behaviors
- Hallucination
- Thoughts of suicide
- Thoughts of harming oneself or others
- Excessive weight gain or weight loss
- Unexplained anger or irritability
- Detachment from loved ones
- Medically unexplained physical symptoms (psychosomatic) such as headaches, jaw pain, stomach pain, or joint stiffness.

Effect of Aging on Biopsychosocial Functioning

The **biopsychosocial model** proposes multiple causes from three main groups (biological, psychological, and social/environmental) that can contribute to mental health disorders. **Biological factors** are related to the body's physiological responses and may present in the form of fluctuations in heartbeat, sweating, shortness of breath, digestive issues, or issues with brain function.

Biological factors are also linked to genetics. One may have predisposed vulnerabilities to mental health disorders due to inherited traits or a history of mental health disorders within one's family. Although biological factors may heighten one's vulnerability to mental health issues such as stress and anxiety, they are not enough to substantiate a mental health diagnosis.

Psychological factors refer to cognitive processes, such as thoughts, beliefs, one's view of an experience, and one's view of self. Thought process can shape the view of self in turn, shapes the sense of stability and control across environments and has a direct impact on how a person functions. Specifically, cognitive processes or psychological factors determine whether a person perceives a situation as threatening or non-threatening and reacts accordingly.

Social or environmental factors are present in one's immediate physical surroundings and social systems such as work, school, home, and peer group. A person's social environment is significantly influenced by the aforementioned biological and psychological environments. For example, their level of stress may be directly and

simultaneously affected by conditions in the workplace and by a peer group. The stress may present with physiological symptoms (such as muscle pain), negatively contributing to one's overall health and wellness.

Biopsychosocial Responses to Illness and Disability

Receiving a diagnosis of a serious physical illness is life changing in many ways. Along with the many physiological impacts of the illness, such as pain and tiredness, there are many psychological and social factors that influence a person's ability to cope with the new diagnosis. Parenting, careers, and intimate relationships are just a few areas that may be impacted.

One's lifelong aspirations are challenged and may have to be adjusted with the reality of a foreshortened future. Some illnesses may bring feelings of guilt or shame, if related to unsafe sexual behaviors, drug use, smoking, overeating, or other unhealthy behaviors. Depression is a common response to a diagnosis of illness, which may reduce motivation to comply with treatment. It could also cause the person to withdraw at a time when support is important or reduce one's confidence in asking others for needed assistance.

Many illnesses have an emotional component, and symptoms can be triggered or exacerbated by stress. In addition to counseling or the use of antidepressant medication, taking an active role in treatment and finding a support group of others dealing with the same illness has been proven helpful. Marriage and family therapy may be useful as well since serious illness impacts all the people who are close to the patient.

Psychotropic and Non-Psychotropic Prescriptions and Over-the-Counter Medications

Psychotropic prescription medications are used to treat disorders such as schizophrenia, psychosis, depression, anxiety, bipolar disorder, attention deficit disorder, and a variety of mood disorders. Common antipsychotics include the brand names Abilify, Risperdal, and Seroquel. Possible side effects of antipsychotic medications include fatigue, weight gain, nausea, vomiting, anxiety, and gastrointestinal discomfort. Common mood stabilizers include the brand name Depakote and a variety of lithium-based medications. Possible side effects of mood stabilizers include gastrointestinal discomfort, weight gain, and fatigue. Common antidepressants include brand names Celexa, Lexapro, Zoloft, Prozac, Elavil, Tofranil, and Parnate. Possible side effects of antidepressants include nausea, weight gain, sexual dysfunction, sleep disorders, and gastrointestinal discomfort. Common anti-anxiety medications include brand names Ativan, Xanax, Valium, Lexapro, and Buspar. Possible side effects of antianxiety medications include fatigue, nausea, and gastrointestinal discomfort. Other psychotropic prescription medications include Vyvanse, which manages attention deficit disorders and hyperactivity, and Lyrica, which prevents seizures.

Non-psychotropic prescription medications are used to treat non-psychological disorders, such as hormonal disorders. The most common non-psychotropic prescription medications include the brand names Lipitor and Crestor (which lower cholesterol levels), Synthroid (which manages hypothyroidism), Ventolin (which manages asthma), and Nexium (which manages acid reflux). The side effects of these medications vary based on pre-existing conditions but can include appetite dysfunction, nausea and vomiting, gastrointestinal discomfort, sleep problems, jitters, dry mouth, and fatigue.

The most commonly used over-the-counter medications include cough, cold, pain relief, and fever-reducing medications. These include the brand names Tylenol, Motrin, Aleve, Advil, Mucinex, Sudafed, and Claritin. Major side effects are typically only associated with over-the-counter cough and cold medications and can include extreme drowsiness. Other commonly used over-the-counter medications include those that treat acid reflux, constipation, and diarrhea.

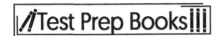

Indicators of Somatization

Somatization refers to physical and physiological manifestations of mental, emotional, and psychological conditions. Somatization most commonly occurs when a client does not have the coping tools or capacity to manage mental, emotional, or psychological stressors. There may or may not be physical or physiological indicators of the symptoms that the client says they feel; however, the symptoms feel extremely real to the client. If a client visits a medical doctor reporting physical or physiological symptoms for which the doctor can find no tangible cause, this may be an indicator that the client is experiencing a somatoform disorder.

Common somatoform symptoms include pain, muscle stiffness, nausea, fatigue, gastrointestinal disorders and discomfort, the experience of losing a function or sense, and hypochondriasis. When investigated from a biopsychosocial perspective, these symptoms often correspond with anxiety, stress, or trauma. Pediatric patients often report somatoform symptoms if they feel neglected, scared, or in need of attention. Therapeutic interventions often involve cognitive behavioral therapy, including introspective practices, the development of healthy coping mechanisms, and the development of problem-solving skills. Therapy may extend to the family unit in pediatric cases, as a shift in parenting style or the provision of parenting support can often help alleviate the pediatric patient's symptoms.

Indicators of Feigning Illness

Feigning illness refers to individuals acting, for deceptive purposes, as though they have symptoms of a physiological, psychological, or social disorder. They may feign illness for an external purpose, such as gaining a reward or avoiding punishment. For example, it is possible that a client who is undergoing a divorce feigns symptoms of spousal abuse to gain more from the proceedings. A client who is charged with homicide may feign a mental illness in order to change the outcome of their sentencing. Feigning illness can also take place for internal reasons.

For example, a client may be struggling with a personal situation, such as a lack of employment or lack of a romantic relationship. They may feign symptoms they present as the cause for their problems. It can be difficult to concretely pinpoint when someone is feigning illness, and it is important not to undermine clients or accuse them of falsifying symptoms that could be real from their perspective. Clients who are truly feigning illnesses may have trouble maintaining the symptoms or relaying them accurately over long periods of time, may have visible circumstances that would indicate that having an illness would be beneficial for their situation (such as someone who is trying to claim disability work benefits), or their client systems may report that the client shows no symptoms outside of intervention sessions.

Basic Medical Terminology

Basic medical terminology can help the practitioner determine the relationship between an individual's physiological and psychological health. It can also help practitioners work seamlessly in multidisciplinary teams with health care professionals such as psychiatrists and nurses. There are ten primary biological systems in the human body, and learning certain prefixes and suffixes can help one understand which systems are related to common medical conditions and terminology.

Cardiovascular System

The **cardiovascular system** circulates blood through the body via the heart. It uses arteries to bring oxygen and nutrients to the organs of the body and veins to take away waste from the organs. Related terms include:

- **Cardi-/Cardio-**: heart
- **Angi-**: vessel
- **Veno-**: vein

80

- **Hem-/Hemo-**: blood
- **Thromb-**: clot
- **Atherosclerosis**: hardening of the blood vessels
- **Angina pectoris**: chest pain
- **Arrhythmia/dysrhythmia**: abnormal heart rhythms (e.g., too fast or too slow)
- **Ischemia**: insufficient blood flow, which can lead to angina or heart attack

Digestive System

The **digestive system** removes nutrients from consumable energy sources through the mouth, esophagus, stomach, and intestines. It removes wastes from the body through the intestines and bladder. Related terms include:

- **Gastr-/Gastro**: stomach
- **Hep-/Hepato-**: liver
- **Chol-**: gall
- **Cyst-/Cysto-**: bladder, sac
- **Emes-**: vomit
- **Gastroesophageal Reflux Disease (GERD)**: a condition where stomach acid reverses into the esophagus and causes severe burning and inflammation
- **Cirrhosis**: progressive liver disease, often caused by alcoholism
- **Crohn's Disease**: a chronic, painful bowel or intestinal disease marked by constant inflammation
- **Peritonitis**: inflammation of the abdomen

Endocrine System

The **endocrine system** uses hormones to regulate complex functions like growth, reproduction, and metabolism. Related terms include:

- **Thyro-**: thyroid
- **Aden-**: gland
- **Hypo/hyperthyroidism**: a condition where the thyroid makes too little or too much thyroid hormone, resulting in metabolic and energy issues

Integumentary System

The **integumentary system** consists of skin, hair, and nails to protect the internal organs from external damage. Related terms include:

- **Adip-**: fat
- **Lip-**: fat
- **Cutaneo-**: skin
- **Derm-**: skin
- **Melan-**: black, dark
- **Seb-**: sebum, oily
- **Melanoma**: a type of skin cancer
- **Dermatitis**: inflammation of the skin
- **Kaposi Sarcoma**: usually fatal skin tumor

Lymphatic System

The **lymphatic system** is a network of vessels that promote the body's ability to fight infection and disease. Related terms include:

- **Blast-/-blast**: bud or germ
- **Lymph-**: clear fluid
- **Phag-**: eat
- **Lymphoma**: a malignant condition of lymph tissue
- **Metastasis**: the spreading of cancerous cells, usually through lymph

Musculoskeletal System

The **musculoskeletal system** enables the body to physically function and provides support for it. Related terms include:

- **Oste-**: bone
- **Chondr-**: cartilage
- **Arth-**: joint
- **Myel-**: bone marrow
- **Ten-**: tendon
- **Burs-**: bursa
- **Myo-**: muscle
- **Arthritis**: loss of mobility and cartilage in joints
- **Osteoporosis**: loss of calcium in bones resulting in structural weakness

Nervous System

The **nervous system** is responsible for communication between the brain and the muscles, resulting in physiological action and tangible sensation. Related terms include:

- **Ceph-**: head
- **Myel-/Myelo-**: spinal cord
- **Neur-/Neuro-**: nerve
- **Multiple Sclerosis**: a disease where nerve fibers lose their insulation and ability to communicate with muscles, often leading to paralysis or other sensory problems
- **Epilepsy:** recurring seizures or convulsions
- **Aphasia**: loss of speech

Renal System

The **renal system** comprises primarily the kidneys, which filter waste from the blood. Related terms include:

- **Neph-**: kidney
- **Ren-**: kidney
- **Ur-/-uria**: urine
- **Pyel-**: renal ducts
- **Nephrosis**: diseased kidneys
- **Nephrolith**: kidney stone
- **Urethritis**: inflamed urethra, which affects the expulsion of urine
- **Enuresis**: uncontrollable bladder and urine expulsion

Reproductive System

The **reproductive system** includes sexual organs responsible for conception and maturation of a fetus. Related terms include:

- **Orchid-**: testes
- **Test-**: testes
- **Andr-**: male
- **Hyst-**: uterus
- **Colp-**: vagina
- **Men-**: menstruation
- **Mammo-**: breast
- **Masto-**: breast
- **-pareunia**: intercourse
- **Prostate-Specific Antigen**: a protein which, in high levels, may indicate prostate cancer in males
- **Endometriosis**: excessive, hardened uterine tissue that can cause abdominal bleeding and painful menstruation in females
- **Pelvic inflammatory disease**: inflamed uterine tubes in females
- **Dyspareunia**: painful sexual intercourse

Respiratory System

The **respiratory system** brings oxygen into the body and releases carbon dioxide out of the body through the lungs. Related terms include:

- **Rhin-/Rhino-**: nose
- **Laryn-**: larynx
- **Trach-**: trachea
- **Bronch-**: lung
- **Pne-/Pneu-**: breathing, lungs
- **Pulmo-**: lung
- **Emphysema/Chronic Obstructive Pulmonary Disease (COPD):** a lung condition where the progressive deterioration of the membranes results in the inability to exchange oxygen
- **Cystic fibrosis**: a genetic disease resulting in abnormal mucous production, lung infections, and lung scarring
- **Pneumoconiosis**: any lung disease in which pollutants become trapped or lodged in the lungs

Indicators of Behavioral Dysfunction

Ideas about what is normal versus what is abnormal with regard to behavior are society-dependent. People tend to equate *normal* with "good" and *abnormal* with "bad," which means that any behavior labeled as abnormal can potentially be stigmatizing. Use of person-centered language is one way to reduce stigma attached to abnormal behavior or behavior health issues (e.g., saying "a person with schizophrenia," rather than "a schizophrenic.")

The **"Four Ds" of Abnormality** assist health practitioners when trying to identify a psychiatric condition in their clients. Deviance marks a withdrawal from society's concept of appropriate behavior. **Deviant** behavior is a departure from the "norm." The *DSM-5-TR* contains some criteria for diagnosing deviance. The second "D" is dysfunction. **Dysfunction** is behavior that interferes with daily living. Dysfunction is a type of problem that may be serious enough to be considered a disorder. The third "D" is distress. **Distress** is related to a client's dysfunction. That is, to what degree does the dysfunction cause the client distress? A client can experience minor dysfunction and major distress, or major dysfunction and minor distress. The fourth "D" is danger. **Danger** is characterized by danger to self or to others. There are different degrees of danger specific to various types of disorders. **Duration** is

83

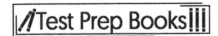
sometimes considered a fifth "D," as it may be important to note whether the symptoms of a disorder are fleeting or permanent.

Placement Options Based on Assessed Level of Care

A client's need for care can fall on a wide spectrum. Some clients may comfortably live in their own residence but attend regularly scheduled meetings with a social worker to receive care. Other clients, after being appropriately assessed, may require institutional care where they can receive medical and therapeutic support as often as needed. Institutional care may be a long-term or short-term solution for a client. The level of care required for a client is assessed by examining a number of self-sufficiency factors, such as the presence of any formally diagnosed developmental disabilities, physical disabilities, or mental disorders.

Additionally, the client's ability to communicate needs, IQ level, ability to complete self-care tasks (such as dressing, toileting, grooming, etc.) alone or with assistance, and risk of voluntary or involuntary harm to self or others will also be taken into consideration. Based on the client's health and caretaking needs, they may receive outpatient services (such as regular therapeutic appointments), inpatient services (such as a behavioral program that lasts for a predetermined period of time), assisted living in a facility such as a nursing home, or in-home support (such as a home health nurse). Regardless of where a client falls on the care spectrum, services for mental wellness and adjusting to this new context of life will likely be beneficial to care.

Organizational Functioning

In order to ensure an organization is achieving and maintaining its mission, goals, and objectives, it should undergo regular assessments to review performance and outcomes. Often, **external audits** (such as those from an independent group or a regulating body) are designed to assess organizational functioning. They are normally performed at regular intervals as preventative quality measures, and they may be performed more frequently if any noncompliance issues arise or if a social work institution is not meeting established performance benchmarks. Internal audits performed by workers in the organization can help gauge the organization's performance and whether there are any areas that should be remedied before an external audit. Noncompliance or lack of performance by an organization can result in fines, penalties, or micromanagement from a regulating agency.

Depending on the size of the social work institution, the type of social work that is performed, and the time and resources that are available for performing evaluations, the organization may also be assessed for factors that go beyond auditing compliance lists. These aspects may include how well its main processes work (through quality focused assessments such as value mapping and waste analysis) and the types of resources that are available in the institution (such as workers' credentials, types of services offered, and technological capabilities). Almost all social work organizations will be assessed for the outcomes it produces. This includes simple data outcomes, such as the total number of clients served in a region, to more complex outcomes, such as how many client interventions led to a defined, successful outcome.

Data Collection and Analysis Methods

Qualitative data can be collected through interviews, observations, anecdotes, and surveys, and by reviewing literature and other relevant documents. Qualitative data collection methods are often subjective and cannot be generalized to larger samples or populations. Quantitative data can be collected from experiments, recordings of certain events and timed intervals, surveys in which an answer choice must be selected for each question, data management systems, and numerical reports. Quantitative data methods are often objective and abstract, and they can be generalized to explain relationships between variables in large populations.

To analyze data, researchers must ensure all collected data are relevant to the questions being posed; are accurate; come from a credible, unbiased source; and are complete. Often, all "cleaned" data sets are entered into a

computer-based data management system software from which analyses and inferences can be calculated. **Clean data sets** can be accurately described for relationships between variables and to make simple observations. They can also be used to answer related hypotheses or propose new ideas and inferences based on visible relationships. Often, these can be applied to explain behaviors, phenomena, or other questions related related to a large population.

Treatment Planning

Methods to Involve Clients in Intervention Planning

Practitioners should always treat the individual as the expert on the individual's life, and while practitioners should gather relevant external and collateral information, they should make all efforts not to allow these sources to supersede information provided by the individual. Practitioners should involve the individual as much as possible in problem identification and resolution planning by asking about details about the individual's life, any presenting issues and what might be causing them, what kinds of changes the individual would like to make, how these changes might enrich quality of life, and real and perceived fears.

All of these details should be acknowledged, respected, valued, and referred to when planning and implementing interventions. Practitioners should also tailor interventions to highlight and utilize established strengths and resources of the individual.

Cultural Considerations in the Creation of an Intervention Plan

An intervention's success depends in part on whether the intervention plan is aligned with the individual's cultural experience. All individuals are part of cultures with specific traditions, habits, and norms. These can vary by race, ethnicity, immigration status, income level, geographical location, or social status. It's important to take culture into context in order to show respect for the individual's way of life, tailor interventions to be easily understood, create trust and cooperation, and avoid wasting time or resources. Cultural contexts can be understood through researching the community, reading literature or periodicals from the area, and networking with people in the setting.

Intervention/Treatment Modalities

When utilizing a holistic approach for client assessment and treatment planning, practitioners should utilize evidence-based research to support the selected interventions and treatment modalities. The interventions and treatment modalities selected will be based on a number of things, including the client's current level of functioning (based on the biopsychosocial assessment), level of care needed, presenting symptoms, and the practitioner's background. Here are some things a practitioner will want to consider when constructing interventions or treatment modalities:

- Are the selected interventions evidence-based?
- Do the selected interventions arise from a strengths-based perspective specifically tailored around the client's strengths, interests, and needs?
- Do the associated risks with the selected interventions outweigh the possible positive outcomes?
- Is the selected intervention culturally-sensitive and culturally-appropriate?
- Did the client participate in the construction of the intervention selection and/or consent to it?
- Does the practitioner feel comfortable and well-versed in the selected intervention to increase the levels of intensity as needed and provide a continuity of care for the selected modalities?
- Does the selected intervention coincide with the client's financial ability to pay?

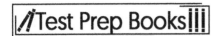

Intervention, Treatment, and Service Plans

Creating SMART objectives allows for data-driven and measurable intervention plans. When creating objectives, practitioners should be able to measure the desired behavior that is exhibited, the number of times the desired behavior is exhibited over a period of time, the conditions in which the desired behavior must be exhibited, and progress from the undesired behavior to the desired behavior through baseline evaluation and evaluation at pre-determined intervals.

Theories of Trauma-Informed Care

Trauma-informed care refers to providing interventions in a way that accounts for the possibility that a client has had traumatic experiences. The definition of trauma will be relative to the client, but common experiences include major loss, assault, abuse, manipulation, neglect, major injury or accident, and major life change. If these events occur during vulnerable periods in a client's life (such as early childhood), symptoms associated with trauma may be more pervasive or exacerbated. Personal trauma often drives mental health and behavioral conditions, so understanding a client's history and the influence of any experienced trauma is a critical component of providing effective care. Experiences of multiple or repeated trauma are associated with higher rates of substance use and other health problems. These can present with additional coinciding and related risk factors, such as poverty, infectious disease, homelessness, or lack of personal support.

The **trauma-informed model of care** encourages all practitioners who work with clients experiencing mental or physical health issues to recognize the influence of traumatic experiences. This model helps practitioners assess the level of risk assumed by clients and provides preventative interventions to help mitigate risks at different trauma levels. The client's perspective of how the traumatic event occurred (e.g., unexpectedly or expectedly, from a stranger or loved one); the time during the lifespan in which the event occurred; and other cultural, social, or personal factors determine the level of risk faced by the client. Reactions to traumatic events may manifest less subtly than obvious problems such as substance use. They can present as anxiety, pain, muscular tension, elevated heart rates or cortisol levels, depression, headaches, and so on. Therefore, allowing room for the consideration of prior trauma when working with all clients broadens the scope of interventions that practitioners choose to employ.

Approaches to Trauma-Informed Care

Trauma-informed care systems ensure that trauma and its effects are understood by health services providers and that signs and symptoms of trauma are recognized even when not explicitly stated by the client. Trauma-informed care means that trauma-informed practices are integrated into all procedures of the care system. Incorporating these aspects into care involves ensuring a sense of safety and security for the client and the client's family. Trauma-informed care also ensures that the client feels they can trust the social worker and that all procedures are communicated and transparent. It provides a network of support, empowers the client to collaborate with their health care providers to develop a suitable intervention, and encourages the client to ask questions and voice concerns at any time. Trauma-informed care also accounts for each client's specific personal history, cultural and social norms, and other unique factors. Interventions encourage respect, self-efficacy, and hope for future outcomes, and they can identify various behaviors that are used as coping mechanisms for specific instances of trauma. Trauma-informed care is a model that is encouraged with any social services client, but it is especially beneficial for survivors of abuse, those experiencing eating disorders or addiction, or those who grew up in poverty or violence.

Immigration, Refugee, or Undocumented Status on Service Delivery

Immigrants, refugees, and undocumented individuals often have the highest need for social services but also have the most barriers to effectively receiving support. Immigrants often face the stress of leaving their home country and assimilating into a completely new culture, economy, and lifestyle. While a social worker can help navigate

these changes to set the foundation for a new life, immigrants often experience language barriers or simply may not realize such services exist for their use. Social workers may need to actively advertise their assistance and understand the background and culture of the immigrant in order to help.

Refugees often have the same stresses and barriers that immigrants have, but often they have also left violent or destructive situations in their home country. They may be happy to be safe, but they may also have deep feelings of sadness, especially if their families were affected (such as through death of a loved one or the necessity of leaving family members behind). While many immigrants come on work visas, refugees may have no means to make money and may need help navigating welfare benefits. There may also be feelings of discomfort in receiving these benefits. Social workers should be especially sympathetic to the diverse reasons behind an individual's refugee status.

Undocumented individuals may feel scared to seek out social services, fearing reprisal or deportation, even though social services can be an avenue to help undocumented families change their status to documented. Social workers who hope to help these groups should focus on building trust and creating spaces of security and safety.

Crisis Plans

Any client who visits a social worker may experience a personal crisis at any time. A **crisis** is defined as any instance where the client is unable to cope with an event in a healthy, resolution-seeking manner. While all social workers should have a general plan developed for unexpected client crises (such as calling for backup support or an emergency contact), a tailored plan should be developed during the initial sessions with the client based on what the client's needs are. To promote a sense of responsibility, accountability, empowerment, and engagement, the client should be invited to collaborate in developing this plan. Developing a **crisis plan** may include discussing the client's possible stress and crisis triggers as well as determining the client's best solution for diffusing a crisis situation (such as employing trusted family members, utilizing a security item, managing therapeutic medications, and so on).

This plan should be reviewed at regular intervals with the client to ensure it is still valid and does not need revisions to account for new triggers or resolved behaviors. Finally, should a crisis arise, social workers should be as transparent as possible about implementing the crisis plan. They should clearly communicate the steps they are taking as they take them, and invite the client to engage in the plan as well (if it is possible). Social workers should be mindful to note the context and present situation of the crisis, so that they can provide the best support in that moment. If the social worker tries to push the client too far in taking responsibility during a crisis or is too overbearing when the client would like to practice self-sufficiency, the crisis intervention may backfire and create a long-term barrier between the client and the social worker.

Discharge, Aftercare, and Follow-Up Planning

An important part of treatment planning is discharge planning. There are numerous reasons that services for a client may end. Clients may feel that they no longer need the services, that they are not compatible with the social work practitioner providing the services, that an increased level of care is needed that is beyond the scope of the practitioner, or they may have successfully met goals for treatment.

Discharge planning should begin with the onset of the initial assessment for the client. The practitioner should not delay discharge planning, as discharge may occur at any time. Making the client aware of the choices for discharge and the discharge planning process empowers the client during treatment. It also provides continuity of care for the client.

The main purpose of **discharge planning** is to develop a plan of care that goes beyond the current treatment sessions to promote success once services have concluded. In the event that the client is going to a higher level of care or to a different professional, effective discharge planning is useful in disseminating pertinent information

about the client to assist in continuity of care and effective treatment. In this sense, the current practitioner should prepare to become a collateral source linked to the client's level of care for the next professional.

In addition to benefiting the other practitioners the client may meet with, effective discharge planning benefits the client as well. If services have been completed successfully and the client has met the stated goals, then discharge planning ensures that the client has a plan to sustain a stable level of function and maintain the successes achieved. This is particularly useful with clients who suffer from substance use or other addictive behaviors, as effective discharge planning can prevent relapse.

Upon the conclusion of the client discharging from services, a discharge summary should be created and placed in the client's file. The **discharge summary** should include the following information:

- Reason for discharge
- Description of treatment goals and the degree to which they were met
- Client's response to the interventions
- Description of the client's levels of functioning
- Baseline
- Progress during treatment
- Functioning at discharge
- Recommendations for follow-up care
- Links to community resources
- Appointment dates for other providers (if available)
- Provision of additional contacts, client supports
- Description of potential risks post-discharge
- Contact information for post-discharge support and crisis intervention

Follow-Up Techniques in Social Work

At the final session, the social worker and client can schedule a follow-up session at a predetermined time to evaluate the client's continued progress after termination. Another option is to propose a time to meet and alert the client that the worker will contact the client to schedule a follow up. The follow-up session enables the social worker the opportunity to determine how well the client has progressed and to determine the effectiveness of the intervention(s) used during sessions.

Techniques Used to Evaluate a Client's Progress

Treatment evaluation is a necessary part of direct practice. Social workers should strive to exercise best practice techniques by using evidence-based practice evaluation. It is beneficial for clients to see the progress they have made, while simultaneously providing information to funders and insurance companies that typically require documentation and outcome measures for reimbursement of services. Other benefits include providing indicators that interventions should be modified or that treatment is complete and termination is warranted. Several factors are important in the evaluation of a client's progress, including identifying specific issues to be addressed; creating appropriate goals, objectives, and tasks; using effective and relevant techniques and tools to measure success; and routinely documenting progress.

Client progress may be measured using a quantitative or qualitative approach used in research. **Quantitative measures** relate to the rate of occurrence or severity of a behavior or problem. When performing quantitative evaluation, first establish a baseline, which is a measurement of the target problem, prior to intervention. **Qualitative measures** are more subjective and reflective of the client's experience (information is gathered largely from observation and different forms of interviewing) and provide a view of whether progress is being made.

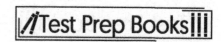

Methods, Techniques, and Instruments Used to Evaluate Social Work Practice

Evaluation is an important component of any field of study, as it allows practitioners to understand which processes are working well and providing results. Evaluation also allows one to identify areas of opportunity and areas for improvement. The process often utilizes data and consumer feedback, and it focuses on processes that are in place and specific desired outcomes of the practice.

Social workers should continuously evaluate their practice. This evaluation begins with what exactly they would like to evaluate. An evaluation typically focuses on processes (such as clinical intake, client satisfaction, time spent with clients, frequency of sessions, type of intervention) and outcomes (such as were specific goals met for a client, how many clients return after being discharged). Many healthcare organizations provide evaluation tools for social workers, such as benchmark reports that provide client satisfaction responses or practice outcomes. Additionally, social workers can employ pre-tests before an intervention to serve as a baseline data set, and they can employ a post-test to measure changes from the baseline. Social workers can also administer surveys, Likert scale questionnaires, or specific intervention evaluation assessments to the client or client system.

These tools can measure quantitative results as well as provide an option for anecdotal or testimonial information. Entrance and exit interviews with the client or the client system can also provide a wealth of evaluation information. When evaluating clients face-to-face or through a survey, it's important to create an environment that fosters comfort, open dialogue, and honesty. Clients may feel pressured to provide positive evaluations if they are answering directly to the social worker, or if they feel as though a satisfaction survey that they are completing can be traced back to them. This can bias the evaluation process and produce skewed results.

Objective and Subjective Data

Both objective and subjective data are used during the assessment and treatment processes. The client provides their perspective on what happened and the correlated feelings and experiences felt, which is the **subjective data**. Subsequently, the social work practitioner uses the information and may ask finding questions to better understand where the client is emotionally, while teasing out facts related to the client's situation. These facts are **objective data**.

The information from both the subjective and objective data is combined to formulate a concise, yet comprehensive, assessment for the client. In some note-taking practices, the identification of the subjective and objective data along with assessment formation is required. This style of documentation is known as the **SOAP method**, an acronym that stands for Subjective, Objective, Assessment, and Plan. Another note-taking style that focuses on the subjective and objective data is the BIRP documentation method. **BIRP** stands for Behavior, Intervention, Response, and Plan. It is not as commonly used as SOAP.

Methods to Interpret and Communicate Policies and Procedures

Social workers have direct contact with clients and are in strategically critical positions to develop, implement, evaluate, and communicate policies and procedures. **Policies and procedures** allow clients and employees to be aware of treatment and agency goals, objectives, resources, and limitations. Policies can sometimes be a barrier to client services, so social workers must be aware of this possibility and point out these barriers when necessary.

Factors in policy and procedure development:

- Front line workers should be involved policy and procedure development since they are in the best position to determine and evaluate how clients are affected.

- Policies should be clearly written and communicated to clients/workers with copies available for distribution. Workers should receive periodic training on current policies and procedures.

- Policies should be in the best interest of clients, but also protect the agency and staff.

Factors to consider when evaluating the effectiveness of policies and procedures:

- The origins of the policy and/or procedure, including values and the related ideology
- Client reactions, thoughts, and feelings about the policy
- Alignment with social work ethics and values
- Intentional and unintentional consequences and benefits
- Regular re-evaluation to ensure policies and procedures are still relevant and in the best interests of clients, workers, and the agency

Research Design and Methods

Basic and applied research are two separate categories of systematic investigation. **Basic research** aims to expand knowledge, although the new knowledge may not have any immediate application in the real world. Basic research can often lead to new ideas and theories. Basic research can explore, explain, or describe existing or potential ideas, with the end goal of simply understanding or creating new information. **Applied research** is conducted with the specific aim of answering a question or solving a problem. It is often used by business entities, scholars, and non-profit organizations to gather and analyze data relating to a very specific inquiry.

Basic and applied research designs can be qualitative (where qualities of interest are examined) or quantitative (where measurements of data are examined to statistically explain relationships between variables). **Qualitative data methods** include performing case studies on a specific entity, observation, interviews, and developing and confirming narratives about a phenomenon. These techniques are commonly employed in social work cases and interventions, where human behavior, family history, relationship history, environmental interactions, and other subjective variables are examined and manipulated to support a client's health outcome.

Quantitative methods measure two or more variables and concretely examine the relationship between them. **Correlational design** is a quantitative method that examines two or more variables to determine the influence one variable has on other variables (such as the relationship between age and IQ). **Causal comparative design** examines groups with similar features and differences to understand factors that may influence the similarities and differences. Experimental design establishes one control group as a baseline and conducts an experiment on another group to quantify the influence of the experimental factor. Control and experimental groups may be randomly assigned or assigned with a purpose (such as employing a sample of 21-year-olds in order to examine a specific behavior in this age range). Some designs use both quantitative and qualitative methods; these are called mixed research designs.

Assessing Reliability and Validity in Social Work Research

Reliability is used to describe whether a measurement method produces the same results over a long period of time and across different users. The reliability of a measurement method is analyzed through **inter-rater reliability** (if multiple researchers can use the method the same way), **test-retest reliability** (when measurements stay the same even when the method is used multiple times by the same person), **parallel forms reliability** (measuring the same results even when slight variations in the method exist), and **internal consistency reliability** (how consistent responses to the measure are). A strong measurement method performs well across all four of these reliability techniques.

Validity is used to describe how well a measurement method works to collect the data it is designed to collect. **Face validity** is used to describe how well a measurement method appears to be collecting desired information to the participant who is using the method. This is believed to influence participants into responding accurately. Construct validity is used to describe how well a specific variable is measured (as opposed to other measures that may be present). **Criterion validity** is used to infer performance. **Formative validity** is used to study outcomes and

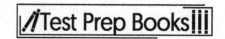

determine how to improve a measure or program. Sampling validity is used to describe how complete a sample is in order to eliminate bias.

Measurement methods can have high reliability and low validity, and vice versa. A strong research metric will be high in both reliability and validity.

Practice Quiz

1. Which of the following is NOT a critical part of the client interview?
    a. Building rapport
    b. Verifying payment
    c. Starting where the client is
    d. Use of encouraging, neutral questions

2. What types of questions can limit insight into the client's problems during an interview?
    a. Open-ended questions
    b. Clarifying questions
    c. Note taking
    d. Closed-ended questions

3. Which of the following does NOT affect client behaviors and responses during the interview?
    a. Practitioner's clothing
    b. Practitioner's speech pattern
    c. Practitioner's eye contact
    d. Practitioner's pitch of speech

4. The client's chief complaint may include all of the following EXCEPT?
    a. Factors from the past that influence their current level of functioning
    b. A previously resolved issue
    c. Collateral resources that describe or validate the problem
    d. Client's description of the overarching problem or issue

5. An example of information included in the social part of the assessment is?
    a. Demographic information pertaining to the client
    b. Factors influencing the current level of functioning
    c. Interaction with peers, work, and home environment
    d. Previous or current diagnoses

See answers on the next page.

Answer Explanations

1. B: Verifying payment is not a critical part of the client interview. Payment may occur before the interview process or may be pre-determined based on the work setting. Choice A, building rapport, happens at all stages of the client interview and is an important characteristic of interviews. Choice C, starting where the client is, is another important feature of the interview and is part of empowering the client by hearing things from their perspective. Choice D, the use of encouraging, neutral questions, is also part of empowering the client and moves the conversation forward, encouraging the client to share.

2. D: Closed-ended questions can limit insight into the client's problems during the interview because they deter answer explanations. Open-ended questions (Choice A) encourage discussion and help the social worker gain insight into the client's problems. Choice B, clarifying questions, can also help the social worker gain insight because he or she provides alternate explanations to problems, as well as validate that the client is being heard. Choice C, note taking, is an effective way for the social worker to record information during the interview.

3. A: Practitioner's clothing does not affect client behaviors and responses during the interview. Practitioner's speech patterns, eye contact, and pitch of speech (Choices B, C, and D) may all affect a client's behaviors and responses during the interview process because the client may mimic the rigid body language of the practitioner and become defensive.

4. C: This question asks the test taker to determine which of the four answer choices is not included in a client's chief complaint. Let's look at what may be included in a client's chief complaint. The text says the following:

Chief complaint is the client's version of what the overarching problem is, in their own words (Choice D). The client's description of the chief complaint may include factors from the past that the client views as an obstacle to optimal functioning (Choice A). It could also be an issue that was previously resolved but reoccurs (Choice B), thus requiring the client to develop additional coping skills.

We can see that Choices A, B, and D are all represented describing the client's chief complaint. Thus, Choice C is the only option not included in a client's chief complaint, which is the collateral resources that describe or validate the problem.

5. C: Interaction with peers, work, and home environment are examples of information included in the social part of the assessment. Choice A, demographics, is incorrect because this does not give insight into the client's social life and is part of the identification stage of the assessment. Choice B is incorrect because the client's current level of functioning is assessed during the mental status exam. Choice D is incorrect because previous or current diagnoses would be information given during the medical component of the assessment process.

Psychotherapy, Clinical Interventions, and Case Management

Therapeutic Relationship

Components of the Social Worker-Client Relationship

The relationship between the social worker and the client or client system is influenced by a number of components. These include the type of emotion that is shown by the parties during sessions, the general attitude toward the working relationship (e.g., positive, supportive), and the value each party places on the working relationship. The social worker should ensure that empathy, sympathy, and acceptance of the client and client system are shown during sessions to help foster a positive relationship. These aspects can be further supported by the social worker's initiative to build rapport with the client, such as through allowing the client to openly express feelings, work at a pace that feels comfortable, and encouraging them to shape and make decisions related to the intervention.

Additionally, a number of external tools may be a vital part of the social worker/client relationship. These include tools and documents that provide information related to the client's personality and behavior and items such as assessments, medical history, family history, current living situation, socioeconomic situation, and personal goals for the intervention. All of these items can help the social worker shape the intervention for the client. These might include items such as assessments, medical history, family history, current living situation, socioeconomic situation, and personal goals for the intervention.

Building and Maintaining a Helping Relationship

As the principal conduit for client change and acceptance, the social worker/client relationship is primary to the problem solving and therapy process. If the social worker cannot develop a positive relationship with the client, the change process is hindered. The worker/client relationship should be based on trust, empathy, and acceptance by both parties in order to facilitate growth. Some clients may have difficulty building trust with the social worker, and the social worker may need to be patient with the client in order to make treatment goal progress. If the social worker cannot develop an appropriate trusting, empathetic, and accepting relationship with the client, the social worker should seek supervision. In some cases, the social worker will need to transfer the client because it will be very challenging for the client to make progress if trust does not exist. Social workers should be alert for countertransference issues in the relationship with the client and address these issues promptly if they occur.

Principles of Relationship Building

Rapport building begins during the initial contact the social worker has with the client, a crucial time for establishing trust and harmony. After building rapport, the client and the social worker can begin working on client issues and continue developing the relationship on deeper levels. The relationship that the client has with the social worker is representative of the relationships the client has in other areas of life; the social worker needs to engage with the client within this framework to effect the greatest change.

Termination of the relationship occurs when the client and the social worker have reached treatment goals. Even though the relationship is terminated, the client may feel warmly toward the social worker, and congruence and empathy may still be part of the relationship. Some clients may require maintenance sessions to continue stability, but when termination is the next clear stage in the relationship, psychotherapy sessions should end.

Power and Transparency in the Social Worker-Client Relationship

Throughout their careers and in specific interventions, social workers should always remain aware of the power differential that is likely to exist between themselves and their clients. As the main person guiding the intervention, social workers inherently have more power in the relationship. Additionally, social workers may have more education, more independence, a clean legal record, better finances, or some other privilege that may make the client feel uncomfortable, ashamed, or defensive (especially when the client is involuntarily in the session, such as court-ordered cases). Awareness is one fundamental component of ensuring that this power dynamic doesn't have a negative effect.

Transparency is another fundamental component, as it allows the client to feel like an equal who is involved in the problem-solving process. Social workers can foster transparency in the working relationship by openly discussing areas of privilege they may have, sharing as much information as they can about the problem-solving process and how it may be of benefit to the client, and empowering the client to take as much of the process as possible into their own control (such as through independent decision-making). When possible, the social worker should avoid hiding information or being unclear about why certain processes of interventions are being pursued.

Social Worker's Role in the Problem-Solving Process

The **problem-solving therapeutic model** serves to teach clients how to manage stressors that come in life. Often clients do not possess skills that allow them to effectively navigate negative events or emotions without increasing personal harm. The goal of the problem-solving model is to teach clients the skills necessary to deal with negative life events, negative emotions, and stressful situations. In particular, goals of this model should be to assist clients in identifying which particular situations may trigger unpleasant emotions, understanding the range of emotions one might feel, planning how to effectively deal with situations when they arise, and even recognizing and accepting that some situations are not able to be solved.

The social worker, however, may be an instructional guide to facilitate problem solving for the client. Because problem-solving skills are one of the primary methods of resolving issues and often are skills that clients lack, the social worker may need to model them for the client so that the client can then develop their own skills. Social workers need to maintain empathy and congruence with the client during the problem-solving process, and even though they may have verbally instructed or modeled problem-solving methods, they need to maintain rapport in the relationship.

Roles and Responsibilities of the Social Worker and Client in the Intervention Process

Clarifying the roles and responsibilities of the social worker, the client, and the client system in the intervention process can reduce the chance of miscommunication, misunderstanding, and interventions not working as intended. This clarification process can be developed during the intake process and initial sessions by actively listening to what the client hopes to achieve, and working together to develop a step-by-step intervention methodology. When possible, the stages, objectives, and milestones of the intervention should be documented in order to have an available reference point, drive accountability, and reduce any confusion around the expectations of all involved parties.

The problem-solving approach to interventions is a commonly used framework to cover these points. This is a **seven-stage model** that encourages active listening and engagement techniques (such as eye contact and other receptive body language); fostering trust and collaboration with the client (such as by showing genuine interest in the client as a person, rather than just in the context of the issues at hand); working together to identify the problem to be addressed and possible solutions, introducing allies in the resolution processes (such as clinical providers, a yoga or meditation teacher, or other experts that could help the client); developing a documented resolution plan and actively engaging all parties to follow it (such as through accountability cues, positive

95

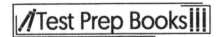

reinforcement, and celebrating small victories); and support for sustaining the desired behaviors until the client is capable of terminating the intervention.

While one can be hopeful that the client and client systems will be cooperative and willing in this framework, that is not always the case. Clients may show distrust, anxiety, fear, or apathy, especially in the beginning. Often, the most important role of the social worker is building trust with the client and the client system. The social worker should continue to encourage a trusting, collaborative relationship until the time-of-service termination.

Acceptance and Empathy in the Social Worker-Client Relationship

Empathy is being able to relate to client circumstances and direction without the social worker actually experiencing it themselves. Sympathy differs from empathy in that **sympathy** is compassion for the client without having experienced the client's state of being. Empathy involves "being with" the client in their time and frame of mind. It involves connecting to the client on a visceral level while still maintaining some objectivity. Because empathy is the framework on which social work practice is built, it is imperative that social workers be empathetic with their clients. Those who cannot be empathetic should seek additional supervision or counsel in order to do their work effectively or refer the client to another worker.

Diversity in the Social Worker-Client Relationship

Attitudes and Beliefs
Social workers should be culturally aware of their attitudes and beliefs. This requires a keen awareness of their own cultural background and gaining awareness of any personal biases, stereotypes, and values that they hold. Practitioners should also accept different worldviews, be sensitive to differences, and refer minority clients to a practitioner from the client's culture when it would benefit the client.

Knowledge
Practitioners should have the appropriate knowledge of different cultures. Specifically, practitioners must understand the client's culture and should not jump to conclusions about the client's way of being. Throughout their careers, social workers should be willing to gain a greater depth of knowledge of various cultural groups and update this knowledge as necessary. This includes understanding how issues like racism, sexism, and homophobia can negatively affect minority clients. Practitioners should understand how different therapeutic theories carry values that may be detrimental for some clients. Social workers should also understand how institutional barriers can affect the willingness of minority clients to use mental health services.

Cultural Skills
Social workers should be well-versed in cultural skills. They must be able to apply interviewing and counseling techniques with clients and should be able to employ specialized skills and interventions that might be effective with specific minority populations. Practitioners should be able to communicate effectively and understand the verbal and nonverbal language of a client. They also should take a systematic perspective in their practice, work collaboratively with community leaders, and advocate for clients when it's in their best interests.

When working with clients from diverse backgrounds, practitioners should be able to shift their professional strategies. Below are techniques and strategies social workers should keep in mind when working with clients of different cultures.

Various Cultural and Racial Backgrounds

- Have appropriate attitudes and beliefs, gain knowledge about the client's background, and learn new skills as needed.

- Encourage the client to speak in their native language and arrange for an interpreter when necessary.

- Assess the client's cultural identity and how important it is to the client.

- Check accuracy of any interpretations of the client's nonverbal cues.

- Make use of alternate modes of communication, such as writing, typing, translation services, and the use of art.

- Assess the impact of sociopolitical issues on the client.

- Encourage the client to bring culturally significant and personally relevant items.

- Vary the helping environment to make it conducive to effective work with the client.

Various Religious Backgrounds

- Determine the client's religious background in the beginning sessions.
- Check personal biases and gain information about the client's religion.
- Ask the client how important religion is in their life.
- Assess the client's level of faith development.
- Avoid making assumptions about the religion.
- Become familiar with the client's religious beliefs, important holidays, and faith traditions.
- Understand that religion can deeply affect the client unconsciously.

Client's Developmental Level on the Social Worker-Client Relationship

A client's development level will vary from client to client, and it may even vary for the same client over the full course of an intervention. Therefore, the social worker should make no assumptions about the client's ability to cope, the way the intervention will be accepted and utilized, or any other aspect of the working relationship. These factors should be assessed upon intake and at regular intervals thereafter, the frequency of which may vary on a case-by-case basis.

Assessments should holistically take into account the client's development, including age, psychological factors, emotional factors, social factors, acute personal conditions (such as an impending divorce or recent refugee status) that may temporarily impact the client's functioning, and any other scope of development that may be appropriate for the client's need. For example, a client who has a history of violent behavior and a history of playing physical sports with extreme contact may find it beneficial to undergo neurological development assessments. By viewing the client through a holistic perspective, social workers can ensure interventions are appropriate across all domains of development; if so, the interventions are more likely to be effective and received positively by the client.

Domestic, Intimate Partner, and Other Violence on the Helping Relationship

Any type of abuse in a client's life can impart symptoms of trauma to the client. These symptoms may be subtle in nature, or they may be relatively obvious to the social worker. Obvious indicators of abuse include physical marks; chronic muscular or stomach pain (as a result of trauma or stress); consistently dressing in high-coverage clothing, even in cases where it seems abnormal (such as a hot day); or particular body language when the abuser is in the room or attending a session. Most abusive relationships occur as a manifestation of dysfunctional power and control tactics. If the client is an abuser, it may be difficult for him or her to be guided by a social worker, as there may be an experience of a loss of control or power. Abuse victims may feel distrustful or fearful of the social worker

and the helping relationship; they also may be uncomfortable discussing their abuser in a negative light. This can be a setback to the intervention process, and social workers may need to spend extra time fostering rapport and building a trusting relationship with these types of clients.

Verbal and Nonverbal Communication Techniques

Social workers use verbal and nonverbal communication techniques to engage clients in completing treatment goals. Verbal communication is vital to the social worker/client relationship, and social workers should be skilled at greetings, summarization, reflection, and the conveyance of new information to the client. The client may misconstrue a social worker's body language if it does not represent openness and trust. Likewise, the social worker needs to be adept at analyzing the client's body language in order to move forward. Clients use both verbal and nonverbal communication to convey their story to the social worker, and communication techniques used by the social worker can be modeled to teach the client improved communication. Clients should be instructed to recognize their own communication techniques in the context of the relationship with the social worker. Clients who are withdrawn or isolated may need especially sensitive communication with the social worker in order to better communicate verbally and nonverbally.

In order to build a strong helping relationship with the client, the worker must learn to use effective verbal and nonverbal techniques. These skills are necessary throughout the treatment process and especially during assessment and engagement.

Congruence in Communication

Social workers need to be congruent—in agreement and harmony—with client feedback and encourage clients' self-direction. Social workers and clients begin treatment by enhancing congruence in communication so that mutually agreed upon goals may be developed for the client. The social worker should be invested in the therapeutic relationship and able to participate in a way that assists the client in becoming more self-aware. If a social worker is not congruent with the client, then treatment progress may be hindered and the client should be referred to another worker who is a more appropriate fit.

Obtaining and Providing Feedback

There are several ways social workers can receive feedback. It can come in the form of evaluation by another social worker during supervision, or from a client during treatment. Obtaining feedback is an important means to improve a social worker's skill and ensure effective treatment for clients. Feedback from clients may be formal or informal. Clients may offer unsolicited feedback verbally or non-verbally during treatment, using words, body language, or tone of voice. Social workers must be sensitive to the messages clients are expressing to decipher how to interpret feedback that may not be clear.

When seeking feedback from a client, the social worker should ensure the method is appropriate to the skills, resources, and abilities of the client (e.g., in writing, by mail, text, in person, etc.).

Factors to consider when obtaining feedback from clients:

- Social workers may consider a client's progress toward a goal or lack thereof as a type of feedback. If treatment is not progressing as expected, the worker should evaluate and make adjustments as necessary.

- Always be clear why the information is needed and ensure client confidentiality to the fullest extent possible.

- Feedback can be sought at different times throughout the treatment process to ensure reliability and consistency.

- Workers should seek feedback regardless of whether it is expected to be negative or positive. All feedback should be viewed as a learning tool to enhance treatment and worker skill.

- Factors to consider when receiving feedback during supervision/consultation:

- Social workers can benefit from feedback during supervision or consultation, especially with difficult clients/cases or at significant times in treatment, such as termination.

- When discussing cases, client confidentiality should be protected as much as possible, and client consent to release information should be acquired.

The Intervention Process

Interviewing Techniques

Interviewing is common in social work. An interview should always be focused and have a purpose—this is often to gather data, make a diagnosis, and provide therapy. An interview can be used to discuss behavior patterns, ensure the practitioner and the individual are discussing the same presenting issues, bring attention to presenting issues, or provide new perspectives on presenting issues. Interviews are generally verbal, although the practitioner should be mindful of observing non-verbal communication. While the questions of the interview should be planned, the practitioner should be able to tailor the questions based on the individual's needs.

There are several communication techniques beneficial to the social work practice other than the basic interview process used to gather general demographic and presenting problem information:

Furthering
A technique that reinforces the idea that the worker is listening to the client and encourages further information to be gathered. This technique includes nodding of the head, facial expressions, or encouraging responses such as "yes" or "I understand." It also includes accent responses, whereby workers repeat or parrot back a few words of a client's last response.

Close/Open-Ended Questions
Depending on the timing or information the worker is seeking to elicit from the client, one of these types of questions may be used. Close-ended questions, such as "How old are you?" will typically elicit a short answer. Conversely, open-ended questions, such as "What are your feelings about school?" allow for longer, more-involved responses.

Clarifying and Paraphrasing
This is when social workers ask a client for clarification to ensure they understand the client's message. Clarifying also includes encouraging clients to speak more concretely and in less abstract terms to provide clearer messages. When paraphrasing, workers should convey a message back to the client to ensure an understanding of the client's meaning.

Summarizing
This is similar to paraphrasing, but summarizing includes more information. It's frequently used to help focus the session and allow the worker to summarize the overall messages, problems, or goals of the client.

Active Listening
Active listening involves using facial expressions, body language, and postures to show that the worker is engaged to the client. Workers should display eye contact and natural but engaged body movements and gestures. An example would be sitting slightly forward with a non-rigid posture. As with all communication techniques, social workers

99

should be aware of cultural differences in what is appropriate, especially related to direct eye contact and posturing.

Methods of Summarizing Communication
Social workers may paraphrase and echo clients' verbal statements to acknowledge their feelings. Summarizing may involve reflecting back the statements made by the client to clarify what the client has said. Social workers also must summarize communication in order to provide sufficient records of the session. Further, during the end of the session, the social worker may wish to clarify goals and homework assigned for the next week so that the client is clear on the changes that need to take place.

Methods of Facilitating Communication
Social workers may facilitate communication with the client by verbally encouraging communication or by addressing the client with constructive information concerning the case. Social workers need to recall information concerning the client from session to session in order to facilitate communication and move forward with the client. Clarifying what the client has said and the client's feelings helps not only to ensure the social worker clearly understands what is being communicated, but also lets the client know that the social worker is engaged and actively listening. Development of trust with the client may facilitate additional communication, and social workers should be sensitive to the trust-building process because it is the cornerstone of the helping relationship. Social workers may provide clients with homework outside of a session that facilitates communication during the next session.

Mandated clients, including court ordered clients or clients ordered to counseling from child protective services, may face challenges in communicating with the social worker because they do not choose to be in treatment. Developing trust with these clients to facilitate communication is especially important for progress to be made. It's helpful to acknowledge the client's feelings and possible frustration about the mandated treatment. Clients who require out-of-home placement need clear communication with the social worker to clarify what is happening and make appropriate psychological adjustments to their circumstances.

Using Bias-Free Language in Interviewing
When interviewing a client, a social worker must be careful to eliminate all personal bias from their language. This relates to all subtle negative phrasing related to race, ethnicity, socioeconomic status, gender, gender identity, life choices, disability, or psychological disorders. The job of the social worker is to support the client without bias, always promoting the client's self-identity. Phrases or expressions that demean or stereotype a particular group of people should never be used. Similarly, labeling someone can be hurtful, especially in cases where that label has a negative connotation or stigma attached to it. Sometimes it may even be appropriate for the social worker to ask the client how they wish to be identified or addressed. Inclusive and affirming language should be used when talking about all groups of people and especially when talking to or about the client. Terms that are known to be offensive or degrading should always be avoided.

The Phases of Intervention and Treatment

The **treatment intervention process** consists of four stages. There is some crossover between stages, and the activities of each stage may occur at other times during the process. For instance, the assessment and evaluation phases of intervention are ongoing throughout treatment. Here are the four stages:

Engagement and Assessment
During this stage, the worker focuses on relationship and rapport building with the client. The worker gathers data, assesses the client's history and systems, and identifies problems and challenges.

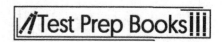
Goal Identification and Intervention Planning

This stage consists of the client and worker collaborating to identify goals to be accomplished. Plan of care/treatment is developed and the contract is implemented.

Implementation

The caseworker implements selected interventions and tasks. The client works toward identified goals. During this stage, the plan is frequently reviewed by the worker in collaboration with the client to assess progress toward goals. Adjustments are made by either party if necessary.

Termination and Evaluation

The social worker should begin the termination phase at the onset of services, since the client may abruptly terminate services for various reasons. It is within best practice guidelines and the best interest of both social worker and client to be prepared for service termination. The social worker should inform the client about the termination guidelines once services begin. Moreover, goal attainment is assessed and evaluation of interventions occurs. The social worker should also review the plan for maintenance of acquired skills while follow-up procedures are discussed and implemented.

Problem-Solving Models and Approaches

When working with clients to develop problem-solving skills, workers must first engage and prepare clients by discussing the benefits of improving such skills and encouraging clients to commit to the problem-solving process during the goal setting/contracting phase.

Steps in the problem-solving process:

Assess, Define, and Clarify the Problem

As with goal setting, social workers should assist clients in clearly determining and defining the specific problem. Workers should focus on the current problem and ensure that clients do not become distracted by other past or current difficulties. Examine specific aspects of the problem, including behaviors and the needs of those involved.

Determine Possible Solutions

Social workers should lead the discussion among participants to determine possible solutions and encourage client(s) to refrain from limiting options at this point. The purpose is for clients to gain practice in solution development. In the case of family work, all capable members should be allowed to offer solutions and should feel safe to do so without fear or criticism from other members.

Examine Options and Select/Implement a Solution

Workers should assist clients in examining the benefits and drawbacks of each possible solution and choose an option that best meets the needs of those involved.

Evaluate and Adjust

Social workers should help clients to determine the success of the solution. Client(s) can use a practical form of tracking solution effectiveness (charts, logs, etc.). If it is determined that the solution is not working, the client can return to the solution-generating stage.

Client's Role in the Problem-Solving Process

Whenever possible, social workers should invite their clients to take a collaborative perspective in designing interventions, establishing objectives, and developing program goals. This allows the client to feel empowered and

101

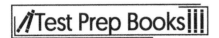
engaged as an active member of the problem-solving process. These factors are associated with higher incidences of positive outcomes, as they encourage clients to feel accountable for their behaviors, actions, and personal changes.

Collaboration should begin at the intake process. This is a period in which the social worker can make assessments, but they can also get information directly from clients about why they are in the session and what they hope to achieve. The social worker can also ask clients the steps they believe they need to take to reach their desired outcomes. While clients may or may not provide useful or feasible answers, this process still sets the tone that allows clients to feel acknowledged and involved in their own care.

In the intake session or in the sessions that immediately follow, the social worker can invite the client to develop SMART objectives to reach their goals. This may also include establishing accountability tools, documenting plans of action to address potential barriers and how to overcome them, and identifying any other support protocols that clients may need for their individual situations. Depending on the client's specific case, this process may take one session or may take much longer. Social workers should continuously show patience, compassion, and a welcoming desire to engage the client in the process.

Engaging and Motivating Clients/Client Systems

When determining a client's motivation, the engagement and assessment stage is crucial. When clients voluntarily seek services and/or are facing a crisis, the commitment and motivation will likely be high. **Non-voluntary clients** are identified as those who are seeking assistance based on pressure outside of the legal system (e.g., a woman gives her spouse an ultimatum to get help or she will leave). When working with non-voluntary or involuntary clients who are mandated legally to seek treatment, the social worker must help determine client-identified problems. This should be in addition or complementary to the presenting problem. The worker and client collaboratively should create a treatment plan that addresses both types of issues.

Additionally, the worker must help the client overcome any negative feelings of anger or mistrust about treatment. With all clients, appropriate relationship-building between the worker is a necessary part of engagement and motivation. Clients must feel they are in a safe, empathetic environment. They also should experience a sufficient level of trust for the social worker in order for treatment to be effective. To create an effective treatment relationship, the social worker must project an attitude free of judgment; recognize the client's individual attributes, strengths, and abilities; and encourage the client's right to be an active participant in their own treatment.

Engaging and Working with Involuntary Clients/Client Systems

When working with involuntary clients, motivation levels can be improved by helping the client realize they have options. Even if services are mandated by a government agency, the client can choose to accept the consequences of not participating. Therefore, agreeing to adhere to the mandate is still a choice. When setting goals and treatment planning, ensure that the client's identified problems are included along with the mandated goals. Attempts to protect a client's right to self-determination should be practiced as much as possible (e.g., encouraging a client's participation in goal setting, problem identification, and priority setting, etc.).

Limit-Setting Techniques

Although it may be difficult for social workers to develop the ability to set limits with clients, it is necessary for treatment to be effective. Many clients struggle with the ability to follow rules and maintain healthy boundaries. In addition to ensuring the treatment process progresses smoothly, when workers set limits, clients also learn to develop helpful life skills. This is especially important with involuntary clients receiving legally mandated services that cannot be modified or negotiated. Other ways to set limits include ensuring the maintenance of an appropriate client-worker relationship, refusing a client request to give misinformation to a legal institution/employer, and saying no if a client asks for monetary loans.

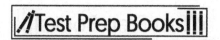

Role-Play Techniques

Role-play is a type of modeling and is also called behavior reversal. This technique enables clients to view the different ways a person may handle a challenging situation. It also allows a client to view a non-tangible behavior in a more tangible way. When clients practice skills and develop new and more productive methods of coping, they are able to take an active role in treatment, increasing their sense of empowerment and self-determination.

Role Modeling Techniques

Role modeling, which offers the client a real-life view of desired target behaviors, can be an important tool to learn new skills. The social worker can request that clients demonstrate the behavior before modeling it, thereby allowing the worker to assess a client's current skills and abilities. Social workers can demonstrate a coping model showing the skill or desired behaviors, including difficulties, anxieties, or challenges. The worker can also demonstrate a mastery model, which shows confidence and competence with the desired behaviors. Each method has benefits and drawbacks. In coping mode, the client and worker can process the interaction and identify improvements or changes that can be made to the desired behaviors or actions. There are several types of modeling:

- **Symbolic Modeling**: client watches a visual representation of the modeled behavior (i.e., video, TV, images)
- **Live Modeling**: client watches while a person performs the behavior
- **Participant Modeling** or **Guided Participation**: client observes the model performing the behavior and then performs the behavior and/or interacts with the model
- **Covert Modeling**: client visualizes the desired behavior

Harm Reduction for Self and Others

Clients who are in immediate danger of self-harm should be referred to a local emergency room or hospital immediately. Clients who are a danger for self-harm may develop a no-harm contract with the social worker, even though this may not be legally binding. Clients who engage in self-harm may find relief in applying ice to the area of harm, snapping a rubber band, or using colored markers instead of sharp objects. Social workers also need to engage clients in changing distorted thinking related to harm reduction. Clients who are at risk for harm to others may need to be hospitalized or placed in protective custody. Social workers who are aware that the client is at risk of harming a specific victim have a duty to warn the potential victim and report this threat to the appropriate authorities. This mandate originated with the **Tarasoff case** involving a client who was not reported to the prospective victim and then proceeded to kill her. This is a mandatory legal requirement when a client threatens a specific victim.

Teaching Coping and Other Self-Care Skills to Clients

Social workers may act in the role of teacher to instruct clients about coping and other skills. Coping skills may include relaxation techniques, deep breathing, time out, and improved communication skills. Common diagnoses that often require the instruction of coping skills include stress reduction, anxiety, and major depression. Clients may be able to utilize coping and acceptance skills for these diagnoses because they are frequently chronic, and clients will need to cope with them on an almost daily basis. Clients often need to learn a plethora of new skills to manage their issues and complex problems, and they and the social worker should collaborate on coping and other skills to manage these circumstances. Social workers can partialize and brainstorm with clients concerning coping and other treatment skills. Clients sometimes need detailed instructions in order to succeed with treatment goals. Clients need to be engaged in therapy outside of sessions and learn how to cope when the social worker is not present, so assigning clients homework between sessions is a method for building skills. While the social worker may offer suggestions to the client for coping and other skills, the client is ultimately the most effective arbiter of their own treatment.

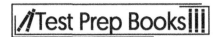

Self-Monitoring Techniques

Client self-monitoring can be a useful technique for turning subjective qualitative information into more quantifiable data. Clients may engage in self-assessment techniques and practices that include journaling, questionnaires, and evaluations. Clients collect data about goals, objectives, and the targeted behavior. This technique collects important information about client progress, but it also adds to clients' feelings of empowerment and self-determination as they become collaborators in treatment. Clients can either track information related to thoughts or behaviors or can use more formal charting techniques. Social workers should assist clients with defining and identifying which type of information to track and then demonstrate how to use the selected tracking technique. Self-monitoring methods serve several purposes. As clients become more invested in treatment, their awareness of strengths and areas in need of improvement may also increase. This will enable the client to monitor behaviors as they occur, allowing for the development of insight related to behavioral change.

Conflict Resolution

Social workers may engage in conflict resolution with clients by acting as a mediator or advocate. Mediators work with clients to intervene in the conflict and develop helpful solutions that reflect all parties involved. For example, the social worker may act as a mediator in family or couples therapy conflicts. Social workers may also work with clients on developing their own conflict resolution skills through methods such as reflection, role-playing, and empty chair techniques. Social workers may also encourage clients to practice the use of **metacommunication**, which is communication about the behaviors and reactions of their regular and possibly dysfunctional method of interactions or communication. Sometimes the client is in conflict with the social worker and transference issues must be resolved before progress can be made. Social workers and clients need to be in collaboration concerning treatment goals and modalities so that conflict is reduced.

In some cases, agencies contract with mediation services outside the agency to assist clients in resolving conflicts. **Professional mediators** are trained in mediation techniques and are paid by the agency for their services. They can be the final step of resolution when the agency cannot resolve client conflict. Child protective services agencies sometimes use professional mediators to reduce or eliminate conflict in cases involving juveniles.

Crisis Intervention and Treatment Approaches

A **crisis** can occur whenever a client is in physical danger or has an extreme emotional need that goes unmet. For example, suicidal threats or ideation qualify as a crisis situation. When a crisis arises, the very first concern is always safety. It is important to get the client into a safe situation, protected from themselves or others. After safety is established, it is then possible to assess the level of need and what should happen next in order to best assist the client.

Another important strategy is **de-escalation**. When there is a crisis, extreme emotions are usually involved. If possible, a client should be guided through relaxation techniques to help calm them down. Oftentimes, a calm and neutral party who can facilitate a conversation or listen to the client empathetically, but without feeding the emotion, will automatically de-escalate the situation. Confrontation or matching the client's emotions will escalate the situation. Allowing the client to communicate the situation fully may help them to become less emotional and more focused on the facts. At this point the client may be able to focus on the next steps and specific tasks that need to be done. If possible, help the client to regain emotional control so that extreme options such as restraints are unnecessary.

In cases where a client is suicidal, it is important to establish if there is a suicide plan or means of committing suicide in place. These two things will determine the severity of suicidal ideation and how at-risk the client is. If it is determined that a client is at imminent risk of suicide, they should be admitted to the hospital or a mental health facility for their own protection.

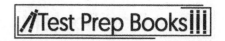

Creating **crisis plans** ahead of time, in collaboration with clients, may assist them in preventing crisis situations or more quickly regaining control when the crisis arises. If clients have been part of the planning process, they may feel empowered, even when their emotions are overwhelming them. Part of the plan should be to identify the potential triggers or warning signs and have immediate steps that can be taken to avoid a crisis. This could be engaging in relaxation strategies or calling a supportive friend, family member, or clinician.

Anger Management Techniques

Anger management is a fairly common treatment goal for clients, so social workers need to be familiar with **anger management techniques**. Clients may manage anger by counting to ten before responding to a situation, taking a time out from the situation to reduce intensity, or practicing deep breathing techniques. Clients may also benefit from vigorous physical exercise to reduce anger. If clients are involved in vigorous exercise, they may need to consult with a physician for approval. Clients may also engage in thought stopping techniques to alleviate anger. Thought stopping sometimes involves the use of guided imagery, such as a stop sign, to reduce moments of intense emotion or thinking.

Stress Management Techniques

Social workers will often encounter clients with stress related problems and should be well versed in **stress management techniques** to offer clients suggestions for this issue. Social workers may engage clients to practice relaxation techniques in order to manage stressors. Clients may engage in physical exercise at their physician's discretion to relieve stress. Deep breathing exercises are also beneficial for relieving stress. To reduce stress, clients may use treatments such as cognitive behavior therapy or rational emotive therapy to change fallacious thinking patterns and distorted perceptions. Clients may be stressed concerning basic needs and social workers can link clients to services in the community to assist them with these issues. If clients are at the safety and physical stages of the hierarchy of needs, these stressors should be addressed before other issues are included in the therapeutic process.

Out-of-Home Displacement

Out-of-home displacement is considered one of the most stressful adjustments a person can experience in their lifetime. It often leads to homelessness, an inability to work, and permanent loss of meaningful personal items. Out-of-home displacement also usually results from a distressing event to begin with (such as a natural disaster, a divorce, immigration from a poor situation in another country, flight from a war zone or other humanitarian crisis, job loss, and so on). Alongside the long-term consequences, individuals can face considerable internal and external struggle as a result of out-of-home displacement.

The intensity of struggle is correlated with four distinct factors: how far the individual is displaced, the type of housing (or lack thereof) to which they are displaced, how many times the individual has to move, and how long the individual has to stay in displacement housing. Another important variable is whether or not separation from family members, close friends, or other important community members occurs. Clients may deal with general psychological distress, post-traumatic stress disorder, acute or long-term poverty, adjustment stress disorder, and unhealthy coping mechanisms, such as substance use.

Children are more profoundly affected and become vulnerable to future risks of obesity, substance use, and chronic disease. It is also important to note, however, that while many clients who experience home loss or displacement experience health and wellness issues that impact them in the long term, a fair number also self-report feeling an increased sense of resiliency and self-efficacy, a strong sense of community and gratitude for receiving aid from others, and hope for the future as their situation begins to improve.

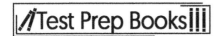
Policies and Procedures that Minimize Risk

Often, the clients and client systems that require the services of a social worker are already in a vulnerable place. Therefore, minimizing additional risk to individuals, families, groups, and their associated organizations and communities (such as places of employment and recreation) is an important component of providing care. To ensure that policies and procedures minimize additional stress, burden, discomfort, or suffering on the part of the client and client systems, practices should employ the constructs of the National Association of Social Work's Code of Ethics in their policies and procedures.

Practices should utilize a sense of transparency, empowerment, and respect in all service procedures. These factors support clients and their systems in playing an active role, when possible, in the services they receive. Policies and procedure should ensure that all services offered have the overarching goal of benefiting clients or client systems, maintain the dignity and self-respect of the client and client systems, and emphasize the importance of cultivating healthy human relationships and the effects those have on recovery.

As social workers implement interventions and treatment, they should always keep lines of communication open with their clients, foster and nurture trust, and continue their educational efforts to ensure they are delivering the highest quality of care at each session. All client intake work should include an informed consent process, and it should engage the client in developing portions of the intervention plan. Social workers should treat all clients of all backgrounds with open-mindedness, without judgment, and with the client's desired intervention outcomes at the center of all interactions.

Social workers may work with clients of different cultures, and social workers should respect the opinions and boundaries that these differences bring to treatment. If a social worker runs into a situation that falls outside the scope of the practice, such as the requirement of clinical intervention for a client, there should be policies in place to address such a situation, and social workers should feel comfortable referring to avenues of care outside of their scope.

Psychotherapies

Social workers need skills in a broad spectrum of areas, including case management, advocacy, and political change. Social workers also need to be versed in psychotherapy modalities so as to enhance client engagement in the change process. **Psychotherapy modalities** originated with the "talk therapy" based on Sigmund Freud's work and include, but are not limited, cognitive behavioral, narrative, psychodynamic, solution focused, and behavioral therapies. It is up to social workers to decide which psychotherapies are most effective for their clients and should be pursued. Agencies may favor a particular type of psychotherapy that the social worker should learn. Insurers may favor psychotherapy modalities and social workers need to consider this in their work with clients.

Psychoanalytic and Psychodynamic Approaches

Psychodynamic approaches engage clients in discovering how their unconscious drives affect their conscious lives. Unconscious drives include sexual and aggression drives that may be unknown to the client on a conscious level. Clients engage in stream of consciousness discussion with the therapist, and the therapist acts mostly as a listener. There is also a focus on dream interpretation in psychodynamic approaches, in which clients are encouraged to discuss their dream states with the social worker. Psychodynamic approaches originate with Freud's "talking cure," in which Freud encouraged clients to attend sessions several times a week.

There are several psychoanalytic organizations in the United States devoted to psychodynamic training. These schools usually have multiyear programs to train new psychoanalysts. While psychodynamic approaches may not encompass the entirety of a client's experience, they are useful for certain clients and may be integrated into psychotherapeutic treatment along with other approaches.

Carl Jung's Psychoanalytic Theory

Jung's theory is similar to Freud's psychoanalytic theory, with differences related to the purpose of the libido, the unconscious, and behavioral motives. Libido is a psychic energy that motivates individuals.

Jung theorized two parts to the unconscious:

- **Personal unconscious**: contains information not accessible to the conscious mind
- **Collective unconscious (transpersonal)**: the memories from a person's ancestors that the individual has from birth

Jung identified this collective unconscious into four main archetypes.

- **Persona**: the artificial self that an individual shows to the world to hide who they really are
- **Anima/Animas**: the masculine qualities that women express to society and the feminine qualities that men express to society
- **Shadow**: similar to Freud's id, signifies raw needs and desires
- **Self**: the unconscious and conscious mind come together to form a unified whole, occurs as a consequence of individuation

Cognitive and Behavioral Interventions

Cognitive Approaches

Cognitive approaches to the social work process involve changing the way the client thinks in order to facilitate progress and problem-solving skills. Cognitive approaches tend to be evidence based and favored by insurance carriers, as they are efficacious for a variety of client issues, including substance use and personality disorders. Cognitive approaches focus on changing maladaptive thinking and cognitive distortions, and thus may help clients engage in behavior change. Cognitive distortions involve fallacious thinking patterns engaged in by the client, such as black-and-white thinking. Types of cognitive approaches may include cognitive behavior therapy, rational emotive behavior therapy, and solution focused brief therapy. There are many modalities of cognitive therapies and social workers should become familiar with—and implement—them when necessary.

Behavioral Approaches

Behavioral approaches, which originated with **Skinner and Pavlov**, include methods of changing and motivating client behaviors toward reaching constructive goals. The underlying concept is that if clients can change behavior, they may also alter the way they think. Skinner and Pavlov believed that all behavior is learned, and they believed in conditioning. Tokens may be awarded for positive behavioral changes in the client; this occurs in what is called a token economy. **Cognitive behavioral therapies**, which focus on both the cognition and the behavior of the client, are considered evidence-based and are favored by managed care insurers.

Strengths-Based and Empowerment Strategies and Interventions

Empowerment is a strengths-based modality, and the goal is that all clients should feel empowered based on their personal identities. Clients need to feel in control of most of their lives and circumstances, and this is what empowerment permits. Working from a strengths-based perspective empowers clients to facilitate change in their own lives. Social workers may seek to empower clients by focusing on strengths and bolstering clients' social constructs. Clients may need to be empowered from a racial, ethnic, religious, gender, or age perspective because they have suffered discrimination in these areas. Social workers may act as political advocates in these realms to combat social oppression affecting clients. The social worker should take into account the differences each client possesses due to their personal race, religion or circumstance and use these differences as strengths.

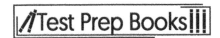

Goal-Setting Techniques

Goal setting is a necessary factor in both the treatment and evaluation of direct practice. Social workers should work collaboratively with clients to determine goals. To be effective, goals need to be specific, measurable, achievable, realistic, and timely. They also should be directly related to the target problem. During the assessment process, begin identifying possible goals for treatment. Depending on the identified issues, goals may focus on desired behavioral, cognitive, or emotional changes.

Reciprocal goals are complementary goals agreed upon by members of a system related to the same target problem (e.g., a father's goal is to offer more compliments to his son, while the son agrees to increase verbal acknowledgement of his father's positive feedback).

Shared goals are when members of a system choose the same goal that addresses an identified problem (e.g., spouses each agree to communicate needs more frequently).

Contracts

Once goals are determined, a contract is the next step to engage the client in services. Contracts can be formal or informal, and written or verbal depending on the policies of the agency and the nature of treatment. A **contract** between client and worker provides a set of expectations and guidelines for treatment. Clients should be made aware that the contract is a commitment by both parties but not a legal document. Components of the contract include goals, assignments of tasks, timeframes, frequency of sessions, methods for determining progress, and how updates or revisions of the contract can occur. Other items that can be included are lengths of sessions, financial arrangements, and procedures for cancelling appointments.

Partializing Techniques

Partializing means to break down into smaller steps. Clients sometimes need partializing techniques to address complex problems such as trauma, grief, or even personality disorders. A social worker can partialize with the client by encouraging the client's suggestions about solving the problem or making a written list. Partializing assists the client in reaching treatment goals in a more organized and efficient fashion. Case management of the client's goals may also include partializing techniques so that the client does not encounter stressors in addition to the problem-solving process. Clients with complex cases may benefit from partializing techniques because they can focus on one step at a time and avoid becoming overwhelmed with treatment goals. Clients may learn partializing techniques from the social worker and then learn to implement them in their own lives so that they can partialize issues that they encounter at home.

Assertiveness Training

Assertiveness training is an intervention that can be used in multiple settings with an assortment of interpersonal difficulties. This type of training helps individuals learn to express their emotions, thoughts, and desires, even when difficult, while not infringing on the rights of others. There are ways in which individuals can assert themselves, including saying no to a request, having a difference of opinion with another person, asking others to change their behavior, and starting conversations. Social workers must respect cultural differences when working with clients to develop assertiveness skills. For example, some cultures feel it is inappropriate for women or children to assert themselves. Role-play is an effective technique to help clients develop assertiveness skills.

Task-Centered Approaches

Task Centered Practice is comprised of a practical, evidence-based intervention that lasts for six to twelve sessions (short term). Task Centered Practice can help resolve problems related to daily living tasks, e.g., lack of basic needs, interpersonal/social relationships, role performance, and decision-making skills. This method is client-driven, with

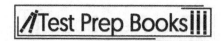

the social worker acting as a guide or collaborator. A specific problem is identified with an associated goal to be accomplished. Afterward, the social worker assists the client in identifying and conquering smaller tasks to resolve the problem. Subsequently, the assessment phase is vital to this process as both client and social worker identify issues, strengths, and resources, and work together to define goals/tasks. The Task Centered Practice model also places emphasis on contracting, carefully planned task implementation, evaluation, and termination.

Psychoeducation Methods

Psychoeducation refers to any form of training or instruction that is provided to clients and the client system as a part of understanding mental health or psychological issues and treatments. Its goal is to support clients experiencing mental illnesses, their families, and their networks while eliminating the stigma that has been associated with mental health issues for decades. Psychoeducation methods include explaining potential causes for specific mental health issues, understanding the challenges of specific mental health issues, explaining how support systems can acknowledge and cope with not only a client's mental health condition but also their own caregiving stress, teaching coping skills, building resiliency, and overcoming in ways that are accessible. This form of education can occur in group settings, seminars or webinars, and in individual or family sessions.

It can also be presented through newsletters, other media, and formal courses. It may be offered in home, online, in hospitals or other healthcare facilities, in community centers, or at conference venues. It is not considered treatment, but it is a beneficial complement to clinical care. It promotes positive and inclusive language, eliminates shame and fear around mental illnesses, creates educational value, fosters network support and understanding, and acknowledges a variety of feelings and responses to mental health conditions. Psychoeducation techniques are associated with reduced inpatient and hospitalization rates for clients with mental health conditions. Psychoeducation is correlated with clients' self-reported feelings of acceptance and increased family support. Family and friends self-report a better understanding of their loved one who may have a mental health condition, a better understanding of their role in providing positive support and care, the ability to draw healthy boundaries for themselves, and relief from learning and utilizing self-care techniques that reduce caregiver stress.

Group Work Techniques and Approaches

Group work can be defined as a goal-directed intervention with small groups of people. The intention of this work is to improve the socioemotional and psychoeducation needs of the individual members of the group through the group process. There are two types of groups in social work: therapeutic and task groups. **Task groups** are created to perform a specific task or purpose. These groups differ in the amount and type of self-disclosure, confidentiality, and communication patterns. There are several types of treatment groups, including support, educational, and therapy groups. Groups can also be long-term or short-term, depending on the type and purpose.

Groups can be open or closed. **Open groups** are ongoing and allow for new members to enter at any time. Open groups are typically used for support and life transitions. There are challenges to this type of group, since the members are at different stages in the group process. The frequently changing membership can be disruptive to the group process because members may not feel as emotionally safe to share with others. **Closed groups** are time-limited, and new members can only join during the beginning stage. The advantages to this type of group are more engagement and better trust by the members, since the group process is more stable. A disadvantage is that if several members leave the group, the group process may not be as effective. There are several variations by theorists that describe the stages of group development. A general method of categorizing the group process uses stages—the beginning, middle, and end. Each stage is classified by different activities, processes, and tasks:

Beginning Stage
Social workers determine the group's purpose, members, objectives, and other logistical tasks (time, location, etc.). Group formation occurs at this stage as new members come together. The social worker fosters a safe and trusting environment by establishing acceptable group norms. As group members become more comfortable, conflicts arise

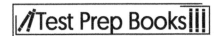

as power and control behaviors emerge. Group roles and alliances begin to form. The worker's role is to help guide the group through these challenges and process any conflicts that arise within the group.

Middle Stage

This stage is where most group work is done. Members share information, openly address issues, and work through conflicts. Some groups do not make it to this stage for several reasons, including member dynamics and a lack of investment by the group members. Group cohesion or the connectedness of the members is extremely important at this stage. The role of the worker is to help members focus on methods and the meaning of communication, working through group differences and confronting members when necessary. Workers should also help develop more intensive levels of cohesiveness while building on member individuality.

End Stage

Group members come to resolutions on the issues addressed during the group process. Members may have strong reactions to termination, especially if there was a high level of cohesion developed during the group process. The social worker should lead the group in discussing feelings about termination and be aware of negative reactions that may surface. When these types of emotions occur, social workers should address any challenges that arise with members. The social worker should also help group members identify and reflect on the skills learned in the group process and how those skills can benefit the members with future challenges.

Working with Individuals in the Group Context

It is the role of the social worker to encourage all members to participate in the group process. The worker can solicit feedback from each member of the group throughout the group process. Clients typically take on various roles during group treatment. **Roles** can be defined as functions that the individual members of the group are fulfilling or performing that facilitate the group process. Some roles include that of a clown, scapegoat, mediator, etc. The worker must be aware of the roles of each individual and how those roles are affecting the group so interventions can be made when necessary.

Family Therapy Models, Interventions, and Approaches

One of the main goals of family therapy is to allow each family member to function at their best while maintaining the functionality of the family unit. When working with families, the social worker must do the following:

- Examine and consider all systems affecting a family and each individual member to determine problems, solutions, and strengths and also consider the functionality of the family subsystems.

- Respect cultural, socio-economic, and non-traditional family systems and not automatically define those systems as dysfunctional if they are not the norm. The overall and individual family functioning should be accounted for.

- Work to engage the family in the treatment while considering the specific traits of the family (i.e., culture, history, family structure, race, dynamics, etc.).

- Assist in identifying and changing dysfunctional patterns, boundaries, and family problems.

Important Concepts

Boundaries: Healthy boundaries around and within the family must exist for families to function effectively. The boundaries must be clear and appropriate.

Emotional Proximity and Distance: This refers to the amount of emotional and physical space that each family member needs to effectively function.

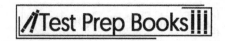

Enmeshed: Boundaries are unclear and pliable. Families that have very open boundaries within the family unit may have very fixed boundaries between outside forces and the family.

Disengaged: Boundaries are rigid with little interaction and emotional engagement. Families that are disengaged within the family system tend to have very open boundaries around the family unit.

Family Hierarchy: The power structure within the family. For families to function effectively, there must be a clear delineation of authority. There must be an individual or individuals who hold the power and authority in a family system. In a traditional family, this should ideally be located within the parental system.

Homeostasis: Family systems should maintain homeostasis or remain regular and stable. When life events become too stressful and the family can no longer function as it normally would, the state of homeostasis is threatened. This is usually when many families seek help.

Alliances: Partnerships or collaborations between certain members of a family. When alliances exist between some members of a family, it can lead to dysfunction (e.g., parent and child have an alliance that undermines the parental subsystem).

Couples Interventions and Treatment Approaches

Many couples enter treatment after experiencing long-standing problems and may seek help because all other options have failed. One of the goals of couple's therapy is to help clients develop effective communication and problem-solving skills so they can solve problems throughout and after treatment. Other goals include helping the couple form a more objective view of their relationship, modifying dysfunctional behavior/patterns, increasing emotional expression, and recognizing strengths. Workers should create an environment to help the couple understand treatment goals, feel safe in expressing their feelings, and reconnect by developing trust in each other. Interventions for couples are often centered on goals geared toward preventing conflicting verbal communication and improving empathy, respect, and intimacy in a relationship. Therapeutic interventions, along with exercises, are designed to help couples learn to treat each other as partners and not rivals. Cognitive Behavioral Therapy is also used when working with couples. It uses cognitive techniques to help change distorted thinking and modify behavior.

Permanency Planning

Juvenile clients who are in danger within their families of origin and/or in foster care may benefit from permanency planning. Clients whose parents have terminated parental rights may be adopted into their foster home or put up for adoption by the state. While the first goal of social workers is to reunite juveniles with their family of origin, this is not always possible due to harmful circumstances in the home. Native American juvenile clients, for instance, are bound by the **Indian Child Welfare Act (ICWA)** when making considerations for permanency planning. ICWA regulations favor the placement of the child with Native families so that the child does not lose contact with their heritage.

Adults who are at risk of abuse and neglect may require permanency planning. Vulnerable adults may be reported to Adult Protective Services agencies. Adult foster care has become more popular in the last few decades and may be an option for at-risk adults. Group homes are another form of permanency planning for vulnerable adults, but the quality of these homes varies. The social worker should make careful screening of these facilities.

Mindfulness and Complementary Therapeutic Approaches

Complementary therapeutic approaches, such as mindfulness, meditation, yoga, exercise, spending time in nature, music therapy, and art therapy can provide emotional, physical, and mental relief for clients who are struggling to cope with adverse events. **Mindfulness** is the act of paying purposeful attention to specific or general events

111

without attaching feelings, judgment, or reason to the events. It can be practiced during a specific time set aside for it, it can be incorporated in increments, or it can be an ongoing behavior throughout one's day. This practice allows clients a way of introspecting and reducing external stimuli, and it is an evidence-based method of stress reduction.

Meditation, another evidence-based method of stress reduction, can include mindfulness as a component. Meditation encourages the practitioner to focus on thoughts and repetitive mental patterns in order to clear them, relax the mind, and improve physiological indicators of stress (such as deeper and slower breathing rates, lowered heart rates, and reduced muscular tension).

Yoga incorporates meditation, focused breathing exercises, and movements to promote mental clarity and strength, improve circulation and respiration, reduce muscular tension, and connect with one's mind and body. Under the guidance of well-trained instructors or a certified yoga therapist, clients can take group or private sessions that are tailored to and address common counseling issues, such as trauma, grief, post-traumatic stress disorder, aging, physical changes, and so on.

Different forms of exercise can have a therapeutic effect, including strength and resiliency building (both mentally and physically), stress reduction, and the management of chronic disease indicators (such as excess weight or blood lipid levels). Group exercise can also be a way to build community and support through a shared, wellness-oriented interest. Finally, exercise programs often support clients in the practice of setting and achieving goals. While this may start off as a primarily physical practice, a number of mental and emotional benefits (such as improved moods and higher self-esteem), introspection, and behavior change often follow suit. Other types of recreational activity, such as creating art, listening to musical sounds and vibrations, and spending time in nature are associated with positive changes at the cellular level.

Follow-Up Techniques

At the final session, the social worker and client can schedule a follow-up session at a predetermined time to evaluate the client's continued progress after termination. Another option is to propose a time to meet and alert the client that the worker will contact the client to schedule a follow up. The **follow-up session** enables the social worker the opportunity to determine how well the client has progressed and to determine the effectiveness of the intervention(s) used during sessions.

Time Management Approaches

Social workers can effectively manage their time through a number of organizational methods. These may include daily prioritization of tasks for the day (such as urgent tasks versus tasks that can wait until the next day), ensuring that all meeting and phone calls with colleagues are scheduled with objectives in mind (such as with the use of a meeting agenda), breaking more tedious tasks into chunks, and planning in a way that works best for one's personality. For example, one person may enjoy making weekly color-coded schedules of tasks with gaps available throughout the week for unexpected assignments that come up; another may prefer to manage tasks daily in a simple list style, with flexible room built in per day. While no schedule can be absolutely rigid, as unforeseen circumstances are guaranteed to arise from time to time, a schedule that is guarded and respected by the social worker fosters effective time management. It is important to decline non-urgent tasks or responsibilities if one's schedule is booked, while ensuring there is space in one's schedule to assist with unanticipated emergencies.

Community Organizing and Social Planning Methods

The **social change process** is one in which interested groups (i.e., community members, lawmakers, businesses, government agencies, community organizations) can work together to create change or solve an identified community or societal problem. Collaborative social planning increases the chances of positive change and allows community members to take ownership of the change and resulting policies. It also encourages the community to

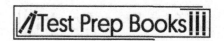
become more energized and more likely to make positive changes in the future. The role of the social worker as a leader in this process includes the following:

- Community engagement
- Problem identification
- Organization and engagement of community members
- Identification of resources, challenges, and solutions
- Creation and implementation of a plan
- Evaluation and follow-up

Measurable Objectives for Client Intervention, Treatment, and Service Plans

Goals in intervention plans should be **SMART**—Specific, Measurable, Achievable, Relevant, and Time-bound. Devoting specific attention to the measurability of a goal requires mutual agreement between the client and practitioner.

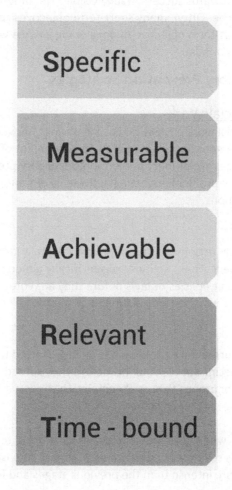

Key recommendations are as follows:

- Measurable terms used in writing the goals should be based on the criteria of the type of desired behavior or action to be demonstrated (and how often), in order to achieve the proposed solution(s).

- Positive, action-oriented language should be utilized when describing the methods that an objective will be measured by. For example, the client should "plan" or "attend" a social gathering. Success of the stated objective will be "demonstrated" or "evidenced" by actually attending or planning a social gathering of some kind. The use of action-oriented language with specific targets assists the practitioner in more effective data collection.

- Objectives should be both short and long-term.

- Short-term objectives should only be a few weeks in length.

- Long-term objectives should be broken down into incremental, small chunks so as not to overwhelm the client and to make progress towards success readily visible. The time-frame for completion should align with the nature of the objective. Often, many short-term objectives can make up one long-term objective or goal (for example, the short-term objective of developing a twice-weekly exercise habit leads to a long-term objective of losing five pounds).

Primary, Secondary, and Tertiary Prevention Strategies

Emphasis on Prevention in Social Work

During the past few decades, the social work profession has increasingly moved toward a prevention-focused service distribution model. This movement has resulted in the development of a **three-stage model of prevention** in social work practice. These three stages are primary prevention, secondary prevention, and tertiary prevention. Each stage assesses the severity of the problem impacting individuals or groups and provides appropriate and evidence-based social work interventions.

Primary Prevention

The **primary prevention stage** includes actions that practitioners take to address the potential causes of a problem before the problem occurs for the client. These actions are specifically aimed at getting rid of a problem's root cause, such as advocating against unfair policies or laws before they are voted upon or take effect. This type of prevention focuses on meeting the needs of the population at an almost universal level.

Secondary Prevention

The **secondary prevention** stage occurs when a problem has already started to impact a person or group. Actions to be taken involve attempts to stop specific social problems before they spread and cause further harm. These actions are designed to help any individuals or groups that are beginning to show symptoms of increased problem severity.

Tertiary Prevention

The **tertiary prevention** stage occurs when both previous stages have failed to address the problem. These actions are designed to decrease a problem's severity through remedial service provision that will decrease its lasting effects and duration. This stage is more intense than the previous stages and focuses on individuals that are most impacted by the problem.

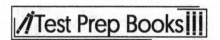

Visualizing the Three Stages of Prevention

These stages can be visualized as three parts of a pyramid. The wide base of the pyramid represents primary prevention, as these are more universal services that reach the broadest portion of the population. The middle of the pyramid represents secondary prevention, in which more prevention services are applied to a smaller portion of the population. The top of the pyramid represents tertiary prevention, with the highest degree of prevention services for the smallest percentage of the population.

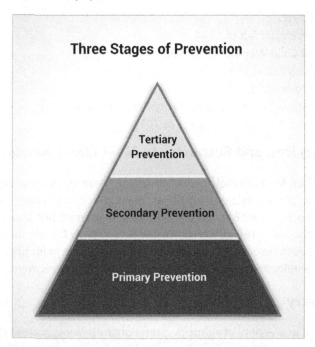

Three Stages of Prevention

Tertiary Prevention

Secondary Prevention

Primary Prevention

Client Readiness for Termination

When clients have made significant progress on the treatment plan, goals, and objectives, the worker can begin planning for termination. Depending on the identified goals and objectives, a standardized assessment can be used to determine how much progress has been made. Social worker practices vary depending on what level of goal attainment should be completed before termination (i.e., some, most, all). Other options can be offered to the client for continued work and learning such as groups, workshops, and reading materials. In many instances, services are terminated due to limitations by insurance or other funding sources. It is extremely important in these circumstances that the worker assists the client in locating additional resources that can be used following service termination. When preparing clients for termination, workers should discuss the following topics with the client:

- Initial reasons for requesting help
- What skills the client initially lacked that led to initiating services
- Skills developed as a result of treatment and how those new skills will help the client with future challenges
- Ways the client will continue to build on the newly developed skills
- Social worker and client feelings about termination

Service Delivery and Management of Cases

Impact of the Political Environment on Policy-Making

Social welfare legislation can have a dramatic effect on social work practice. Some legislation may help solve social problems that social workers encounter and other legislation may create more problems, challenges, and barriers

through which social workers must help clients navigate. To be effective, social workers must be knowledgeable about legislative measures that affect clients. Another possible role of a social worker is that of legislative advocate, which is working to change, modify, or create legislation for the benefit of a group of people.

Significant Social Welfare Legislation:

- Civil Rights Act of 1964
- Older Americans Act of 1965
- The Child Abuse and Prevention Act of 1974
- Adoption Assistance and Child Welfare Act of 1980
- Americans with Disabilities Act of 1990
- The Family Medical Leave Act of 1993
- The Health Insurance Portability and Accountability Act of 1996 (HIPAA)
- The Patient Protection and Affordable Care Act of 2010

Advocacy for Policies, Services, and Resources to Meet Client Needs

Social workers must help clients understand their needs versus the services and resources available to them. Workers must be knowledgeable of the services available at their agency and in the communities in which their clients live. It is the role of the worker to assist clients in obtaining resources, but also to help clients understand their options and their right to choose or refuse which resources to access. Clients should receive assistance in identifying the pros and cons of each resource. They should also be involved in identifying and seeking resources as much as possible to foster the development of self-determination and empowerment.

Methods of Service Delivery

Social workers may be employed in a variety of agencies. Some organizations, such as hospitals or government entities, employ diverse professionals. Other types of organizations, such as direct service non-profits or private practice agencies, maintain predominantly social services staff. Agency policies directly and significantly impact the working environment, the services provided, and, as a result, the effectiveness of the care clients receive. All agencies should have a mission statement that gives the agency purpose and serves as an umbrella for the agency's smaller goals and objectives. Agency policies must be in the best interest of the client and must support the ethical guidelines to which social workers adhere. They must also be clearly written and available to workers and clients where appropriate. Social workers and all those providing care to clients should be able to help shape policy development to ensure consistency with client and worker needs and protection. Policies must address the following:

- Appropriate confidentiality, consent, and information protection
- Case management and supervision
- Cultural competency guidelines
- Professional development and ongoing trainings
- Anti-discriminatory/diversity practices

Components of Case Management

Clients frequently experience difficulty navigating everyday life problems and systems. One of the roles of a social worker is to help link clients with needed services and resources. To perform this role effectively, social workers must have a thorough knowledge of available local resources to aid the client.

When acting in the case manager role, social workers help clients define, locate, and access needed services and resources. Additionally, social workers must often interact with other professionals, including external resources to

ensure the client's needs are met. In the case management role, social workers also make referrals directing the client to the appropriate resource for needed services. The worker acts as a manager, following up with the client on a regular basis to ensure the client is following through with their case plan. Workers may also serve as an advocate in this role, working on behalf of the client if any barriers to resources are met.

Process of case management:

- Assessing needs and client engagement
- Creating an intervention plan of care that includes goals, needed services, and timelines
- Administering the plan
- Monitoring progress and reassessing the plan at fixed intervals
- Termination of services
- Evaluation and follow-up

Case Recording, Documentation, and Management of Practice Records

Accurate case recording is an integral part of social work practice. It is necessary to accurately document clients' information for effective treatment and protection of confidentiality. It is also required to protect the agency from possible legal ramifications and to ensure reimbursement from funders. Client records should be kept up-to-date, objective, and completed as soon as possible to ensure accuracy of information. Social workers should assume it is always possible that records may be requested as part of legal proceedings. Treatment notes should always be clearly written and only include information necessary to the client's treatment to protect confidentiality as much as possible. Social workers must also adhere to any state or federal legal requirements related to storage, disclosure of information, release of client records, and confidential information.

Establishing Service Networks or Community Resources

Due to limited funding and resources and a rapidly growing demand for services, establishing service networks to maximize community resources has become a necessary part of social work practice. Social workers and social service agencies frequently create partnerships, collaborations, or networks to bridge gaps in service and provide a comprehensive system of care for clients. These collaborations can be formal with the use of a comprehensive intake process and service or memorandums of agreements between programs. Partnerships can also be informal, in which workers routinely refer clients to specific providers. When establishing new community resources, social workers must first perform a community assessment, which involves examining existing resources, community needs, and demographics.

Employee Recruitment, Training, Retention, Performance Appraisal, Evaluation and Discipline

Employee recruitment, training, retention, performance appraisal, evaluation, and discipline are primary responsibilities of an organization's human resources department. However, a worker's direct supervisor, manager, or other team leader plays a role in these aspects as well. An effective team leader will know which skillsets and personality traits are needed to fill roles on the team. The leader will communicate this need to human resources, which will then develop a job posting and pursue recruiting and interviewing efforts to find a competent candidate. Once a candidate is selected, offered a job, and has accepted the job, human resources will normally provide generalized training about the organization (such as more detail about the mission and vision, employee benefits, company culture, ethics courses, and so on). The team leader or a lateral colleague will provide on-the-job training and support until the new employee is established.

Depending on the job, extra training may also be required (such as certification or licensures) during a specified period after hire. When so much time and resources are committed to a new employee, retention becomes

117

important for preventing waste. Retaining employees begins in the hiring process, by ensuring the candidate is truly a good fit for the role and the workplace culture. Retention continues by ensuring the employee remains satisfied with their job, work environment, and compensation. Performance appraisals and evaluations should take place at regular intervals to review the employee's current work and future goals and to keep organizational expectations transparent. If an employee is performing poorly or acting inappropriately, disciplinary measures such as coaching, demotion, suspension, or termination of the employee may be required from both the team leader and a representative of human resources.

Case Recording for Practice Evaluation or Supervision

Social workers must document their practice with the client. Social workers document sessions with clients as well as client legal mandates, such as visitation with minors in state custody. Documentation may be a combination of narrative and quantitative descriptions, depending on agency requirements. Records should be kept confidential either electronically or in a physical location. New laws require that all records be electronic, and they are called electronic health records. These records must be confidential as stated in the Health Insurance Portability and Accountability Act of 1996 (HIPAA). It is crucial for the social worker to maintain accurate documentation.

Evaluating Agency Programs

Different types of evaluation methods can be used to evaluate agency programs. A needs assessment looks at existing processes and services to determine whether a need exists. This **needs assessment** is usually a systematic investigation utilizing concrete planning strategies, evidence, case studies, interviews, and other methods of information synthesis. A **need** can be defined as perceived (what is believed to be needed), expressed (what is asked for), or relative (this term used primarily in the context of socioeconomic inequities between classes, races, genders, or other defined groups). A **formative or summative assessment** is usually conducted on a pilot study of a program, or during the planning phase of a program, to ensure that it will likely produce the desired outcomes.

If it appears that the program will not produce the desired outcomes during the formative evaluation, changes can be made or the program can be discarded before further resources are unintentionally wasted. A **cost effectiveness evaluation** examines various ways a program could be conducted to determine which route minimizes the resource cost while maximizing desired results. This is a way to minimize or eliminate unnecessary costs and maintain lean processes. A **cost-benefit analysis** examines all associated monetary costs over a set period of time in order to determine whether the associated costs outweigh the projected benefits in the end, or vice versa. An **outcomes assessment** examines a program for the effects that resulted in participants. Often, desired effects are listed as part of the program objectives during the planning phase. Outcomes assessments may check if program objectives were met. They may also look at program effects on a broader scale, such as whether the program is considered an overall success and should be repeated.

Effects of Program Evaluation Findings on Services

Often the urgency of immediate client services takes precedence over program evaluation, but evaluation is a necessary step in ensuring that an organization provides effective and affordable services for clients. Program evaluation can be conducted during the formative stage of a program in order to establish the best objectives and methods, but it can also be summative, evaluating outcomes of the program at a later stage. Summative evaluations can be used to determine what changes should be made or even if the program should continue.

Different types of evaluation methods can be used to evaluate agency programs. A **needs assessment** looks at existing processes and services to determine whether a need exists. This needs assessment is usually a systematic investigation utilizing concrete planning strategies, evidence, case studies, interviews, and other methods of information synthesis. A need can be defined as perceived (what is believed to be needed), expressed (what is asked for), or relative (this term used primarily in the context of socioeconomic inequities between classes, races, genders,

or other defined groups). A formative or summative assessment is usually conducted on a pilot study of a program, or during the planning phase of a program, to ensure that it will likely produce the desired outcomes. If it appears that the program will not produce the desired outcomes during the formative evaluation, changes can be made or the program can be discarded before further resources are unintentionally wasted. A **cost effectiveness evaluation** examines various ways a program could be conducted to determine which route minimizes the resource cost while maximizing desired results. This is a way to minimize or eliminate unnecessary costs and maintain lean processes. A **cost-benefit analysis** examines all associated monetary costs over a set period of time in order to determine whether the associated costs outweigh the projected benefits in the end, or vice versa. An outcomes assessment examines a program for the effects that resulted in participants. Often, desired effects are listed as part of the program objectives during the planning phase. Outcomes assessments may check if program objectives were met. They may also look at program effects on a broader scale, such as whether the program is considered an overall success and should be repeated.

Techniques Used to Evaluate a Client's Progress

There are several techniques to evaluate client progress, including self-reporting by the client, quantitative measures that are collaboratively discussed by the social worker and the client, and narrative approaches that utilize a textual basis for describing progress. Social workers may ask the client scaling questions to measure client mood and/or progress. Client progress should be measured at regular intervals in order to assist with treatment planning and intervention efficacy. Clients should be informed of progress, and social workers should develop progress notes to reflect client progress. Social workers need to be aware of client progress and compliance in order to accurately measure the steps the client is taking to move forward.

Quality Assurance

In social work, **quality assurance** is the practice of ensuring that services rendered meet established criteria and deliver intended, beneficial outcomes. Quality assurance practices review procedures in place to ensure they lead to high caliber service delivery, to identify gaps that need to be addressed, and to prevent errors before they are made.

Methods of quality assurance include program assessments, benchmarking, social worker evaluations, and internal and external audits. Program assessments and social worker evaluations often utilize a list of standardized best practices; actual processes are compared to the standardized best practices to determine compliance. **Benchmarks** are clear, quantitative indicators of performance that serve as a standard for outcomes. Program evaluations may compare program outcomes to benchmark metrics to determine how well the program is performing. If there is a large gap, the program may undergo quality improvement procedures (such as a gap analysis or root cause analysis) to determine what is causing the discrepancy. Once this has been determined, a **plan-do-study-act cycle** (PDSA, a quality-oriented test of change) can be implemented to see whether benchmark indicators improve.

Auditing is a regular practice in the social work field. **Auditing** is conducted on processes performed as well as on the actions of the social worker to ensure ethical conduct and high levels of competence. For example, during licensure application and renewals, social workers' educational histories are audited to ensure they meet licensure and continuing education requirements. Audits may be conducted internally by the organization in which the social worker is employed or externally by regulatory bodies. The NASW performs comprehensive audits nationally, while state or local appointed boards and associations may audit for other requirements.

Consultation and Interdisciplinary Collaboration

Leadership and Management Techniques

Leading and managing teams requires a range of organizational and interpersonal skills. An effective leader can clearly develop a vision for a preferred future state as well as develop strategies to make the vision a reality. An effective leader must also be able to identify key stakeholders who are necessary to reach the vision and keep them actively engaged throughout the operational process. These tactics require that the leader is self-motivated, is able to think uniquely to solve problems, and has a desire to develop and attain a feasible end result. However, a single leader cannot accomplish a vision alone. Therefore, leaders must be able to communicate the vision and motivate their team to take the actions that are necessary to reach the desired goal.

Leaders should be individuals who the team can trust and feel comfortable supporting. The most effective team will be one where leadership vision and team motivation align; however, this arrangement may not always be the case in a work setting. Therefore, a leader must know how to make projects seem of value to the employee, know which tasks are a good fit with an employee's personality type, and understand what motivates a team member's work. When managing a team, leaders may fall on a spectrum of laissez-faire (hands-off and relatively unstructured) to autocratic (which involves a high-level of micromanaging). Most successful leaders manage their teams by falling somewhere in the middle—establishing clearly defined goals and strategies and hand-selecting appropriate workers to execute tasks, but allowing their team members to have a sense of autonomy and creativity over their delegated responsibilities.

Models of Supervision and Consultation

In social work, supervision takes place when a more experienced professional mentors or coaches an emerging professional in fieldwork, practical application, or other service delivery settings. This requires strong interpersonal skills, a sense of respect, and open communication between both parties. The supervisor should be able to provide supportive instruction and guidance without arrogance and condescension; the supervisee should be receptive to instruction and have an honest desire for professional growth and learning. Some commonly used models of supervision in the social work setting include **individual-oriented** types of supervision, in which the supervisor may ask the supervisee to reflect upon their interactions with different clients or their personal judgments and biases that may have arisen during a session. The supervisor may also present the supervisee with different forms of research and data and ask the supervisee to utilize the evidence to structure interventions. Finally, the supervisor may provide coaching related to the supervisee's development, by establishing small objectives that lead to larger professional goals.

In **peer-oriented** and **group-oriented** approaches, lateral-level colleagues (perhaps with the aid of one or two supervisors) learn from one another by sharing clinical experiences and lessons, new research and literature, or other professional development opportunities. This may take the form of team meetings at the beginning or end of the day, social events where work can be discussed, or conference settings. In some workplaces, individual, peer, and group models may be integrated to provide a more holistic sense of supervision.

Consultation can take place in any interaction that a social worker has with a client, regardless of setting or context. Consultation can primarily be divided into organizational, program, educational, mental health, and clinical cases. These can take place one-on-one with an individual or in group therapy settings.

Educational Components, Techniques, and Methods of Supervision

Social workers should expect to continuously learn. Educational components include staying abreast of new and emerging research and methodology in the field, brushing up on less-used skills, learning from mentors and more experienced social workers, and ensuring that one's practical expertise is up to the most recent standards.

Supervisors or managers may choose to ensure that social workers who report to them have the time and resources to continuously learn, that they can learn materials for their needs, and that they feel comfortable addressing any gaps in their education with their superiors in order to resolve the discrepancies.

Techniques for learning may include visual techniques (such as books, videos, newspaper articles, and journal articles), listening techniques (such as lectures, seminars, podcasts, and audiobooks), or hands-on techniques (such as field work or practicums with a mentor). Some learning opportunities include tactics from all three learning techniques.

Supervisors may choose to be more involved in their team's education, or they may be more distant and allow their team members to pursue their educational goals and requirements independently. An effective supervisor will allow their team members to introspect as to what may be the best educational route for them and provide space coupled with guidance and support for team members in achieving their goals. Effective supervisors will also ensure that the professional goals individual team members are seeking align with the goals of the group as well.

The Supervisee's Role in Supervision

Although the focus is often on the supervisor's role of ensuring that clients are provided with ethical services by training and evaluating the supervisee, the supervisee's role in supervision is not passive. The social worker should fully engage in the process of supervision and use this relationship to grow and improve. In order to do that, the supervisee must be willing to discuss areas of ethical or legal concern that have arisen in their interactions with clients. They must also be ready to honestly address their own struggles and identify their learning needs, and seek the help and advice of the supervisor. This can only happen effectively through genuine self-assessment, which flows from a real desire to become a better social worker. The process of self-assessment in supervision can help them see any biases or weaknesses that may be holding them back from fully meeting their clients' needs. If the social worker is defensive or resistant to the supervisory relationship, then they will make little progress.

Factors to consider when receiving feedback during supervision/consultation:

- Social workers can benefit from feedback during supervision or consultation, especially with difficult clients/cases or at significant times in treatment, such as termination.

- When discussing cases, client confidentiality should be protected as much as possible, and client consent to release information should be acquired.

Identifying Learning Needs and Developing Learning Objectives for Supervisees

Supervisors must ensure that their team members are competent and ethical, that they deliver service effectively, and that they are satisfied with their performance and work environment. Supervisors may audit or review performance with their team members to ensure that standard competency and operational requirements are met. If gaps exist, supervisors may choose to develop training that addresses them. Speaking directly with team members individually or as a group can also help supervisors to find out where personal learning concerns or interests lie. In general, supervisors should ensure that their team is knowledgeable about current literature and able to deliver social service to the highest acceptable quality, that their team understands the legalities and risks of their work, and that all team members perform professionally and ethically in any given situation.

When choosing to develop learning objectives that are not based on any existing gaps, supervisors may focus on new and emerging research, skill sets, or modalities that their team may want to use in their practical work. They may also choose to focus on improving current processes to enhance the client experience; often, this practice may focus on areas that are important but may not regularly get attention in the day-to-day routine tasks (such as writing competence, leadership skills, business skills, and so on). Supervisors may choose to teach learning

121

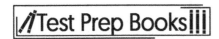
objectives in a workshop or other interactive format, conduct online trainings, or engage in field work as a learning modality.

Elements of Client System Reports

Elements of client reports may include developmental history, family history, substance use information, medical history, the presenting problem, and recommendations. There are a variety of elements of client reports that may be required by the agency. With the advent of electronic records, client reports are often built into the software that the agency uses. Client reports may also be in **DAP** (data, assessment, plan) format or in the model of **SOAP notes** (subjective, objective, assessment, and plan). Reports are at the agency's discretion, and the social worker should use the format that is required by the agency to develop client reports.

Elements of a Case Presentation

Elements of a social work case presentation may include identifying data, the presenting problem, history of the presenting problem, medical/psychiatric information, significant personal and/or social information, impressions and summary, and recommendations. This format is only one model to choose from. There are many formats for a case presentation, and the social worker needs to make sure that they are following their agency's or organization's case presentation format.

Principles and Processes for Developing Formal Documents

Social workers may need to develop formal documents that are used for a broad range of functions; therefore, it is important to develop writing and communication skills that can be employed in a variety of professional contexts.

Social workers may be expected to write grant and research proposals for securing external funding for practical and applied work. They may need to write brochures or pamphlets that advertise their practice (especially if they are running their own business), explain types of interventions, or promote community initiatives. Social workers may need to communicate through letter or email correspondence regarding a client's progress. In these instances, they must be careful to explain clinical concepts in ways the client can understand from simply reading the correspondence without the social worker there to answer any potential questions.

Additionally, written correspondence with the client must always remain appropriate and in compliance with HIPAA and other privacy concerns. Social workers may be required to provide their superiors with weekly, monthly, or annual reports about the work they performed. They may also need to maintain regular reports of individual client progress updates or milestones. Social workers can be expected to provide evaluation reports on processes and outcomes utilized in their cases. Depending on the field of work (such as government agency, private institution, medical setting, et cetera), the requirements for reporting and evaluation may vary significantly.

Finally, today's social workers can expect to maintain some degree of technological capability and have the ability to leverage web platforms and social media. Web platforms can provide an avenue for blogging or other information sharing that makes people aware of the work of social institutions. Social media posts can provide this avenue as well, and they can also serve as another point of connection for clients and colleagues. Social media can be an important tool in business-building and networking. It is imperative that social workers maintain a respectful, professional online presence that maintains both the trust and privacy of their potential clients.

Consultation Approaches

Although it may lead to possible conflict due to differing perspectives, opinions, and approaches to treatment, the use of consultation assistance from an expert in a related field can be extremely beneficial to an individual's treatment. The **NASW Code of Ethics (2.05)** specifically addresses consultation with other disciplines. Accordingly,

workers should seek consultations with other areas when it benefits clients. When seeking consultation, social workers should maintain client confidentiality to the greatest extent possible, only releasing necessary information. When seeking consultation, the worker should seek competent colleagues and only consult with those who are appropriately qualified. Additionally, the worker should ensure the guidelines are clear for the consultation process by defining goals, the presenting problem, and the role of the consultant(s). In line with the code of ethics, social workers also may provide consultation or supervision. When providing consultation, workers must also be knowledgeable in the focus area and always maintain appropriate and culturally sensitive boundaries.

Methods of Networking

Networking in social work can be defined in different ways. One type of networking occurs when social workers connect with colleagues and other professionals to improve services and skills. External collaboration with community resources and colleagues with similar goals enables social workers to learn about available resources and to provide opportunities for developing relationships with others who have a similar purpose.

Additionally, social workers may also help develop connections between clients, organizations, or other groups. This networking assists with the acquisition of support, skill development, and the facilitation of ongoing learning related to resources. Networks are typically more informal than official organizations and can therefore sometimes be more easily accessed by individuals.

Interdisciplinary and Intradisciplinary Team Collaboration

Interdisciplinary team collaboration refers to a group of professionals with different skillsets and perspectives working toward a common goal (such as a social worker, a psychiatrist, a job counselor, and a life coach working together to support an unemployed client). Intradisciplinary team collaboration refers to a group of professionals from the same field but with varying backgrounds working together (such as a team of three veteran clinical social workers and two entry-level clinical social workers who are establishing a new program in their organization).

Interdisciplinary teams can support a client holistically. Because they work together, they may offer smoother operating processes than a client would experience if they sought the services of each team member individually. Social workers may be placed in interdisciplinary teams by their superiors, or they may refer clients to colleagues in different fields and voluntarily choose to collaborate on the client's intervention. Regardless, communication channels and communication itself must be clear, open, and purposeful when working with other professionals. All team members should be clear about their roles in the client's intervention, and the client's positive outcomes should be the primary goal of the collaboration. Intradisciplinary teams may tend to understand each other's perspectives better. This type of team dynamic most commonly occurs in organizational shifts or in supervisory or mentoring relationships.

Basic Terminology of Other Professions

Social workers may need to work with professionals in a number of other fields to support their clients. Therefore, it is important to have a basic understanding of some of the terminology that is used in the professions with which social workers most commonly collaborate. These include the criminal and legal fields, since social workers may often support legal cases such as those of abuse, negligence, divorce, and child custody. Social workers should understand basic legal terms so that they can provide relevant support to the clients as well as to the other professionals involved in the case.

Socials workers often collaborate with educators in the school setting, and they work with children who may be in a vulnerable position. In these contexts, social workers should understand the values of the school system and the laws that school systems must follow when working with children, and they should ensure that social work does not detract from the child's educational experience.

123

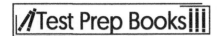
Social workers may commonly collaborate with or refer patients to professionals in the medical field. They may need to understand basic medical and health terminology associated with their client's conditions. They may need to understand the impact that clinical issues may have on both the client's current behavior and desired outcomes. For example, a social worker may see a client who has severe depression linked with alcoholism. A physician may diagnose the client with stage 4 cirrhosis; the social worker will need to understand the severity of this diagnosis and how it will impact the client's depression and future sessions with the social worker. When in doubt, the social worker should ensure that their working relationships allow clarifying questions to be asked. Asking questions as needed will allow the social worker to fully understand any unfamiliar contexts and to serve the client.

Influencing Organizational and Social Policy

Social workers may act in a macro capacity for the common public good and serve as policy advocates or provide leadership in the policy change process. There are many types of societal influences that can affect social policy.

Cultural

Societal perceptions or beliefs can shape policy. For instance, a general belief that children should have access to health care can aid in the development of child health care laws. Additionally, the media can bring problems/issues to the forefront and have a huge impact on public opinion, which can then influence policy development.

Economic

Lack of or an availability of resources has a significant impact on policy development. Additionally, those who control the resources also impact how policy is shaped.

Institutional

The capabilities, resources, and structure of government offices affect policy development. The institutions that create and implement policies have to be able to do so in an effective manner for those policies to be successful.

Social

The social environment, including events or situations such as recessions, wars, or poverty, all affect how policies are developed.

Legal

Existing laws and policies can influence future trends in policy development. New policies may or may not be adopted, depending on how they complement those already in existence and the current social climate. Legal events may also influence new policies.

Political

The political climate directly influences social policy, since the parties in control of governing bodies directly affect which policies and laws are implemented and repealed.

Availability of Community Resources

There is a wide range of community resources available, making it confusing for some clients to navigate the system and identify what would be most helpful for them. Therefore, a case manager plays a critical role in helping the client to find and utilize the community resources that would be most beneficial. When seeking resources, it is

useful to look at the different domains of life—physical, psychological, emotional, spiritual, and educational—and then compile a collection of resources that may be useful for the client in each of these domains.

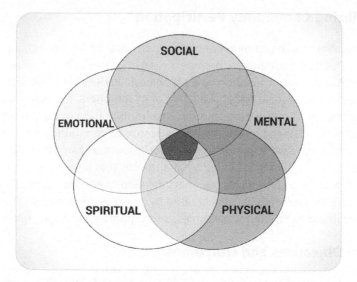

Physical needs can include food, shelter, clothing, or medical care, and there are many government programs available for these needs, such as free health care, affordable housing, and food stamps. For the elderly or disabled, their greatest need may be related to the accessibility of physical resources. In that case, the delivery of meals through Meals on Wheels or transportation services may be the most appropriate recommendation. Another help would be prescription assistance programs offered by some pharmaceutical companies to those with low income, which provide medications for free or at reduced cost. Other resources for the elderly can be accessed through the Administration on Aging and other local departments for elder care.

Ensuring the provision of adequate emotional and psychological services would first involve making sure the client is receiving emotional support from family and friends, or getting involved in support groups with others who have similar struggles. For the elderly, there may be community centers with programs to help seniors connect with each other and stay active. When it comes to finding the right psychological resources, both therapeutic and psychiatric, there are many options, so the client must be involved in the process of deciding what type and format of therapy would be best.

An often-overlooked area of whole-person care is the spiritual needs of the client. In addition to providing spiritual support, religious organizations are often nonprofits that can assist the client in physical or emotional ways as well. Fraternal organizations may provide similar benefits to a person, offering emotional, social, and spiritual components.

Educational resources should not be disregarded, especially in the case of someone who has mental or physical health needs. Whether formal training or informal learning through the library or online, there are many resources for gaining knowledge in almost any area. As discussed, education related to the individual's specific health needs is a crucial element of self-management care, client activation, and empowerment.

Calling United Way's helpline at 211, checking the U.S. government website, or conducting an internet search are easy and effective means of identifying the relevant community resources in the client's locality. Collaborating with other service providers can also make use of those who already know the client and can also prevent overlap in the provision of services. Finally, and perhaps most importantly, help the client to find resources through the people and organizations with whom they are already connected. Not only does this encourage self-determination and

empowerment by helping the client see how many resources they already have in their life, but many clients will be most comfortable with places and people they already know.

Techniques for Mobilizing Community Participation

Limited resources in communities make community member participation in social change movements vital to the success of the community. Mobilizing community members is an important part of creating macro-level change. The community develops a sense of self-determination when it takes an active role in removing barriers, creating needed services and resources and advocating for the rights of its members. Members are encouraged to participate in problem identification, goal setting, and resource mobilization to create change. When community members become engaged in the change process, the overall sense of community empowerment increases. There are some challenges with community participation in which social workers can assist. Community members may lack necessary skills, or there may be barriers created by institutions that operate in the community. Social workers can serve the role of educator to help community members develop needed social organizational skills. The worker may also serve as an advocate to overcome barriers created by larger systems and institutions. Workers must engage a community and mobilize its strengths, resources, and support systems to create positive changes.

Establishing Program Objectives and Outcomes

When developing a social work program, objectives should be developed for each process that is used or evaluated and for each outcome that is desired or evaluated. Often, a funding source will require that certain process and outcome objectives are evaluated in order for the organization to receive funds; this often provides a practice with some objectives to manage. When objectives are not tied to a funding source, programs may decide to develop them based on a needs assessment or the program's service interest and capacity. These may be inspired by evidence-based research, successful outcomes in other programs, or data collected from focus groups. They may also be tailored to a specific case. A logic model is a useful tool to map out what the program hopes to achieve, the inputs it requires, and the expected outputs. It can also be used at the end of a program to map out the actual intervention and analyze how it compared to the expected plan.

Process objectives set standards for procedures, activities, and other implementation constructs of the social work program. Outcome objectives set standards for what exactly the program hopes to achieve. All objectives should follow SMART criteria. This means that any objective that is set forth should be Specific (the action to be taken and the person to perform the action are clearly stated), Measurable (changes can be measured and analyzed), Achievable (the objective is realistic for the client, the social worker, and the available resources), Relevant (the objective relates to the desired overall goal), and Time-bound (the objective can be achieved in a specified time period).

Governance Structures

The **National Association of Social Workers (NASW)** is considered the most reputable association for the field of social work. NASW sets the tone for the field's standards, competency requirements, and public and legislative initiatives. It also provides social workers with resources to stay current on emerging research and news and with which to continue their social work education.

Other important governance structures in the United States that social workers may deal with depend on their field of practice. Social workers who work in a small, private setting may only have a single office manager to whom they report. If a social worker owns their own practice, they may choose how they establish the organization's reporting hierarchy. Social workers who work as part of a large government agency, such as a case worker for a state's Department of Child and Family Services, may work with a more bureaucratic structure that involves a supervisor, manager, division director, agency director, and the state governor. Social workers who work as part of a national

non-profit may have a large, hierarchical governing structure similar to that of a state or federal agency, whereas social workers who work in local non-profits may be part of a lateral leadership system.

Often, nonprofit and government groups will collaborate with one another or with private companies to lead social work initiatives. Therefore, social workers may need to be flexible in how they adapt to the governance structures of the organization they are serving while still maintaining the standards established by the NASW.

Formal and Informal Power Structures in the Decision-Making Process

Organizations are typically run as hierarchies of power. The higher in power level a position is, the more likely it is to be involved in decision-making. Formal power structures are those that are listed in the organizational chart, such as the chief executive officer of an organization. The higher on the chart the position is listed, the more power that position has in decision-making. In small organizations where workers are more close-knit, this structure may be less strict. However, there are likely to be distinguished key players who primarily execute decisions (such as the company founder, or the person who is in charge of all operations). In informal power structures, key power wielders may not be officially listed as having high-ranking positions on an organizational chart, but they can still influence important decisions or the opinions of formal power structures. For example, informal wielders of power could be a mid-level employee who oversees a critical project, business associates who refer the most clients to the organization, or an entry-level employee who has the most knowledge about a niche topic in the field.

Accreditation and/or Licensing Requirements

In the United States, social work accreditation and licensure requirements vary by state. Therefore, aspiring social workers should ensure they follow standards set forth in the state in which they hope to practice.

The **Council on Social Work Education (CSWE)** is the main accrediting body for higher education programs in social work, and the majority of states require that social workers receive undergraduate or graduate degrees from universities whose social work curriculum is CSWE-accredited in order to become a licensed professional. CSWE-accredited programs ensure that coursework includes not only information related to competencies established by the NASW, but that an emphasis is placed on ethics, professionalism, and practical application. Most states do not allow aspiring social workers to take board examinations without proof of a CSWE-accredited degree.

Other licensing information pertains to the type of social work a person hopes to do and the education they have received. Clinical social workers have different licensing requirements. Some states require post-graduate education in social work before licensure can be obtained. Other levels of licensure require practical and field work for a designated period of time. While board scores may be transferred across state lines, licensure is a separate process in each state that reviews both the worker's education and working experience comprehensively.

Practice Quiz

1. What kind of records are required today in social work practice and social workers should become proficient at using them within the scope of their practice?
   a. Economic
   b. Political
   c. Electronic
   d. Paper

2. Which BEST describes a definition of client advocacy?
   a. Helping clients recognize and then use their strengths, resources, and systems to obtain goals
   b. Working on behalf of clients to remove barriers and obtain needed resources and/or services
   c. A short-term treatment usually lasting four to six weeks and is implemented when a client enters treatment following some type of traumatic event that causes significant distress
   d. Helping to link clients with needed services and resources

3. Which is NOT a method of working with involuntary clients?
   a. Helping clients to recognize participation is still a choice
   b. Including a client's goals in a service plan along with mandated goals
   c. Protecting a client's right to self-determination
   d. Refraining from getting a client's consent in treatment since participation is mandatory

4. Which of the following is an aspect of the psychosocial approach to treatment?
   a. Unique to the field of social work and allows it to stand out from other professions
   b. Used when clients experience a state of disequilibrium, are out of balance, and can no longer function effectively
   c. Emphasizes the concept of problems of living
   d. Short-term, practical, and evidence-based intervention

5. Which component of the problem-solving process is left out of these steps?
   1. Assess, define, and clarify the problem
   2. Examine options and select/implement a solution
   3. Evaluate and adjust

   a. Emphasize contracting and carefully planned task implementation.
   b. Determine possible solutions.
   c. Social worker functions as a collaborator to assist the client in identifying smaller tasks.
   d. Social worker identifies issues, strengths, and resources.

See answers on the next page.

Answer Explanations

1. C: Electronic records are required today in the social work field. Social workers should be familiar with electronic health records and prepare to use them in today's environment. Medical records in all fields are now electronic, and the systems of documentation vary. Some electronic health records are software based and others are Internet based. Social workers should have some computer proficiency in order to use electronic records systems.

2. B: Client advocacy is working on behalf of a client to remove barriers and obtain needed resources and/or services. Choice *A*, client empowerment, is helping clients to recognize and then use their strengths, resources, and systems to obtain goals. Choice *C*, crisis-intervention approach, is a short-term treatment usually lasting four to six weeks and is implemented when a client enters treatment following some type of traumatic event that causes significant distress. Choice *D*, case management, is helping to link clients with needed services and resources.

3. D: It is important that social workers always acquire client consent, even when working with involuntary clients. Guidelines about client consent are mentioned throughout the NASW Code of Ethics. When working with involuntary clients, social workers should help clients to recognize participation is still a choice, include a client's goals in a service plan along with mandated goals, and protect a client's right to self-determination.

4. A: The psychosocial approach is unique to the field of social work and allows it to stand out from other professions. Choice *B* is related to the crisis intervention theory, whereby clients experience a state of disequilibrium and are out of balance. Choices *C* and *D* are related to task centered practice, which emphasizes concepts of living and is a short term, practical, and evidence-based intervention.

5. B: Determining possible solutions is the second step in the problem-solving process. Choices *A, C* and *D* are components of task centered practice, which includes: contracting and carefully planning task implementation, along with the social worker functioning as a collaborator to help clients identify issues, strengths, resources, and smaller tasks.

Professional Values and Ethics

Professional Values and Ethical Issues

Legal and Ethical Issues Related to the Practice of Social Work

Social workers are, by nature, helping professionals. In theory, they are much like other helping professionals such as counselors or family therapists. The goal of the field of social work is not only social justice but also improving the lives of individuals through empowerment and advocacy. Social work maintains a person-focused perspective that stipulates that the profession strives to "meet people where they are," not forcing ideals and decisions onto those in need, but instead using their own values to empower them to make changes.

The social work profession has a set of values that governs how social workers do their jobs. These values are the root of the social work profession and lay the groundwork for everything that social workers do. These six values are: service, social justice, dignity and worth of the person, importance of human relationships, integrity, and competence.

In order to meet the needs of the various populations served by social workers, there are certain rules and regulations regarding ethics that social workers must follow. The National Association of Social Workers (NASW) has a Code of Ethics that serves to educate social workers on how they should conduct themselves.

The NASW Code of Ethics has six core purposes. These purposes are:

- To establish the core values on which the mission of social work is based

- To provide a set of ethical standards for social workers, as well as specific information regarding different ethical dilemmas

- To help identify information that social workers should take under advisement when ethical conflicts may exist or when an ethical dilemma presents itself

- To provide standards that can be used by others to ensure accountability and responsibility by those in the profession

- To inform new social workers about core issues relating to the mission of social work and to the ethical standards of the field

- To provide the rules and standards that social workers can use to evaluate the conduct of others in the profession

Ethical Dilemmas

Ethical dilemmas occur when three different conditions are met in a situation. The first is that the practitioner must make a decision. If the situation does not require that a decision be made, then there isn't an ethical dilemma. The second is that there are different decisions that could be made or different actions one could take. The third condition is that an ethical ideal will be conceded no matter what decision is made.

One type of ethical dilemma occurs when you have a situation in which two ethical principles are conflicting. This is a pure ethical dilemma because either choice of action involves conceding one of these principles, and there is no way to keep both principles intact. Another type of ethical dilemma occurs when ethical principles conflict with values and/or laws. In these types of situations, a social worker's values may conflict with an ethical principle, and a decision must be made.

130

Once you have determined which kind of ethical dilemma you are facing, there are steps to take in order to reach a conclusion and, ultimately, the resolution of the dilemma. The NASW lays out steps that should be taken when attempting to resolve an ethical dilemma.

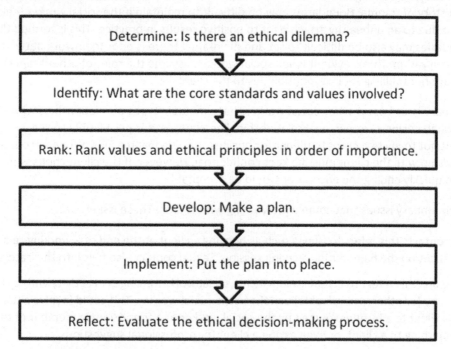

The Client's Right to Refuse Services

As per the NASW Code of Ethics, the client has the right to refuse all or a portion of social work services and utilize self-direction at any point. During the intake process, social workers should address this possibility with the client and also inform the client fully about the possible ramifications of refusing services. Clients may need outside service linkages from the social worker during the termination process; they may also choose to continue service but decide to work with a different social worker or in an entirely different social or health field.

Social workers should be respectful of clients who terminate services before completing the problem-solving process, and they should remain detached and objective during the termination without taking any critical feedback too personally. Rather, this can be viewed as a learning opportunity to understand different types of clients better. It is important to note that not all clients can voluntarily cease services. For example, court-appointed social work sessions often cannot be terminated by the client. In these cases, the social worker may have difficult interactions with the client and face resistance, especially if the client truly does not want to be in the session. Additionally, clients who are unable to make decisions due to a medical reason (such as a mental condition that inhibits decision-making) may voice opposition to the treatment, but they cannot be the actual person who terminates treatment. This is usually left to a proxy, such as a legal representative or family member.

Professional Boundaries

Difficulties in Setting and Maintaining Professional Boundaries in Social Work
Professional boundaries in social work are clearly defined limits on the practitioner-client relationship that provide a space for the creation of safe connections. Some helpful things to keep in mind include: the line between being friendly and being friends; being with the client versus becoming the client; and understanding the limits and responsibilities of the social worker role.

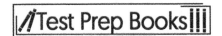
Conflicting values occur when the social worker's values and knowledge about best practices are at odds with the client's values, history, relationships, or lifestyle. **Vicarious trauma** may happen when a social worker experiences symptoms of trauma after listening to a client's experience. These symptoms may arise due to the practitioner sharing a similar history of trauma. Boundaries may be difficult to maintain if the social worker feels that they need to rescue the client due to an unhealthy attachment to positive results in practice. This is termed the **rescuer role**. Professional boundaries may also be difficult to set and maintain if there is poor teamwork between colleagues in the social work organization. This is evident when social workers assume the roles of other team members because they believe they are not fulfilling their responsibilities to the client.

Professional boundary issues occur when social workers have multiple types of relationships with a client. This may include a professional, business, or personal relationship. For example, it is permissible to see a client out in public at a restaurant, but not to invite a client to dinner for business or personal reasons. When encountering a client in public, the relationship with the client must be kept confidential. However, if the client chooses to say hello, saying hello in return and quickly ending the encounter would be acceptable.

There are several boundary issues that come with working with clients. These issues are:

- **Intimate contact**: This refers to things such as hugging a client at the end of a working relationship, or patting a client on the hand during a crying session. Sexual contact also falls into this category.

- **Personal gain**: This refers to instances in which a social worker engages in activity with a client that results in a monetary (or otherwise valuable) benefit to the social worker. This could involve situations such as referring a client to a business owned by the social worker or a friend/family member of the social worker, selling something to a client, or even asking a client for professional suggestions.

- **Emotional and dependency issues**: This refers to instances in which a social worker's own personal issues cause the social worker to have impaired judgment, possibly resulting in other boundary issues, such as a dual relationship with the client.

- **Altruistic instincts**: In some instances, a social worker's own good intentions and concerns for a client can result in boundary violations and confusion about the relationship between the social worker and the client. An example of this would be going to a client's bridal shower or retirement party.

Strategies for Setting and Maintaining Professional Boundaries in Social Work

Despite these difficulties, social workers must set and maintain boundaries with their clients and colleagues to ensure an effective practice. Practitioners should consistently monitor how their professional boundaries enhance or harm relationships with clients, colleagues, supervisors, and administrators. They must also gauge the impact of their boundaries on the amount of time they devote to work, their ability to cope with stress at work, and the amount of time and energy that they spend on extraneous activities and relationships.

There are several strategies for building and maintaining appropriate professional boundaries and relationships. First, practitioners should examine their motivations for giving extra time and attention to a client. If a social worker treats one client differently, this indicates that the boundary may be overextended. Social workers can manage this situation by determining whether the services provided are in line with the client's care plan, the organization's mission, the job description, and scope of practice.

Social workers should also avoid encouraging clients to contact them through personal channels. Clients should use the channels of communication set in place by the organization, such as work email, voicemail, cell phones, pagers, receptionists, and on-call staff, and procedures for after-hours referrals to 911, emergency rooms, or mental health crisis centers. Extending the professional boundaries of the social worker role puts colleagues and the organization at risk for failure. It also sets an unfair expectation that other colleagues will extend their professional boundaries. If boundaries are inconsistent between colleagues and within the organization, then clients may become confused and distrust the entire organization.

132

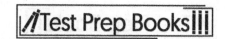

A third strategy for building appropriate professional boundaries is establishing clear agreements with clients during the initial sessions about the role of a social worker and the dynamics of a client-practitioner relationship. When warning signs indicate that healthy boundaries may be in jeopardy, social workers must address the issues with the client clearly, quickly, and sensitively. This involves clarifying the roles and boundaries with the client and asking the client to restate these boundaries to ensure understanding.

A fourth strategy is limiting self-disclosure about the social worker's personal life to information directly related to the client's goals. If there is a dual relationship between the social worker and client, the practitioner must preserve the client's confidentiality, physical security, and emotional well-being in social situations.

A fifth strategy is avoiding social media within professional practice. Practitioners should not connect with clients on social media. This includes adding clients as friends on Facebook or following clients on Twitter. To prevent conflicts of interest, social workers should use discretion and limit the amount of online information that is made available to the public or to social network connections. Social workers also shouldn't attempt to access online information about clients without prior informed consent. Finally, practitioners shouldn't post negative information about colleagues or the organization online.

A sixth strategy is for social workers to foster strong work relationships with their colleagues at the organization. These connections will help practitioners cope with stresses, think through questions of ethics and professional relationships, and help maintain a sense of humor. Practitioners should be sensitive to signs of bullying in the workplace, as each practitioner deserves respect and dignity to ensure social justice for others. It's important that social workers use appropriate channels of supervision and consultation to determine appropriate boundaries in difficult situations. Supervision can also be useful when trying to remedy concerns with existing organization procedures that address or inhibit client needs.

A final strategy for maintaining professional boundaries is ensuring appropriate self-care. This includes taking time for nurturing oneself throughout the workday, maintaining a regular work schedule, and taking time away from the office each day to refocus. Practitioners should limit communication when they are away from work to ensure time for rejuvenation, especially during vacations or personal time. They must also be aware of how they handle work stress and monitor how often they take work home. This includes physical work, emotional strain, or hyper-vigilance about work situations. If a practitioner consistently struggles to maintain professional relationships and work boundaries, they should seek supervision or outside mental health counseling.

Ethical Issues Related to Dual Relationships

Dual relationships are clearly outlined in the **NASW Code of Ethics**. The Code of Ethics states that social workers should not engage in dual relationships with clients or former clients in which exploitation of the client may occur. The Code of Ethics does recognize that there might be situations where dual relationships are unavoidable. For example, a social worker might have two jobs, one of which involves providing group therapy to survivors of sexual abuse. It is possible that a member of the aforementioned therapy group could become an employee or client at the social worker's second place of work. In these types of situations, the Code of Ethics suggests that the social worker establish clear boundaries that are sensitive to the client/former client.

Under no circumstances should a social worker ever become involved in a sexual relationship with a client. In addition, the Code of Ethics establishes that social workers must avoid sexual relationships with anyone who is related to or has a close personal relationship with a client or former client. The Code of Ethics also states that social workers should not become involved in sexual relationships with former clients because of the high risk of harm that may occur with such relationships. If, however, a social worker does become involved in a sexual relationship with a former client, the social worker is responsible for demonstrating that the former client entered into the relationship without manipulation or exploitation. The Code of Ethics also specifies that, due to the obvious risk of

133

harm, a social worker should not provide professional services to anyone with whom the social worker has had a previous sexual relationship.

Situations called "**boundary crossings**" are when a social worker does not intend to create a dual relationship but inadvertently does so, as would be the case were a clinician to self-disclose personal information during a therapy session. This is distinguished from a **boundary violation**, which occurs when a dual relationship is established that is inherently coercive or manipulative and therefore harmful to the client. What are some clues about whether a boundary crossing is unethical?

- It hinders the social worker's care.
- It prevents the social worker from being impartial.
- It exploits or manipulates the client or another person.
- It harms clients or colleagues.

Dual relationships are sometimes unavoidable in practice, particularly in small communities. However, it is possible to avoid dual relationships that involve boundary violations and ethical violations.

Self-Disclosure Principles and Applications

To build professional boundaries, it is recommended that social workers limit self-disclosure about their personal lives to information directly related to the client's goals. If there is a dual relationship between the social worker and client, the practitioner must preserve the client's confidentiality, physical security, and emotional well-being in social situations.

Obtaining Informed Consent

When disclosing information due to legal requirements, it is always important to discuss the situation with the client. It should be noted that the social worker should evaluate their own safety when discussing disclosure of confidential information with the client. If the social worker believes the situation to be unsafe if/when the client learns of the disclosure, then it is not necessary to alert the client prior to disclosing the confidential information. This is something that should be discussed in detail with clients during the informed consent process and throughout the relationship.

One of the difficulties associated with breaking confidentiality to protect a third party is that the threat isn't always clearly established. If a client discloses during treatment that he is going to go home and stab his neighbor, this is clearly a plan of intended harm. However, what about an HIV-positive client who fails to warn sexual partners of her HIV status? What if the client fully understands the risk to her partners and has no intention of disclosing her status? This is a situation that would require thorough documentation, thoughtful debate, and possibly conferencing with colleagues to decide upon the best course of action.

Confidentiality also becomes more complicated when a social worker is working with two or more people, either in a family or group session. All participants must agree that any information shared within the context of treatment will be kept confidential and not shared with others. However, the social worker should stress with clients that they cannot force other members to abide by the confidentiality agreement and that breach of confidentiality is a risk.

Documentation

Keeping accurate client records has many purposes, such as documenting the history and treatment of a client, getting insurance reimbursement, and providing social workers a historical account of client sessions. The information contained in a client record can also be used to evaluate the effectiveness of services. Client records, when combined with other evaluation tools (e.g., client satisfaction surveys, reactions to treatments, accomplishments of goals), can be an effective method of evaluating treatment progress. Supervisors may review

client records to evaluate the effectiveness of the treatment process, social worker performance, and client progress, or to ensure documentation is being completed accurately and on time. When reviewing client records for evaluation, ethical standards must always be upheld.

The NASW Code of Ethics specifically addresses guidelines for using client information for evaluation, including:

- Protecting confidentiality to the fullest extent possible
- Accurately reporting information
- Protecting clients from harm
- Obtaining required client consent for all uses of their information (e.g., supervisory review, reimbursement)
- Making clients aware that the consent can be withdrawn without punishment

Termination

Termination of the relationship occurs when the client and the social worker have reached treatment goals. Even though the relationship is terminated, the client may feel warmly toward the social worker, and congruence and empathy may still be part of the relationship. Some clients may require maintenance sessions to continue stability, but when termination is the next clear stage in the relationship, psychotherapy sessions should end.

In the case of a client choosing to prematurely terminate services, the social worker should clearly explain the risks to the client and also carefully document all meetings and interactions to protect against legal ramifications. **Abandonment**, which refers to the social worker terminating services prematurely without adequate reason or in an improper manner, is considered malpractice and can lead to lawsuits. When the social worker decides to end the working relationship, they must ensure that the client is adequately prepared and warned about the end of services and that the client is emotionally equipped to deal with the termination. Social workers can refer clients to other types of providers, who can continue working with the client after their own services have ceased. If a social worker needs to terminate services early, such as in the case of leaving a job, they should connect the client to a new social worker who can continue to provide the same level of services.

Death and Dying

Some clients have documented clear wishes about their death and dying (advance directives), while others do not. In these cases, social workers may be called upon to provide information and counsel to the client and client system. This can be an emotional process, and social workers should show compassion, sympathy, and respect as the client and the client system adjust to the news. Terminal clients are allowed to take comfort measures, such as hospice services, but are not allowed to take any external measures that would intensify or speed up the dying process (such as requesting a lethal medication dose).

Terminal clients may choose to refuse treatment and pass away naturally; while this process may hasten death, it is considered a natural and acceptable alternative to prolonging the dying experience with intervention, and it is also considered the client's choice. Terminal clients may choose this route if they have made peace with the decision and with their family and friends, if they want to remove a physical and financial burden from loved ones, and if they are ready for the process. Still, in such a case a social worker could provide guidance to ensure the client truly understands the process and consequences of their decision. With a do not resuscitate (DNR) order, a client chooses to refuse services if their cardiopulmonary system ceases to work.

In clients who are unable to make decisions (such as those who are in a permanent vegetative state), the next of kin or a legal appointee may make medical decisions on the client's behalf. This may include taking the client off life support, if applicable. This can be a highly contentious situation if family members or legal proxies do not agree on the best course of action. This situation can be avoided by preparing advanced directives, which document the client's wishes in such contexts.

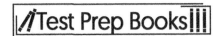

Research Ethics

Research performed on living creatures, especially humans, is always scrutinized for ethical concerns. Such research often uses experiments for which the outcomes are unknown. Therefore, it is possible that any research performed on a person may have unintended, unwanted, or otherwise harmful psychological, physiological, emotional, or social effects. Research ethics are intended to protect participants, ensure that research is being conducted for some public benefits, and ensure that participants who are involved have been provided with informed consent. Informed consent involves explaining to an individual, in as much detail as possible, the processes of the experiment or study and all potential side effects or outcomes and giving an individual the opportunity to make an educated decision independently about participation in such a study. Informed consent also documents the fact that the participant may leave the study at any time. Informed consent paperwork is usually signed by the participants, the researcher, and an independent third party. Some controversy still exists over research that affects vulnerable populations, such as those with psychological disorders, the elderly, children, the poor, and others who cannot easily make objective decisions or could be persuaded by experiment incentives (such as gift cards or the like).

An **Institutional Review Board (IRB)** is any independent group that reviews research and clinical trial designs that have human participants to ensure there are no potential ethical violations. IRBs are accredited by the US Food and Drug Administration. These groups can request changes, additions, and eliminations to any study proposal; they can also completely deny a proposal for approval. Without IRB approval, research designs cannot come to the experiment phase. While research is in session, IRB committees conduct regular audits to ensure compliance is still intact. Noncompliance can result in heavy fines, penalties, criminal investigation, and termination of a study.

Supervision and Management

Supervisors and managers should always be aware of the hierarchical power they wield over subordinates, and they should ensure that their leadership does not take advantage of this dynamic. Behaviors that would be unsuitable in a lateral colleague may be ignored in a supervisor if a subordinate feels their job or work environment would be in jeopardy should a complaint be filed.

Interpersonal work dynamics between supervisors and subordinates should ensure that the supervisor treats subordinates with professional respect and support, even when they are challenging them to grow professionally or learn more. It is critical to not become domineering in this regard. Additionally, if a supervisor needs to coach a subordinate on performance, this should be done privately rather than in front of other colleagues. On the other hand, supervisors also need to make sure that their relationships with subordinates do not become overly friendly or intimate. Supervisors should avoid confiding overly personal details to subordinates or pursuing romantic relationships in the workplace. Not only could this cause extreme discomfort for colleagues, it could also be reported for harassment. When in doubt, supervisors can refer to the NASW Code of Ethics to drive not only their service delivery, but also their interactions in the workplace.

Social Worker Safety

Social workers are often in high-risk situations, working with high-risk populations. The threat of violence or other personal safety issues is relatively high compared to other fields of work. Implementing policies and procedures that help protect social workers during their workday can help mitigate some of this risk. This includes the provision of an avenue to report unsafe settings or clients, and if necessary, to terminate working relationships in which the social worker does not feel safe without fear of workplace reprisal. Reviewing the daily processes of service delivery can help identify areas where risk management techniques may be necessary.

Since social workers work in a number of different places—office settings, jails, courtrooms, family homes, community centers, hospitals, and so on—they should treat each session individually and assess safety risks each time. This assessment may include an overview of the location, the ability to receive emergency services quickly,

136

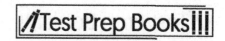

other available workers who may be able to help in an emergency, and the state of the client at each visit (even if it is someone the social worker has treated for some time). Social workers should also protect their personal boundaries, such as not allowing clients to call or visit them at home, not sharing personal information in person or online, and maintaining protocols to address client emotions that could lead to violence. (Examples include shouting at or threatening the social worker. While these are not physical assaults, they are still verbal and emotional violence toward the social worker, and they could escalate.)

Confidentiality

Use of Client Records

Issues relating to confidentiality include the storage and maintenance of records and charts. All confidential material should be kept in a secure location and locked at all times. For example, if a social worker takes a clipboard into client rooms to make notes for later documentation, that clipboard should be locked in a drawer when not in use so that no one can turn it over and see confidential information when the social worker is away from their desk. With the use of electronics and computers, there should be policies in place to lock computers when away to avoid anyone seeing notes or other confidential information. Collaboration between colleagues in which clients may be discussed should be done behind closed doors to avoid anyone else hearing the conversation.

Social workers are to provide clients with reasonable access to records. Social workers are permitted, however, by the Code of Ethics to withhold all or part of the client record from the client if the social worker determines there is a great risk of harm in releasing the information. In these cases, it is important to fully document the request, whether the records were released, and the rationale for either releasing or not releasing them.

There may be instances in which a social worker is sued for malpractice. In these cases, the Code of Ethics states that it is permissible for the social worker to share confidential client information to aid in self-defense, but only so far as is necessary to adequately defend oneself.

Throughout the development of a professional relationship in social work, it is important to keep case notes and records for several reasons. Case notes are important in the process of conceptualizing the case and the client's needs. They can help the practitioner pull together their thoughts when making a diagnosis. Case records also serve as a measure of the standard of care and subsequently can be used in court to show adequate client care. They help social workers determine whether clients have made progress and remember what the client said from visit to visit, and they can be used when a practitioner seeks supervision about the case. In addition, case notes are needed by insurance companies, agencies, and schools to support the treatment that is provided to clients.

Legal and Ethical Issues Regarding Confidentiality

Social workers have a duty to protect confidential information of clients. Ethically, client information should not be discussed with anyone other than the client. Legally, a client has a right to keep their medical and therapeutic information confidential. The **Health Insurance Portability and Accountability Act of 1996 (HIPAA)** requires that medical information (including therapeutic and mental health information) be protected and kept confidential. However, there are certain limitations to confidentiality. These generally involve risk of harm to the individual being served as well as to others.

Social workers are not as protected as some other professionals when it comes to confidentiality and often find themselves being called to testify in court cases related to their clients. There are also certain situations in which social workers may have to release confidential information to protect the client or satisfy the duty to warn.

Providing services to minors can be challenging when it comes to confidentiality issues, especially since the legal rules and regulations vary from state to state. At times, there can be a conflict between the social worker's feeling

of ethical responsibility to maintain the privacy of the minor and the legal right of parents to be informed of issues discussed. Adolescents in particular may discuss concerns with a social worker that they do not want their parents to be aware of, and it can be a violation of trust if these issues are subsequently revealed to parents. It is imperative that at the start of treatment, the expectations of the social worker's relationship with each person are discussed with the parents and minors, as well as the benefits and limits of confidentiality.

Minors should never be promised confidentiality when the social worker cannot keep that promise, but the privacy and individuality of the minor should be maintained as much as possible. In cases where private information about the minor is going to be revealed, social workers should always inform the minor. This holds true whether it is with the client's consent, mandated reporting, or due to the parent utilizing their right to information.

With technology being utilized extensively by helping professionals, confidentiality of electronic information is another important issue. Counseling sessions are now being provided by telephone, video chat, and online simulation, and these media open new possibilities for information abuse. If a practitioner provides a video therapy session, they should be aware that it is possible for the client to have someone else in the room, off-camera, without informing the clinician or other participants. The same could be true with electronic communication such as texting or email. There is no way to know if a client is forwarding electronic information to third parties without the clinician's knowledge.

Mandatory Reporting

Some clients may disclose intent to harm themselves. It is necessary in these situations to fully assess suicidal intent and determine if the client is serious about carrying out a plan for self-harm. It might be sufficient, in cases where a client has considered self-harm but has no clear plan, to complete a safety plan with the client. The safety plan will outline what the client agrees to do should they begin to experience the desire to engage in self-harm. However, if the client has a clear plan of action and access to items necessary to carry out the plan, then confidentiality should be broken to protect the client. This would involve notifying police and having the client committed for observation for their own protection.

In addition to protecting clients from themselves, social workers also have a duty to warn third-party individuals if there is threat of harm. Duty to warn was established by the **1976 case Tarasoff vs. Regents of the University of California**. In this case, a graduate student at the University of California-Berkeley had become obsessed with Tatiana Tarasoff. After significant distress, he sought psychological treatment and disclosed to his therapist that he had a plan to kill Tarasoff. Although the psychologist did have the student temporarily committed, he was ultimately released. He eventually stopped seeking treatment and attacked and killed Tarasoff. Tarasoff's family sued the psychologist and various other individuals involved with the university. This case evolved into the duty to warn third parties of potential risk of harm. Satisfying the duty to warn can be done by notifying police or the individual who is the intended victim.

Because ethical dilemmas can involve legal situations, they may also have legal consequences for a social worker or necessitate involving the legal system. For example, a client may disclose that he frequently drinks large amounts of alcohol and then drives his children to school. Ethically, there is an obligation to keep what the client has said in confidence. However, the client's children are being placed in a situation in which they are in great danger of being injured or harmed. Due to laws protecting the welfare of children, the social worker would need to make a report to Child Protective Services. In some states, if someone has a good faith reason to believe that a child is being neglected or abused and does not report the situation, that person may face a civil lawsuit and even criminal charges.

It's important to note as well that social workers are considered mandated reporters in all states. This means there is a legal and ethical obligation to break confidentiality to report any signs and symptoms of child and elder abuse. In some cases, it will be impossible to know for sure if abuse or neglect is happening. Often the social worker will

have only a small amount of information that may raise concerns but must make a report so that an investigation can occur. A social worker cannot be held liable for reports made in good faith to Child Protective Services or Adult Protective Services.

Liability is another legal issue that social workers may sometimes face. Clients can sue a social worker for malpractice. When a social worker is sued, the liability does not stop with the social worker. In lawsuits, a social worker's supervisor can be named as a defendant, and liability can extend as far as the head of the agency that employs the social worker. Agencies that provide social services carry malpractice insurance for this very reason. It is good practice, however, for individual social workers to also carry malpractice insurance for extra protection.

Ethical and Legal Issues Regarding Mandatory Reporting of Abuse

Mandatory reporting laws require social workers, and other professionals, to report any suspected abuse or neglect. This means that any professional who has a suspicion of abuse or neglect of a child or a vulnerable adult must legally make a report to either Child Protective Services or Adult Protective Services. Note that some states, such as Tennessee, have laws that require all citizens to report suspected abuse or neglect, making everyone a mandated reporter.

Often when abuse or neglect is suspected, the concern about breaking confidentiality is at the forefront of the mind of the social worker. During informed consent, this requirement to report any signs of abuse or neglect should have been disclosed to the client. When such breaks in confidentiality occur, they can damage the relationship. In some cases, it may be necessary or appropriate to disclose to the client that a report is being made. For example, if a new mother has tested positive for cocaine and the infant has tested positive for cocaine while in the hospital, the infant will remain in the Neonatal Intensive Care Unit due to withdrawal. Disclosing to the mother that a report is being made, and why it's being made, could prepare her and create an opportunity to speak further with her about treatment options and other important considerations. It's important to note that social workers who fail to report suspected abuse or neglect can be subject to civil penalties and/or prosecution.

Professional Development and Use of Self

Professional Values and Principles

Values are ideas or beliefs that guide an individual's thoughts and actions. The values that a person holds have their basis in the moral foundation to which they were exposed in childhood and adolescence. **Moral foundations** can include anything from family-specific beliefs and religious moral codes to the ethics and laws of society. As an individual gets older, they are increasingly exposed to new value systems that coincide or challenge their existing values. When someone must consider adopting one value system over another, this is called a **value conflict**. Value conflicts may occur when someone makes new friends, engages in romantic relationships, joins a new community, attends a new school, and accepts a new job.

The process of acquiring values is important for social workers to keep in mind when working to understand where their own values and their clients' values originated. Social workers should be aware of their own moral codes, values, biases, and prejudices to avoid conflict with the treatment they are providing to clients. The process of acknowledging and controlling personal values in social work practice is called **value suspension**. Self-awareness is a vital part of ensuring that one's personal values and beliefs do not intrude on the social worker/client relationship. It may be necessary to seek consultation from a supervisor or colleague in situations where one's personal values or beliefs conflict with those of the client and when those feelings cannot be resolved. In extreme cases where consultation and self-reflection cannot remedy the conflict, termination of the social worker/client relationship and referral to another therapist may be necessary.

All professions are built upon a foundation of values and guided by ethical codes. At times, these values trump that profession's empirical knowledge base. The focus of the social work profession is providing care and improving

society rather than simply defining and explaining existing problems. To these ends, social workers must apply the knowledge and skills in other fields, including sociology, philosophy, law, and psychology.

Social workers must distinguish between and cater to social and individual morality. Individual morality describes the behavior of one person in private or specific people in public roles. Social morality is the wide range of behaviors that create and contribute to public life and impact greater society. Social workers must recognize the interplay between these types of morality and advocate when their absence creates social injustice.

Below are the three main values in social work.

Preserving Human Rights

Social workers are charged with preserving the rights of all people. This means taking a compassionate, holistic view of the individuals that social workers serve and advocating for them when society cannot meet their needs. Still, it's important that clients retain the power to make decisions about the direction their lives will take. The social worker can guide clients, but the clients maintain the ultimate decision. Only when clients pose a risk to the well-being of others should social workers intervene on their behalf. Social workers should take a strengths-based approach in their practice and help their clients develop and use their personal strengths to achieve their goals and compensate for weaknesses. The ultimate goal of social work is to provide clients with the tools they need to empower themselves to make their own decisions and enhance their personal health and the well-being of their family, community, and the greater society.

Advocating for Social Justice

Social workers advocate for justice and fair treatment for those they serve. Practitioners should challenge prejudice and discrimination against their clients to model good moral judgment and to uphold anti-discrimination laws. Practitioners must also inform those in power when they become aware of policies that violate anti-discrimination laws or unethical practices. In this role, social workers are agents of social change who help improve society for future citizens.

Social workers should celebrate the diversity of their clients and the communities where they work. This includes identifying differences and similarities between cultures and maintaining an "open door" policy to all individuals in need of assistance. These practices are intended to promote a society inclusive to all individuals and groups, regardless of their personal characteristics, values, or beliefs. Practitioners must identify resources in their community and their own organization that best serve their clients. Social workers should use good moral judgment to make sure that these resources are given equally to their clients and are tailored to the specific needs of those they serve.

Following the Ethics and Morality of the Profession

Practitioners must follow the profession's code of ethics and act with honesty, compassion, and dignity. Social workers should be familiar with the most recent version of the social work code of ethics, which contains the values and principles endorsed by the practitioners and researchers in the field. They should apply these principles in practice and evaluate how they can be tailored to their specific communities. Practitioners should also be respectful of clients and colleagues by acting with sincerity and good moral judgment. This includes setting and following professional boundaries with clients and coworkers, following the profession's ethical code, and taking responsibility for their actions.

Professional Objectivity

While social workers should show empathy toward a client, it is also important that they remain objective and do not become enmeshed in the social worker/client relationship. Enmeshment occurs when the social worker is overly involved with the client's emotional life, and it may harm the client. Social workers must demonstrate professional objectivity with the client to avoid countertransference, which occurs when a social worker redirects their emotions

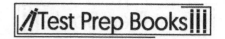
onto the client. In addition, social workers can engage in professional objectivity by recognizing that the client is the party who needs to do the majority of the work in the relationship. It is difficult to maintain professional objectivity when enmeshment occurs, and social workers should seek supervision if they cannot maintain professional objectivity with the client.

Social workers must also ensure that they're competent to fulfill any job that they are assigned before practicing with clients. This includes being a life-long learner and reviewing relevant research literature related to their therapeutic approaches and the clients they serve. Practitioners should also use evidence-based practices in their work with clients whenever possible. Practitioners should behave in morally responsible ways, advocate for their clients when they are faced with discriminatory practices or policies, practice self-care to ensure that they are effective in their work, and only work within the scope of their practice.

Protecting Client Self-Determination

Social workers realize that clients have a right to lead their lives as they see fit, making their own decisions based on their values. Issues may arise when the values of clients do not align with how others believe clients should behave or live. Social workers must advocate on the behalf of clients with other professionals to ensure that their values are at the core of any plan. It is the job of the social worker to work with the client to aid in goal creation and identification that is congruent to the client's values.

There are situations in which promoting client self-determination may cause conflict between the client, social worker, and other professionals. For example, if a client has entered a hospital due to medical issues arising from alcohol abuse, healthcare professionals may recommend that the client attend an alcohol and drug rehabilitation facility for treatment. However, if the client does not wish to seek treatment, then the social worker should advocate on their behalf and help to devise a plan that honors the client's wishes. Exceptions to this value would be when a client needs protection from self-harm or harming others. In this situation, the social worker must act in accordance with legal and ethical standards to do no harm versus promoting the self-determination of the client.

Client Competence and Self-Determination

Social workers realize that clients have a right to lead their lives as they see fit, making their own decisions based on their values. Issues may arise when the values of clients do not align with how others believe clients should behave or live. Social workers must advocate on the behalf of clients with other professionals to ensure that their values are at the core of any plan. It is the job of the social worker to work with the client to aid in goal creation and identification that is congruent to the client's values.

There are situations where promoting client self-determination may cause conflict between the client, social worker, and other professionals. For example, if a client has entered a hospital due to medical issues arising from alcohol abuse, healthcare professionals may recommend that the client attend an alcohol and drug rehabilitation facility for treatment. However, if the client does not wish to seek treatment, then the social worker should advocate on their behalf and help to devise a plan that honors the client's wishes. Exceptions to this value would be when a client needs protection from self-harm or harming others. In this situation, the social worker must act in accordance with legal and ethical standards to do no harm versus promoting the self-determination of the client.

Social Worker's Own Values and Beliefs on the Social Worker-Client Relationship

Social work as a profession prides itself on practitioners putting personal values aside, even when those values conflict with client values. Social workers must not engage in discriminatory practices or condone the discriminatory practices of others. For example, if a social worker is personally uncomfortable with same-sex relationships, but has a gay or lesbian client, the social worker will need to take steps to evaluate their own values and beliefs. The social worker must ensure that personal feelings are put aside in order to appropriately meet the client's needs. Self-

awareness is a vital part of ensuring that one's personal values and beliefs do not intrude on the social worker/client relationship. It may be necessary to seek consultation from a supervisor or colleague in situations where one's personal values or beliefs are in conflict with the client and when those feelings cannot be resolved. In extreme cases where consultation and self-reflection cannot remedy the conflict, termination of the social worker/client relationship and referral to another therapist may be necessary.

Social Worker's Own Values and Beliefs on Interdisciplinary Collaboration

Reflecting on one's personal values and beliefs in order to maintain objectivity and reduce biases when providing treatment for clients is a fundamental component of the NASW's Code of Ethics. Providing treatment as part of an interdisciplinary collaboration (such as part of a team consisting of medical professionals, allied health workers, financial experts, legal experts, and other professionals that support a client) is becoming more common in the field of social work. It can be difficult to manage all competing interests, as each professional on a collaborative team will bring a different perspective with different ideas for the most effective treatment. While a social worker may focus primarily on psychosocial factors that influence a client's life, a doctor may focus more on the client's physical health, and a financial expert may focus on providing the client with better financial resources.

Therefore, working in collaborative groups requires keeping the client's desired outcomes for the intervention as the primary goal of the interdisciplinary team. Documenting the client's goals and mapping out each professional's objectives can help mitigate the effects of professional and personal biases. Additionally, a documented plan can help establish clear job roles for each professional so that a single set of values does not take over the full scope of the intervention. When interdisciplinary collaboration accounts for these factors, the benefits of providing the client with multiple skill sets and perspectives can be tremendous.

Transference and Countertransference in the Social Worker-Client Relationship

Transference occurs when the client consciously or unconsciously relates feelings, thoughts, or emotions to the social worker because the social worker reminds the client, in some way, of a person from a past relationship. Transference by clients toward the social worker often occurs during the course of treatment and the client needs to be made aware of transference issues and how to reduce them. If clients are experiencing transference with the social worker, they may also be experiencing transference in other relationships in their lives, and this needs to be addressed. Transference is a common occurrence for many clients and can be a useful tool in therapeutic treatment to develop both healthier relationships and a productive relationship with the social worker.

Countertransference occurs when the social worker identifies the client with someone from the social worker's past. Social workers must work through countertransference issues while assisting the client in recognizing and coping with transference situations. If social workers recognize countertransference, they may want to seek the assistance of a supervisor to work through countertransference issues. Transference and countertransference may be useful for the social worker and client to experience because they may impact other areas in the relationships of both.

Transference and Countertransference Within Supervisory Relationships

Transference and countertransference are used to describe how projections occur in an interactive relationship. Transference occurs when supervisees project certain attitudes, values, beliefs, or feelings onto their supervisors; countertransference occurs when supervisors project certain attitudes, values, beliefs, or feelings onto their supervisees. Depending on the intensity or type of projections that take place, transference and countertransference experiences may impact the boundaries, mentoring relationship, or professional collaboration that takes place between supervisors and supervisees. Transference and countertransference experiences may also occur as a result of temporary situations the supervisor or supervisee find themselves in, and interactions that occur afterward may have a long-lasting impact.

For example, a supervisee may have heard from a colleague a long, emotional story about harassment from another supervisor. Upon meeting with their personal supervisor, the supervisee may project irrational feelings of anger, fear, or resentment on the supervisor for the rest of their working relationship. Additionally, supervisors must take care to examine supervisees when they are working with clients. Transference and countertransference can take place unexpectedly between social workers and their clients, and it can have similar impacts on the intervention process. Finally, overly positive transference and countertransference experiences can be somewhat problematic as well. They may unwittingly place one person on a pedestal, result in an insincere mentoring relationship, or cause feelings of disillusionment in supervisees when they see their supervisors make an error.

Transference and countertransference experiences can be minimized by openly discussing their potential in the beginning of a professional relationship. By discussing the fact that both parties are vulnerable to this experience, both parties can become more self-aware and reflective about occurrences and how to handle them. This sets the stage for professional and collaborative growth, transparency, and effective communication.

Safe and Positive Work Environment

Social workers have an emotionally and physically taxing job; therefore, a safe and positive work environment is crucial in supporting social workers in their jobs and in doing their best work. A safe and positive work environment is characterized by processes that foster work-life balance; good boundaries between work and personal life; a culture of respect and ethical behavior toward colleagues and subordinates; just compensation for tasks performed; support for the social worker's personal and professional development; and a zero-tolerance policy for threats, violence, harassment, or bullying in the workplace. Additionally, a documented process that allows social workers to express feelings of unsafety (whether with coworkers or with clients) and established avenues for resolution are other ways to ensure a positive and safe work environment. Social workers should feel comfortable employing these avenues without fear of consequences from colleagues or supervisors. Finally, leadership should ensure their workers feel comfortable communicating their professional goals, successes, and obstacles; leadership should also provide opportunities that support professional goal achievement or resolution to overcome obstacles.

Social Worker Self-Care Principles and Techniques

Due to the highly emotional, interpersonal, and empathic demands of the social work field, social workers must employ and sustain self-care practices to protect their personal health. Without self-care, social workers are highly susceptible to burnout and compassion fatigue—two risks that occur when working in a field that often provides exposure to disheartening humanitarian situations, abusive intrapersonal relationships, and cases that, for bureaucratic or personal reasons, take a long time to resolve. Unchecked, these experiences can lead the social worker to feel detached from work and hopeless toward cases or to consistently experience the ill effects of chronic stress. **Self-care practices** may include establishing boundaries between one's work and personal life, having a regular meditation practice or other mental exercises that are shown to soothe the nervous system, eating a healthy diet and engaging in regular physical exercise (as these behaviors decrease inflammation in the body and reduce stress hormones), and having a trustworthy support system of friends and colleagues.

Introspective exercises, such as daily journaling, can provide the social worker with a better understanding of which activities bring stress to their lives and which activities bring peace. By knowing these, the social worker can bridge the gap to reduce stress in areas they can control, such as setting a clear cut-off time for answering emails or scheduling personal activities that bring them joy. They can adopt healthy coping mechanisms for the areas in which they are unable to control factors that might contribute to their stress, such as an emotional case or external funding issues.

Burnout, Secondary Trauma, and Compassion Fatigue

Sometimes it may be necessary to seek supervision if the social worker experiences burnout, secondary trauma, compassion fatigue, countertransference or the inability to develop a trusting relationship with the client. Although the focus is often on the supervisor's role of ensuring that clients are provided with ethical services by training and evaluating the supervisee, the supervisee's role in supervision is not passive. The social worker should fully engage in the process of supervision and use this relationship to grow and improve. In order to do that, the supervisee must be willing to discuss areas of ethical or legal concern that have arisen in their interactions with clients. They must also be ready to honestly address their own struggles and identify their learning needs, and seek the help and advice of the supervisor. This can only happen effectively through genuine self-assessment, which flows from a real desire to become a better social worker. The process of self-assessment in supervision can help them see any biases or weaknesses that may be holding them back from fully meeting their clients' needs. If the social worker is defensive or resistant to the supervisory relationship, then they will make little progress.

Factors to consider when receiving feedback during supervision/consultation:

- Social workers can benefit from feedback during supervision or consultation, especially with difficult clients/cases or at significant times in treatment, such as termination.

- When discussing cases, client confidentiality should be protected as much as possible, and client consent to release information should be acquired.

Impairment is a professional issue that should be addressed swiftly. Impairment occurs when a social worker's personal problems (e.g., mental health conditions, difficult life circumstances, or alcohol/drug use) have an impact upon their practice. The Code of Ethics states that social workers should seek to rectify their impairment by consulting with colleagues or supervisors, seeking their own treatment, limiting work, and/or terminating client relationships until the impairment has been fully addressed. In the event that a colleague is suffering from some sort of impairment, a social worker should address the concern with the colleague and encourage the colleague to rectify the issue. If the issue continues without proper attention, the social worker should go through appropriate channels to seek additional help for the colleague and to prevent consequences to clients. The same is true if the social worker feels there has been unethical behavior by a colleague. The social worker should discuss the behavior with the colleague and possibly with a supervisor. If a colleague is unfairly accused of unethical behavior, assisting the colleague in rectifying the situation is the best course of action.

Evidence-Based Practice

Social workers can use **Evidence-Based Practice methods** to ensure effective treatment for clients. This type of practice uses both research and clinical knowledge. Social workers using evidence-based practice will choose interventions that have scientifically documented effectiveness. With this method, workers also evaluate chosen interventions throughout treatment to ensure a successful outcome.

Research Terms

Independent variable: a factor changed or controlled when conducting an experiment or research

Dependent variable: a factor that is dependent on the independent variable and that is observed for changes as the independent variable is manipulated

Randomized controlled trial (RCT): a quantitative study that uses participants or subjects who are chosen randomly to participate

Reliability: the consistency of a measure, or the likelihood the same result will be achieved each time a measure is used

Validity: reflects whether a test, tool, or study is measuring what it intends to measure

External validity: the ability of a study to be generalized to other people or circumstances

Internal validity: refers to cause and effect; one question that can be posed: Are the effects of the study caused by the intervention?

Professional Development Activities

Professional development activities are a vital component of continuing education and ensuring social workers remain competent over the course of their careers, especially as public needs and norms shift. Social workers can find a plethora of continuing education courses, seminars, and trainings at the college or university from which they received their degree. Often, these are free or discounted for alumni. The NASW provides various free to for-cost opportunities on their website, including a portal which allows the user to filter opportunities by date, topic, location, and cost. The web site also provides online courses that can be done at home, free teleconferences in which to learn from peers, online articles, and links to new scholarly literature.

The NASW also invites professionals to write and advocate for issues on behalf of the organization, which allows social workers to hone research and writing skills while also promoting themselves professionally and serving causes about which they are personally passionate. Networking and conferences are another way to meet and learn from peers and develop professionally. Additionally, employers may provide free or discounted opportunities for social workers to pursue professional development activities. This may include providing activities such as in-house workshops or sponsoring to attend conferences or trainings.

In order to maintain licensure, social workers must pursue a certain number of continuing education hours per designated time cycle. Therefore, all social workers can inherently expect to continuously develop as professionals as long as they are continuing to renew their licenses. The specifics of continuing education are determined by the state issuing the license and the type of license that is held. Certain licenses may also require that all or a portion of the continuing education credits cover specific topics.

Practice Quiz

1. Interdisciplinary collaboration is commonplace in social work. To avoid conflict, there are steps that can be taken to promote a smooth working relationship. The first step is to advocate. What does this mean within the context of interdisciplinary collaboration?
   a. Educating team members about the role of the social worker
   b. Standing up for the social workers when other team members try to keep them from being heard
   c. Making sure everyone on the team hears what the social workers have to say
   d. Asking team members to remember that everyone has strengths they bring to the table

2. At every level of professional development, it is important to continually participate in education opportunities. Why is this important to the values of social work?
   a. Continuing education is necessary in order to maintain a level of competence in the area of expertise that the social worker practices.
   b. Continuing education is required to maintain licensure, and licensure ensures that the social worker is regarded as a capable professional.
   c. Conferences and learning situations provide networking opportunities that can aid in interdisciplinary collaboration.
   d. Education is an ongoing personal journey.

3. Alex is a social worker in the Emergency Room where Lucas, who is homeless, frequently visits for ailments of varying severity. The Emergency Room staff advise Alex that he must find somewhere for Lucas to go. Alex speaks at length with Lucas, who states that he has no friends or family with whom he is in contact. Lucas tells Alex that he has lived at shelters before and that he doesn't like the rules that must be followed. Lucas declines a bed at the local shelter. Alex discusses this with Lucas' doctor and nurse and both become adamant that Lucas must go to a shelter; sleeping on the street is not acceptable. Alex facilitates a discussion between medical personnel and Lucas in which Lucas maintains that he does not intend to go to a shelter. Eventually, Alex asks to speak privately with the medical personnel, and he advocates strongly on Lucas' behalf, stating that Lucas has made his decision. Was Alex's course of action correct?
   a. No. If the doctor felt that a shelter was necessary, then Alex's responsibility was to listen to the doctor and to convince Lucas to go to the shelter.
   b. Yes. Having a private conversation with the medical staff was the best solution, so that Lucas didn't hear the discussion.
   c. Yes. By advocating on Lucas' behalf, Alex was protecting his right to self-determination.
   d. No. Alex should have asked to call Lucas' relatives on his behalf to convince them to take him in.

4. When working in an interdisciplinary collaboration, what should be kept in mind to ensure a seamless working relationship?
   a. Educate, Communicate, Experience, Skill levels, Conflict
   b. Advocate, Understanding, Common Ground, Differences, Conflict
   c. Advocate, Communicate, Experience, Skill levels, Closure
   d. Educate, Understanding, Common Ground, Differences, Closure

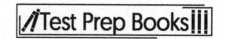

5. What is the purpose of the emphasis on understanding systems within the field of social work?
   a. To help increase the amount of field experience that a social work student participates in because only so much can be learned in the classroom.
   b. To better understand a client's place in society so that the social worker can help increase social understanding and make connections.
   c. To learn about diversity within family and social systems so that all clients receive unbiased and respectful care.
   d. To help the social worker advocate for clients on the local, state, and national levels by understanding the programs available.

See answers on the next page.

Answer Explanations

1. A: In this context, *advocate* means that the social worker will educate the rest of the team about the role of the social worker. Often the professional goals and vision of social work differs from that of other disciplines. The social worker should educate team members about this and attempt to gain understanding.

2. A: Competence is the reason that social workers need to be continually educated. This is important so that the social worker can provide the services in which they are trained and remain up-to-date on research and practice.

3. C: Alex was correct in protecting Lucas' right to self-determination. Lucas had made it clear several times that he had tried going to a shelter in the past and did not like the restrictions. He preferred a freer life that allowed him permission to do as he pleased. If Lucas had been suffering from some sort of medical issue that would make him unsafe, then Alex would have needed to explain all the information to him so that he understood his choices. If Lucas still decided to avoid the shelter, then that would have been his right.

4. B: The things to remember when working with an interdisciplinary collaboration are Advocate (educating team members about the role of the social worker), Understanding (striving to understand the other disciplines by asking questions about their roles, functions, and goals), Common Ground (attempting to find things in common that would contribute to better collaboration), Differences (recognizing that differences exist between disciplines and their goals and approaches), and Conflict (striving to approach conflict directly and with sensitivity and respect).

5. B: The field of social work places an emphasis on understanding systems because once the practitioner understands a client's place in society, then he or she can help increase the client's social understanding and make connections to help meet treatment goals. Understanding the client from an individual, family, and social system perspective sets the foundation for an understanding system. The other choices describe other emphases in the field of social work, such as the emphasis on field experience, the emphasis on advocacy at the local, state, and national levels, and the emphasis on maintaining effectiveness in practice.

ASWB Clinical Practice Test #1

1. A social worker is doing a biopsychosocial assessment of a new client. When the social worker asks about the client's social development, biological development, and medical history, the client says he can't remember because he was just a kid. How should the social worker proceed?
   a. Ask the client about his earliest memories.
   b. Ask the client if he has relatives who could help him remember.
   c. Ask the client's permission to request his school and medical records.
   d. Move on to the next section of the interview.

2. Sammantha is a 74-year-old woman who has been coming to your office for support with grief following the death of her husband. After nearly 50 years of marriage, Sammantha finds that she is struggling to manage her home and finances. "Herman did all of this," she says during your most recent session. "I feel lost. I don't know how to pay bills. I don't know how to change the filters on the furnace. How can I survive on my own?" Sammantha also shares that she is struggling with advanced arthritis in her joints. You work with Sammantha to recognize that she'd benefit from an assisted living facility and begin to support her in navigating this process. What is the BEST way to describe the social worker role you are fulfilling here?
   a. Enabler
   b. Advocate
   c. Broker
   d. Facilitator

3. According to family life cycle theories, what is the primary task that needs to be accomplished during the launching stage?
   a. Finding one's lifestyle and life partner
   b. Establishing a marital system
   c. Accepting adult children's independence
   d. Transitioning from a marital system to a family system

4. What is the FIRST thing a social worker should do to assist a client with sexual dysfunction?
   a. Ask whether the client has experienced sexual abuse.
   b. Refer the client for a medical evaluation.
   c. Assess the client for depression and anxiety.
   d. Ask about medications, lifestyle, and stress.

5. What provides social workers with additional resources for their clients and within their scope of practice?
   a. Socializing
   b. Networking
   c. Partying
   d. Conversations

6. Jane is a 35-year-old woman who is considering trying for her first child. She was sexually abused by a male relative as a child, and she has heard that this means she will become an abuser herself. She wants to know if it is wrong for her to have a child given her past. What should the social worker tell her?
   a. The idea that abuse survivors are more likely to perpetuate abuse is a myth.
   b. The cycle of abuse applies to physical but not sexual abuse.
   c. Being a victim does not mean she will automatically become an abuser.
   d. Having children is not recommended for abuse victims.

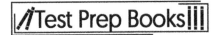
7. Jim is a 42-year-old male with no previous psychiatric history who suddenly developed severe psychotic symptoms. His wife found him scratching at his arms to the point of bleeding because he was convinced there were bugs under his skin. He tore apart the house trying to find the source of the bugs, which he could hear inside the walls. According to his wife, he had been in good health prior to this incident except for a stuffy nose, which she attributed to the long hours he was putting in at work. Based on this information, what is the MOST likely cause of Jim's symptoms?
   a. Schizophrenia
   b. Depression with psychotic features
   c. Bipolar I disorder
   d. Substance-induced psychosis

8. A social worker is evaluating Mr. X, a 48-year-old white, male client whose physician referred him after a recent check-up found no medical basis for his symptoms. Mr. X reports that his wife died unexpectedly six weeks ago. Initially, he was sad and preoccupied with thoughts about her, but he was coping with the support of friends. About three weeks ago, he started feeling much worse. He has been feeling down, tired, and hopeless every day. He reports trouble sleeping, loss of appetite, and trouble concentrating. He no longer feels any pleasure from his favorite hobbies. He says that he feels guilty, like he's letting everyone down, even though he can't provide any evidence that he has done anything wrong. According to the *DSM-5-TR*, what is the MOST appropriate diagnosis for Mr. X?
   a. Bereavement disorder
   b. Dysthymia
   c. Major depressive disorder
   d. Adjustment disorder with depressed mood

9. A licensed clinical social worker in private practice is considering restructuring her fees to include a sliding scale based on income. She also plans to reserve a few hours a week to provide treatment pro bono (free of charge) to clients who would otherwise be unable to pay for services. Would this fee structure be ethical?
   a. The sliding scale would be ethical, but pro bono services would be unethical.
   b. Pro bono services would be ethical, but the sliding scale would be unethical.
   c. Both the sliding scale and pro bono services would be ethical.
   d. Neither the sliding scale nor pro bono services would be ethical.

10. A social worker is working with a family with dysfunctional dynamics. One parent misuses methamphetamine, and the other has a poorly managed personality disorder. This year, the family experienced unexpected financial hardship, and they are struggling to pay for basic necessities. Two months ago, one of the three children in the family started struggling with performance and behavior at school. Using a family systems approach, how would the social worker explain the child's problems at school?
   a. The child's problematic behavior is adding stress to the family system and causing the dysfunctional family dynamics.
   b. The dysfunctional family dynamics are stressing the child and causing the problematic behavior.
   c. The child is repeating a transgenerational pattern of poor academic performance; it is a learned behavior.
   d. The child is most likely developing a personality disorder because they have an increased genetic risk from their parent.

11. A social worker is evaluating a middle-aged male client who is applying for long-term disability due to symptoms that interfere with his ability to work. The man arrives dressed in an unusual robe and states that six months ago, he suddenly began hearing voices telling him that he is Jesus. During the interview, he periodically pauses, turns his head to the side and says, "hold on, I'm hearing one right now," then reports what the voice said to the social worker. He is articulate, has good hygiene, and is oriented to time, place, person, and situation. The man has no history of medical or psychiatric conditions. He says he does not have any difficulties with mood, concentration, thinking, or motivation. When asked about visual hallucinations, he says that a large, cartoonish bunny rabbit appears to him sometimes. Which diagnosis is the MOST likely explanation for the man's symptoms?
   a. Brief psychotic disorder
   b. Schizophrenia
   c. Factitious disorder
   d. Malingering

12. A social worker is running a psychoeducation group for men with substance use disorders. During the first meeting, one of the participants states, "everyone knows junkies can't be trusted." How should the social worker respond?
   a. Discuss stigmatizing language and provide alternative vocabulary.
   b. Ask the participant why he believes this to be true.
   c. Pull the participant aside and explain that the word *junkie* is offensive.
   d. Do not react and see how the rest of the group responds.

13. Susan has been seeing a client, Christine, for about six months. Christine has three young children and a previous drug addiction. Susan suspects that Christine may be using again and decides to confront her at their session. When Christine arrives, she appears to be under the influence, and she has her 2-year-old with her. Susan also notices that the 2-year-old is covered in bruises. When she comments on the bruises, Christine becomes defensive. Christine has disclosed in the past that she sometimes gets so angry at her small children that she feels like she could beat them, but that she never would. What is the ethical concern?
   a. Christine has disclosed past drug abuse and violent thoughts toward her children. Susan now suspects both are occurring, but she would have to break confidentiality to report her suspicions.
   b. Christine may be on drugs again, but she's already been defensive with Susan, so it will be difficult for Susan to bring it up without damaging their relationship.
   c. Christine has made disclosures in the past regarding drug use and also seems to need childcare so she can go to therapy. Susan knows a good babysitter who can help, but also knows that would be establishing a dual relationship.
   d. Christine seems to be neglecting her children. Christine could possibly use education about parenting issues. Susan isn't sure if Christine would be open to a referral for parenting classes.

14. A social worker notices that one of her clients sometimes comes to therapy restless, talking quickly, and with dilated pupils. Other times he appears irritable and tired. He has been sniffling constantly for two months, which he attributes to a lingering cold. He has been getting into trouble for missing work. He used to be involved in several community groups but has stopped participating. His wife recently confronted him about the fact that he is often up late into the night then falls asleep randomly during the day. She checked their bank account and discovered that he has been spending large amounts of money that he refuses to explain. What is the MOST likely explanation for this client's behavior?
   a. Psychosocial stress
   b. Alcohol use disorder
   c. Cocaine use disorder
   d. Narcolepsy

151

15. You are a social worker providing therapy in a community mental health setting. You are completing a biopsychosocial and intake assessment with a new patient who is a 65-year-old male seeking therapy for symptoms of depression. His symptom report includes a recent decline in concentration, increased forgetfulness, and increased frustration when completing tasks. What should you suggest FIRST?
    a. Refer him to a psychiatrist for a medication evaluation.
    b. Begin a treatment plan to use CBT techniques to address his depression.
    c. Recommend he see his primary care provider to rule out a medical cause.
    d. Provide support and validation around the challenges of aging.

16. A social worker is trying to decide whether to use self-disclosure with one of her clients. She and the client are both single mothers, and she thinks disclosing this might help her client feel less alone. She has considered the potential benefits and harms to the client, but she is still not sure what to do. What should she do NEXT?
    a. Test the waters by making a small self-disclosure and see how the client reacts.
    b. Ask the client if it would be helpful to hear about the social worker's experience.
    c. Err on the side of caution and do not make the disclosure.
    d. Obtain supervision to determine if the disclosure is professionally justified.

17. Which of the following tools is MOST useful for taking a family history?
    a. Ecogram
    b. Genogram
    c. Medical records
    d. Family tree

18. A 52-year-old Asian American man is seeking treatment for alcohol use disorder and depression. Which one should be treated FIRST?
    a. Whichever disorder started first
    b. Alcohol use disorder
    c. Depression
    d. Both at the same time

19. Martin is a social worker in a pediatrician's office. He is conducting an intake assessment for a 13-year-old patient named Jordan during her first appointment. While she is filling out the intake questionnaire, Jordan asks if everything she shares will be kept private. How should Martin respond NEXT?
    a. Ask her why she is asking about this during the intake.
    b. Explain there is confidentiality between social workers and their patients.
    c. Explain the mandated reporting obligation and limits to confidentiality.
    d. Inform her legal guardians about her confidentiality concerns.

20. A licensed clinical social worker is planning to move to a different state and practice social work there. She wants to know whether she can transfer her license. Who should she contact?
    a. The National Association of Social Workers (NASW)
    b. The Council on Social Work Education (CSWE)
    c. The social work board of the state she lives in now
    d. The social work board of the state she is moving to

21. Which type of delusion involves a fixed, false belief that innocuous things in the environment have special, personal meaning, often related to the person's destiny?
    a. Delusion of reference
    b. Delusion of control
    c. Grandiose delusion
    d. Persecutory delusion

22. Jason is a social worker who is meeting a new client for the first time. The client is a woman named Hilda with intellectual disabilities whose mother is her court-assigned legal guardian. Hilda is able to communicate well, care for herself, and work a part-time job. She and her mother sought the guardianship because Hilda is unable to manage her finances, but otherwise her mom stays out of her business. Hilda comes to the initial meeting and begins telling Jason her story. What is the BEST way for him to respond?
   a. Tell Hilda that he wants to hear more, but first he needs her mom to sign some papers.
   b. Wait for Hilda to finish telling her story, then explain the informed consent documents and have her sign them.
   c. Talk to Hilda about how treatment works, her rights, and situations where he must share her information with her mom. Get her mom's informed consent and Hilda's assent.
   d. Excuse himself for a moment. Ask his supervisor to make a determination about whether Hilda or her mom should provide informed consent.

23. Juan is a social worker helping his client Karen, who came to treatment because she frequently has angry outbursts and doesn't understand why. Juan wants Karen to do some homework, including keeping a log of when the outbursts occur, what was happening, how she was feeling, and what she was thinking. Karen is reluctant because she says she wants to stop having outbursts and doesn't want to write about them. How can Juan explain that self-monitoring would be beneficial to her treatment?
   a. Keeping the log will increase her discipline and make her feel empowered.
   b. Doing homework is required for her treatment plan.
   c. Writing about the outbursts will cause them to happen less frequently.
   d. It will clarify what causes the outbursts and what can be done to reduce them.

24. Erika is a social worker in the hospital's emergency department. She is tasked to meet with a patient named Betty to assist with discharge planning. Betty is an 80-year-old woman who has been living alone and recently received a life-limiting diagnosis that will require her to have more support in place to maintain her safety. Betty is adamant she does not need any assistance. Erika's initial goal is to identify sources of support she may already have in place. What tool would be MOST helpful?
   a. Ecomap
   b. Genogram
   c. Columbia Severity Rating Scale
   d. Needs assessment

25. A teenager encounters a bully on the way home from school. The bully says demeaning things, trips the teen, and laughs. The teen is too afraid to say anything in the moment and simply continues on with his head down. The teenager arrives home and finds his 8-year-old sister playing in his room. Normally, he doesn't mind when she does this, but for some reason, today, he is irate. He screams at her, grabs her roughly, and marches her out of the room as she protests that he is hurting her. What psychological defense mechanism is the teenager demonstrating?
   a. Displacement
   b. Sublimation
   c. Projection
   d. Repression

26. A social worker is meeting with her client Teresa, an 80-year-old who lives with her son. Teresa is uncharacteristically quiet and seems uncomfortable. She tells the social worker that her son came home drunk yesterday, which was completely out of character. When she asked for her medication, he threw the bottle at her, leaving a bruise. He refused to help her get dinner, change her diaper, or transfer her from her wheelchair to her bed, so she spent the entire night sitting up, hungry, and in soiled clothing. This morning, her son apologized profusely and promised it would never happen again. The social worker tells Teresa that she is worried about Teresa's safety at home. Teresa panics and begs the social worker not to get her son in trouble. She has lived in that house for 60 years and would be devastated to leave. What should the social worker do?

    a.   Do safety planning with Teresa and monitor the situation in case the son's behavior escalates.

    b.   Request that the son come to some sessions with Teresa to work on improving the relationship.

    c.   Request that the son seek therapy individually to manage his frustration and alcohol consumption.

    d.   Inform Teresa that the social worker is going to report the son for elder abuse and make the report.

27. Jan is a 25-year-old woman whose mother died of cancer last year. She has been meeting with Clara, a social worker, for weekly therapy sessions to work through her grief. In one session, Jan tells Clara that she is so grateful that they met and that she has come to think of Clara as her new "mom." How should Clara respond?

    a.   Thank Jan for the compliment. Jan's statement indicates that they have developed a strong therapeutic relationship.

    b.   Ask Jan who else in her life she considers a "mom" figure to get her thinking about the rest of her support network.

    c.   Clarify the role of the social worker with Jan. Her comment indicates that she may be too dependent on Clara.

    d.   Note the comment in Jan's client file and seek supervision to figure out the best way to respond.

28. Claudia is a social worker at a group home. She has a new client, Jacob, who has been unwilling to share anything with her during their sessions and has been struggling to integrate with the other residents. She thinks that it would be helpful to speak with the case worker at his last group home placement to find out ways to better support him. What should she do FIRST?

    a.   Contact the case worker to request his records before Jacob's next session.

    b.   Get Jacob's permission to contact the case worker and have him sign a release of information.

    c.   Tell Jacob that contacting the case worker is a required part of the intake process and request her phone number.

29. A social worker is telling her supervisor about a recent play therapy session with a 4-year-old boy. During the session, the boy announced, "I have a pee pee," pulled down his pants, and pointed to his genitals. He then stated, "Daddy does too, but you don't because you're a girl." The social worker is concerned that the boy's behavior might be a sign of sexual abuse. What should the supervisor tell her?

    a.   She should make a report to child protective services with the information she has.

    b.   She should tell the mother that the father might be abusing the boy.

    c.   She should assess the child for developmental delay, as four is too old for this behavior.

    d.   She should not worry because the boy is displaying typical behavior for a 4-year-old.

30. What is the purpose of an Institutional Review Board?

    a.   To review journal articles submitted to peer-reviewed academic journals

    b.   To investigate accusations of social worker misconduct

    c.   To approve and monitor research studies that involve human subjects

    d.   To ensure social work degree programs meet ASWB standards

31. A social worker is meeting with a new client who states that her main goal is to expand her social circle, with a secondary goal being to work toward a promotion at work. During the assessment, the client reveals that she has diabetes, but her blood sugar is not well-managed because she cannot afford her insulin. The social worker tells her that they need to get her medically stabilized before they can work on her other goals. The client is unhappy with this, saying that she came to treatment to work on her social and professional issues, not her medical condition. How should the social worker respond?
    a. Agree to work on the professional goals first because a promotion and increase in pay will make insulin affordable.
    b. Transfer the client to another therapist who will be comfortable with her priorities.
    c. Tell her that according to Maslow's hierarchy, her priorities are incorrect.
    d. Explain how managing the diabetes will facilitate her other goals and vice versa.

32. In an initial meeting with a new client named Mary, a social worker asks what brings her in for treatment. Mary states that she has been having panic attacks. When the social worker asks her about the panic attacks, Mary starts talking about her childhood, then jumps to an issue she had several years ago at work, then mentions an aunt who she believes had an eating disorder. How can the social worker help Mary focus and articulate her chief complaint?
    a. Explore the meaning of her childhood experiences.
    b. Ask for more details about the issue that happened at work.
    c. Ask about her current relationship with her aunt and how her aunt is doing now.
    d. Ask her about her experience with panic attacks over the last two weeks.

33. Carla is seeing a routine patient in a private-practice setting. The patient is Daniel, a 14-year-old male who has been seeking counseling for depression. Daniel states that he has been experiencing suicidal thoughts. What should Carla do FIRST?
    a. Make a contract for safety.
    b. Hospitalize Daniel in an inpatient setting.
    c. Conduct a thorough risk assessment.
    d. Call Daniel's parents to notify them of what he disclosed.

34. Jill, a social worker, is co-running a psychoeducational group about healthy relationships with a new colleague named Martha. Lately, Martha has been unprepared, late, and moody. She has even made several inappropriate, cynical jokes about relationships during group, which made the clients uncomfortable. Another colleague, a close friend of Martha, mentioned to Jill that Martha is going through a difficult divorce. Jill wonders if this might account for her strange behavior. What should Jill do FIRST?
    a. Tell her supervisor about Martha's behavior and its impact on the clients.
    b. Ask for advice from the other colleague who knows Martha better.
    c. Find ways to be supportive without bringing up Martha's personal issues.
    d. Tell Martha her concerns and help Martha develop a plan to address them.

35. A social worker wants to know more about a client's perceptions, needs, motivations, and conflicts. The social worker presents the client with a series of pictures and asks the client to use their imagination and tell stories about what might be happening in the pictures. Which assessment tool is the social worker using?
    a. Beck Depression Inventory (BDI)
    b. The Minnesota Multiphasic Personality Inventory (MMPI)
    c. Thematic Appreciation Test (TAT)
    d. Myers-Briggs Type Indicator (MBTI)

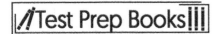

36. A social worker has a private practice and contracts with an agency to run a therapy group once a week. One of her private therapy clients expresses interest in joining the group. The social worker believes that the group would be helpful for the client and is not aware of any similar groups in the area. What should the social worker do?
   a. Apologize and explain that this would constitute a dual relationship and would therefore be unethical.
   b. Continue private therapy and advocate for the agency to start another group that the client could join.
   c. Allow the client to join the group after clarifying boundaries regarding group vs. individual therapy.
   d. Offer to refer the client to another social worker for private therapy so that the client can participate in the group.

37. Carter is a social worker providing services to families experiencing grief and loss. He is meeting with Shirley, a 70-year-old recent widow. In their first session, she begins to cry as he asks his basic assessment questions and instead wants to spend the session telling him about how she met her husband many years ago. What should Carter do FIRST?
   a. Explain the importance of completing the biopsychosocial assessment and continue with questions.
   b. Listen actively and engage with Shirley's story about meeting her husband.
   c. Refer her to a grief group offered by the agency.
   d. Provide education on grief and loss and its impact.

38. According to Piaget's theory of cognitive development, people reach the formal operations stage at age 11. The formal operations stage is characterized by all of the following EXCEPT:
   a. Magical thinking
   b. High-level abstract thinking
   c. Planning for the future
   d. Hypothetical thinking

39. A white social worker is assigned a new client from the Hmong ethnic group. In the initial meeting, the client walks in and says, "I don't think this is going to work. No offense, but I just don't think a white lady can understand where I'm coming from. Can I talk to another social worker?" How should the social worker respond?
   a. Point out the things that the social worker and client have in common and ask if the client is willing to try to overcome their differences.
   b. Refer the client to a social worker of color, a Hmong social worker if possible.
   c. Tell the client what she knows about the Hmong people to demonstrate her cultural competence.
   d. Acknowledge the cultural difference and ask the client if they would be willing to explore it together.

40. A social worker attends a conference about art therapy and decides it would be a good addition to the services she offers in her private practice. She attends a training course and receives a certificate of completion. She then updates her website to reflect that she is now an art therapy practitioner. Is this ethical?
   a. Yes, because she attended a conference and completed a training course.
   b. Yes, because the training course provided a certificate of completion.
   c. No, because art therapy practitioners must complete an internship after training.
   d. No, because she didn't consult with a supervisor/consultant with art therapy experience.

41. A social worker is holding a session with a grief and loss group, and it's the second week. Members are each sharing an update from their week. Group member Patricia sits with her arms crossed, looking at the floor, and doesn't seem to be showing any signs of listening or participating with her peers. She exhibited this behavior last week as well. What is the BEST way to approach this behavior?
   a. Ignore the behavior and allow her to participate at her own pace.
   b. Other group members should provide gentle encouragement to Patricia.
   c. The social worker should start asking Patricia pointed questions during group time.
   d. The social worker should ask Patricia after the session if she still wants to participate.

42. Josh is hired as a manager in a large social work agency. The agency recently received negative feedback from clients and employees regarding safety. He is assigned to review the agency's policies and flag anything that could be contributing to the problem. Which of the following policies should he flag as MOST likely to create an unsafe environment?

    a. If a client needs to meet with a social worker after normal business hours, the social worker must arrange for at least one other person to be in the office.

    b. There is a "three strikes, and you're out" rule regarding client outbursts; services will be terminated after three incidents of yelling, violence, or abusive behavior.

    c. Social workers may only communicate with clients during business hours via work phone or email. Using social media or other personal channels is not allowed.

    d. Group supervision is provided for free by the agency. If an employee wants individual supervision, the agency can provide recommendations but not funding.

43. Monica is a young woman who was born in the United States to Mexican parents. She has friends from several different Latin American backgrounds. She considers herself Chicana, and her ethnicity is an important part of her life. According to Ferdman and Gallegos's model of Latino identity development, which lens or orientation BEST describes Monica's relationship to her ethnic identity?

    a. Undifferentiated

    b. Subgroup identified

    c. White identified

    d. Latino identified

44. Laura is an elementary school social worker. She is meeting with a 7-year-old student named Sarah who has been sent to see her due to a change in behavior in the classroom. During the meeting, Laura notices that Sarah has a bruise on her arm. What should Laura do NEXT?

    a. Call Sarah's pediatrician to inquire about this injury.

    b. Ask Sarah about the injury and conduct a risk assessment.

    c. Contact child protective services and make a mandated report.

    d. Refer Sarah to counseling for her behavior changes.

45. Which of the following statements about professional boundaries is MOST accurate?

    a. It is the responsibility of the social worker alone to set and maintain professional boundaries.

    b. Professional boundaries are co-created by the client and the social worker.

    c. Professional boundaries are determined by the practice setting (i.e., agency, school, etc.).

    d. Setting professional boundaries is primarily a concern for social workers in private practice.

46. Greg is a social worker who utilizes the Gottman Method with the couples that he works with. He has been working with a couple who are seeking support in improving their communication after experiencing some trauma within their family. Which intervention is Greg MOST likely to use?

    a. Greg will focus on conflict resolution and improving communication.

    b. Greg will focus on understanding potential attachment issues.

    c. Greg will focus on identifying and changing patterns of interaction.

47. Mikhail is a licensed clinical social worker. Mikhail's boss tells him to take over a therapy group for veterans with PTSD. Mikhail does not have experience or training in this area, but he does not want to disappoint his boss. Mikhail determines that he is facing an ethical dilemma. Which core social work values are in conflict?

    a. Integrity vs. service

    b. Competence vs. service

    c. Importance of human relationships vs. competence

    d. Service vs. importance of human relationships

48. Jasmine is a social worker at an outpatient counseling center for adolescents. She is meeting with a client, Miranda, and Miranda's mother for a session. Miranda is 16 years old and has been in counseling since her parents became concerned with certain behaviors such as spending a lot of time with her friends, trying out different identities, and spending less time at home than she used to. She acknowledged that Miranda is continuing to do well in school and has not gotten into any trouble. After listening to them both, Jasmine explains that some of this behavior is normal for someone Miranda's age and that peer relationships and identity development are critical pieces of adolescence. Which theory BEST supports Jasmine's explanation?
    a. Social learning theory
    b. Erikson's stages of psychosocial development
    c. Attachment theory
    d. Piaget's cognitive developmental theory

49. Josie is a social worker in a community mental health center. She is meeting with a new client to conduct an intake assessment. The client is Robert, a 28-year-old man who is seeking counseling for anxiety. Josie asks questions about Robert's medical and psychiatric history, recent stressors, relationships, substance history, trauma history, and current mental status. What is the MOST important factor Josie should have also asked about?
    a. Employment status
    b. Education history
    c. Strengths and resources
    d. Political affiliation

50. What is the relationship between gender and self-esteem?
    a. Men tend to have higher self-esteem than women during middle adulthood.
    b. Women tend have higher self-esteem than men during adolescence.
    c. Gender does not affect self-esteem.
    d. Women tend have higher self-esteem than men throughout the lifespan.

51. Andre is a social worker who recently started work at a large agency with a much higher volume of clients than his previous job. His caseload always includes at least 25 clients and sometimes as many as 50. In the beginning, he was struggling to remember details about his clients and felt that this was negatively affecting his ability to build rapport. He started jotting down little personal details in each client's records that he could refer to before each meeting. He noted things like favorite foods, religious beliefs, friends' and relatives' names, jokes made by clients, and unusual things about each client's appearance to help him remember who they are as people, not just where they are in the treatment process. Andre explains this new system during supervision. How should his supervisor respond?
    a. Clarify the ethical standards for documentation and help him find a new way to remember clients.
    b. Congratulate him on using good problem-solving skills to overcome his difficulties.
    c. Ask to see his client records to ensure these personal details are being documented appropriately.
    d. Suggest other strategies he could try in addition to the personal notes to help remember clients.

52. Jennifer is 43 years old and started substance use counseling last week. She has been struggling with alcohol misuse for approximately 13 years and has had intermittent periods of sobriety. During her first session with the social worker, she says, "I don't like who I am after I've been binge drinking. I can't seem to stay on top of my responsibilities, and I know my kids are frustrated with my flakiness. It's just… there is a feeling I get when I first start to drink that makes me feel so relaxed, like my problems are so much smaller. That is hard to give up." Considering the stage of change that Jennifer appears to be in, what is the BEST way the social worker can support Jennifer?
    a. Support Jennifer in setting clear and manageable treatment goals.
    b. Engage Jennifer in identifying harm reduction strategies surrounding binge drinking episodes.
    c. Identify warning signs for relapse so that they can be prepared early on in treatment.
    d. Build on Jennifer's realization that there is an issue to increase change talk.

53. Carmen is a social worker at a community mental health center. She is conducting an initial session with Josh, a 30-year-old patient seeking services for anxiety treatment. Josh shares that he has been struggling financially and this is a contributing factor to his increased anxiety. Josh works as a mechanic in town and asks if Carmen would be able to trade mechanic services to subsidize the cost of his sessions. What is the BEST response?
    a. Carmen should accept the offer for services in lieu of payment but explain to Josh that a contract needs to be drawn up to ensure informed consent.
    b. Carmen should explain that social workers cannot accept services for payment but offer the option to waive his insurance copay to make services more affordable.
    c. Carmen should explain the agency policy on sliding scale services and assist Josh with an application for financial assistance.

54. For many years, Abraham Maslow, who developed the hierarchy of human needs, described self-actualization as the highest level of achievement. In later years, he adjusted the model in order to add another level, which is referred to as what?
    a. Peace and serenity
    b. Spiritual attainment
    c. Self-determination
    d. Self-transcendence

55. Leo is a social worker at a pediatrician's office. He runs a weekly group for new parents to provide education and support their transition to parenthood. Leo educates parents on how important it is for infants to have a consistent caregiver upon whom they can depend for care and comfort. He also teaches them that it's normal and healthy for babies to become distressed when the caregiver is separated from them and display relief when the caregiver returns. He focuses on the importance of this caregiver relationship for the first three years of a baby's life. What is the MOST relevant reason why Leo is teaching this topic?
    a. To educate parents on this topic because if infants do not bond to their caregivers during infancy, this behavior cannot be fixed during later childhood
    b. To educate parents on the importance of the attachment relationship that is developed during infancy and is critical for future development
    c. To make sure that parents choose a preschool that will support their baby's development as they grow older
    d. To make parents aware that babies thrive when parents make them independent as soon as possible during infancy

56. A local hospital is working towards improving their ability to provide trauma-informed care. They have received a grant for funding this project and training on where to begin. They plan to implement several changes to complete this goal. Which change would NOT be aligned with the theory of trauma-informed care?
    a. Installing better lighting in the parking area, waiting room, and hallways
    b. Training only clinical and client-facing staff on the impact of trauma
    c. Implementing universal trauma screening practices
    d. Including clients in the decision-making process about planned changes

57. Gregory is 23 years old and has been coming to counseling for about three weeks to address his anxiety. You've noticed that Gregory often needs to pull out his phone during sessions, reportedly to respond to texts from his husband. Gregory confides that he experiences increased contact from his partner when he's not with them and finds that he's often fielding accusations that he's lying about what he's doing. Today, Gregory arrives to the session with noticeable bruising on his neck and appears depressed. What is the BEST approach to take?
    a. Inform Gregory that he is in an abusive relationship and offer nearby domestic violence shelters.
    b. Conduct the session as normal and wait for Gregory to bring up any concerns.
    c. Gently prepare Gregory to delve into this topic and then ask direct questions about his safety.
    d. Let Gregory know that you might have to report his injuries to the proper authorities.

58. According to the *DSM-5-TR*, selective mutism is categorized with which type of disorders?
   a. Anxiety disorders
   b. Neurodevelopmental disorders
   c. Depressive disorders
   d. Trauma and stressor related disorders

59. Abe is a social worker at a partial hospitalization program that provides mental health treatment for adults. He is working with Claudia, a woman receiving treatment for a mood disorder who has not been progressing in her recovery. During a recent session, Claudia states that she does not wish to take psychiatric medication and refuses Abe's recommendation that she pursue a higher level of care. What should Abe do FIRST?
   a. Conduct a risk assessment to determine if Claudia is at risk of harming herself or others.
   b. Respect Claudia's right to autonomy and self-determination and support her decisions about her care.
   c. Set up a meeting with Claudia's parents to discuss their concerns and goals for her treatment.
   d. Request that the program's psychiatrist declare Claudia incompetent to make her own care decisions because she is not behaving in her own best interest.

60. Jan is a social worker at a counseling center for children. She is meeting with the parents of her new client, a 4-year-old boy named Ryan. His parents are concerned because he has an imaginary friend with whom they often hear Ryan playing with and talking to. His parents report that he does not seem bothered by these interactions and appears to be having fun. His parents ask Jan what they should do to stop this behavior because they are worried that it poses a problem for his development. What is the BEST response?
   a. Suggest that Ryan requires further psychological testing to determine the reason why he developed an imaginary friend.
   b. Explain that Ryan needs more social interactions; he likely created this imaginary friend because he does not have friends in real life.
   c. Educate the parents that this is developmentally normal and likely something he will age out of on his own.

61. Juan is a social worker in a busy emergency room setting working an overnight shift. He is the only social worker available during this shift. His manager asks him to triage the patients waiting and intervene accordingly. What does Juan need to do?
   a. Assess the severity of each situation and prioritize the patient with the highest or most acute needs to be seen first.
   b. Contact other hospitals and send patients elsewhere to be seen, as their facility is too busy.
   c. Quickly meet with each patient in the order they arrived in order to fit everyone in during his shift.

62. Celia is seeing a social worker for help with anxiety that started after she was involved in a public scandal. The social worker thinks he could provide treatment more effectively if he knew more about what happened. He knows that a quick internet search would turn up all the details. Would it be ethical for him to look up Celia's name on the internet?
   a. Yes, but only to look for information that directly relates to her treatment.
   b. No, that would be a violation of her privacy.
   c. Yes, but only if he seeks supervision and he and the supervisor agree that it is necessary for treatment.
   d. Yes, but only with Celia's permission.

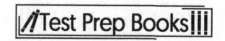

63. Emily is a social worker for an agency that works with seniors. She is conducting a family care plan meeting for a patient named Edith, a 75-year-old woman who has lived alone since she lost her spouse last year. Edith's children are also present for the meeting. Edith's children do not think that she should continue living alone and would like her to move into a facility. Edith refuses, stating that her independence is important to her and that she wants to remain in her home. Edith states that her doctor has cleared her of any health concerns, and she does not plan to leave her home unless it becomes necessary to do so. How should Emily respond?
   a. Ask Edith's children if any of them would be willing to move in with her and care for her so that she doesn't have to move.
   b. Offer to tour nursing home facilities with Edith so that she is aware of her options in case her circumstances change.
   c. Explain to Edith that she needs to listen to her family's input and accept their concerns about her living independently at her age.
   d. Support Edith in her goal of maintaining her independence and discuss what supports will enable her to do so.

64. A social worker is meeting with a client who has been managing symptoms of depression and anxiety for several months. This 34-year-old lost his dream job recently and has become largely reclusive and noncommunicative with friends and family. He is expressing thoughts of hopelessness and shares that his support system has largely disintegrated over the last year. He shares that playing video games is the only thing that he enjoys doing. His unemployment ends soon, and he wishes that he could find another job that he feels as passionately for as he did his last position. What should the social worker do FIRST in this situation?
   a. Identify local job fairs and create goals surrounding attendance.
   b. Explore the client's feelings surrounding the loss of his dream job.
   c. Explore the client's love for video games.
   d. Assess safety surrounding suicidal ideation.

65. Which of the following may be a dysfunctional family pattern?
   a. Scapegoating a child
   b. Affirming a child
   c. Undermining a child
   d. Disavowing a child

66. Which two phases indicate client readiness for change?
   a. Precontemplation and contemplation
   b. Action and termination
   c. Contemplation and preparation
   d. Maintenance and recycling

67. Linda is a social worker at a children's mental health agency. She has been working with Jayce, a 7-year-old boy, for six months to provide treatment for anxiety and behavioral challenges at school. Jayce's parents recently got divorced, and his mother has custody of him. Linda has met Jayce's father several times between his treatment and other interactions in the community, and the two of them have acknowledged a mutual attraction and are interested in pursuing a romantic relationship. How should Linda proceed?
   a. Refer Jayce to a different social worker at her agency so the romantic relationship does not create a conflict of interest or dual relationship.
   b. Linda should not pursue the relationship because it would not be in the best interest of Jayce or his care.
   c. Consult her supervisor to receive clinical supervision regarding this relationship and ensure that it's appropriately documented per agency policy.
   d. Disclose the relationship to Jayce's primary guardian and discuss boundaries and limits to confidentiality to avoid the relationship negatively impacting Jayce's care.

161

68. Hannah is a social worker at a children's grief center. She is working with a 7-year-old girl named Lily whose father died six months ago. Lily has been struggling with the loss, and it's impacting her school performance, relationships, and behavior. Hannah is meeting with Lily's mother to discuss ways to support her. Which suggestion would be MOST appropriate?
    a. Avoid saying the word *death* at home because this can be scary for a child of Lily's age.
    b. Allow Lily to miss school when she's having a difficult day and request make-up work as needed.
    c. Ensure that Lily does not see other family members grieving so she doesn't have more to worry about.
    d. Work with Lily to stick to her routine and avoid any further changes.

69. What is the term for the period of months or years prior to the onset of psychosis during which a person experiences gradual changes in their perceptions, thoughts, feelings, and behaviors?
    a. Acute phase
    b. Prodromal phase
    c. Premorbid phase
    d. Residual phase

70. Julie is a social worker providing counseling services at a veteran's health clinic. She meets with Tyler, a 40-year-old veteran who has been referred by his primary care provider for counseling for PTSD after returning home from combat. Tyler spends most of the session pacing around the room and turning his chair around to look towards the doorway. What should Julie do FIRST?
    a. Conduct a PTSD screening using the standardized assessment tool.
    b. Work with Tyler to write a treatment plan and set goals for counseling.
    c. Refer Tyler to the agency psychiatrist for a medication evaluation.
    d. Offer options such as moving chairs, going for a walk together, or opening the door.

71. Yara is a 27-year-old woman that is in her fourth session with a social worker. She has been struggling off and on with an opioid addiction since a traumatic car accident when she was a senior in high school. She suffers from PTSD and finds it difficult to navigate social situations. She entered therapy following a one-week stay in a psychiatric facility last month after she attempted suicide. Yara has been utilizing therapy well to process past trauma, which she has never done before. She has continued to use fentanyl on a regular basis. What is the BEST way to support Yara?
    a. Ensure that Yara has access to Naloxone and test strips.
    b. Assess Yara for suicidal ideation.
    c. Educate Yara on the dangers of withdrawal and provide contacts for detox facilities.
    d. Refer Yara to group substance use therapy.

72. Which of the following is NOT a common characteristic of a perpetrator of abuse?
    a. Uses/abuses drugs or alcohol
    b. Has a learning disorder
    c. Tends to be controlling toward others
    d. Has a history of mental illness

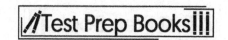

73. Vera is a social worker at a community mental health clinic. She uses a strength-based approach in her practice. She is meeting with Marcus, a young man in his twenties who has been receiving mental health treatment. In their most recent sessions, Marcus tells Vera that he does not feel like things are ever going to improve and that he does not see the point of continuing with counseling. What should Vera do?
   a. Help Marcus understand the connection between his past difficulties and the challenging pattern in which he is currently stuck.
   b. Educate Marcus that sometimes counseling can cause discomfort before symptoms improve and assure him that this is a normal aspect of treatment.
   c. Terminate services to respect Marcus's autonomy and decision making.
   d. Highlight the progress Marcus has made and discuss the ways he has overcome challenges in the past.

74. Damon is a social worker in a hospital setting who is asked to conduct a risk assessment for a 70-year-old male patient named Harold. Harold's doctor is concerned about his mental health due to statements he made during his appointment about having thoughts of suicide. Which risk factor would be the MOST likely to prompt the need for further intervention before a safe discharge could be planned?
   a. Harold lives alone.
   b. Harold has access to firearms at home.
   c. Harold recently lost his job.
   d. Harold has a history of depression.

75. You are a social worker working with a family to increase positive communication and strengthen familial bonds. The family consists of two parents and two teenagers. This is your second session with the family. You have explained to them that your style of work reflects a narrative therapy-based approach. What is the NEXT thing you should do to move the family forward in treatment?
   a. Work with the family on identifying strengths as well as helpful ways they've navigated past conflicts.
   b. Establish a safe space for each member to share their perspective.
   c. Break down the most recent conflict the family has been navigating into manageable parts.

76. Kris is a social worker at a community health center. She is meeting with Anh, an elderly female client who was referred for social work services by her primary care provider. Anh speaks some English, but her primary language is Vietnamese. When Kris meets with Anh for an intake, Anh is struggling to understand the consent forms provided in English. Kris offers to reschedule with an interpreter, but Anh says her daughter is waiting for her in the parking lot and she can translate. What should Kris do NEXT?
   a. Kris should respect Anh's right to self-determination and allow her daughter to translate the session to ensure that she has informed consent.
   b. Kris should reschedule the session as soon as possible with a qualified interpreter and provide forms in the primary language of Vietnamese.
   c. Kris should discuss the pros and cons of Anh's daughter translating the session and how this may impact confidentiality and rapport.

77. Holly is a social worker at an adoption agency, and she provides counseling to adoptees and their families. She is meeting with the family of Brian, a 4-year-old boy who was orphaned as an infant and then adopted at six months old. Brian's parents are concerned because he is struggling behaviorally, and they do not feel like he responds to them consistently. Brian's parents explain that he often seems scared or withdrawn, and he rarely engages with other family members, although he seems to be observing them closely. Brian's parents ask what they could have done wrong because they do not understand why he is acting this way. What should Holly do FIRST?

    a. Provide education around early attachment and the impact that Brian's previous trauma is likely having on his behavior.

    b. Explain that Brian needs more consistency at home, and the parents need to develop a behavioral plan to reflect his needs.

    c. Refer Brian to a psychiatrist for a medication evaluation as counseling alone will likely not address his symptoms.

    d. Educate Brian's parents that all children who are adopted experience these symptoms and give them strategies to adapt to his behavior.

78. Cathy is working as a social worker in a substance use treatment day program. She has been seeing her client Thomas, a 30-year-old male, for several months. His goal is to stop his alcohol use, and they have spent several sessions working through planning and preparation stages of what this would look like. In their last session, Thomas stated he was ready to take action and begin attending AA. Since then, Thomas has canceled most of his sessions and has not been engaging when he does show up to the program. What should Cathy try NEXT?

    a. Refer Thomas to a group to try a different treatment environment.

    b. Ask Thomas about what has been getting in the way of going to the AA meetings.

    c. Discontinue treatment due to missing sessions.

    d. Offer to attend AA meetings with Thomas to ensure he goes.

79. Excessive sleepiness, untreated medical problems, excessive hunger, and reports that no one is around to provide care are indicators of what?

    a. Physical neglect

    b. Biological assessment flaws

    c. Sexual neglect

    d. Starvation

80. Hector is a social worker at a hospital. He is contacted by John, a 60-year-old man who is a former patient. John is requesting his records from his meetings with Hector. What should Hector do NEXT?

    a. Seek supervision and consultation from his primary supervisor as well as the hospital leadership team to determine how to proceed in an ethical manner.

    b. Inquire the reason for the request of records before releasing them.

    c. Document the request for records in John's file and release them in accordance with the hospital's policy.

    d. Explain that records are rarely shared because reviewing one's records can be detrimental and is only allowed in extraordinary circumstances.

81. A social worker is working in a case worker role within a child welfare program. They are assigned a case involving a 4-year-old girl who was removed from her mother's care and placed in kinship care due to concerns with the mother's alcoholism and ability to maintain a safe environment for her daughter. The social worker learns that the mother has just been discharged from her inpatient treatment program and is engaged in ongoing counseling and parenting classes. What should the social worker do NEXT?

    a. Set up a meeting with the mother to establish parenting time goals.

    b. Recommend that the child be placed in kinship care long-term, given the risk of relapse.

    c. Send a request for records to the inpatient treatment program.

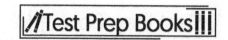

82. Morgan is a social worker with a hospice agency and is working with a 50-year-old patient named Lucy. Lucy has a terminal illness and has been seeing Morgan for support and to process this news. Lucy shared that her children are visiting this week and tells Morgan she has not told them about her illness and does not plan to. How should Morgan respond FIRST?
    a. Respect Lucy's right to make this decision and not discuss it again.
    b. Tell Lucy she will need more support as she declines and that she needs to tell her children now.
    c. Ask Lucy to share more about this decision and what she is feeling and thinking.
    d. Inform Lucy's medical team that she is in denial about her illness.

83. What is the primary difference between atypical and typical antipsychotics?
    a. Atypical antipsychotics were developed decades after typical antipsychotics and generally have fewer side effects.
    b. Typical antipsychotics were developed decades after atypical antipsychotics and generally have fewer side effects.
    c. Atypical antipsychotics were developed decades after typical antipsychotics and generally have more side effects.
    d. Typical antipsychotics were developed decades after atypical antipsychotics and generally have more side effects.

84. Troy is a social worker who provides marriage counseling services. He is meeting with Sarah and Jacob, a couple who has been married for 20 years. Their children have both recently moved out of their home for college, and they are seeking counseling because they feel like their marriage is struggling with this transition. Troy is helping them determine strategies to work on this goal. Which intervention would be LEAST appropriate?
    a. Redefining their relationship and connection as a couple rather than as parents of young children
    b. Discussing their hopes for the future and what they are seeking in this next phase of life
    c. Working on ways to continue parenting and being involved in their children's lives on a daily basis
    d. Reflecting on their friendships and community and identifying if there are changes they would like to make

85. Rob is a social worker in a private practice setting. He does not accept insurance payment for sessions and utilizes a fee-for-service model. Rob has all of his clients sign consent paperwork explaining his payment structure when they begin care. He is meeting with Heidi, a 40-year-old patient whom he has been seeing for depression treatment. Heidi has had an overdue balance for the past six weeks of sessions and has not paid. Rob has spoken to her about this several times and explained that it may result in termination. What should Rob do FIRST?
    a. Continue meeting with Heidi because it would be unsafe and unethical to discontinue treatment of someone with a mental illness due to their inability to pay and assist her with a Medicaid application.
    b. Conduct a risk assessment to determine if Heidi is at risk of harming herself and others and assess the current severity of her depressive symptoms.
    c. Make a contract with Heidi to waive the overdue fees in exchange for a comparable trade of services through her business as a massage therapist.
    d. Immediately terminate services due to non-payment and document the steps taken to rectify the situation and the client's failure to respond.

86. During a mental status exam (MSE), assessing the client's cooperation is an example of what MAIN element of the MSE?
    a. General appearance
    b. Mood and affect
    c. Speech
    d. Level of consciousness

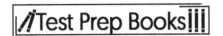

87. Fran is a social worker at a nursing home. She is working with an 85-year-old resident named Lillian who was referred to counseling for symptoms of depression. Lillian has been sharing some of her concerns, which include feeling a lot of regret over her life choices. She feels some bitterness over her strained relationship with her family, and she often wonders if she should have done things differently. What is the BEST explanation for the cause of Lillian's feelings?
   a. Lillian is experiencing the stages of grief associated with the aging process.
   b. Lillian is struggling with the integrity vs. despair stage of development.
   c. Lillian is struggling with the intimacy vs. isolation stage of development.
   d. Lillian is experiencing major depressive disorder, which is common in nursing home patients.

88. Your client is a 27-year-old woman named Helena who is seeking support to manage anxiety following her return to work after taking parental leave. Helena has two children under the age of 3 and works a full-time job as an events coordinator. She presents as nervous and verbose in sessions, wringing her hands and biting her lip throughout your interactions with her. She shares with you that she is worried that she is wasting your time and that her problems don't compare to "real mental health issues." What should you focus on FIRST?
   a. Psychoeducation surrounding anxiety and negative thought patterns
   b. Suggest a peer group where Helena might feel more accepted.
   c. Validation for the importance of addressing her anxiety and continued direct engagement

89. Steven is a licensed clinical social worker who has just started working as a therapist on a military base. He learns during orientation that he is expected to fill out monthly progress reports for each client and deliver them to the client's commanding officer. The progress report form includes questions about diagnosis, treatment plan, substance use, and medications. The purpose of the form is to identify soldiers who might need to be removed from field operations temporarily to protect them and the rest of their team from harm. Is this policy ethical?
   a. It is unethical because it violates a client's right to confidentiality.
   b. It is unethical because the commanding officers are not social workers.
   c. It is ethical because it protects the clients and other soldiers from harm.
   d. It is ethical because social workers on base must comply with military rules.

90. Jim is a social worker at a hospital. He is meeting with Melanie, a woman whose mother recently passed away unexpectedly after a surgery. He provides Melanie with support and resources surrounding this loss. Melanie tells Jim that she has two young children, and she is not sure how to tell them about the death. How should Jim respond?
   a. Encourage Melanie to be honest and use concrete, age-appropriate language to explain that their grandmother died.
   b. Suggest that Melanie wait to tell the children until after the funeral, as it would not be appropriate for young children to attend.
   c. Offer to conduct a home visit to tell the children himself, as this discussion requires professional expertise and sensitivity.
   d. Tell Melanie that she should not display any tears or emotional response as she tells the children because such displays may worry them.

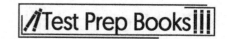

91. Grace is a social worker who works at a large outpatient counseling center in an urban city center. She is assigned to meet with a new client, Margaret, for an intake. During the first session, she realizes that Margaret is her 2-year-old daughter's pediatrician. What is the BEST response?
    a. Ask Margaret if she's comfortable seeing Grace since she will also be seeing Grace's daughter for pediatric care.
    b. Notify the pediatric practice of the dual relationship and have them transfer Grace's daughter to a different provider.
    c. Seek supervision to determine if this is an instance in which a dual relationship would be ethically allowable.
    d. Acknowledge the situation to Margaret and have her transfer to work with a different social worker at the counseling center.

92. Your client is a 67-year-old woman who has been living with her cousin and his family for the past two months. She arrives to the session today distraught and shares that her cousin asked her to start paying rent starting next month. Your client shares that it's clear that her family hates her. She also states the belief that she will be homeless within the week. You have been working with this client for several months and know that she can be prone to feeling overwhelmed easily by small demands. After ensuring safety, what is the BEST approach to take with your client?
    a. Remind the client that she can be prone to overreact to situations.
    b. Make a chart to separate the facts of the situation and her resulting feelings.
    c. Provide a list of emergency housing options in the area.

93. Nathan is a school social worker who has been asked to meet with Jill, a 14-year-old student who has been suddenly skipping class and arguing with peers. Her teachers are worried about this change in behavior. During their meeting, Jill discloses that she has been experiencing abuse from a family member who lives in her home. Nathan supports Jill through this disclosure, but she becomes upset when he explains the need for a mandated report and asks him not to do this. How should Nathan proceed?
    a. Agree to wait until tomorrow so Jill is able to discuss this issue with her family.
    b. Provide emotional support while explaining the importance of her safety, and file a report with child protective services immediately.
    c. Contact the school principal to decide how to proceed and set up a meeting.
    d. Call the local police to report a crime and file a police report.

94. The methods used to develop an intervention/treatment plan are problem definition, problem causation, _____, and obstacle/risk identification.
    a. objective development
    b. risk assessment
    c. solution identification
    d. information gathering

95. Jennifer is a social worker at a clinic that provides services for clients struggling with substance abuse. She provides individual and group therapy services. In a meeting with her supervisor, she states her belief that the agency needs to do more to address the crisis of substance use in their community from a macro level. Which change would BEST meet this need?
    a. Hiring more clinicians so they can provide counseling services to more people
    b. Advocating at the state level to change a state policy that limits access to housing for many of their clients
    c. Starting a support group for family members of people struggling with substance use
    d. Educating staff on different treatment modalities to ensure that everyone is providing evidence-based care

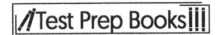
96. Gabe is a social worker in a private practice setting. He is meeting with Veronica, a 50-year-old female client whom he has been working with for several months. Veronica shares that she is contemplating divorce because she just learned her spouse has been having an affair. Veronica was tearful during the session and talked about feeling alone and like no one in her life understands what she is going through. Veronica asks Gabe if he has ever been married. What is the BEST response?
   a. Honestly answer her question about his marital status and redirect the conversation back to her shared feelings about loneliness and lacking support.
   b. Refuse to answer the question and explain to Veronica that this question violates a personal boundary in the social worker/client relationship.
   c. Tell the patient that he was previously married but it also ended due to infidelity and that he knows how she feels and can empathize.
   d. Acknowledge that he was previously divorced and that it can be very difficult to cope, and refer the patient to the helpful divorce attorney he utilized.

97. Dawn is meeting with a new client who was referred for therapy services. The client is a 60-year-old woman named Elsa who states that she has been experiencing chronic pain and that it is impacting her quality of life. Elsa states that she has been seen at many different hospitals, and no one has been able to assist her. She states she is not interested in having further testing. As Dawn listens to her story, she notices several inconsistencies and contradictions. Dawn begins to suspect Elsa is feigning illness. What should Dawn do NEXT?
   a. Contact Elsa's medical provider team to gather collateral and background information to better understand her medical history.
   b. Inform Elsa that your assessment is that she's feigning illness and provide education on getting help to treat this condition.
   c. Engage in active listening, ask open-ended questions, and build initial rapport with Elsa.
   d. Refer Elsa to a support group for individuals with chronic pain to improve her coping skills.

98. Regina is a 43-year-old woman struggling with chronic pain and an opioid addiction, and she recently had her children removed from her home and placed with a family member. She is a new client on your caseload at an outpatient clinic. After completing an initial assessment with you, she breaks down and tearfully shares with you, "I just can't get a handle on life lately. It feels like I'm just spinning out and there is no stopping it. My rent is two months overdue, I don't know how to quit taking these pills, and I'm never going to see my children again." What is the BEST approach to use in this situation?
   a. Focus on a plan for reunification with her children, as this will provide the best motivation for change.
   b. Refer her to a detox program for completion before continuing sessions with her.
   c. Ask which concern she would like to start with.
   d. Validate her feelings and create an itemized plan to address her concerns in order of urgency.

99. Leslie is a social worker at a psychiatric hospital. She was working with an adult male patient named Randy until he passed away a few months ago. Leslie receives a message from Randy's daughter, who identifies herself as his next of kin and requests that Leslie provide her with her father's treatment records and answer some questions about how he had been doing prior to his death. What is the BEST response?
   a. Request documentation to verify the daughter's identity before speaking to her and releasing Randy's records to her.
   b. Do not respond to the request or provide information about the client to his daughter.
   c. Inquire as to why the daughter needs the records to determine if the situation meets the criteria for releasing information on a deceased patient.
   d. Call the daughter and explain that the records can't be shared, but offer to meet with her and provide grief support.

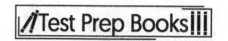

100. A social worker is supporting a mother and father whose 13-year-old son, Henry, is currently hospitalized in a long-term inpatient program following a suicide attempt. The social worker is empathizing with the parents' shock and despair after this attempt occurred. The mother shares, "We never even talk about suicide at home. I don't understand how this was on his mind." Based on the statement, what is the social worker's NEXT intervention?
   a. Empathize and allow the mother to continue to share her feelings.
   b. Discuss common myths surrounding suicide.
   c. Facilitate a dialogue between Henry and his parents.

101. Meg is a social worker for a home health agency. She is meeting with a family of three adult siblings who have been sharing the responsibility of caring for their father as his dementia diagnosis has been worsening over the past few years. The family is experiencing increased conflict over differing opinions on care goals and whether the father should remain home or move to a nursing facility. What should Meg try FIRST?
   a. Assist the family in applying for financial assistance.
   b. Facilitate a family meeting to discuss their goals.
   c. Connect the siblings to a caregiver support group.

102. Olivia is an 18-year-old client who is in treatment at a college counseling office. She has been in treatment for about five weeks, following her transition to a college that is four hours from home. Olivia attends sessions once a week. What is the BEST way to measure her progress in treatment?
   a. Measure the decline in depressive symptoms as reported by Olivia.
   b. Compare the client's ability to participate in treatment more openly to her initial session.
   c. Assess her current level of functioning compared to when she initially began treatment in relation to her goals.

103. Jordan is a social worker with a child welfare agency. He is tasked with finding a foster placement for a 6-year child named Jessie who recently came into foster care after she was removed from her home. She is currently in an emergency foster placement. Jessie does not have any known behavioral needs or mental health conditions, but she is understandably struggling with the removal. Jordan is discussing the different placement options with his supervisor and trying to make a decision with Jessie's best interests in mind. Assuming all settings have been deemed safe, which would be the MOST supportive placement choice?
   a. Kinship care
   b. Residential facility
   c. Therapeutic foster care
   d. Group home

104. Julia has been working with her client Vincent to provide therapy services for a few months. Together they have developed a treatment plan to work on Vincent's goal of reducing his anxiety and increasing his healthy coping skills. Vincent has begun to work on multiple interventions towards his goal, including practicing mindfulness and meditation techniques, continuing with CBT during their therapy sessions, and learning about his triggers for anxiety. What should Julia do NEXT for Vincent's treatment?
   a. Discuss imminent discharge planning with Vincent.
   b. Refer Vincent to an anxiety support group to further work on these strategies.
   c. Create a safety plan with Vincent.
   d. Work with Vincent to assess how these changes are going.

105. When the client provides their perspective on what happened and the correlated feelings and experiences felt, it is known as what?
   a. Measurable data
   b. Objective data
   c. Subjective data
   d. Planning data

169

106. Jessina is the facilitator of a supervision group that meets twice a month. The members of her group are all in entry-level social work positions within the same large organization and often utilize this group for debriefing first-time experiences within their respective roles. In her group this week, one of the supervisees confesses to having strong romantic feelings for one of her clients. The supervisee has not disclosed this to the client but is overwhelmed with how to manage this. What should Jessina do FIRST in this situation?
    a. Facilitate an open discussion with the supervisee surrounding ethical concerns.
    b. Report this social worker to the board.
    c. Support the supervisee in transitioning this client off their caseload.
    d. Ask the supervisee to not discuss this topic in a group setting.

107. Hayley is a social worker at a community health center. She recently began working with Lou, an older man who is a veteran and has a diagnosis of PTSD. Hayley has limited experience working with this population. What should she do NEXT?
    a. Refer Lou to a more experienced provider and not take any further referrals for patients who are veterans.
    b. Engage in consultation and professional development on evidence-based approaches for trauma treatment and working with veterans.
    c. Attend a support group at the local veteran's center to learn more about their experiences firsthand to better relate to Lou.
    d. Obtain supervision to process her feelings of incompetence so they do not get in the way of providing effective treatment.

108. Which of the examples listed depicts obtaining information from a collateral source?
    a. An initial verbal consultation conducted with a potential client
    b. A self-report assessment filled out by the client
    c. An official medical report brought by the client to their first session
    d. The client draws a picture illustrating their current mental state during a session

109. Andrea is a social worker at a partial hospitalization program for adults. During a group she is running, one of her clients makes a comment about wanting to harm himself. The client is Ron, a 50-year-old man. Upon further risk assessment, it's determined that Ron requires a higher level of care, as he discloses that he is having thoughts of suicide with a plan and intent to act upon his thoughts. Which setting would be MOST appropriate for Ron right now?
    a. Short-term psychiatric hospitalization
    b. Long-term residential program
    c. Intensive outpatient program

110. Kari is a social worker at an agency that provides services to adult survivors of domestic and interpersonal violence. She runs a support group that meets monthly. During a recent session, one of the women in the group shares about her experience with her former partner. The woman tells the group that she was unsure if her experience was considered interpersonal violence because she did not experience physical abuse. The woman shares that it was difficult to leave her former partner because she did not have access to household finances, was not allowed to have a credit card, and didn't have access to all of her identity and personal documents. Which response would be MOST appropriate?
    a. Providing validation and education on the many aspects of interpersonal power and control, including the financial abuse described
    b. Telling the woman that she experienced financial abuse and filing a mandated police report regarding this crime
    c. Referring the woman to a financial literacy program to reduce the likelihood of this happening to her again
    d. Providing psychoeducation on the hierarchy of the dynamics of violence and how behavior will always escalate from financial abuse to physical

170

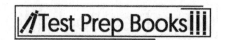

111. Mila is a social worker in the court system who works as an advocate for victims of violent crimes. She has been in her role for several years when she begins to experience recurrent nightmares, hypervigilance, headaches, and trouble sleeping. She goes to see her primary care provider, who confirms that there are no physical health concerns. Mila is unsure what is happening to her, as nothing in her life changed to prompt these issues. What should Mila do NEXT?
   a. Mila should set better boundaries with her clients and colleagues because she's showing signs of fatigue, burnout, and being overworked.
   b. Mila should take a leave of absence to prioritize her mental health and self-care and be transparent with her clients about the reasons why.
   c. Mila should seek supervision and support regarding the signs of vicarious trauma she is displaying.
   d. Mila should compartmentalize her feelings while at work because it's important to be fully present when working with clients who have survived traumatic experiences.

112. Which medication is commonly used to treat depression in people with bipolar disorder?
   a. Sodium valproate (Depakote)
   b. Carbamazepine (Tegretol)
   c. Lamotrigine (Lamictal)
   d. Lisdexamfetamine (Vyvanse)

113. Joelle is a social worker with a community-based hospice agency that focuses on keeping patients in their homes for end-of-life care. Joelle is meeting with Margaret, an 80-year-old woman who is being cared for at home by her family. Margaret tells Joelle she wishes she were dead. What should Joelle do NEXT?
   a. Contact mental health crisis services to coordinate psychiatric hospitalization.
   b. Inform Margaret's family of the concerns and develop a safety plan.
   c. Ask Margaret to share more about how she's feeling and conduct a risk assessment.
   d. Tell Margaret that she needs to stay strong for her loved ones.

114. Jason is a social worker at a pediatric ward in a hospital. He is called to meet with Noel, a 13-year-old girl. Noel has a younger brother with a serious and chronic medical condition who has been hospitalized repeatedly. When Jason meets with Noel, she expresses anger that her parents missed her recent birthday because her brother was in the hospital again. Noel shared feelings of frustration and resentment about the situation. What should be Jason's FIRST response?
   a. Provide validation and space to process these feelings because they are normal responses to this family dynamic.
   b. Help Noel find gratitude for her health and understand that her parents need to focus on her brother due to his illness.
   c. Refer Noel to therapy as these feelings are abnormal and indicate a possible mental health condition of depression or anxiety.
   d. Meet with Noel's parents for a family meeting to work on strategies to both children.

115. Bill is a social worker in a private practice setting. He has been working with Helen, a 40-year-old woman, to provide treatment for anxiety. The treatment has been primarily cognitive behavioral therapy. Helen tells Bill she feels that she would like to try something else and asks if he can provide an alternative somatic therapy she read about. This treatment is not evidence based, and Bill is not trained in this model. How should Bill respond?
   a. Educate Helen that there is no evidence that this treatment is effective, so she should not pursue it and should continue with the approach that's best supported by research.
   b. Explain that he will need to contact Helen's insurance provider to confirm that they will authorize coverage for this alternative therapy before he can provide it during their sessions.
   c. Obtain informed consent and then agree to provide this therapy in order to honor Helen's right to self-determination.
   d. Support Helen's choice to pursue any resource she believes will be helpful to her, but explain he would not be able to be the one to provide this alternative approach during their sessions.

116. Which approach integrates knowledge about the prevalence, effects, and triggers of trauma into all elements of the service delivery system?
   a. Trauma-specific services
   b. Trauma-informed care
   c. Trauma-sensitive practice
   d. Universal trauma screening

117. Jackie is a social worker with a home hospice agency. Part of her role is to support family caregivers who care for their loved ones at home. She is meeting with Georgie, an older woman who has been caring for her mother who has had dementia for about a year. Georgie states that she has been feeling burnt out, and she frequently worries about how they will be able to afford her mother's increasing care needs. Georgie tells Jackie that they have incurred significant medical debts, which really concern her. Georgie asks for Jackie's assistance in tackling this issue. Which intervention would be MOST appropriate?
   a. Refer Georgie to counseling to help her process the stressors of caregiving.
   b. Set up a private home health aide to give Georgie a weekly break from caregiving.
   c. Assist Georgie in applying for state-based financial assistance.
   d. Help Georgie apply for a state-funded nursing home facility for her mother.

118. Malcolm is a social worker in the emergency department. He is asked to meet with Joe, an older man with safety concerns upon discharge. Joe appears to be experiencing homelessness, and his speech and presentation appear disorganized. What assessment should Malcolm utilize to gather more information to inform next steps?
   a. Mental status exam
   b. Minnesota Multiphasic Personality Inventory
   c. Potential Stressful Events Interview
   d. Beck Depression Inventory

119. You are a counselor at an on-campus counseling office at a local university. Your client, a student of the university, dies suddenly. A week later, the family reaches out to you to request copies of the student's counseling records. They share that they are trying to understand the client's frame of mind before they died in an effort to gain closure. What should you do NEXT?
   a. Offer a family session to discuss the client's final weeks.
   b. Refuse the request for records.
   c. Consult with another counselor at your office.
   d. Determine the laws surrounding the release of medical records.

120. Amira is a social worker at an outpatient counseling center for children. She is meeting with Luke, a 9-year-old boy referred for services following difficulties at school. He is telling her about a difficult peer situation, and Amira notices that Luke is able to reflect on how his peers felt about his behavior during their conflict. He was able to talk about the fact that not everyone thinks and feels the same way as him all the time. However, when Amira asks Luke how he might handle a similar conflict in the future, he struggles to engage with this part of the conversation. What is the MOST likely reason that the future planning part of the session was difficult for Luke?

    a. Luke is demonstrating signs of a cognitive developmental delay.

    b. Luke is in the concrete operational stage of development and is struggling with abstract thought.

    c. Luke is in the preoperational stage of development and utilizes magical thinking.

    d. Amira asked Luke to complete more tasks in a short period of time than is developmentally appropriate.

121. Jenny is a social worker who works for a mobile emergency crisis program. She is called to the home of John, a 24-year-old male whose outpatient provider suggested he contact mobile crisis services for support with a recent increase in thoughts of suicide and self-harm. Jenny conducts her risk assessment and finds John to be safe to remain in the community and is now working with John to create a crisis intervention plan. Which would NOT be an appropriate goal for this plan?

    a. Increase John's support and healthy coping skills to safely manage his thoughts and feelings.

    b. Connect John to an intensive outpatient program for a higher level of care.

    c. Create a safety plan for future crisis situations.

    d. Assist John in getting a new job, as he identified this as a source of stress.

122. The Jones family has very fixed boundaries with the outside world. They limit their interactions with people and systems outside the family unit. Forming relationships with people outside the family is seen as a betrayal and is discouraged. What type of relationship dynamics are likely occurring within the family?

    a. Differentiation

    b. Disengagement

    c. Enmeshment

    d. Triangulation

123. Jo is a social worker with a home visiting program for senior citizens. She is meeting with Ruth, an 80-year-old woman who has lived alone since her husband passed away last year. Ruth has been struggling with changes to her body and mobility following a recent hip surgery. She tells Jo that this has been very difficult on her as she always took good care of her body in the past. What should Jo do NEXT?

    a. Validate Ruth's feelings, explain that it's unusual for someone of her age to experience these types of changes, and coordinate a referral to a physical therapist.

    b. Validate Ruth's feelings, conduct the PHQ-9 to assess for major depressive disorder, and initiate a referral for mental health services.

    c. Validate Ruth's feelings and connect her to a grief support group for bereaved spouses through the local senior center.

    d. Validate Ruth's feelings, normalize the changes occurring with her health and aging, and discuss coping strategies.

124. Abigail is a social worker working with a 30-year-old man with generalized anxiety disorder. The man is struggling immensely to cope with the anxiety he gets leading up to each work week. He finds that Sundays are progressively getting more challenging to handle, as he is so worried about going to work. Abigail is supporting this client with identifying the thought patterns that lead up to Sunday in order to replace them with more functional thinking and gain control over his emotions. Which therapy approach is Abigail MOST likely taking?

    a. Psychodynamic therapy

    b. Cognitive behavioral therapy

    c. Dialectical behavior therapy

    d. Humanistic therapy

173

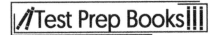

125. Iris is a social worker at a child welfare agency. She is working with Kim, a 13-year-old girl who is in foster care. Iris and Kim have worked together for many years and have a good rapport. Iris is leaving her position for a new job and is worried about how this will impact Kim, who already struggles with insecure attachment due to her history. What should Kim do NEXT?

    a. Get approval from her supervisor to remain available to Kim as needed after she transitions out of her role to decrease feelings of abandonment.

    b. Prepare Kim for the upcoming transition and facilitate a warm handoff to the new social worker.

    c. Give Kim her personal contact information to stay in touch after she leaves the agency.

    d. Wait until her last week at the agency to notify Kim of the change to avoid causing her anxiety about the upcoming transition.

126. A hospital is trying to save money in its budget. The hospital wants to know whether it makes financial sense to continue having social workers in the emergency department. What type of program evaluation would help them determine whether employing the social workers saves or loses them money?

    a. A needs assessment

    b. A cost-benefit analysis

    c. A SWOT analysis

    d. An outcome assessment

127. Holly is a social worker in a short-term psychiatric hospital facility. It is her job to assist with discharge planning for patients in the facility. Holly is working with Lydia, a 21-year-old woman who has been hospitalized for the past two weeks with a goal of medication management and diagnostic clarity. Lydia is her own guardian and found to have capacity, but her parents provide support and are present for her discharge planning meeting. During the meeting, Lydia states she does not agree with the plan for discharge to a residential facility. What should Holly do FIRST?

    a. Ask Lydia's parents what their wishes are for her next steps at discharge.

    b. Inform Lydia that she must go to the residential facility as she is not safe to discharge otherwise.

    c. Ask Lydia to share what she is feeling and listen to her concerns.

    d. Request that the doctor conduct a competency exam to decide if Lydia can make her own care decisions.

128. A social worker runs a group for people struggling with eating disorders. The group has been meeting weekly for seven weeks and has established a safe and supportive environment. A group member is recounting a recent relapse into her disorder and is struggling to share without crying. The social worker lets her know that crying is normal and that she should take her time in sharing. What technique is the social worker using?

    a. Linking

    b. Cognitive reframing

    c. Active listening

    d. Validation

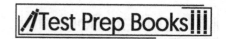

129. Alex is a social worker with the child welfare department. The agency has been seeing a shortage of foster parents, which has caused youths in foster care to be placed further from home or be separated from their siblings. The social workers at the agency feel that this is negatively impacting children and families. Alex engages in advocacy with the state legislature to change the requirements for foster parents to make the role accessible to more people. Which level of change is this?
    a. Micro
    b. Mezzo
    c. Macro

130. What is the purpose of a compliance audit?
    a. To ensure that local, state, and federal regulations are being followed
    b. To verify that a social worker is meeting their licensing requirements
    c. To monitor the extent to which a client is following their treatment plan
    d. To improve the quality of services provided to clients

131. Polly is a social worker at a partial hospitalization program for adults with mood disorders. She has been working with Jack, a 25-year-old man with bipolar disorder, for the past few months and they have a strong relationship. Jack's symptoms have been escalating recently, and the team has been concerned about him and is working with him to hopefully avoid hospitalization. Polly is scheduled to have two weeks off to deal with some personal and medical matters. Jacks asks if he can contact her if it's an emergency during that time because she's an important part of his support system. What is the BEST response?
    a. Reschedule her time off to later in the month to be available for Jack during this critical time in his treatment.
    b. Explain that she cares about him but will be unavailable during her time off, work with him to create a safety plan, and connect him to the covering social worker.
    c. Obtain permission from her supervisor to be available only for a crisis situation, and set boundaries with Jack regarding what would meet that criteria as well as whom he should contact otherwise.

132. Dana is a social worker at a large hospital. She is conducting training for the medical staff on the impact of trauma and adverse childhood experiences. Her goal is to make sure that staff members such as physicians and nurses are educated on this issue. What is the BEST answer as to why this training is important?
    a. Adverse childhood experiences are linked to chronic health conditions and worsened health outcomes throughout the lifespan.
    b. Medical staff should be asking all patients about their histories with trauma and mandating counseling.
    c. Patients who have experienced adverse childhood experiences are more likely to be involved in a malpractice suit, so staff should be prepared.
    d. All patients with a history of trauma require a social worker to conduct a risk assessment during their hospitalization.

133. Gretchen is working with a family who has lost their home to an area wildfire. The family is devastated, and the social worker is tasked with supporting them to create a plan to move forward after this loss. What is the MOST important thing Gretchen should support this family in initially understanding?
    a. They might find that the normal coping mechanisms they'd use in everyday life are temporarily ineffective.
    b. They need to engage in ongoing therapy or else the crisis will just feel ongoing.
    c. They will likely never reach the level of functioning they had before the fire occurred.

134. Susan is a social worker at a community mental health agency working with a 17-year-old high school student named Ryan. Ryan was referred by his school counselor due to increasing challenges with academics and behavior at school. Among his symptoms, Ryan reports restlessness, mood swings, difficulty focusing, and impulsivity. Ryan and the school staff who made the referral report that these issues began six months ago. Which diagnosis can be ruled out?
   a. Attention-deficit/hyperactivity disorder
   b. Bipolar disorder
   c. Major depressive disorder

135. Mariana is a social worker at a psychiatric residential program. She is participating in a treatment team meeting for Jack, a 20-year-old patient who is struggling with mental illness. The goal of the meeting is to discuss barriers to discharge, and Mariana is asked to give her input. Which response BEST represents a person-in-environment framework?
   a. Jack requires psychiatric medication management and further diagnostic testing to diagnose and treat his mental illness before he can be discharged.
   b. Jack would benefit from setting up supportive housing, case management, psychiatric care, and employment resources as part of a safe discharge plan.
   c. Jack needs to take responsibility for his behavior and the ways he created some of these problems before discharge can be successful.
   d. Jack should further explore his childhood and early attachment through psychotherapy to help him better understand his behavior in preparation for discharge.

136. A social worker wants advice from her supervision group about a client she is treating. With the client's permission, she provides the group with a summary that includes the client's characteristics, biopsychosocial history, diagnoses, presenting problem, assessments and impressions, treatment plan, and progress so far. What is it called when a social worker shares this information about a client to improve their care?
   a. Case recording
   b. Quality assurance
   c. Case presentation
   d. Interdisciplinary collaboration

137. Lars is a social worker with a child welfare agency. He is working with a family impacted by the foster care system. His clients are biological mother Maya and her 10- and 6-year-old daughters who have been in foster care for the past year. Maya has completed all requirements in the parenting plan set by Lars, and there's an upcoming court date to determine permanency planning. Which recommendation would likely be the BEST for the children?
   a. Kinship care
   b. Reunification
   c. Adoption
   d. Residential facility

138. Marietta is a social worker within a large school system. She has been tasked by the administration to conduct a thorough analysis of new policies that will impact students and their families throughout the community. Which step should the social worker take FIRST?
   a. Conduct informal interviews with teachers, caregivers, and students within the community.
   b. Look into the potential impacts of these policies on the community.
   c. Delve into the historical background of the issues that led to the creation of these policies.
   d. Assess alternative policies that could be more effective.

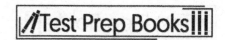

139. Leah is a social worker tasked with running an educational program for other providers on the prevention of child sex trafficking and exploitation. She is teaching about how to recognize signs of trafficking and to identify potential victims. Which statement should she include in her presentation?
    a. All child trafficking is coordinated by gangs or organized criminal groups.
    b. Children who are victims of trafficking are almost always homeless girls.
    c. Children must be held physically captive by a third party to be legally considered victims of trafficking.
    d. Money is not always exchanged during instances of child trafficking or exploitation.

140. Portia is a social worker at a community mental health clinic. She is conducting an intake assessment with her new patient, a 50-year-old male named George who is seeking counseling services for depression. The sessions are going smoothly until Portia asks George about his history of substance use or abuse, and he shuts down and says he does not see why this is relevant. What should Portia do NEXT?
    a. Tell George she respects his decision not to share and do not bring this up again.
    b. Ask George if he has an issue with substance use.
    c. Be transparent about why she is asking and acknowledge this is a difficult topic.
    d. End the session due to George not cooperating with the treatment expectations.

141. You are a social worker at an outpatient mental health practice and are working with a 10-year-old girl. Your approach has been immensely validating and empathetic, and the child appears to be comfortable engaging with you during sessions. Lately, she has appeared sad and withdrawn, which is a contrast to her normal presentation. You are working with her to identify these feelings and normalize them. What is the NEXT thing you should do?
    a. Create a plan to address sad feelings over time.
    b. Administer the Patient Health Questionnaire-2 (PHQ2).
    c. Make a good faith report to Child Protective Services (CPS), given the child's drastic change in presentation.
    d. Speak to the child's caregiver(s) about the concern.

142. What is the goal of building rapport with a client?
    a. Laying the foundation for a relationship based on mutual trust, empathy, and acceptance
    b. Gaining an understanding of the client's presenting problem
    c. Deciding if the social worker wants to work with the client
    d. Completing the informed consent process

143. Sergio is a 45-year-old who has been in his current position for four months. He is working with a social worker on challenges in communication with his peers at work. He reports struggling with shyness and feelings of isolation. His social worker asks him to consider a time in which he did have a successful communication with a colleague, even if it was brief. What method of treatment is the social worker likely using?
    a. Solution-focused treatment
    b. Psychodynamic therapy
    c. Cognitive behavioral therapy

144. Jared is a social worker at a middle school who is meeting with Leon, an 11-year-old sixth grade student. Leon recently started at the middle school after being placed in foster care. Leon's teachers report that he is struggling to focus in his classes, and his academic performance has suddenly dropped. Jared plans to meet with Leon regularly to provide extra support. What is the MOST likely cause of Leon's struggles at school?
    a. Leon is showing the signs of an autism spectrum disorder and would benefit from further testing.
    b. Leon is experiencing the developmentally normal academic decline that occurs during the transition from sixth to seventh grade.
    c. Leon is experiencing adverse effects from traumatic experiences and removal from his home.

177

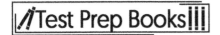

145. Alex is a social worker at a nursing home. She is meeting with Violet, an 80-year-old resident who has reported a change in mood. Violet has been living at the facility for several years and was previously very involved in their social activities and has several family members nearby who visit often. Recently, Violet has withdrawn from many of these activities and tells Alex she is feeling depressed. When Alex asks about recent changes, Violet reports that she went on a new medication recently. What should Alex do FIRST?
    a. Recommend that a doctor examine Violet to rule out a medical cause and medication side effects.
    b. Contact Violet's children to inform them of the concerns and suggest they visit more often.
    c. Create a treatment plan with Violet to meet weekly for CBT sessions to address the depression.
    d. Recommend that Violet be evaluated for antidepressant medication.

146. Donna is a social worker in a small rural community where she runs a private practice. She has been in recovery from an alcohol use disorder for 20 years. She attends an AA meeting one evening and shares a bit of her story. Afterwards, she is approached by Henry, a client who was also present. Henry didn't know that Donna was also in recovery and is upset by the situation. He has questions about Donna's recovery and says that he wishes she'd felt comfortable telling him about it. He wants to discuss this during their next session. This program is the only AA group in their county. What should Donna do NEXT?
    a. Apologize and agree to transfer Henry to a new social worker so they can both continue to attend the AA program without creating a dual relationship.
    b. Consider the conflicting ethical dilemmas presented, determine how to prioritize them in her response to do the least harm, and seek consultation on this issue.
    c. Explain to Henry that she will not discuss this further with him because she's uncomfortable with the level of self-disclosure and that this violates client/social worker boundaries.
    d. Agree to meet with Henry to answer his questions about her recovery in order to preserve the therapeutic relationship because the Code of Ethics indicates that the value of human relationships should be prioritized in this scenario.

147. Jen is a social worker at a skilled nursing facility. She is meeting with Ellie, an 85-year-old resident who recently moved into the facility. Jen has been engaging in rapport building and get-to-know-you activities with Ellie, as she does with all new residents. Which activity would BEST support Ellie's current psychosocial stage of development?
    a. Helping Ellie with advance directive paperwork to make her end-of-life and medical wishes known
    b. Facilitating conversations with Ellie focused on reflection and life review
    c. Assisting Ellie in an application to Medicaid to help subsidize the cost of her nursing home care
    d. Contacting Ellie's children on a monthly basis to provide updates on how she is doing at the facility

148. Andrew is a social worker at a community mental health clinic. He has been meeting with his patient Mark for several months but does not feel like they are making much progress treating Mark's symptoms of depression. Mark is a 22-year-old man who was referred by his primary care provider for symptoms of depression. After consulting his supervisor, Andrew decides to suggest that Mark would be better served by a dual diagnosis program. What does this recommendation indicate?
    a. Mark is struggling with both substance use and depression.
    b. Mark needs inpatient hospital level of care.
    c. Mark has both medical and psychiatric symptoms that need treatment.
    d. Mark requires a medication management program.

149. Joy has been in treatment for social anxiety with a social worker, Ursula, for about three weeks. Last week, Ursula asked Joy to walk to her local coffee shop and order her coffee instead of having it delivered to her home. Joy agreed to the assignment at the time, but during her session today, she reports that she did not attempt the assignment. What should Ursula do NEXT?
    a. End the session early and ask Joy to attempt the assignment before returning.
    b. Assign an alternative assignment.
    c. Explore potential barriers to completing this homework.

150. Maura is a licensed social worker who works with a mobile crisis program meeting with Jane, a 40-year-old woman who called for support due to feeling overwhelmed. After conducting a thorough biopsychosocial and risk assessment, Maura determines that Jane is safe to remain in a community setting and works with her to develop a safety plan, connect her to increased support, and set up a counseling referral with a first appointment later in the week. What does Maura need to do NEXT?
    a. Document her assessment, intervention, and safety plan.
    b. Contact Jane's primary care provider to update them on the situation.
    c. Obtain supervision to discuss this case and her assessment.

151. Whitney is a social worker working with a sex offender program out of her local community mental health organization. This job has always been fulfilling, but she has found lately that her patience is limited, and she's struggling to find compassion for the clients she serves. She has been reflecting on her capacity to do her job effectively and is overwhelmed with how to manage these feelings. What is the BEST way for Whitney to approach this situation?
    a. Take vacation time from work.
    b. Explore new positions.
    c. Begin to journal her feelings before and after work every day.
    d. Bring up her concerns in supervision.

152. Marcus is a social worker with a home health agency that works with elders living in the community. He is facilitating a family meeting with his patient Darlene and her daughter Kathy, who is her live-in caregiver. Darlene is an 80-year-old woman diagnosed with dementia, and Kathy has been caring for her for many years as her illness progressed. In prior meetings, they have both shared that their goal is for Darlene to remain at home. During the meeting, Kathy shares she is feeling overwhelmed and cannot do this anymore. What should Marcus do NEXT?
    a. Refer Kathy to the agency support group for caregivers of dementia patients.
    b. Contact Elder Protective Services to inform them that Darlene is without a caregiver.
    c. Begin the process to place Darlene in a nursing home.
    d. Provide support and active listening to Kathy and ask her to share more.

153. Which social work interviewing technique is used to bring together important points that have been discussed, reflect on progress made, and ensure that the social worker and client are on the same page at the end of a session?
    a. Asking open-ended questions
    b. Validating
    c. Clarifying
    d. Summarizing

154. Georgina is a social work supervisor at an outpatient mental health organization. She notes that her supervisee, Jules, benefits from experiencing in a very hands-on manner and would rather process experiences after they happen rather than leading up to them. Jules has a strong intuition and seems excited at the prospect of doing and trying new things. Because of this, she tends to schedule their supervision for the end of the week, at which time they are able to process the week more in depth. According to David Kolb's stages of learning model, which learning style has Georgina learned that Jules BEST matches?
    a. Diverging
    b. Accommodating
    c. Assimilating
    d. Converging

155. Jeff is a social worker in a psychiatric hospital, conducting a diagnostic assessment on a recently admitted patient named Heather. Heather is being treated for symptoms of depression, and her hospitalization is focused on stabilization of symptoms and medication management. Jeff is considering a diagnosis of either major depression or dysthymia. What question would BEST help him rule out the less accurate diagnosis?
   a. Asking about how long symptoms have been present for
   b. Asking about changes in appetite and sleep
   c. Asking about comorbid substance use
   d. Asking about depressed mood

156. A social worker is working with a client who has great difficulty saying no to his boss's requests, even when the requests are unreasonable and result in the client being overwhelmed by extra work. The social worker shows the client a video of a conversation between a boss and an employee in which the boss is pushy, but the employee remains assertive. What type of modeling is this?
   a. Live modeling
   b. Symbolic modeling
   c. Covert modeling
   d. Participant modeling

157. Krista is a social worker in the juvenile justice system who is providing court-ordered counseling to Nicole, a 13-year-old female client. During their first session, Nicole tells Krista that it wasn't her choice to be here and that, although she's required to come to the sessions, she won't be talking. Nicole presents as angry and frustrated, sitting with her arms crossed in the chair furthest away from Krista. What should Krista do FIRST?
   a. Validate Nicole's emotions and offer choices on how to spend the session.
   b. Explain the consequences if she chooses not to engage in the mandated therapy.
   c. Ask Nicole to fill out the standard biopsychosocial assessment form together.
   d. Share her own history of juvenile justice involvement to build rapport.

158. Jorge is a social worker who has been meeting with a 17-year-old client, Mark, for three weeks to address anxiety. During session, Jorge asks about Mark's upcoming symphony band performance. Mark becomes visibly anxious during the conversation and begins to cry. He is hyperventilating and struggling to engage in conversation. What is the BEST approach for Jorge to take in this situation?
   a. Jorge should stay quiet and offer space for Mark to collect his thoughts.
   b. Jorge should dial 911 to access EMS services for Mark, as hyperventilating can be dangerous.
   c. Jorge should vocalize that Mark is likely having a panic attack and is safe. Then Jorge should offer a grounding exercise.

159. Nadia is a social worker who manages the social services department at a large hospital. She is in a meeting with the management team to discuss changes to improve care for patients who have experienced trauma. Nadia suggests implementing universal trauma screenings and providing mandatory education to all hospital employees on the signs and impact of trauma. What model is informing Nadia's suggestions?
   a. Trauma-focused cognitive behavioral therapy
   b. Trauma-informed care
   c. Systems theory
   d. Social learning theory

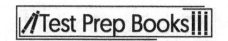

160. You are working in a rural community that is experiencing high rates of poverty. You are new to a position in a grassroots organization that is focused on community organizing. Other members of your team are locals who have lived in the area for several years. What is the FIRST step you should take?
    a. Utilize your team members to conduct outreach to community members.
    b. Organize a fundraising event to build a community center.
    c. Bring these concerns to local government officials to increase funding toward this issue.
    d. Conduct a needs assessment to clearly identify needs and available resources.

161. Which psychotherapy modality is MOST effective for clients with borderline personality disorder?
    a. Psychodynamic therapy
    b. Dialectical behavior therapy
    c. Exposure and response prevention therapy
    d. Cognitive behavioral therapy

162. Simone is a social worker who provides family therapy and counseling. She is meeting with the Robinson family today for their second session, and they are continuing to work on their assessment before discussing treatment goals. The Robinson family consists of two parents and daughters that are 14 and 11 years old. During the session, the family members begin to argue, and scapegoat much of the tension onto the recent behavior of the older child. The child also expresses frustration with the situation and says she doesn't want to participate. How should Simone respond?
    a. Offer individual counseling sessions to each family member until they feel ready to meet together.
    b. Explain they need to work together to set goals or things will not improve.
    c. De-escalate the immediate conflict, and reflect back what she has observed.
    d. File a Child Protective Services report due to ongoing family conflict and fighting.

163. Vanessa has been hired to evaluate and improve policy for a mental health organization. She is starting by conducting an ethics audit, so her first step is to establish a dedicated committee. What should Vanessa's NEXT step be?
    a. Collect data from reports, policies, interviews, etc.
    b. Establish which policies are low, moderate, and high risk.
    c. Conduct a needs assessment for the organization.

164. Jared is a social worker at a partial hospitalization program for adults. He is meeting with Michael, a 30-year-old patient receiving therapeutic services for anxiety. He is working with Michael to set goals and develop a treatment plan for their time together. Michael sets a goal to use mindfulness several times a week, engage in weekly CBT therapy groups, and participate in sessions with Jared three times a week. Jared also educates Michael on the benefit of trying an anti-anxiety medication to assist with his recovery and offers to make a referral to the program psychiatrist as another part of the treatment plan. Michael refuses, stating that he is not interested in any medication at this time. How should Jared respond?
    a. Explain that this is standard protocol and works well for most patients.
    b. Respect Michael's decision not to take medication at this time.
    c. Tell Michael that he may not be as successful in his recovery without medication.

165. A client expresses that he does not understand why he engages in a particular behavior. The behavior goes against his moral values, makes him uncomfortable, and causes shame and guilt. According to psychoanalytic theory, which term describes the client's behavior?
    a. Preconscious
    b. Unconscious
    c. Ego-syntonic
    d. Ego-dystonic

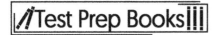
166. Teagan is a social worker in a recovery program for opioid addiction. She is meeting with a client, Brittany, to complete an initial assessment. The client is enthusiastic about moving forward, expressing the desire to move into more stable housing and to work toward getting her cosmetology licensure. What is the FIRST step that Teagan should take?
    a. Order a comprehensive lab panel to screen for substances.
    b. Gather information about Brittany's strengths, needs, and available resources.
    c. Create a comprehensive plan that targets Brittany's stated goals.

167. A social worker is conducting group therapy with women who struggle with alcohol misuse. One woman says that it seems like the local addiction treatment center was made for men, and the rest of the group agrees. The social worker helps them identify the specific ways that the treatment center is not meeting their needs as women. The social worker reminds them of previous group discussions about the unique strengths and abilities they have as women, and together they discuss how they wish the treatment center would acknowledge and build on these strengths. The group decides to work together to advocate for the creation of more inclusive treatment services and asks the social worker for help finding resources to support their efforts. What type of approach is the social worker using?
    a. Harm reduction
    b. Crisis intervention
    c. Empowerment
    d. Behavioral

168. Ann is a social worker in the emergency room. She is asked to meet with Lila, a 13-year-old patient who is being treated for a broken wrist that will require surgery. When Ann arrives at her room, she finds that Lila's parents are not present. Lila is with an older man named Chris, who states he is a friend, and Lila refuses to provide parental contact information even when Ann explains that her parent or guardian needs to consent to the procedure. Ann asks to meet with Lila alone and explains this is protocol, but Chris states he would like to stay with her, and Lila agrees. What should Ann do?
    a. File a Child Protective Services report and request that a worker come to the hospital.
    b. Contact the hospital legal team to find out if there are options for Lila to consent as a minor.
    c. Ask Lila about how she broke her wrist and what caused them to come to the hospital.

169. Lora is working with her local government to facilitate a program to make Naloxone readily accessible to the community. It is the end of the fiscal year, and this program is being assessed to determine funding. Lora's job is to advocate to the board of directors for increased funding allocation for this program. What is the MOST effective method to do so?
    a. Complete an ethics audit.
    b. Collect testimony from community members.
    c. Use goal attainment scaling.
    d. Conduct a summative evaluation.

170. What is a technique used in assertiveness training?
    a. Not taking no for an answer
    b. Using "you" statements
    c. Indirect communication
    d. Using "I" statements

Answer Explanations #1

1. C: When clients are unable to recall information about their early history, the social worker should request permission to pursue secondary data, like school and medical records or interviews with relatives. Choice *A* is incorrect because exploring the client's earliest memories is not likely to elicit the kind of information the social worker needs. Choice *B* is incorrect because the social worker will be able to get more comprehensive, relevant, and objective data by consulting secondary sources rather than instructing the client to ask his relatives. Choice *D* is incorrect because developmental history can have important impacts on the client's current functioning. The social worker should try to uncover this information rather than just skipping it.

2. C: The correct answer is Choice *C*. A broker supports clients by connecting them with appropriate services and resources in the community. Choice *A* is incorrect, as this is a role focused on increasing social functioning, such as by cultivating hope, setting goals, and focusing on behaviors and relationships. Choice *B* is incorrect, as this role encompasses speaking up on behalf of a client or client system. Choice *D* is incorrect, as this role specifically refers to leading in a group setting, such as in group therapy.

3. C: Family life cycle theories describe the development of family systems in terms of stages that families progress through over time. During the launching stage, the children have grown up and are establishing themselves as independent adults. The relationship between parents and their children shifts to accommodate these new roles. During this stage, the parents might also start taking on caregiver roles as their own parents age. Choice *A* is incorrect because finding a suitable lifestyle and life partner happens during the first stage: unattached young adult. Choice *B* is incorrect because establishing a marital system occurs during the newly-married couple stage. Choice *D* is incorrect because transitioning from a marital system to a family system happens during the family with young children stage. Family life cycle theories can provide insight into the challenges that families commonly confront at different times. However, these models are based on a very narrow view of what a family is and do not take into account the many different types of families that are common today. It is important for social workers to remember that each individual and family is unique.

4. B: Sexual dysfunction describes problems with sexual desire, performance, or both. It can be caused by medical, psychological, and lifestyle factors. The first thing a social worker should do to assist a client with sexual dysfunction is refer them to a physician for a medical evaluation. It is important to determine if there is a medical problem first before exploring other potential causes. If problems persist after medical explanations are ruled out, then it would be appropriate to explore psychological factors, Choices *A* and *C*, or lifestyle factors, Choice *D*, that may be contributing to the problem.

5. B: Networking may provide social workers with additional resources to assist their clients. Networking may be performed at conferences, meetings, and trainings. Networking may also be interdisciplinary in nature, and the worker may network with medical, legal, and psychological professions. The social worker may network within the capacity of their employment scope. Networking is a vital part of social work. It can be helpful to reach out to those met while networking during difficult cases.

6. C: The social worker should reassure Jane that being a victim does not mean she will automatically become an abuser. It is not a myth that abuse survivors are more likely to perpetuate abuse, and the social worker should be honest about that. The cycle of abuse is real and occurs with all types of abuse. However, being at an increased risk does not mean that it is destiny. Most survivors of abuse do not hurt their children, and many abusers were not abused as children. Processing the trauma of the abuse, healing attachment problems, and learning coping, communication, and self-regulation skills can all help abuse survivors prepare for parenthood. It would be inappropriate, unethical, and harmful to recommend that someone not have children because they are a victim of abuse.

183

7. D: Jim's symptoms are most likely substance-induced. Jim's age, lack of psychiatric history, lack of medical conditions, and sudden onset of psychotic symptoms make a primary psychotic disorder like schizophrenia, Choice *A,* highly unlikely. Psychotic disorders usually develop in men during their teens and twenties. Sudden onset schizophrenia in a 42-year-old male is extremely unusual. Additionally, the chronic stuffy nose, long hours working, and hallucination of formication ("bugs under the skin") are indications that he may be using cocaine or another stimulant drug. Choices *C* (bipolar I disorder) and *B* (depression with psychotic features) are incorrect because Jim has no history or current symptoms of a mood disorder.

8. C: According to the *DSM-5-TR*, Mr. X meets the full criteria for major depressive disorder. For at least two weeks, he has been experiencing at least five depressive symptoms, and at least one symptom is depressed mood or loss of interest/pleasure. This represents a change from his previous functioning and is not related to a medical disorder. In a previous edition of the *DSM* (*DSM-IV*), major depressive disorder was not diagnosed within two months of a death. This was called the "bereavement exclusion," which has been eliminated in the *DSM-5-TR*. This is due to the recognition that, although grief and depression share some features, they are distinct conditions. Clients who meet the full criteria for depression should be offered appropriate treatment regardless of whether the depression occurred in the context of grief. Choice *A* is incorrect because bereavement disorder is not a diagnosis. Choice *B* is incorrect because dysthymia is chronic depression that occurs over at least two years. Choice *D* is incorrect because adjustment disorder with depressed mood is diagnosed when someone experiences depressive symptoms in response to a psychosocial stressor but does not meet the full criteria for major depressive disorder.

9. C: The NASW Code of Ethics provides guidance on how to set fees for social workers in private practice. It states that fees must be "fair, reasonable, and commensurate with services," and that fees should take into consideration "a client's ability to pay." Offering reduced fees on a sliding scale to low-income clients is one way to set fees ethically and fairly. The NASW Code of Ethics was updated in 2017 to include guidance on offering pro bono services. Specifically, the section on the social work value of service encourages social workers to offer at least some services pro bono. Pro bono means "for the public good," and in this context refers to providing services without charging a fee. For these reasons, both a sliding scale and pro bono services are ethical and even encouraged in the profession.

10. B: Family systems approaches view family dynamics through the lens of system theory, which considers how different parts of the family interact and shape each other. Using this approach, the child's behavior is seen in the context of the family dynamics. Sometimes one member of a family will manifest symptoms of the entire family's dysfunction. This person is called the scapegoat or symptom bearer and is often incorrectly blamed for the family's problems. The child's symptoms are a result of family dysfunction, not a cause of the dysfunction. To improve the child's symptoms, the social worker must help the family repair its dysfunction. Family systems theory also considers the role of genetics, parenting, and social learning, but from the information given in the example, none of these is the best explanation for the child's problems. Because the child's symptoms arose immediately following recent changes in the family's stress level and finances, it is more likely that changing family dynamics are responsible.

11. D: The man's symptoms are best explained by malingering, which involves faking symptoms for external gain. In this case, the man is faking delusions and hallucinations to obtain long term disability, so he doesn't have to work. Choice *A* is incorrect because his alleged symptoms have lasted longer than one month. Choice *B* is incorrect because his alleged symptoms are not consistent with schizophrenia or any actual psychotic disorder. For example, the symptoms began suddenly, with no prodrome, in a middle-aged male with no psychiatric or medical history. He has no negative symptoms, no mood symptoms, no cognitive symptoms, and no difficulty with hygiene. Choice *C* is incorrect because factitious disorder involves faking symptoms when there are no obvious external rewards.

12. A: Psychoeducation involves providing information to help clients understand their problems. Psychoeducation helps clients learn about the nature of the problem, its causes and effects, and different treatment options and resources that are available. One purpose of psychoeducation is to provide clients with the vocabulary they need to

talk about their experiences. In the example, the participant used the word *junkie*, which is stigmatizing, ill-defined, and not a useful way to describe a person's situation. Because this is the first group meeting, it is important for the social worker to set the tone, make it clear that stigmatizing language is unhelpful and unwelcome in the group, and provide alternative vocabulary to foster a more effective discussion.

Choice *B* is incorrect because it challenges the participant's beliefs rather than addressing the real issue, which is the participant's choice of words. Choice *C* is incorrect because the situation is an opportunity to get the whole group on the same page about language. Also, pulling the participant aside might make them feel singled out and does not reassure the rest of the group that this type of language will not be used in the future. Choice *D* is incorrect because this is the first meeting of the group, so the social worker should create a safe atmosphere and establish rules and expectations for the group. A failure to react communicates that stigmatizing language is acceptable, which could make other participants feel unsafe and unwilling to participate.

13. A: Susan has knowledge that Christine has a history of drug abuse. Christine has shown signs of possible relapse. Susan also has safety concerns for Christine's children based on what she has seen and the way Christine has behaved. Due to her concerns, a good faith report is warranted, which will require that Susan break confidentiality to report the suspected child abuse and neglect.

14. C: Cocaine use disorder is most likely because of the client's combination of physical symptoms (sniffling, dilated pupils, restlessness, talking quickly, irritability, sleep disturbance, mood, and attitude changes) and increasing negative life consequences (missing work, arguing with his wife, overspending, and withdrawal from previous activities). Choice *A* is incorrect because his behavior is causing problems rather than the circumstances of his life causing stress. Choice *B* is incorrect because, although alcohol use disorder shares similar negative consequences, the physical signs are different. The sniffling, dilated pupils, and talking quickly are especially indicative of cocaine use. Choice *D* is incorrect because narcolepsy is a medical condition that causes daytime sleepiness but not any of the other issues he is having.

15. C: The correct answer is Choice *C*, recommend he see his primary care provider if he has not done so already to rule out any medical explanation for these changes. It is critical that social workers are able to recognize when patients report changes or symptoms that could have a medical explanation and have them ruled out by a medical provider. This patient shared symptoms that may be related to depression but could also be neurological changes related to medical illness or disease. While the other answers listed could be appropriate responses in the future, the first step is for the patient to consult with his primary care provider to ensure these symptoms do not have an organic cause.

16. D: The social worker should obtain supervision to discuss the situation. She should only proceed if they determine together that it is professionally justified. In general, social workers should always consult a supervisor before making a self-disclosure. Choice *A* is incorrect because it still involves a self-disclosure that the social worker is unsure about. Choice *B* is incorrect because it is not the client's decision whether the social worker uses self-disclosure. Choice *C* is incorrect because it does not help the social worker determine if self-disclosure would help the client. It also does not provide the social worker with an opportunity to improve their services by learning how to manage the situation if it comes up again in the future.

17. B: A genogram is a tool that can be used to identify patterns in a family. It is a visual representation of a client and their family that tracks generational patterns of behavior, emotions, relationships, psychosocial functioning, and tendencies. Choice *A* is incorrect because an ecogram is a visual representation of a client and various aspects of their environment. Choice *C* is incorrect because medical issues are only one of many components of a family history. Choice *D* is incorrect because it does not cover the depth and breadth of information that a genogram does.

18. D: The man is suffering from co-occurring alcohol use disorder and depression. The most effective treatment for co-occurring disorders is integrative treatment, which address both at the same time. Many people, including

185

healthcare professionals, assume that substance use disorders must be treated before other issues can be addressed, as in Choice *B*, but this is not accurate. In fact, treating co-occurring disorders one at a time is not only less effective, but it can cause symptoms to worsen. This is because treatment requires change, which is stressful, and it can cause the person to increase their use of other maladaptive behaviors to cope. Treating both disorders at once allows the treatment team to monitor and respond to behavioral changes that arise during treatment.

Choice *C* is incorrect because treating his depression before treating the alcohol use disorder is unlikely to be effective. Excessive alcohol consumption contributes to depression since alcohol is a central nervous system depressant. Alcohol can also interact with antidepressants. Choice *A* is incorrect because the disorders should be treated simultaneously. Some people believe that if disorder started first, then it must have caused the other disorder, and so treating the first disorder will naturally fix the second. Although this may be true in some cases, it is impossible to determine causality with certainty. The man in the example may have started drinking to deal with his depression. Conversely, the drinking could have caused his depression. However, it is also possible that the two disorders are not causally related and would have both occurred anyway. Regardless of which assumptions one makes about what caused the disorders and how they are related, it is always best to treat both at the same time.

19. C: The correct answer is Choice *C*, explain the mandated reporting obligation and limits to confidentiality. Social workers have an obligation to make a mandated report if they learn that someone may be at risk of harm to themselves or others, or if they are experiencing harm. This is especially true if the harm is coming to a minor or vulnerable person. While it's true that there is usually confidentiality, Martin is obligated to answer Jordan honestly here. While asking why she's asking this may be helpful, it should not be his first response.

20. D: The social worker should contact the social work board of the state she is moving to. The board can help her navigate the process of becoming licensed to practice in the state. Different states have different licensing requirements. Some states allow social workers to simply transfer their licenses, while others have additional requirements that need to be fulfilled first. Choice *A* is incorrect because the NASW sets the standards for the social work profession as a whole, while state boards oversee licensing in their state. Choice *B* is incorrect because the CSWE is the body that accredits social work education programs. A degree from a CSWE-accredited program is a basic requirement for social workers. Choice *C* is incorrect because the social work board in the state the social worker lives in now deals with licensing in that state. They would not be able to help her navigate the licensing process of the state she is moving to.

21. A: A delusion of reference is a fixed, false belief that people, things, and events in the environment have special, personal meaning. People with psychotic disorders sometimes experience this type of delusion. An example would be a person believing that a TV news bulletin, song on the radio, or conversation between strangers are full of personal messages. Choice *B* is incorrect because a delusion of control is a false belief that one's body is being manipulated or controlled by an outside entity, like a marionette. Choice *C* is incorrect because a grandiose delusion involves a false belief that one is extremely wealthy, powerful, intelligent, or otherwise exceptional. Choice *D* is incorrect because a persecutory delusion involves a false belief that one is being persecuted, monitored, or harassed by another person or organization.

22. C: Hilda's mother is her court-appointed legal guardian, which means that Hilda cannot legally provide her own informed consent for treatment. The social worker should still have the informed consent conversation with Hilda (including the role of her mother), make sure she understands, and seek her assent. Then, the social worker should have a similar conversation with her mother and have her mother sign the informed consent documents. Choice *A* is incorrect because even though Hilda can't provide informed consent, she should still be given all of the relevant information in language that she understands. It is especially important for her to understand the limits of her confidentiality and her mother's access to her records. Choice *B* is incorrect because Hilda cannot legally sign the informed consent. Also, the social worker should not listen to Hilda's entire story before obtaining Hilda's assent and her mother's consent. Choice *D* is incorrect because consulting a supervisor is not necessary; the legal, ethical, and organizational standards are clear that Hilda's mother must provide informed consent.

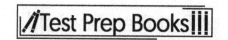

23. D: When assigning homework, it is important for social workers to clearly explain why it is important and how it connects to the client's goals. Keeping a log of the outbursts will reveal patterns that Karen may not be aware of and clarify why the outbursts occur. This information will allow Karen and Juan to collaborate on a treatment plan that will effectively reduce the outbursts. By explaining this, Juan is making a connection between doing homework and achieving her goal of reducing the outbursts. Logging behaviors, feelings, and thoughts is an example of client self-monitoring. Self-monitoring techniques can be used to translate vague, subjective experiences (e.g., "I have outbursts, but I don't know why") into data that can be acted on (e.g., "When I feel disrespected, I lose control; it happens more frequently and severely if I am hungry or tired").

In this example, an intervention might focus on techniques for managing the feeling of being disrespected as well as creating a routine that ensures she is well-rested and eating regularly. Choice *A* is incorrect because even though doing the homework is likely to make Karen feel more involved and empowered in her treatment, telling her this without explaining why the homework is important is not likely to increase her motivation to do it. Also, increasing discipline is not one of the goals of her treatment. Choice *B* is incorrect because telling Karen that homework is required for her treatment plan does not help her understand why it is important. It also makes the treatment plan sound like something imposed on her rather than something she is collaborating on. Choice *C* is incorrect because the goal of tracking the outbursts is not to reduce the outbursts but to understand why they occur so that they can intervene effectively.

24. A: The correct answer is Choice *A*, ecomap. An ecomap explores the client's relationships, community support systems, and the strength of these connections and highlights areas where support could be increased. This could be useful in assessing her natural supports that may already exist and starting a conversation about the resources needed in a collaborative and non-judgmental manner. A genogram would only focus on family relationships, which may not be relevant for her. A needs assessment would not be appropriate, as this is a tool for program development. The Columbia Scale may be a useful tool in her overall assessment but would focus on suicide risk factors, not specifically examine her support system.

25. A: Psychological defense mechanisms are strategies used to manage unacceptable feelings and impulses. People are usually not aware that they are using a defense mechanism in the moment; it is more of a reaction than a choice. The teenager's behavior is an example of displacement. He felt angry at the bully, but he was scared. Expressing his anger to the bully directly felt unsafe, so instead he displaced that anger onto a safer target—in this case, his little sister. Sublimation involves channeling unacceptable feelings into healthy, acceptable outlets. For example, if the teenager returned home and went for a run to get his anger out, that would be sublimation. Projection involves attributing one's own unacceptable feelings to someone else. For example, perhaps the bully feels weak, and this is unacceptable to him. Instead of confronting these feelings, he might project them onto others by bullying them for being weak. This is his mind's attempt to deal with the feelings of weakness without having to admit or fully experience them. Repression involves pushing unacceptable feelings away. People can repress feelings to the point where they experience amnesia and have trouble remembering certain painful experiences.

26. D: Social workers are mandated reporters, which means that by law they have to report suspected elder abuse. This situation poses an ethical dilemma because Teresa does not want her son to be reported; however, the law is clear that the social worker must make the report. It is important to inform Teresa so that she won't be taken by surprise.

27. C: Clara should clarify the role of the social worker with Jan. It is not the role of the social worker to become a client's support system. The fact that Jan thinks of Clara as a maternal figure indicates that she has become dependent on Clara, which will ultimately inhibit her progress in therapy. Choice *A* is incorrect because although it might be tempting to see Jan's comment as a compliment, the comment is actually a sign that there may be problems in the therapeutic relationship. Choice *B* is incorrect because it does not address Jan's dependency on

Clara. Jan's goal is to work through her grief, not to find a replacement for her lost mother. Choice *D* is incorrect because Clara does not need to consult with a supervisor before addressing the comment.

28. B: The correct answer is Choice *B*, obtain Jacob's permission to contact the case worker and have him sign a release of information. Social workers need client permission and a signed release of information to contact collateral or past providers. This is an appropriate step in an assessment, but Claudia needs to obtain Jacob's permission to do so. He is allowed to refuse in this situation.

29. D: The supervisor should reassure the social worker that the boy's behavior is normal and developmentally appropriate, and it does not indicate abuse or sexualization. Children between ages two and five are curious about their bodies and do not feel embarrassed about nudity. It is normal for children this age to learn names for their genitals and to understand that males and females have different bodies. Nothing about the boy's behavior warrants a report to child protective services, Choice *A*. The fact that the child knows his father also has a "pee pee" does not indicate that the father is abusing the boy. It would not be appropriate to tell the child's mother that the father might be doing something inappropriate based on the information given, Choice *B*. Choice *C* is incorrect because the boy's behavior is totally normal and expected for his age. If the behavior were to persist into the child's elementary school years, it would start to become a cause for concern about the child's development.

30. C: Institutional Review Boards (IRBs) approve and monitor research studies that use human subjects. The NASW Code of Ethics encourages social workers to contribute to the development of knowledge in the profession, and doing research is one way to accomplish this. Social workers conducting research on human subjects have an ethical obligation to protect those subjects from harm and must obtain IRB approval before beginning the study. IRBs can approve a study, recommend changes, and monitor the study process for any ethical concerns that may arise.

31. D: The social worker should provide psychoeducation on diabetes and explain how managing the condition will facilitate her social and professional goals. The social worker should also explain how leaving the diabetes untreated will create obstacles, making it more difficult to achieve her current goals and creating new problems at the same time. Showing the client Maslow's hierarchy could be helpful depending on the client's learning style. However, the goal is not to convince the client that the therapist is right and she is wrong, Choice *C*, but rather to help her draw connections between her physical health and other aspects of her life. Transferring the client to another social worker should not be the first response because it does not help the client to understand and improve her situation, Choice *B*. The social worker could compromise by agreeing to pursue some aspects of her social or professional goals and her medical condition simultaneously. However, this should not be framed as pursuing a promotion so the client can pay for insulin, Choice *A*. This is backwards; the social worker should find other resources to make the insulin affordable so that the client is healthy enough to pursue a promotion.

32. D: The social worker should encourage Mary to focus on how the panic attacks have been affecting her over the past week or two. This is the initial session, so the social worker should identify Mary's chief complaint and get a sense of her current situation. It could be that the other topics Mary brought up are related to her current problem, but that should be explored later when discussing Mary's history as part of the biopsychosocial assessment. Choices *A*, *B*, and *C* are incorrect because they should be discussed in the context of Mary's social history after the chief complaint has been identified.

33. C: The correct answer is Choice *C*, conduct a thorough risk assessment. A thorough and evidence-based risk assessment is indicated here due to Daniel's statement. While hospitalization, a safety contract, or involving his family may or may not be necessary based on the outcome of that risk assessment, they would not be the first step. More information is needed before choosing the appropriate intervention.

34. D: According to the NASW Code of Ethics, if a social worker believes that a colleague's ability to provide service to clients is compromised, they must first go directly to that colleague with their concerns and help them develop a

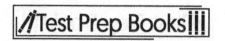

plan to address them. This applies to cases where a colleague is impaired by a substance, an illness, or another stressor (in this case, divorce) that affects their ability to do their job.

35. C: A Thematic Appreciation Test (TAT) is used to explore a client's perceptions, needs, motivations, conflicts, and desires. The pictures are intentionally ambiguous, and the client's reactions to them can uncover subconscious information that the client may not be aware of. Choice *A*, Beck Depression Inventory (BDI), is a relatively short test that asks a series of questions to determine the level of depression symptoms the client is currently experiencing. Choice *B*, the Minnesota Multiphasic Personality Inventory (MMPI), is an extensive personality test that asks a series of questions to assess the client's level of psychopathology. Choice *D*, Myers-Briggs Type Indicator (MBTI), is a personality test that asks a series of questions to assign clients a personality type based on four dimensions (extraverted/introverted, sensing/intuition, thinking/feeling, and judging/perceiving). The result is an MBTI type, such as INTJ.

36. C: The social worker should establish boundaries with the client regarding the private therapy relationship and the group therapy relationship. Treating a client in private and group therapy is an example of a dual relationship, but according to the NASW Code of Ethics, some dual relationships are unavoidable and can be ethical as long as no harm comes to the client. Terminating with the client would not be ethical. The social worker could advocate for the agency to start another group, but this would not solve the immediate problem of meeting the client's needs.

37. B: The correct answer is Choice *B*, listen actively and engage with Shirley's story about meeting her husband. Social workers use active listening to build rapport, gather information, and meet the client where they are at. In this situation, it's appropriate to pause the assessment and listen to where the client is at right now. While the grief group or education may be helpful interventions in the future, these should not be what Carter does first.

38. A: Magical thinking is associated with the preoperational stage of cognitive development, which occurs between ages two and seven. Magical thinking involves believing events are connected when they are not. Because young children are egocentric, they often believe that they have more influence over the events around them than they actually do. For example, a child calls his sister a name. The sister gets sick. The child believes his sister got sick because he called her a name. As children develop cognitively, magical thinking is replaced by more logical thinking and a better understanding of cause and effect. The formal operations stage is the final stage of Piaget's model. It represents the most mature thinking processes. People who have reached this stage are able to think abstractly at a high level, Choice *B*; effectively plan for the future, Choice *C*; and think hypothetically, Choice *D*. This level of cognitive development allows people to take on adult roles and responsibilities.

39. D: The social worker should acknowledge the cultural difference and see if the client is willing to explore it together. If the client is totally unwilling to work with the social worker, it would be appropriate to refer them to another practitioner. However, she should first try to have a conversation about cultural differences and how they affect the client, the social worker, and the helping relationship. The social worker should demonstrate comfort and curiosity during this conversation, as well as a willingness to acknowledge how her own values and beliefs are shaped by culture.

40. D: It is not ethical for the social worker to call herself an art therapy practitioner because she has not completed all of the steps required to practice ethically in a new area. In addition to study and training, she would also need to consult with and receive supervision from professionals with experience in art therapy. This is important because it provides ongoing support to the social worker as she begins treating clients in this new modality. The other choices are incorrect because attending a training and receiving a certificate is not sufficient to gain competence in a new area, and an internship is not required to practice art therapy.

41. B: The correct answer is Choice *B*. Encouragement from the other group members can facilitate feelings of inclusion and is proven more effective. Choice *A* is incorrect, as when withdrawing behaviors are identified and dealt with early in treatment, there is a greater likelihood of improvement. Choice *C* is incorrect, as a social worker will

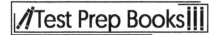

inherently present a power dynamic that can lead to Patricia feeling targeted and under undue pressure to participate. Choice *D* is incorrect, as although this conversation might be helpful down the line, early on in treatment it is more appropriate to encourage participation.

42. B: The policy described in Choice *B* is a red flag for potential safety issues because it requires a client to display unsafe behavior three times before action is taken. A better policy would be to have a clear process for employees to report any unsafe client behavior as soon as it occurs and a clear set of steps for addressing it. All employees should be familiar with this procedure and have confidence that using it will not result in penalty or reprisal from the agency.

43. B: Ferdman and Gallegos's theory of Latino identity development is not a linear model in which people progress from one stage to the next. Instead, it involves six different lenses or orientations through which Latino people come to view their identity. Which lens they adopt is dependent on several factors, including their family, their peer group, and their experiences growing up, going to school, and interacting with social institutions. The model shows that Latino identities are multifaceted, involving a variety of ethnic, racial, and cultural identities. Monica views her ethnicity through the subgroup identified lens. This means that she recognizes the existence of multiple Latino races, and as a Mexican American, she identifies as Chicana. Choice *A* is incorrect because the undifferentiated lens describes people who consider themselves "colorblind," who are aligned with the dominant culture, and who attribute their struggles to personal failure rather than discrimination. Choice *C* is incorrect because the white identified lens describes people who recognize the existence of Latino and white races and identify as white. Choice *D* is incorrect because the Latino identified lens describes people who recognize the existence of Latino and white races and identify as Latino.

44. B: The correct answer is Choice *B*, ask Sarah about the injury and conduct a risk assessment. More information is required here to make a determination about safety and appropriate next steps; therefore, Laura needs to continue her assessment. If she determines that Sarah is at risk of harm, a mandated report may be warranted, but there is not enough information here to determine that yet. Counseling may be useful, but again, it would not be the next step. Laura cannot contact the pediatrician without a release of information from Sarah's parents or guardian.

45. A: Setting and maintaining professional boundaries is the responsibility of the social worker. Choice *B* is incorrect because boundaries are not co-created by the client. Social workers take client characteristics into account when setting culturally appropriate boundaries, but it is not the responsibility of the client to set boundaries. Choice *C* is incorrect because professional boundaries are determined by the social worker, not the setting. Choice *D* is incorrect because setting and maintaining professional boundaries is something all social workers must do.

46. A: The correct answer is Choice *A*. The Gottman Method is focused on improving communication by eliminating harmful language and managing conflict resolution. Choice *B* is incorrect, as this reflects an Emotionally Focused Therapy (EFT) approach. Choice *C* is incorrect, as this describes an approach guided by the Imago Relationship Therapy model.

47. C: The values in conflict are the importance of human relationships and competence. Mikhail wants to maintain a positive relationship with his boss, and he is concerned that saying no to this assignment could harm that relationship. On the other hand, because of his lack of training and experience, he would be practicing outside the scope of his competence.

48. B: Erikson's stages of psychosocial development theory best supports Jasmine's response that Miranda's behavior is developmentally appropriate. This theory breaks human development into age-based stages that build upon each other. Each stage features a key conflict that the individual must overcome as a part of healthy development. The stage for adolescents is *identity vs. role confusion*; and exploring one's identity, craving independence, and valuing peer relationships are core tenets of this stage. Miranda appears to be doing well

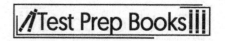

socially and academically, which suggests positive and healthy development for an adolescent. Therefore, this theory affirms Jasmine's explanation of Miranda's behavior.

49. C: The correct answer is Choice *C*, strengths and resources. Social workers need to take care to ask about and identify strengths, resources, and positive connections that clients already have during their assessment and not only focus on problems or challenges. Most social workers take a strengths-based approach, which is the belief that all clients already have unique strengths and resources, and part of the role of the social worker is to identify these and help them be applied. Josie's assessment contained a lot of useful information but did not focus on identifying these types of strengths.

50. A: Research has shown that although men and women tend to follow the same basic pattern of self-esteem throughout the lifespan, certain differences can be observed. Self-esteem tends to be high in early childhood and then declines through later childhood and adolescence. In adulthood, self-esteem steadily rises in both men and women; however, men tend to have higher self-esteem than women during this period. As adults continue to age, the difference between men's and women's self-esteem decreases; by very old age, women's tends to be higher than men's. Gender is one factor that affects self-esteem throughout the lifespan, but it is important to remember that these are population trends, and every individual is unique.

51. A: The supervisor should explain to Andre that it is unethical to include extraneous personal information about clients that is unrelated to treatment in a client's record. Client records are not merely notes to aid the social worker. Under certain circumstances, they can be seen by the client, other professionals, or the courts. A good general rule is to not include anything in a client file that one would not want to read aloud in court. Although Andre's method clearly helped him with memory, it is not ethical, and the supervisor must help him find a different solution to replace his current one.

52. D: The correct answer is Choice *D*. Jennifer is in the contemplation stage of change, as although she is identifying concerns with her current behavior, she is still weighing the pros and cons of engaging in change. The best thing a social worker can do for her is continue to support her in this process to increase change talk. Choice *A* is incorrect, as this approach is used in the preparation stage, when a client is fully ready to make a change. Choice *B* is incorrect, as this is usually a tactic reserved for the precontemplation stage, in which a client is unwilling to explore change or recognize there is an issue. Choice *C* is incorrect, as this approach should be used when the client has already made the change and is working to maintain their progress.

53. C: The best practice for social workers is to not accept bartered services or goods in lieu of payment for social work services. While there are rare and specific situations where this may be allowed, it is generally considered an unethical practice that places the client at risk for exploitation or harm. Option *C* is the best choice because the social worker is not accepting bartered services but is acknowledging the challenges of the client's financial situation and offering options to assist. Utilizing agency services for financial assistance is the more ethical choice. Choice *B* is incorrect because it is also not allowable to waive the copay when utilizing insurance coverage unless this has been specifically allowed by the insurance provider.

54. D: Maslow devised his last level during his later years and referred to it as self-transcendence. Achievement of this goal relies on experiencing a greater sense of spiritual growth and practicing one's beliefs on a deeper level. Previously, self-actualization was the ultimate achievement in Maslow's hierarchy of needs. In later life, as he worked on his own spiritual evolution, he believed this went beyond the process of self-actualization and deserved to be added to his original model of human needs. Self-transcendence refers to elevating one's self to a state of spiritual enlightenment in which there is greater clarity and understanding of certain spiritual truths. Choices *A* and *B* are factors that contribute to the self-transcendence level, but these are not listed in Maslow's hierarchy of needs theory.

55. B: Leo is running a group founded on a belief in attachment theory, which is a key approach to parenting and healthy infant development. This is an accepted theory in social work practice. Attachment theory is grounded in the importance of developing a strong and reliable bond between infants and their primary caregiver; this bond is the foundation for future healthy relationships and mental health. Choice *A* is incorrect because, while it is true that attachment in infancy impacts attachment as children age, it's not true that nothing can be done to change or address early disruption in attachment to the primary caregiver. Choice *C* is incorrect because although preschool choice may be important for toddler development, this question is focused on strengthening the relationship between the infant and the primary caregiver. Choice *D* is incorrect because attachment theory promotes connection that results in eventual independence but does not endorse immediate independence in infancy.

56. B: The correct answer is Choice *B*, training only clinical and client-facing staff on the impact of trauma. Training all staff, not just clinical or client-facing staff, on the impact of trauma is critical to have in a trauma-informed organization. This includes training for staff such as administrative team members, board members, and anyone else connected to the organization. Universal screening, collaboration with clients, and increasing the physical safety of the environment are all known components of a trauma-informed care model.

57. C: The correct answer is Choice *C*. Questions regarding Gregory's safety are ethically necessary, and prefacing them with dialogue that supports him in feeling prepared to delve into this topic is therapeutically beneficial. Choice *A* is incorrect, as it is inappropriate to label Gregory's relationship as such without processing this with him. Furthermore, suggesting that he leave is not an advisable approach, as this can damage therapeutic rapport if Gregory isn't ready to make this decision. Choice *B* is incorrect, as you have noticed controlling patterns of behavior from Gregory's husband, and Gregory has visible injuries. Choice *D* is incorrect, as this would only be applicable for minors and vulnerable adults.

58. A: Selective mutism is categorized with anxiety disorders in the *DSM-5-TR*, and comorbidity with other anxiety disorders is common. The diagnosis is given when a person does not speak in certain situations, such as at school, for at least one month. The failure to speak must cause difficulty with functioning and cannot be explained by a communication disorder. The person speaks normally in other social situations. Choices *B*, *C*, and *D* are incorrect because they refer to other categories of disorders that are not related to selective mutism.

59. A: The first step for the social worker in this scenario is to conduct a risk assessment to determine if Claudia is at risk of harming herself or others. While social workers strive to prioritize the self-determination of their clients and support their clients' right to refuse treatment recommendations, safety concerns are still the ultimate priority. The primary exceptions to client self-determination are if they are at risk of harming themself or others or if the client has been deemed legally incompetent to make their own care decisions. Therefore, the first thing to do is to assess risk level. Choice *B* is incorrect because the risk assessment needs to be conducted first. Choice *C* is incorrect because Claudia is an adult who is her own guardian; therefore, her family would not be a part of the decision-making process, and including them without her consent would be a breach of confidentiality. Choice *D* is incorrect because while a competency hearing could be necessary, it would be unethical for a social worker to request that the physician declare the patient incompetent. A client who refuses treatment recommendations is not automatically deemed unable to act in their own best interest. There is a strict legal process surrounding this.

60. C: Imaginary friends and magical thinking are common and developmentally appropriate in young children, so Choice *C* is correct. A 4-year-old having an imaginary friend does not prompt further intervention or testing, nor does it indicate a mental health disorder. In Piaget's theory of cognitive development (a widely accepted developmental theory), children between two and seven years old are in the preoperational stage. This stage involves use of imaginative play and imaginary friends, and these behaviors are seen as cognitively normal rather than causes for concern.

61. A: The correct answer is Choice *A*, assess the severity of each situation and prioritize the patient with the highest or most acute needs to be seen first. Triage is the act of assessing crisis situations and prioritizing needs accordingly.

192

This is a term commonly used in hospitals. Standardized assessments and evidence-based risk assessments should be used in this situation to determine the most acute needs and safety concerns.

62. D: The NASW Code of Ethics is clear that it is unethical for social workers to do online searches for information about their clients unless they have the client's consent. This protects clients' right to privacy. The only exception would be if there is an emergency and doing a search is required to prevent harm to the client or others. In Celia's example, there is no emergency, so the social worker must get her permission to do the search.

63. D: The best response is for Emily to support Edith in her goal of maintaining independence. Social workers should always support client autonomy and decision making, but this is especially important when working with geriatric patients. Maintaining independence is important to many people as they age; the other answer choices would take away or diminish Edith's ability to remain independent. While sometimes safety concerns must take priority over clients' desires, that does not appear to be the case here because the question states that Edith's doctor does not have concerns. Social workers who work with elders must be aware of these dynamics and be prepared to educate others and act as advocates for their clients in situations like this.

64. D: The correct answer is Choice *D*. Given the client's symptoms of depression and identified hopelessness, it is pertinent to first assess for safety. Choice *A* is incorrect, as goal setting surrounding finding a job will come later in the process. Choice *B* is incorrect, as delving into the client's feelings should be secondary to the safety assessment. Choice *C* is incorrect, as while this might be a useful tool in identifying the client's passions and tapping into his resilience, it should not come before safety.

65. A: Scapegoating a child occurs when a child is blamed for family problems and for things that are not their fault. This pattern of family dysfunction may happen in families where the problems are not being properly recognized or addressed, and members of the family seek to shift the blame. Affirming, undermining, or disavowing the child are not concepts connected to family dysfunction.

66. C: Contemplation and preparation indicate that the client is ready to make changes. Precontemplation indicates resistance and unwillingness to change. Action phases suggest that the client is already engaged in the change process and not contemplating or preparing.

67. B: There are clear ethical principles for social workers around this issue. Social workers are not to pursue a romantic or sexual relationship with their clients or close relatives of the client, as this has the potential to harm the client and their treatment. Choice *A* is incorrect because this would be acting in the social worker's self-interest, not the child's, which is ethically unacceptable for social work practice. Choice *C* is incorrect because supervision is not needed, as there are clear ethical guidelines surrounding this issue. Choice *D* is incorrect because the relationship would be considered unethical regardless of whether the social worker disclosed it and set boundaries surrounding the relationship.

68. D: The most appropriate suggestion to support a grieving child is to maintain their routine, as this helps create a sense of stability in an unpredictable time. This is especially important for younger children, such as the young girl in this example. Choice *A* is incorrect because it's recommended to be direct and honest with children when discussing death and dying and to use the actual words. Choice *B* is incorrect because missing excess school would not create the needed sense of normalcy and routine. Choice *C* is incorrect because it's healthy and helpful for children to observe the adults in their life experiencing grief, as it helps normalize their own feelings.

69. B: The prodromal phase describes the gradual changes in functioning that occur over the months or years prior to the onset of psychosis. Most but not all people who develop a psychotic disorder experience the prodrome phase, although it is sometimes only apparent in retrospect. During the prodromal phase, people experience a variety of symptoms that may include social withdrawal, difficulty with concentration, mood and sleep disturbances, and neglect of personal hygiene. Choice *A* is incorrect because the acute phase describes the onset of clear

psychotic symptoms. Choice *C* is incorrect because premorbid refers to the period before the illness begins to affect functioning. Choice *D* is incorrect because the residual phase describes the period after the acute phase when the symptoms start getting better. Some people will experience full remission after an episode of psychosis, while others will continue to deal with lingering symptoms.

70. D: The correct answer is Choice *D*, offer options such as moving chairs, going for a walk together, or opening the door. Tyler's behavior is indicating that he does not feel safe or comfortable in this setting, and Julie's assessment should include observing this non-verbal sign of discomfort. Especially for trauma treatment, it is critical that the first step is helping the client feel safe. Until this is addressed and further rapport is built, it would be premature to attempt the other interventions, even if they may be done in future sessions. Working with Tyler to help him feel physically safe and comfortable in the therapy space will help build rapport and a foundation for future work together.

71. A: The correct answer is Choice *A*. Ensuring that Yara has access to Naloxone and test strips is considered harm reduction, which is the best way to help mitigate risk for a client who is unable or unwilling to attain sobriety yet. Choice *B* is incorrect, as this is the fourth session. Yara would have been assessed for safety in the beginning of treatment and should be assessed at regular or required intervals thereafter. Choice *C* is incorrect, as Yara is not actively seeking to abstain from use. Choice *D* is incorrect, as Yara has indicated difficulty with social situations and has not identified a goal of sobriety.

72. B: While the use/abuse of alcohol, a history of mental illness, and a tendency to control others are all risk factors for abuse, the presence of a learning disorder is not. There are many factors that may indicate a potential abuser, but there are no foolproof ways to identify one apart from the evidence of abuse.

73. D: Social workers often use a strengths-based approach with their clients; this approach involves the belief that all people have unique strengths, resources, and resiliency. The role of the social worker is to highlight these strengths rather than just focusing on the problems. Choice *D* is the best example of a strengths-based intervention. Choice *A* takes a psychodynamic lens, focusing on past problems and how they are impacting Marcus in the present. Choice *B* focuses on the problems and positions Vera as the expert, which does not align with a strengths-based approach. Choice *C* respects Marcus's autonomy, but it does not highlight his strengths or utilize his resiliency to help him meet his goals.

74. B: The correct answer is Choice *B*, Harold has access to firearms at home. All of these risk factors (recent loss, lack of social support, and psychiatric history) are relevant and known suicide risk factors. However, having access to firearms at home creates the most imminent risk to Harold's safety and is also the factor here that can be potentially changed. It is critical for Damon to address this access to lethal means in his risk assessment and safety planning for Harold.

75. B: The correct answer is Choice *B*. As a social worker practicing narrative therapy, you'll want to focus on providing space for each member to share their perspective and support the other members to listen and understand. Choice *A* is incorrect, as this reflects a solution-focused approach. Choice *C* is incorrect, as this reflects a systemic approach.

76. B: Social workers are obligated to provide informed consent for all services and treatment, and part of this obligation is to provide the information in the client's primary language to ensure that they understand. Choice *B* is the best option because social workers are ethically obligated to provide a qualified interpreter and not allow family to translate. Choices *A* and *C* are incorrect because family members should not be used as interpreters.

77. A: Infancy is a critical stage, and infants who experience trauma and disruptions in attachment commonly display the behaviors demonstrated by Brian. This is a normal response to the early adversity he survived, and the best response is for Holly to educate his parents on this topic. While consistency may be helpful moving forward, his

parents first need to understand Brian's behavior and be supported in navigating it. Choice C is incorrect because medication is not the standard intervention for these symptoms. Choice D is incorrect because although Brian's symptoms are common in children who experienced a disruption to their early attachment, this is certainly not the experience of all children who are adopted.

78. B: The correct answer is Choice B, ask Thomas about what has been getting in the way of going to the AA meetings. This question is looking at the stages of change model. Even though Thomas stated he was ready to move from preparation to action, his response indicates he may not be ready yet. Asking Thomas about the barriers and taking time to listen to his experience may help provide more information on where he is at and what the appropriate supports are. The other suggestions are not appropriate based on the known information.

79. A: These symptoms are indicators of physical neglect. Physical neglect can be the appearance of always being hungry, excessive sleepiness, or untreated medical problems. Other indicators of physical neglect are parents or caregivers demonstrating lack of interest or suffering from chronic illness. Usually, the home is an unsafe environment for victims who experience physical neglect.

80. C: Social workers are ethically obligated to provide clients with their records when requested, unless there is a significant concern that doing so will cause harm to the client. This is a rare occurrence and would need to be well documented. As John is an adult with no indication that receiving his records would cause harm, the social worker needs to document the request and provide the records. Choice A is incorrect because there's no need for further supervision on this issue; the ethical standard is clear because there is no indication that receiving his records would negatively impact the client. Choice B is incorrect because there is no reason to ask why the client wants his records, and this could be perceived as trying to dissuade him from obtaining the records he has a right to access. Choice D is incorrect because the usual occurrence is that clients have the right to access their records.

81. A: The correct answer is Choice A. Engaging one-on-one with the mother establishes rapport and works toward the eventual goal of reunification. The social worker should eventually work toward increasing unsupervised parenting time to increase the mother's confidence in parenting and sustain the parent-child bond. Choice B is incorrect, as the primary goal of permanency planning is reunification, unless there are specific criteria met to suggest otherwise. In this example, this child's mother is making the necessary choices to comply with treatment. Choice C is incorrect, as although a request for records might be necessary later in the case, the more important step is connecting with the mother.

82. C: The correct answer is Choice C, ask Lucy to share more about this decision and what she is feeling and thinking. Further assessment is needed here to best decide how to support Lucy. While social workers do respect a client's right to self-determination and decision making, Morgan still needs to better understand Lucy's decision to plan the appropriate support. While this could indicate denial, there are many reasons someone may not want to discuss an illness with family, and Morgan needs to obtain more information to understand. Social workers do not tell patients what to do in this situation, and Morgan should not require this.

83. A: Atypical antipsychotics were developed in the 1990s and have been shown to have less severe side effects. Typical antipsychotics were developed in the 1950s. They can be used if atypical antipsychotics don't work for the client, but they usually have severe side effects.

84. C: According to the family life cycle, this couple in the launching children stage. This stage represents a transition from the demands of raising children to being a couple with adult children who live independently. It is common for people to struggle with this transition. The goals for this stage include redefining the couple's relationship and roles outside of daily parenting, building other relationships and hobbies, building adult relationships with children, and engaging in self-exploration. Choice C is correct because it does not align with the goals of this stage.

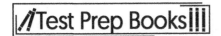

85. B: This question is examining the issue of termination due to non-payment for treatment in a fee-for-service practice setting. The social worker's best first step is to conduct a thorough risk assessment, because social workers cannot terminate for non-payment if a client is at risk of harm to themselves or others. The social worker must determine that is not the case before proceeding with termination. Choice *A* is incorrect because if there is no risk of acute harm and the social worker has both outlined the payment policy and attempted to address this with the client, as is the case here, social workers are ethically and legally allowed to terminate on the basis of non-payment. Choice *C* is incorrect because social workers are not ethically allowed to exchange goods or bartered items in exchange for payment for social work services. Choice *D* is incorrect because the risk assessment should occur prior to the termination.

86. B: During a mental status exam (MSE), assessing the client's cooperation is an example of mood and affect. Cooperation, appropriateness, stability, and demeanor (e.g., flat, bubbly, warm, or restricted) are examples of mood and affect examined during an MSE. Choice *A*, general appearance, is determined by race, age, sex, body build, personal hygiene, and grooming. Choice *C*, speech, is incorrect because its attributes include syntax, rhythm, voice quality, and phrases used. Choice *D*, level of consciousness, includes alertness and presence of fatigue or lethargy.

87. B: Erikson's stages of psychosocial development theory describes healthy development as age-based stages with a central task that one must achieve in order to progress developmentally and emotionally through the life cycle. Based on her age and the conflict described, Lillian is in the stage of integrity vs. despair. This is the life stage in which elders focus on their lives in review. If one does not feel satisfied or at peace with their life choices and relationships, it can result in feelings of despair and hopelessness, as demonstrated here. Choice *A* is incorrect because although grief may accompany aging, Choice *B* is a better reflection of this experience. Choice *C* is incorrect because this is the developmental stage associated with adolescence. Choice *D* is incorrect because the experiences described do not meet the diagnostic criteria for major depressive disorder.

88. C: The correct answer is Choice *C*. By validating the concerns that she is bringing to therapy and continuing to focus on direct engagement, you are building rapport that serves as the foundation for her to feel safe in exploring her anxiety during your sessions. Choice *A* is incorrect, as moving into psychoeducation before building adequate rapport isn't appropriate. Choice *B* is incorrect, as it is your job as the social worker to create an environment that fosters acceptance.

89. A: The policy is not ethical because it violates the client's right to confidentiality. Choice *B* is incorrect because it is irrelevant whether the commanding officers are social workers; sharing private client information without the client's permission is unethical either way. Choice *C* is incorrect because the potential harm is theoretical; it is only ethical to violate a client's right to confidentiality if they pose a clear risk of grave harm to themselves or another person. Choice *D* is incorrect because social workers must abide by the NASW Code of Ethics regardless of the setting in which they practice.

90. A: Social workers often assist people of all ages who are grieving or have experienced a loss. While all children are unique and Melanie should be seen as the expert on her children and their circumstances, best practices when discussing death with young children include being honest and using concrete language that they can understand. Choice *B* is incorrect because it is not a standard recommendation to exclude children from a funeral or other rituals of grieving. Choice *C* would be inappropriate and unnecessary; it would cross a professional boundary, and grieving children would be better supported by a trusted caregiver than an unknown social worker. Choice *D* is incorrect because children benefit from seeing adult caregivers model healthy and normal emotional responses.

91. D: Social workers are expected to avoid dual relationships when at all possible. Dual relationships have potential to cause harm or exploitation to the client. This situation is easily avoidable because it takes place in a large practice with multiple clinicians, and the social worker/client rapport has not yet been established. Therefore, the best choice is to transfer the client to a different provider at the practice. Choice *A* is incorrect because it does not avoid the dual relationship when there is an option to, and the client may not feel comfortable answering this question

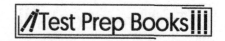

honestly. Choice *B* is incorrect because it breaks the client's confidentiality. Choice *C* is incorrect because the guidelines surrounding when dual relationships are permitted is clear and does not require consultation in this instance.

92. B: The correct answer is Choice *B*. Reality testing with the client can be a useful method, particularly if they are prone to feeling overwhelmed by simple demands. Choice *A* is incorrect, as this approach invalidates the client's experience. Choice *C* is incorrect, as although this might be an eventual step, it is unclear if this is needed without exploring the situation in greater detail.

93. B: The correct answer is Choice *B*, provide emotional support while explaining the importance of her safety, and file a report with child protective services immediately. While Nathan should support Jill throughout this process, her safety is the most important factor here. Because Jill has disclosed abuse that has been occurring in her home, protective services need to be contacted to begin their investigation and determine next steps before she goes home for the school day. While Nathan may need to follow any procedures his school has in place, social workers are all mandated reporters, and he will need to report this information himself. While child protective services may opt to involve law enforcement, the appropriate next step is to follow reporting guidelines and allow protective services to conduct their investigation in accordance with their protocol.

94. C: Solution identification is the third method used to develop an intervention/treatment plan. This is where the practitioner works with the client to suggest solutions to work towards.

95. B: The three levels of social work intervention exist at the micro, mezzo, and macro levels. Micro interventions are those at the individual level, mezzo interventions are at the community level, and macro interventions are at a policy or systemic level. Therefore, Choice *B* is correct because it is the only response focusing on a change of policy rather than providing support to individuals or the community.

96. A: Self-disclosure is a complex ethical issue in social work practice. The general consensus is that self-disclosure has a high risk of harming the client relationship and creating boundary problems, but it can be utilized when it's done so intentionally in the best interest of the client and their treatment. The best option here is Choice *A*, where the social worker honestly answers a brief question and redirects the conversation back to the client and her experience. Choices *C* and *D* are incorrect because it is inappropriate to disclose detailed information about the social worker's own relationship challenges; this could negatively impact the client in many ways, including making her feel as though it's a peer relationship, implying she should support the social worker, appearing to invite a sexual relationship with the client, or seemingly encouraging them to get a divorce rather than supporting their emotional process and helping them cope. Choice *B* would not be unethical, but it may make the client feel alienated or vulnerable for asking the question and therefore impact rapport, making Choice *A* the best selection.

97. C: The correct answer is Choice *C*, engage in active listening, ask open-ended questions, and build initial rapport with Elsa. While there are some potential indicators here of feigning illness, Dawn should first engage in active listening and build rapport with Elsa as she conducts her assessment and develops a plan. Social workers should typically gather information and build a relationship first before jumping into action. While it would be indicated to obtain collateral information from the medical team here, Dawn needs to get Elsa's permission to contact them. Providing education or referring to a support group would be inappropriate as a next step without getting further information to make an informed plan to meet Elsa's needs.

98. D: The correct answer is Choice *D*. Acknowledging and validating Regina's concerns and working hand in hand with her to create a plan to address all of her concerns is the best approach. Specifically supporting her in utilizing a partializing technique to break down the concerns in order of urgency is vital given the complexity of her case. Choice *A* is incorrect, as simply focusing on reunification negates the other issues presented and doesn't meet the patient where she is. Choice *B* is incorrect, as there is not an indication that she is ready to approach detox, particularly with potential housing instability on the table. Choice *C* is incorrect, as given Regina's state of

197

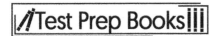

overwhelm, asking her to choose where she wants to start in this moment might increase stress and doesn't utilize your capability as a social worker to help create a plan.

99. B: The principles of confidentiality remain in place, even in the event of the death of a patient. The social worker cannot disclose confidential information or client records without a release of information, legal obligation, or threat of harm to the patient or someone else when a patient is alive, and this continues after their death. Nothing in this example indicates a reason to break confidentiality; the social worker should not even respond because this confirms he was a patient.

100. B: The correct answer is Choice *B*. This is a good opportunity for providing psychoeducation surrounding suicide, given the mother's false belief that not talking about suicide helps to prevent it. Choice *A* is incorrect here, as the situation already indicates that the social worker has been empathizing with the parents. Choice *C* is incorrect, as although this may be a future intervention, it is vital for the parents to gain a better understanding surrounding suicide before moving forward.

101. B: Facilitating a family meeting would be the best first step when working with caregivers and family members who are struggling to agree upon goals and next steps. This dynamic is common when adult siblings share caregiving responsibilities for an aging or ill parent. The family can have differing perspectives and values and/or be at different levels of acceptance regarding the parent's decline. While financial assistance or a support group referral can be appropriate social work interventions to support caregivers, the first step would be to facilitate a family meeting to address the core concerns and needs.

102. C: The correct answer is Choice *C*. The most effective way to measure Olivia's progress is to assess her level of functioning now compared to when she initially began treatment in relation to her treatment goals. Choice *A* is incorrect, as there is no indication that Olivia is in treatment for depression. Choice *B* is incorrect, as there is no indication that Olivia was struggling to participate openly in treatment.

103. A: Kinship care would be the most supportive foster placement choice for Jessie in this scenario. Kinship care is when children are placed with a relative instead of an unknown foster parent. Assuming that there is a safe and reliable kinship caregiver available, this provides the most stability for the child, keeps them connected to their family and culture, and is linked to the best future outcomes for the child. Residential facilities and group homes are institutional settings where the child would not have their own primary caregiver; these would also be more disruptive changes, so these choices are incorrect. Choice *C* is incorrect because therapeutic foster care is a program for children with behavioral, mental health, or developmental needs, which are not indicated in the question.

104. D: The correct answer is Choice *D*, work with Vincent to assess how these changes are going. Monitoring and evaluating how the treatment plan and interventions are going is a critical step in the social work treatment planning process. While discharge planning is another step, it's important for the monitoring and evaluation phase to come first. There is nothing here to indicate that Vincent is in need of a support group or further safety planning.

105. C: Subjective data is when the client provides their perspective on what happened and the correlated feelings and experiences felt. The social worker may use the information to tease out facts related to the client's situation, which is known as objective data, Choice *B*. Measurable data, Choice *A*, and planning data, Choice *D*, are not relevant to the context of the question.

106. A: The correct answer is Choice *A*. The first thing that Jessina has the responsibility to do is to model an open discussion with this supervisee and the group surrounding the ethical concerns involved. Choice *B* is incorrect, as this social worker has not acted on any concerns that are reportable. Furthermore, discussion would be warranted before any reporting occurred anyway. Choice *C* is incorrect, as although this step might need to be utilized later in the process, the first step is discussion. Choice *D* is incorrect, as this is an appropriate topic for discussion within a supervision group.

107. B: Social workers are expected to practice within their areas of competence and expertise, but they also need to be constantly expanding their knowledge to serve their patients. The best next step is to engage in consultation and training to be able to provide the best possible care to this patient. Choice *A* is incorrect because the social worker should first attempt to expand her competence before disrupting his treatment with a new referral. Choice *C* is incorrect because this does not provide appropriate professional development or training on evidence-based care. Choice *D* is incorrect because it's an incomplete response; supervision may be useful here, but supervision alone does not address the issue of professional competence.

108. C: An official medical report brought by the client to their first session would be information from a collateral source. The other three examples show primary sources of information, as all of the information available is provided directly by the client. While the client is still the one physically giving the medical history report to the practitioner, it's considered a collateral source because it was officially documented and then obtained from a secondary source (the client's healthcare provider).

109. A: The correct answer is Choice *A*, short-term psychiatric hospitalization. Based on the information provided, Ron would benefit from hospitalization to provide stabilization, safety, and further assessment. While Ron could require a longer-term setting, such as a residential program, this would not be the first step. Intensive outpatient would also not be appropriate as that is a lower level of care than he currently receives.

110. A: Violence, control, and abuse can take many forms, and this is an area of practice that all social workers should understand. A violent or controlling relationship can include dynamics such as physical abuse, sexual abuse, financial abuse, emotional abuse, manipulation, isolation, or coercion. These dynamics often overlap, but someone does not need to experience all of them to be a victim of interpersonal violence. Validation and education regarding the experiences shared is the only appropriate response. Choice *B* is incorrect because this situation does not warrant breaching confidentiality, and social workers are not mandated reporters of financial abuse of a non-vulnerable adult. Choice *C* would be inappropriate because it suggests that the woman is at fault for the abuse she experienced. Choice *D* is incorrect because it invalidates her experience as a survivor of financial abuse and manipulation, and it's not true that this behavior always escalates into physical violence. Interpersonal violence is a complex topic to which social workers must respond with compassion and knowledge.

111. C: The social worker in this example is displaying signs of secondary or vicarious trauma, which is when professionals who are consistently exposed to the traumatic experiences of their clients begin to experience similar symptoms. This is something social workers must be attuned to in themselves, and the best thing to do is to seek support and supervision. This will both promote the well-being of the social worker as well as help mitigate the impact vicarious trauma can have on client care. Choice *A* is incorrect because boundaries alone will not address the symptoms of secondary trauma, and these symptoms are different from burnout or feeling overworked. Choice *B* is incorrect because while a leave of absence for self-care may end up being needed, she should first seek supervision, and it wouldn't be appropriate to discuss her secondary trauma with her clients. Choice *D* is incorrect because while being present is important, her symptoms need to be addressed, not ignored, for the well-being of both her and her clients.

112. C: Lamotrigine (Lamictal) is a mood stabilizer and anticonvulsant commonly prescribed to treat depression in bipolar disorder. Treating depression in bipolar disorder is a clinical challenge because traditional antidepressants can trigger mania in this population. Lamotrigine is one of the few medications that has been proven effective for bipolar depression. Choices *A* and *B* are incorrect because sodium valproate (Depakote) and carbamazepine (Tegretol) are mood stabilizers/anticonvulsants used to treat mania in bipolar disorder. Choice *D* is incorrect because Lisdexamfetamine (Vyvanse) is a stimulant used to treat ADHD.

113. C: The correct answer is Choice *C*, ask Margaret to share more about how she is feeling and conduct a risk assessment. More information is needed here before making a decision about the appropriate next steps. Joelle works in a hospice setting and is providing end-of-life care; therefore, conversations about end of life and death are

199

to be expected. More information is needed to determine if Margaret is a risk to herself. It may be appropriate to take further action to ensure safety, but these may be normal thoughts that Margaret is having related to her terminal illness. Joelle needs to continue assessing before taking action.

114. A: Noel's feelings are a normal given her situation, so the best choice is for Jason to provide validation, normalization, and support. In families with a seriously ill child, it is a common dynamic for the healthy child to have feelings such as resentment, jealousy, guilt, or anger and to feel as though all parental attention is on the ill child. If left unaddressed, this can negatively impact the entire family system in what is already a stressful time. While a family meeting will likely be needed, Jason should first validate Noel's experience and the feelings she shared. Choice B is inappropriate because it is invalidating and would likely further her feelings of guilt and resentment. Choice C is incorrect because although therapy may be a helpful space to process her feelings and stress, her feelings are neither abnormal nor indicative of mental illness.

115. D: Social workers are ethically obligated to provide services in areas of their competence and strive to provide services that are evidence based. This question balances the competing ethical priorities of competence and promoting self-determination. Choice D is the best choice because the social worker is supportive of the client's goal and treatment interest but holds the appropriate boundary that this would not be a service he can provide, as he's not trained to do so and it's not evidence based. Choice A is incorrect because it's not respectful to the client and doesn't promote her self-determination. Choice B is incorrect because the primary conflict here is not related to billing or insurance. Choice C is incorrect because the social worker cannot provide this therapy due to his lack of training and it not being evidence based.

116. B: Trauma-informed care involves approaching all clients as if they may have experienced trauma, understanding the symptoms of trauma, incorporating knowledge about trauma into all aspects of service delivery, and avoiding practices that could inadvertently re-traumatize clients. Choice A is incorrect because trauma-specific services refer to practitioners and organizations that focus specifically on treating trauma. An organization or practitioner can use a trauma-informed approach without offering trauma-specific services. Choice C is incorrect because it is not a service delivery model. Choice D is incorrect because universal trauma screening is an example of a specific practice that may or may not be used by a trauma-informed practitioner or organization. It is possible to provide trauma-informed care without using universal trauma screenings. There is some debate in the field of trauma-informed care about whether and to what extent universal trauma screenings are helpful or necessary.

117. C: Social workers frequently assist caregivers in navigating what can be a stressful and consuming role at times. While Choices A and B are both common interventions when working with caregivers and would help reduce the emotional toll, neither address the financial constraints with which Georgie is struggling. Choice D is incorrect because although it would help cover the cost of care, it would not address prior medical debt, and Georgie is not asking for her mother to be placed out of the home. Choice C is the only option that offers the general financial support Georgie is requesting.

118. A: The correct answer is Choice A, mental status exam. The mental status exam is a tool used during the social work assessment process that assesses client appearance, orientation, speech pattern, affect, mood, judgment, impulsivity, risk of harm to self or others, cognition, and memory. It is a standard part of the assessment process. The other tools listed are for more specific circumstances than a general screening, as they are intended to diagnose specific mental health conditions or identify a trauma history.

119. D: The correct answer is Choice D. Given the variance of laws within states and individual organizations surrounding posthumous release of medical records, it is vital to understand which laws you are governed by before moving forward with this request. Choice A is incorrect, as it would be inappropriate to disclose any information surrounding the client to the family without proper release. Choice B is incorrect, as there is not enough information to determine that refusal is appropriate. Choice C is incorrect, as although consultation would eventually be warranted, determining the legal mandates surrounding this request is more important.

200

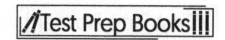

120. B: This question is asking about Piaget's stages of cognitive development, a developmental theory founded on the idea that children progress through distinct age-based stages of cognition from infancy through childhood. Children are in the concrete operational stage from ages seven to eleven, making Choice *B* the correct answer. The hallmarks of this stage include the start of logical thinking and the ability to consider the thoughts and feelings of others. Children in this stage still typically struggle with hypothetical scenarios or more abstract thoughts, as demonstrated by Luke's inability to discuss how he might behave in the future. Luke's age and behavior make the concrete operational stage the only correct choice. Choice *A* is incorrect because his behavior is developmentally normal and not a sign of a delay. Choice *C* is incorrect because he is too old for the preoperational stage and is not demonstrating any traits of magical thinking in his actions. Choice *D* is incorrect because an inability to consider hypothetical scenarios is developmentally appropriate and not related to the number of tasks he is performing.

121. D: The correct answer is Choice *D*, assist John in getting a new job as he identified this as a source of stress. The purpose of crisis intervention is to rapidly assess, build rapport, and set goals to restore the client to their previous state of functioning and stability. Crisis intervention focuses on concrete support and interventions that work quickly to address the current crisis. While getting a new job may be helpful for John in the future, it would not be an appropriate part of the crisis plan at this time. Safety planning, increasing support and coping skills, and connecting John to a higher level of therapeutic services would address the immediate symptoms of the crisis that led to this assessment.

122. C: Enmeshment refers to a relationship dynamic where boundaries are weak and pliable. Enmeshment leads to emotional fusion that prevents individuals from feeling and acting autonomously. Enmeshed families tend to have very rigid boundaries with the outside world to the extent that there is limited engagement with people, activities, and ideas from outside of the family. Enmeshment is dysfunctional; it prevents the family from differentiation. Differentiation, Choice *A*, means that each person can be themselves and act autonomously while still maintaining healthy relationships with family members. Differentiation is healthy. The opposite of enmeshment is disengagement, Choice *B*, another dysfunctional dynamic wherein boundaries inside the family are very rigid. This means that family members are emotionally distant from each other. In disengaged families, boundaries between the family and the outside world tend to be very weak and open. Choice *D* is incorrect because triangulation describes a dynamic where two people experience conflict, and rather than addressing it directly, they recruit a third person into their interaction to reduce anxiety.

123. D: Body image struggles are normal and expected across the lifespan at various ages, and these types of body image concerns are a normal part of the aging process for many people. As the body changes and health conditions cause changes in functioning, many people struggle with the resulting physical and emotional changes. While a physical therapy referral may or may not be warranted, Choice *A* is incorrect because it's not unusual to have changes to physical functioning and mobility in older age, especially after a major surgery. Choice *C* is incorrect because Ruth does not identify her loss and grief as the source of her current challenges. Choice *B* is incorrect because although assessing for depression is important among this population, the scenario focuses specifically on bodily changes, making Choice *D* the better response.

124. B: The correct answer is Choice *B*. Abigail is working to identify dysfunctional thought patterns with her client, which might be leading to unhelpful emotions. Choice *A* is incorrect, as psychodynamic therapy would be delving into this client's past experiences to see how they are impacting current-day issues. Choice *C* is incorrect, as dialectical behavioral therapy is a treatment used with disorders with more intensive emotional patterns, such as borderline personality disorder. Choice *D* is incorrect, as humanistic therapy focuses more on feelings exploration with the client and less on dysfunctional thought patterns.

125. B: Termination is an essential part of social work services, and it's the responsibility of the social worker to prepare clients for this regardless of the reason for termination. The best option is Choice *B*, as the social worker needs to assist the client through this transition and help connect her with the new social worker. Choices *A* and *C* are incorrect because it would not be ethical or allowable for the social worker to remain in touch with a client or

201

continue providing care after they resign from their role. Choice *D* is incorrect because the expectation is for social workers to adequately prepare clients for termination, not avoid the topic. All choices besides Choice *B* put the client at risk of harm.

126. B: A cost-benefit analysis looks at how much a program costs to run and how much money it generates or saves and compares these figures in a cost-benefit ratio. In the example, the hospital would consider the costs associated with employing the social workers (recruiting, hiring, training, salary, benefits, etc.) and the savings associated with the program (reduction in ER readmissions, better patient outcomes, time saved for doctors and nurses, etc.). Choice *A* is incorrect because a needs assessment is used to identify what a person, community, or organization needs. It uncovers gaps in services, barriers, and populations that are not being reached. A needs assessment is often the first step in determining whether a new program is necessary. Choice *C* is incorrect because a SWOT analysis is a way of looking at a person, community, or organization's current strengths, weaknesses, opportunities, and threats. It is a helpful way of identifying strengths to build on, areas that need improvement, potential opportunities for growth, and potential pitfalls to avoid. Choice *D* is incorrect because an outcome assessment looks at whether a program achieves its intended objectives. Unlike a cost-benefit analysis, the emphasis is on program objectives rather than financial value.

127. C: The correct answer is Choice *C*, ask Lydia to share what she is feeling and listen to her concerns. The first step in most social work interventions is to gather more information, understand what the patient is feeling or thinking, and listen actively to them before taking action, which is needed here. Discharge planning does prioritize client safety but is also done collaboratively, so Holly should listen to Lydia's concerns first. She may end up having to still go to the facility, but there should be an active conversation to prioritize her autonomy as much as possible. Lydia's parents are not her guardians, so it is not their decision, and nothing here indicates that Lydia does not have decision-making capacity.

128. D: The correct answer is Choice *D*. The social worker is validating that crying is okay in the context of her situation. This demonstrates empathy and encourages the client to share. Choice *A* is incorrect, as this is a group technique that ties group members' experiences to each other to support connection. Choice *B* is incorrect, as this refers to the process by which the therapist supports the client shifting the way they view a situation. Choice *C* is incorrect, as this refers to the verbal and nonverbal communication cues that one gives to ensure that someone knows you are listening.

129. C: Micro, mezzo, and macro practice are commonly used terms to describe the level of social work intervention taking place. Micro practice focuses on the individual, mezzo is at the community level, and macro interventions are those at the policy or systemic level. Alex's advocacy to change a statewide policy through the legislature would be considered macro level social work practice.

130. A: A compliance audit is a formal review of a practice environment conducted to ensure that local, state, and federal regulations are being followed. Nowadays, social work practice settings are increasingly moving beyond compliance auditing and engaging in more comprehensive auditing processes that focus on quality assurance and continuous improvement. This involves regularly collecting data and making improvements to provide the best quality services to clients, Choice *D*. Choice *B* is incorrect because verifying that a social worker is meeting their licensing requirements is one of the responsibilities of state licensing boards, but it is not called a compliance audit. Choice *C* is incorrect because monitoring the extent to which a client is following their treatment plan is called treatment or progress monitoring.

131. B: While social workers care deeply about their clients, maintaining boundaries and attending to their own self-care needs are essential parts of this profession. The best option here is Choice *B* because it maintains a professional boundary and protects the social worker's ability to focus on their self-care during their time away from work while also promoting support and safety for their client. Options *A* and *C* are incorrect because they do not prioritize the self-care of the social worker, and they reflect poor boundaries.

132. A: Adverse childhood experiences and the impact of childhood trauma throughout the lifespan are well documented through research, such as the ACE study, and they are widely accepted concepts in social work practice. Histories of adverse childhood experiences are linked to poorer health outcomes and physical health concerns across the lifespan, which would be an important area of education for medical providers. Additionally, according to the trauma-informed care model, all employees should be trained on this topic. Choice *B* is incorrect because it is not always appropriate to inquire about a trauma history, and mandated counseling would not be recommended or even allowed in this situation. Choice *C* is incorrect because there is no connection between an ACE history and malpractice suits. Choice *D* is incorrect because a risk assessment is not necessary for every patient who reports a history of trauma to their medical provider; further assessment would only be necessary if there was a cause for concern.

133. A: The correct answer is Choice *A*. According to crisis theory, a major facet of coping with a crisis is that the individual(s) finds that normal coping skills are not effective, resulting in a feeling of disequilibrium. It is helpful for the social worker to support the family in identifying the feeling of disequilibrium so that it is less disorienting. Choice *B* is incorrect, as therapeutic intervention should not necessarily be the primary goal in this case. Choice *C* is incorrect, as with proper intervention, a return to normal functioning is achievable.

134. A: The correct answer is Choice *A*, attention-deficit/hyperactivity disorder. According to the *DSM-5*, ADHD must have symptoms that appeared prior to age 12. Although Ryan's symptoms could meet the criteria for ADHD, he is 17 years old and reports they began six months ago, so this would be ruled out.

135. B: The person-in-environment framework is one of the foundational theories of social work practice. It's rooted in the belief that people cannot be separated from their environments and that their behavior is deeply impacted by their surroundings. Choice *B* is correct because it's looking at environmental factors that may impact Jack's discharge, such as housing, needed services, and employment. It does not discount the need for psychiatric services but rather takes a holistic view that also includes other needs and factors. Choice *A* is incorrect because it is rooted in the medical model and focuses solely on Jack's diagnosed mental health condition. Choice *C* is incorrect as it makes Jack the problem and does not consider any external circumstances. Choice *D* is incorrect because it takes a psychodynamic approach of viewing the barriers through the lens of childhood patterns and attachment.

136. C: The social worker is providing her supervision group with a case presentation. A case presentation is a way of summarizing important information about a client to other professionals to improve the client's care. The client must always give permission before their information can be shared. Case presentations are also used for teaching and learning purposes in social work education and supervision. Case presentations can also be used for evaluation purposes to ensure that the client is receiving the most effective treatment. Choice *A* is incorrect because case recording is the process of documenting a client's treatment, including all interactions with the social worker. Choice *B* is incorrect because quality assurance refers to the systems a practice setting uses to collect data, monitor performance, and improve outcomes. Choice *D* is incorrect because interdisciplinary collaboration involves working together with professionals in fields other than social work. Case presentations can be very useful in interdisciplinary settings because they help other professionals focus on the important elements of a case. However, in the example, the social worker is seeking advice from her supervision group, which means everyone in the group is a social worker.

137. B: Reunification is typically the goal for all out-of-home placements whenever possible. Reunification is when children are returned to the care of their biological parent following a removal. Reunification typically requires successful completion of a parenting plan, and the court also must determine that the home is safe and that the parent can safely care for the child. It is well accepted that if reunification is possible, it is the best option for the child and their development. It should almost always be the goal when engaging in permanency planning.

138. C: The correct answer is Choice *C*. Marietta must have a clear understanding of the issues that led to the implementation of these policies before moving forward with analysis. Choice *A* is incorrect, as although collecting

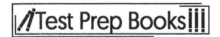

narrative data may be useful down the road, this is not where Marietta should start her work. Choice *B* is incorrect, as although looking into the impact of policies is a future step, this is not where Marietta should start her work. Choice *D* is incorrect, as this implies that an issue has already been found with the policies, but Marietta hasn't completed her analysis yet.

139. D: Child sex trafficking and exploitation involve the exchange of money or other goods in exchange for a commercial sex act. It does not have to involve money itself; sometimes the act is in exchange for a valuable item, housing, or other non-monetary commodity. Choice *A* is incorrect because while some circumstances of exploitation are gang-related, it is also true that traffickers can be friends, family, or a partner of the child. Choice *B* is incorrect because while homelessness is a risk factor, not all victims of child sex trafficking are homeless, and children of any gender can be victims. Choice *C* is incorrect because many victims experience manipulation and psychological abuse without being physically kidnapped or held captive.

140. C: The correct answer is Choice *C*, be transparent about why she is asking and acknowledge this is a difficult topic. During the assessment phase, social workers often have to ask about topics that are personal to clients or sensitive for them to discuss. It is important to be honest about why this is being asked, how the information will be used, and take a sensitive approach in these conversations. While Portia should respect George's decision to share what he's comfortable with, she should at least address this first. This would not be a reason to terminate care.

141. B: The correct answer is Choice *B*. Utilization of the PHQ2 is important here. This screening tool is utilized to detect depression and is an important primary prevention strategy for suicide. Choice *A* is incorrect, as it is important to screen and assess before moving toward intervention. Choice *C* is incorrect, as there is not enough information here to warrant a report to CPS. Choice *D* is incorrect, as this step should be taken after the session is completed but shouldn't precede assessment in the moment with the child.

142. A: The goal of building rapport with a client is to lay the foundation for a relationship based on mutual trust, empathy, and acceptance. A positive relationship is the basis of the helping process and the factor that promotes change and growth. During rapport building, the social worker and client can get comfortable with each other and start to build trust. The social worker can get a sense of how a client feels about seeking help and address any issues or concerns they have. If the social worker has trouble building trust with a client, they should seek supervisory assistance. The supervisor can help the social worker explore any feelings of countertransference that could be negatively affecting the helping relationship.

Choice *B* is incorrect because although the client's presenting problem might come up briefly during the rapport-building process, it is not the goal of rapport-building. Choice *C* is incorrect because the goal of rapport-building is not for the social worker to decide whether they want to work with a client. In general, ethics dictate that social workers should treat any client that they are competent to help. If a social worker is unable to build rapport with a client, they should seek supervision. Only in rare cases should a client be transferred to another social worker. Choice *D* is incorrect because informed consent is a requirement for beginning treatment and must be completed before the social worker focuses on building rapport.

143. A: The correct answer is Choice *A*. Sergio's social worker is trying elicit the exception to Sergio's problem, which is a solution-focused technique. Choice *B* is incorrect, as psychodynamic therapy seeks to delve into past experiences that may have led to current issues. Choice *C* is incorrect, as cognitive behavioral therapy seeks to focus on dysfunctional thought patterns.

144. C: When children experience adversity or traumatic experiences, such as those related to home removal and out-of-home placement, they often struggle in school and in their relationships. Changes in concentration and ability to focus would be expected in this instance. While other causes should always be considered, this is the most likely explanation. Choice *A* is incorrect because it would be very unlikely for an autism spectrum disorder to

204

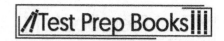

suddenly develop at age 11. Choice *B* is incorrect because this is not a normal or developmentally expected academic decline.

145. A: The correct answer is Choice *A*, recommend that a doctor examine Violet to rule out a medical cause and medication side effects. Whenever there is a concern that symptoms are non-organic and related to medical illness or medication, there needs to be a referral to a health care provider to address this before proceeding further with diagnosis and treatment planning. Social workers can work collaboratively with other health care providers but cannot diagnose medical illnesses or discuss medication side effects themselves, as it's outside the scope of practice. Since Violet stated symptoms began after she started her new medication, this is the first step Alex must take in her care.

146. B: This is a situation that presents a complex ethical dilemma, and as with many ethical challenges, there is not a singular correct or clear answer. Some of the competing issues here are dual relationships, confidentiality, self-disclosure, the social worker's self-care and well-being, integrity, and the therapeutic relationship. It's also important to note that this is further complicated by the rural setting, as dual relationships are more common in small communities. The best option is Choice *B* because it outlines the steps social workers should take when navigating an ethical dilemma. The Code of Ethics does not prioritize any single value; it instead advises that social workers consider the competing concerns and values, seek consultation, and review the literature to help them make a choice that is least harmful and the least likely to create a legal issue of unethical practice. Even if the social worker ended up choosing some of the actions outlined in other choices, this is the clear next step. Choice *D* is incorrect because the Code of Ethics does not prioritize relationships over other values.

147. B: Erikson's stages of psychosocial development assign different tasks to each age-based stage. Elders such as Ellie are in the stage of integrity vs. despair, which is best supported by engaging in reflection and life review. While the other options are appropriate activities and interventions for a nursing home social worker, Choice *B* is the only option that specifically supports her needs from the perspective of psychosocial development.

148. A: The correct answer is Choice *A*. Mark is struggling with both substance use and depression. Dual diagnosis indicates a comorbid mental illness and substance use disorder. Andrew and his supervisor are suggesting that Mark would be better served by a program that addresses both of these concerns simultaneously, which is typically seen as best practice.

149. C: The correct answer is Choice *C*. The best thing that Ursula can do to support Joy in fulfilling her role as the client is to support her in limiting barriers to success. Choice *A* is incorrect, as this is not an appropriate reason to end the session early. Choice *B* is incorrect, as without understanding why the assignment wasn't completed, it is not clear whether or not a new assignment is appropriate.

150. A: The correct answer is Choice *A*, document her assessment, intervention, and safety plan. Maura followed the steps of a crisis assessment and intervention here, but it is critical that she also clearly documents everything she did in accordance with her agency's protocol. Social workers are expected to always document their interventions, assessments, and safety plans in a timely manner. She should not contact Jane's other providers without a release. Supervision might be helpful but is not necessarily required, depending on Maura's licensure and agency policy.

151. D: The correct answer is Choice *D*. This is an important issue to bring up in supervision so that she is not isolated in her experience and her supervisor can support her in exploring where these feelings are stemming from. Whitney has a responsibility to be transparent regarding her self-assessment with her supervisor. Choice *A* is incorrect, as although this might be helpful, it is a temporary solution to a larger issue. Choice *B* is incorrect, as this could be an overcorrection to an issue that could be remedied with other options. Choice *C* is incorrect, as Whitney has already been reflective and has called into question her capacity to do her job, meaning that she has a responsibility to her clients to ensure that she is getting adequate support from her supervisor.

152. D: The correct answer is Choice *D*, provide support and active listening to Kathy and ask her to share more. Marcus's first step needs to be to provide support and listen to Kathy, both to build rapport as well as gather more information to assess the situation. While it's possible Kathy means she will not continue as a caregiver, her emotions are also very normal for a caregiver who is experiencing burnout. There may be other interventions that can support Kathy and Darlene in their goal of keeping Darlene at home, but Marcus first should gather more information and validate Kathy's emotions before acting. Without more information, it's not possible to decide if steps such as contacting elder services or a nursing home placement are necessary, and while a support group could be helpful, it should not be the first step here.

153. D: Summarizing is an interview technique in which the social worker restates the important points of a discussion. Summarizing can be done at any time, but it is especially effective at the end of a session to make sure that the social worker and client are on the same page about how the session went and what the next steps are. Summarizing also helps focus the discussion on important issues to address while highlighting the progress that has been made. Choice *A* is incorrect because asking open-ended questions is a technique used to elicit additional information from a client. Choice *B* is incorrect because validating is a technique used to affirm a client's feelings and statements about their experiences. Choice *C* is incorrect because clarifying is an interview technique that involves paraphrasing what a client has said and asking questions to make sure the social worker understands.

154. B: The correct answer is Choice *B*. Jules appears to have an accommodating learning style, which is hands-on and heavily relies on intuition. Choice *A* is incorrect, as a diverging approach is reflective of needing to see things from different perspectives and working well in groups in which brainstorming occurs. Choice *C* is incorrect, as assimilating refers to a logical and concise approach to learning in which the person benefits from clear explanation prior to moving forward. Choice *D* is incorrect, as converging refers to a problem-solving type of learning style in which the person is very competent at finding practical uses for theoretical ideas.

155. A: The correct answer is Choice *A*, asking about how long symptoms have been present for. While these are both in the family of depressive disorders, the DSM differentiates these diagnoses based on severity and persistence of symptoms. To meet DSM criteria for dysthymia, two of the listed symptoms must be present for at least two years. To meet criteria for major depression there must be at least five identified symptoms, but they only need to have been present for two weeks. Asking about the symptom timeline would help Jeff make the correct diagnosis.

156. B: This is an example of symbolic modeling because the model (the employee) is seen in a video doing the desired behavior (saying "no" assertively). Modeling is a useful technique that helps clients learn or improve skills through observation and imitation. Choice *A* is incorrect because live modeling involves watching a person do the desired behavior in real life. Choice *C* is incorrect because covert modeling involves asking the client to imagine someone performing the desired behavior and describe it in detail. Choice *D* is incorrect because participant modeling involves a real person modeling the desired behavior and then instructing the client to model it as well.

157. A: The correct answer is Choice *A*, validate Nicole's emotions and offer choices on how to spend the session. Social work assessment has many components, and the first step should be to read the client's cues and meet them where they are at. Nicole has made it clear that she is upset at the mandated therapy, so Krista should provide validation and respond to this concern first. Offering choices wherever possible is a useful approach for both mandated clients as well as adolescents. While Krista should be transparent about the repercussions if she chooses not to engage, Nicole's feelings are normal and should be addressed prior to this conversation. Self-disclosure would not be appropriate or indicated at this time. While they will need to complete the assessment, Krista needs to build rapport first.

158. C: The correct answer is Choice *C*. Providing immediate psychoeducation and reminding Mark that he is in a safe place is important, given the stress that panic attacks put on the brain. Offering a grounding exercise that helps Mark to calm his body down is vital. Supporting clients with skills in the moment is an excellent opportunity for practicing the skills and then debriefing after the fact. Choice *A* is incorrect, as although therapeutic silence can

often be helpful, if Mark is in treatment for anxiety and is actively panicking, the more effective option is to support him in self-soothing. Choice *B* is incorrect, as there are no medical components in this question that would lead one to believe that Mark is having a medical emergency. Given the purpose of his treatment, it is more likely that he is having a panic attack, which is not life threatening in and of itself.

159. B: The correct answer is Choice *B*, trauma-informed care. Trauma-informed care is seen by many in the social work field as the best-practice approach for providing services to people impacted by trauma and traumatic experiences. This model includes recommendations for universal trauma screenings and staff education, as well as systemic interventions that improve physical and emotional safety for all staff and clients. Nadia's suggestions would be in line with this model of care.

160. D: The correct answer is Choice *D*. The first step to community organizing is to conduct an assessment to have a clear idea of needs and resources. Choice *A* is incorrect, as although this will be a vital part of the process, this comes after the needs assessment. Choice *B* is incorrect, as jumping straight into staging an event skips several vital steps. Choice *C* is incorrect, as without a needs assessment, one would lack the specific data necessary to advocate to government officials.

161. B: When choosing which psychotherapy modality to use with a client, social workers must consider their competency, the client's needs, agency policy, insurance requirements, and the research evidence. Some types of therapy have been shown to be more effective for certain disorders. Dialectical behavior therapy is an evidence-based psychotherapy treatment for borderline personality disorder (BPD). It was developed by Marsha Linehan, a clinician who also has a BPD diagnosis, and it is considered the best modality for these patients. Choice *A* is incorrect because psychodynamic therapy is aimed at uncovering unconscious motivations and desires that affect behavior. Choice *C* is incorrect because exposure and response prevention therapy is used to treat phobias and obsessive-compulsive disorder. Choice *D* is incorrect because cognitive behavioral therapy helps draw connections between thoughts, feelings, and behaviors.

162. C: The correct answer is Choice *C*, de-escalate the immediate conflict and reflect back what she has observed. During family therapy, observing family interactions can be a critical assessment tool. Simone can use what she's observed to help the Robinson family see patterns and communication styles, and she can help highlight areas of growth with this information. She should de-escalate the immediate conflict but also validate that this may be normal for their family and allow space for everyone's feelings. She should not meet with them separately, as the goal of family therapy is to meet with them as a unit. Nothing here indicates the need for a protective services report. While the goal may be increased cohesion, Simone's role is to observe their family functioning and support them in setting goals, not tell them how to function.

163. A: The correct answer is Choice *A*. Vanessa's committee should gather as much data as possible so that they can establish what needs to be reviewed. Choice *B* is incorrect, as establishing risk level comes after collection and review of data. Choice *C* is incorrect, as a needs assessment is not typically a step within an ethics audit.

164. B: The correct answer is Choice *B*, respect Michael's decision to not take medication at this time. Social workers respect the autonomy and self-determination of their clients at all times unless there is an acute safety concern, which is not the case here. Jared already provided basic education on this option, so he should respect Michael's decision. Treatment planning is collaborative and based on client goals, not determined by the social worker.

165. D: The client's behavior is ego-dystonic because it goes against his ego, the part of his personality that manages the conflict between primal drives and social norms. Ego-dystonic behavior causes a person to feel guilty, unsettled, and anxious. If the behavior was in line with his ego and did not produce feelings of guilt and distress, it would be considered ego-syntonic, Choice *C*. Choice *A* is incorrect because the preconscious is the part of the mind that holds all the thoughts and feelings that a person is not currently focusing on but can be readily accessed when needed.

Choice *B* is incorrect because the unconscious is the part of the mind that holds thoughts and feelings that a person has no conscious awareness of.

166. B: The correct answer is Choice *B*. The first part of an initial assessment is to ensure that one has a clear understanding of the client's strengths, their needs, and the resources they have available to them. Choice *A* is incorrect, as the question indicates a need for an assessment and does not specify the need to test the client for substances. Choice *C* is incorrect, as although this will be a vital step later on in the process, an assessment has to come before the plan.

167. C: The social worker is using an empowerment approach. The goal of empowerment approaches is to help clients access the resources they need to achieve their goals. This approach is strengths-based, meaning it focuses on building clients' abilities, resilience, power, and resources rather than reducing their deficits. Empowerment approaches believe that every client has the ability to make the changes they want to make when they have access to the resources they need. This approach takes into account the impact of discrimination on groups and individuals; clients are encouraged to connect with others who have similar experiences and goals and work together to advocate for their collective needs. The role of the social worker is to help clients identify and build on strengths and access resources. Choice *A* is incorrect because harm reduction seeks to improve health and reduce harms associated with a behavior. Choice *B* is incorrect because crisis intervention approaches focus on stabilizing clients in acute crisis situations. Choice *D* is incorrect because behavioral approaches use incentives to motivate individuals to change their behaviors.

168. A: The correct answer is Choice *A*, file a Child Protective Services report and request that a worker come to the hospital. There are safety concerns here that indicate an investigation is needed and that it needs to occur before Lila leaves the hospital. Lila not being willing to give out her parents' information and being accompanied by a non-relative adult who refuses to leave her side at the hospital are all red flags for possible child trafficking or exploitation. While social workers often ask for more information in this situation, it would not be safe to ask Lila more questions with Chris in the room, so this should wait for the professional expertise of the child protection agency. While there are certain circumstances in some states where minors can consent to some types of health care, this would not qualify.

169. D: The correct answer is Choice *D*. A summative evaluation is a helpful tool to use with programs that require continual funding renewal, as it offers a breakdown of the effectiveness of a program. It offers clear and presentable data, which is necessary when advocating to a board that may not have in-depth knowledge of a certain topic. Choice *A* is incorrect, as an ethics audit is specifically focused on addressing widespread ethical concerns within an organization. Choice *B* is incorrect, as although testimony from community members can sometimes be helpful in advocating for programs, this would not be a good standalone option in a funding discussion, which requires comprehensive data. Choice *C* is incorrect, as this technique is utilized on a smaller scale to measure progress, such as in one-on-one sessions.

170. D: Assertiveness training involves teaching clients to communicate their feelings and needs directly in a way that is respectful of others. Social workers can help clients develop their skills in this area by identifying situations in which the client has trouble being assertive, teaching them strategies, and practicing until assertive communication becomes more natural. Replacing "you" statements, Choice *B*, with "I" statements is a common technique. "You" statements involve blame and put people on the defensive, while "I" statements focus on the feelings of the speaker. For example, the statement, "You always come home late! You obviously don't care about me," could be replaced with "I get worried when you come home late because I'm afraid something has happened to you."

The "I" statement is much more likely to lead to a constructive conversation where both people get their needs met. It is critical for social workers to understand that assertiveness is not the same as aggressiveness. Choice *A* is incorrect because not taking no for an answer is an example of aggressiveness and not respecting others' rights and boundaries. Choice *C* is incorrect because assertiveness is about communicating directly. People are often afraid to

208

communicate difficult or negative feelings directly because they don't want to make the other person feel bad. In the long run, avoiding these conversations usually leads to more problems. Assertiveness training teaches people how to communicate directly without alienating or harming other people.

ASWB Clinical Practice Test #2

1. Tanya is a social worker conducting an intake assessment with Kat, a new patient. Kat is a 40-year-old woman who was referred by her primary care provider for treatment for anxiety and depression. As a standard part of the assessment, Tanya asks about trauma history. Kat hesitates, then shares that she experienced violence as a child but does not wish to discuss this further today. How should Tanya respond?
   a. Validate how difficult that was to share and tell Kat she gets to choose what she's comfortable discussing.
   b. Explain that she needs to file a mandated report with the Child Protective Services agency.
   c. Ask Kat at what age this occurred to get a more detailed history and assessment.
   d. Explain that this history should be explored today as it might be related to her depression and anxiety.

2. Sam grew up with two parents and one sibling. His parents spent money irresponsibly and were frequently unemployed. Sam was a good kid, but his parents blamed him for the family's troubles, including things that he obviously had no control over. Over time, Sam internalized what he was told about himself: he was a bad child, the rotten apple spoiling things for the rest of the family, who were good people trying their best. What role did Sam occupy in his family of origin?
   a. Peacekeeper
   b. Lost child
   c. Problem child
   d. Scapegoat

3. Amy is a social worker for a home health company. She has been visiting her 75-year-old client, Sofia, for about six months. Lately, Sofia's daughter has seemed on edge when Amy is visiting. As Amy approached the house for her most recent visit, she could hear Sofia's daughter yelling at her, along with what she believed to be sounds of Sofia being hit. Amy then observed Sofia holding her arm and saw red marks when Sofia moved her hand. Amy attempted to speak to Sofia about her home life, but Sofia simply shook her head "no." Amy also noticed that Sofia has lost some weight over the last couple of months. Amy has concerns about Sofia's well-being. What should Amy's course of action be?
   a. Amy should continue to observe Sofia and make notes regarding what she sees.
   b. Amy should make a report to adult protective services.
   c. Amy should look at the nursing notes to find out what other health care professionals have observed.
   d. Amy should drop in more often to see if she can catch Sofia's daughter in the act.

4. A social worker has been meeting with Jerry weekly to treat his depression. He sought services voluntarily. After a month of treatment, he announces, "The treatment isn't working. I still feel terrible. This whole thing was a big waste of time and money. I just came to let you know that I'm done, and I'm not coming back." What is the BEST way for the social worker to respond?
   a. Empathize with Jerry's frustration and suggest creating a new treatment plan together.
   b. Explain that treatment takes longer than one month and encourage Jerry to continue.
   c. Explain the risks of terminating without completing treatment and document the encounter.
   d. Apologize and offer to reimburse Jerry for a percentage of the treatment.

5. In an initial meeting with a social worker, Mr. M states that he has been taking Prozac for 10 years for depression. He explains that he has tried to stop taking the medication but always begins taking it again after a couple of days because he feels so terrible. Why is Mr. M experiencing adverse effects when he stops taking Prozac?
   a. Stopping the antidepressant is causing his depression symptoms to return.
   b. He is addicted to Prozac and experiencing withdrawal symptoms.
   c. He is dependent on Prozac and experiencing discontinuation symptoms.
   d. He is psychologically dependent on Prozac and experiencing psychosomatic symptoms.

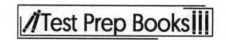

6. Dan tells a social worker that he is having trouble with his 14-year-old daughter, June, who has intellectual disabilities and is nonverbal. Dan states that June recently stopped wanting to go to her day program, which she previously loved. She cries, refuses to get in the car, and starts hitting herself in the head when it's time to go. She has been moody and withdrawn at home. She had a medical check-up recently and was treated for a urinary tract infection but is otherwise in excellent health. What should the social worker tell Dan?
   a. Moodiness, changes in preferences, and withdrawal from parents is typical adolescent behavior.
   b. June should be assessed to see if her intellectual disability has progressed or worsened.
   c. Urinary tract infections can manifest as psychological problems.
   d. June should be assessed to see if she is being abused at the day center.

7. A client with a history of major depressive disorder tells a social worker that she is done with therapy because she is no longer depressed. The social worker observes that the client is excited, talking extremely quickly, and jumping from topic to topic. She tells the social worker that everything changed a little over a week ago when she realized that her destiny was to spread God's love and that she no longer needs to eat or sleep because she is sustained by her devotion. She ordered 1,000 copies of the Bible along with a church organ. The client is unconcerned with the fact that she cannot afford these purchases or fit them in her apartment. Before this meeting, the client described herself as an atheist. What should the client's diagnosis be changed to?
   a. Major depression with psychotic features
   b. Bipolar I disorder
   c. Bipolar II disorder
   d. Schizoaffective disorder

8. A social worker is helping a client who is experiencing a lot of stress at work. The social worker asks the client about specific triggers, and together they identify the following sources of stress: the client is not sure if their boss is happy with their work, the client has trouble managing their time, and the client is worried that one of their coworkers might get a promotion instead of them. What is the next thing the social worker should do to help the client manage their stress?
   a. Teach the client deep breathing techniques.
   b. Ask the client what evidence they have that their coworker will be promoted.
   c. Reassure the client that everyone gets stressed at work.
   d. Help the client identify which parts of the situation they can control.

9. Mr. S came to Alan, a licensed clinical social worker, for help dealing with his depression. After several months of weekly sessions, Mr. S has accomplished his therapeutic goals and no longer experiences symptoms of depression. He states that he is not interested in setting any more goals, but he wants to keep coming to therapy because he enjoys talking to Alan. What should Alan do?
   a. Continue having weekly sessions with Mr. S.
   b. Reduce the frequency of the sessions.
   c. Refer Mr. S to a new therapist.
   d. Terminate with Mr. S.

10. At a neighborhood meeting, residents share that many of their children are struggling at the local public school. Their test scores are low, the school's discipline policy strikes many parents as too punitive, and there is no afterschool programming for children whose parents work. How would a social worker approach this problem using community development theory?
   a. Meet with local politicians and advocate for funding to cover new programming at the school.
   b. Provide individual and family counseling to affected students and their families.
   c. Act as a case manager and help affected families find afterschool options and other resources.
   d. Help the community organize and take collective action to hold the school accountable.

211

11. A social worker has a juvenile client who has recently been removed from his home by Child Protective Services due to multiple reports of parental neglect. The child has been temporarily placed in a group home. What should the social worker's FIRST goal be when working with this child and his family?
   a. To secure the child a permanent place in the group home
   b. To find a permanent foster family for the child
   c. To reunite the family once safety concerns are addressed
   d. To determine if there is a relative the child could live with

12. Which therapeutic modality uses the miracle question?
   a. Cognitive behavioral therapy
   b. Psychodynamic therapy
   c. Solution-focused brief therapy
   d. Person-centered therapy

13. What is the zone of proximal development?
   a. The older neighborhoods surrounding a new development
   b. A child's immediate physical environment at any given moment
   c. A child's developmental level compared to their peers
   d. The tasks a child can do with adult help but has not yet mastered

14. A social worker is assessing a client for an eating disorder. The client states that he eats large amounts of junk food at night several times a week, which causes him shame and distress. To avoid gaining weight, he skips breakfast the following day and spends hours in the gym to make up for the extra calories consumed. He feels like he must complete his workout routine even if he must cancel other plans. The client is an average weight but believes he is "fat." Which diagnosis would be MOST appropriate for this client?
   a. Anorexia nervosa
   b. Binge-eating disorder
   c. Bulimia nervosa
   d. Unspecified feeding or eating disorder

15. A social worker has been providing couples therapy to Mark and Breanne, a middle-aged couple, for three months. One day, Mark is unable to attend the therapy session, and Breanne comes alone. She confides in the therapist that Mark is very controlling. Mark does not allow her to work and instead gives her an allowance. When Mark is unhappy with Breanne, he withholds the allowance to "teach her a lesson." Breanne asks the social worker not to tell Mark that they talked about this. How should the social worker respond?
   a. Encourage Breanne to bring this up in the next session so they can all talk about it together.
   b. Reassure Breanne that they will not tell Mark.
   c. Schedule an individual session with Mark to get his perspective.
   d. Terminate couples therapy and refer Mark and Breanne to individual therapists.

16. A woman tells her social worker that she is worried about her 7-year-old son. She caught the boy talking to himself, and he explained that he was talking to his imaginary friend. The woman is afraid that this means her son is mentally ill. What should the social worker tell the woman?
   a. This behavior suggests that the boy is being neglected or abused.
   b. This behavior indicates that the boy is experiencing psychosis.
   c. This behavior is normal for very young children but is concerning at age seven.
   d. This behavior is normal for the boy's age and development.

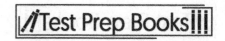

17. Sarah is a licensed clinical social worker in private practice. She receives a subpoena from an attorney requesting one of her client's records. How should she respond?
   a. Claim privilege on behalf of the client.
   b. Ignore the request unless it is accompanied by a court order signed by a judge.
   c. Release the client's records but not the psychotherapy notes.
   d. Inform the client and release the records.

18. Sandra is a social worker who has worked for 10 years at an agency serving survivors of domestic violence. In this time, her workload has been steadily increasing, but her pay and benefits have remained the same. She has had four different managers in the past two years. Increasingly, over the past year, she has been dreading going into work. Her anxiety has been getting worse and causes trouble sleeping. She often has nightmares about things her clients have gone through. She stopped dating and reduced her socializing some time ago because she has started to feel fearful and panicky around men. She used to find it easy to empathize with her clients, but lately she feels frustrated and bombarded by their suffering. What is the MOST likely explanation for Sandra's feelings?
   a. Compassion fatigue
   b. Burnout
   c. Stress
   d. Secondary trauma

19. A licensed clinical social worker is at home supervising a play date between his 6-year-old daughter and Amanda, another 6-year-old girl who has just moved to town. Amanda picks up two dolls and simulates oral sex. The social worker asks what she is doing, and she replies with a sexually explicit description of the activity. Amanda then asks the social worker if he wants to engage in the activity with her. Should the social worker make a report to child protective services?
   a. No, because the incident happened at home and not in the course of practicing social work.
   b. Yes, because the child displayed signs that indicate sexual abuse.
   c. No, because it is normal for children this age to be curious about sex.
   d. Yes, but only after trying and failing to resolve the issue with Amanda's parents.

20. A social worker has a client who has made significant progress on his goals. The last few therapy sessions have been uneventful with no new discoveries. The tone of the sessions has become more relaxed and friendly as they no longer discuss serious issues. What might this change indicate?
   a. The client is losing motivation.
   b. The client has lost trust in the social worker.
   c. The social worker is experiencing countertransference.
   d. The client is ready for termination.

21. Mike is an adult with intellectual disabilities who has been meeting with a social worker for issues related to childhood trauma. During their last session, Mike disclosed an incident of sexual abuse that he had never told anyone. The next day, the social worker received a call from the case manager at the day center Mike attends who said that Mike was uncharacteristically tense all day, even lashing out at staff. The case manager asked the social worker if something was going on with Mike. Mike has signed a release form permitting the social worker to communicate with the rest of his care team, including the case manager. What should the social worker do?
   a. Explain to the case manager that they have been working through trauma, and although Mike is making good progress, he might need extra support for the time being.
   b. Release Mike's records to the case manager and the rest of the care team so they can better coordinate his care.
   c. Do not answer the case manager's question because discussing Mike's treatment information would be a HIPAA violation.
   d. Tell Mike about the case manager's request, discuss the risks and benefits of disclosing treatment information, and help him decide how to respond.

22. Mike is a social worker meeting with his client Lewis, a 60-year-old man whom he has been seeing weekly for several months. During this session, Lewis appears agitated and makes a comment about wanting to hurt his doctor. Mike conducts a risk assessment and finds Lewis has both a plan and intent to harm the doctor. Mike is also aware from previous conversations that Lewis has access to firearms in his home. What does Mike need to do regarding his obligation under duty to warn?

    a. Make a safety plan with Lewis and provide him with crisis hotlines.

    b. File a report to have Lewis's firearms confiscated by law enforcement.

    c. Contact local police and contact Lewis's doctor to inform them of the threat.

    d. Begin the process for involuntary hospitalization due to safety concerns.

23. A social worker is helping a client develop goals for his treatment plan. The client states that his goal is to lose 20 pounds in one month. Is this an example of a SMART goal?

    a. Yes, it meets all the criteria.

    b. No, it is not realistic.

    c. No, it is not achievable.

    d. No, it is not time limited.

24. A woman is concerned about her teenage child, who was assigned female at birth and recently came out as transgender. Her child has begun dating a female classmate; the mother is confused and frustrated, telling the social worker, "I don't understand why he had to transition to date a girl when he could have just stayed a girl and been a lesbian." What should the social worker tell the mother?

    a. It is common for teenagers to go through phases like this, and she should be patient.

    b. Internalized homophobia is making her son think he needs to change his gender to date the girl.

    c. Her son is probably feeling neglected and acting out for attention.

    d. The mother is confusing gender identity and sexuality; they are unrelated.

25. A social worker is providing therapy to a client who has a history of abusing his intimate partners. The client discloses that he has a new girlfriend. The social worker is concerned for this woman's safety, even though the client says the relationship is going well. What should the social worker do?

    a. Discuss the relationship and continue therapy as usual unless the client indicates a plan to harm the girlfriend.

    b. Find a way to contact the client's girlfriend and warn her about his history.

    c. Conduct an internet search on the client to get more information about his past abuse to determine whether his girlfriend is in danger.

    d. Encourage the client to put the relationship on hold until he makes more progress in therapy.

26. Harriet is a social worker at a residential program that provides long-term psychiatric treatment for adults. She is conducting a discharge planning meeting for Owen, a 25-year-old man who has been at the program for a year receiving treatment for anxiety and OCD. His treatment team has determined that Owen is safe to discharge to a lower level of care in a community setting. What level of care would be appropriate for Owen to receive once he discharges?

    a. Intensive outpatient program

    b. Dual diagnosis community program

    c. Inpatient psychiatric facility

27. Claudette is a 24-year-old who is in treatment with you once a week to address stress related to medical school. She is a bright student and typically gets high marks in all of her classes. She has been worried about an upcoming final exam. She remarks during a session, "I know that I'm going to fail this test. This has been the hardest class that I've ever taken." What is the BEST way for you to use cognitive reframing with Claudette?

    a. "I'm hearing you saying that you're having a lot of anxiety about failing, as this class has been challenging. Is that right?"

    b. "Wow—you've nearly survived the hardest class of your career."

    c. "I notice that when you are feeling especially stressed, you catastrophize situations. Do you have past failed exams on which you are basing this belief that you will fail?"

    d. "Final exams can be so incredibly stressful for everyone."

28. What is an example of a positive symptom in schizophrenia?

    a. Poverty of speech

    b. Reduced emotional expression

    c. Lack of motivation

    d. Delusions

29. A client successfully completed treatment but had some difficulty during the termination process, stating that he feared he would backslide without the social worker's support. They agreed to schedule a follow-up meeting to ensure that the coping strategies the client learned were still working. At the follow-up, the client was doing well and had not experienced any returning symptoms. The client kept redirecting the conversation, casually chatting about his life and asking the social worker about hers. At the end of the session, the client stated that he felt an additional follow-up meeting was necessary to make sure he was still on track. Should the social worker schedule another follow-up meeting?

    a. Yes, because the client feels he needs one.

    b. Yes, because it is unethical to refuse a follow-up meeting.

    c. No, because the client shows signs of becoming dependent on the social worker.

    d. No, because the client is behaving inappropriately.

30. Lee is a social worker who is working on a team that conducts research on child development. He is working on a research project that is investigating the link between socioemotional interventions in elementary school settings on adolescent mental health. Lee is tasked with reading up on past studies and the current journal articles available on this topic. What stage of the social work research process is this?

    a. Question formulation

    b. Literature review

    c. Data analysis

    d. Needs assessment

31. You are a social worker in a substance use program. You are assigned 38-year-old Justina, who just completed detox and will now be working with you for weekly sessions. You learn that she is court-mandated to participate as a requirement for keeping visitation with her children, who are temporarily placed with their grandparents. During your first session, Justina walks into your office and says, "I don't want to be here. I'm only meeting with you because I'm sick of dealing with the court taking away my visitation." What is the BEST way to respond?

    a. "You're doing something you don't want to do, working with the program, in order to avoid something happening that would be even worse, like losing visitation. This makes a lot of sense."

    b. "I need you to know that there are limits to confidentiality in our sessions, as I am obligated to report to the courts whether or not you are cooperating with treatment."

    c. "I understand how stressful that must be, but it's important that you aren't just here to appease the courts. You need to be invested in your treatment."

32. Jordan is a social worker in the emergency room. He is meeting with Ryan, an 18-year-old college student who was referred by his therapist at the university counseling center after an outburst on campus where Ryan felt others were out to get him. As Jordan talks to Ryan, he notices that Ryan's speech is disorganized and incoherent at times. Ryan reports he has been hearing voices recently. In the referral from the university therapist, it states that Ryan is no longer going to his classes and has been struggling socially. The referral states these concerns have been going on since he returned from the winter break last month. What is the MOST likely diagnosis?
   a. Autism spectrum disorder
   b. Schizophrenia
   c. Bipolar disorder
   d. Substance use disorder

33. Janet is a social worker at an outpatient counseling center. She is tasked with starting a new group for adolescent girls. She is designing the group based on the needs of their psychosocial developmental stage. The group will be for girls between the ages of 14 and 17, and all referrals will come through school counseling departments. Which activity would be MOST appropriate for the first session?
   a. Communication activities designed to prevent peer-to-peer bullying
   b. An activity on self-exploration, identity development, and values
   c. Education on the risks of using alcohol and substances
   d. An activity exploring their families of origin and familial relationships

34. In which of the following situations can a social worker disclose a client's confidential information to a third party without the client's written permission?
   a. When the social worker is seeking reimbursement from the client's insurance company
   b. When the social worker is consulting with an expert about the client
   c. When the parents of a minor client request access to their child's records
   d. When the social worker is updating an interdisciplinary team about the client's progress

35. Heidi is a social worker at a partial hospitalization program for young adults. She is meeting with Johnny, a 20-year-old patient receiving treatment for depression following a recent hospitalization. During today's group, Johnny states that he still has ongoing thoughts of self-harm. What would help Heidi gather the MOST relevant information to make a decision about next steps?
   a. Collateral contact
   b. Columbia-Suicide Severity Rating Scale
   c. Biopsychosocial assessment
   d. Beck Depression Inventory

36. Roland is a social worker at a child welfare agency who manages a caseload of youth in foster care. He is meeting with Zach, a 15-year-old boy who was recently removed from his home and placed in foster care. Zach is angry about the situation and expresses his frustration to Roland during their monthly visit. He tells Roland that he just wants to go home and that everything feels unfair. He has gotten in trouble for skipping school since his removal and is annoyed by his curfew at his foster home. What is the BEST response?
   a. Roland should validate Zach's feelings and promise that he will be reunified with his family as soon as possible.
   b. Roland should eliminate Zach's visitations with his biological parents to allow him time to adjust.
   c. Roland should move Zach to a school that is closer to his new foster home to help ease the transition.
   d. Roland should validate Zach's feelings and offer him choices whenever possible.

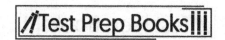

37. A social worker in private practice meets with a new client and learns that he has a very different worldview than she does. The client makes several statements about his beliefs that leave the social worker feeling uncomfortable. She is concerned that empathizing with the client would involve compromising her own values. What should the social worker do FIRST to address this?
    a. Reflect on her personal values and determine if she can put them aside to remain professionally objective.
    b. Consult with a trusted friend for advice on how to work with the client without compromising her own values.
    c. Refer the client to another social worker whose values are more like the client's and who could therefore provide better care.
    d. Update her intake procedure to screen out clients with certain values to avoid this conflict happening in the future.

38. Gracie is evaluating a program within a community center that engages high-risk youth in a summer program about financial literacy. In past years, they have found that enrollment has started out strong but that attendance diminishes as the summer progresses. Surveys administered to all past participants reveals that regular transportation has been challenging. What is the FIRST thing that Gracie should do?
    a. Pass out bus vouchers.
    b. Implement a contract at the beginning of the course that mandates transportation to participate.
    c. Dissolve the program in lieu of a more effective option.
    d. Form a committee involving community center staff and student participants to brainstorm solutions.

39. Sigmund Freud and his daughter Anna developed a lengthy list of defense mechanisms, including denial, projection, rationalization, and sublimation. They proposed that the need for people to employ defense mechanisms was for which of the following reasons?
    a. Because they were dishonest and did not want others to see the real person
    b. Because if they admitted the truth about themselves others would no longer accept them
    c. Because the defense mechanism allows one to avoid perceiving or accepting something very unacceptable about themselves, which they are not yet ready to address
    d. Because using defense mechanisms gives one an emotional advantage over others and makes it easier to exploit them

40. Sienna is a newly graduated social work student who has accepted a job in a child welfare organization. A week into the job, she finds that the needs of those on her caseload are more complex than she had anticipated. The support they need is multifaceted, including mental healthcare, housing stability, food insecurity, and so much more. Sienna feels overwhelmed in navigating her responsibilities to manage her clients' needs. What is the FIRST thing she should do?
    a. Advocate for increased staffing to lighten caseloads.
    b. Step down from the position.
    c. Seek individual supervision.
    d. Set priorities.

217

41. Liza is a social worker at a community mental health clinic. She works with a diverse caseload of patients to provide mental healthcare and treatment. She is working with a new family that identifies with a religion with which she is not very familiar. The family is devout, and their faith is a source of strength for them. What is the BEST response?
   a. Liza should not ask further questions because discussions about religion can be polarizing in the counseling relationship.
   b. Liza should ask questions about the family's experience and values and do her own research about the religion to be better informed.
   c. Liza should ask the family to provide her with educational materials on their religion so she can better understand their experience.
   d. Liza should refer the family to a provider who shares the same religion.

42. A social worker is creating a new website to promote her private practice. She has identified several current clients who she believes could provide testimonials endorsing her services. She plans to discuss the risks and benefits of providing a testimonial with each client, answer any questions they have, and ask them to sign a written permission form if they agree to provide a testimonial. She will make it clear to each client that choosing not to provide a testimonial will not negatively impact their past, current, or future access to her services. Is her behavior ethical?
   a. It is ethical because she is providing full informed consent.
   b. It is unethical because she is not giving all her clients an equal chance to participate.
   c. It is ethical because testimonials allow potential clients to make more informed choices.
   d. It is unethical because asking current clients for testimonials is never ethical.

43. Norah is a social worker at a clinic that serves veterans and their families. She recently began working with Dominic, a 25-year-old veteran who recently returned home from active service. She has had two sessions with Dominic, focusing on her assessment and getting to know him. Dominic reports that he has been doing fine since returning home and does not feel he has many goals for therapy. After the second session, Norah gets a phone call from a woman who states that she is Dominic's mother and that Dominic is not being honest with Norah about how difficult his transition home has been. How should Norah respond?
   a. Provide education to normalize how difficult this transition can be for veterans.
   b. State that she is not able to confirm or deny if he is a patient and that she cannot give out patient information.
   c. Give his mother information on the support group for family members of veterans run by the agency.
   d. Ask the mother to tell her more about how Dominic has been doing so she can complete her assessment.

44. A community organization has received a grant to fund programming related to overdose prevention. The organization is evaluating different program models to determine which one would allow them to prevent the most overdoses using the money they have. What type of evaluation would BEST help them make this decision?
   a. A cost-effectiveness evaluation
   b. A cost-benefit evaluation
   c. An outcome assessment
   d. A process evaluation

45. Don is a social worker who works with incarcerated individuals. He utilizes a systems-based approach in his work with his clients. He is meeting with Jackson, a 20-year-old man who is currently incarcerated. They have been working together for a few weeks. Which activity would be MOST relevant?
   a. Providing co-occurring substance use treatment
   b. Referring Jackson to a group on personal accountability
   c. Exploring Jackson's past and family of origin in the therapy space
   d. Providing case management services to address housing and employment needs upon release

46. Mara is a social worker at a substance use treatment facility. She is working with Ruby, a woman in her early twenties who is receiving treatment for a substance use disorder. Mara is attempting to work with Ruby to decrease her use and find healthier coping skills. Ruby spends most of her sessions talking about how she knows she would be happier and things in her life would improve if she got sober, but states she does not feel ready to set any goals to make these changes. Ruby has been sharing a lot about the problems substances are causing in her life but has not stopped her use at this time. What intervention should Mara try NEXT?
    a. Meet Ruby where she is at by exploring the resistance she is experiencing.
    b. Create a treatment plan with Ruby with a goal of reducing her substance use.
    c. Tell Ruby they will need to stop treatment if she doesn't make changes.
    d. Refer Ruby to a group therapy program since individual sessions aren't working.

47. Bart is a social worker working in a child welfare organization. His position requires that he spend a significant amount of time working one-on-one with parents in developing parenting skills. He shares with his supervisor, Martha, that he is struggling to establish rapport with a parent. This parent initially made disparaging comments about Bart's young age and lack of children of his own and often talks over Bart during sessions. What approach can Martha take to BEST support Bart?
    a. Have another social worker shadow Bert during sessions to provide on-the-job feedback.
    b. Move this client to a new caseload, as the rapport is damaged beyond repair.
    c. Use educational activities during supervision to focus on communication, body language, and conflict resolution.

48. An experienced social worker has had a successful private practice for years. After completing extensive training, she has started offering eye movement desensitization and reprocessing (EMDR) therapy to her clients. Since this is a new area of practice, she is receiving supervision. She was initially excited because her new supervisor has the reputation of being the best in town. He has double the experience of other supervisors in the area and is extremely popular with recent graduates working towards their clinical license. After several supervision sessions, the social worker is frustrated. She feels the supervisor is treating her as if she had never practiced social work before. They seem to be wasting a lot of time reviewing basics that she has already mastered. What should the social worker do?
    a. Find a new supervisor who has more experience with mature professionals.
    b. Discuss her frustration with the supervisor during their next supervision session.
    c. Reflect on why she has such a strong reaction to feeling like her experience isn't being acknowledged.
    d. Notify the board because the supervisor's incompetence could be affecting many social workers.

49. A genogram is MOST useful for what?
    a. Determining the occurrence of behaviors
    b. Establishing peer support systems
    c. Pinpointing significant life events
    d. Understanding life events and familial patterns

50. Howard is a social work professor at a large university who also conducts research studies. He is beginning a new study that will investigate the impact of social media use on anxiety and depression in college students. The study will use both quantitative and qualitative methods to gather data and will involve human subjects. What does Howard need to do FIRST?
    a. Obtain informed consent from the students selected to participate in the study.
    b. Ensure that the study participants are aware that they'll be compensated for their participation.
    c. Complete the approval process with the appropriate institutional review board.
    d. Participate in the peer review process with full transparency.

51. You are a social worker at a practice that employs a solution-focused model of care for clients experiencing substance use concerns. You have been working with a client for six sessions, and they have met all of their goals and graduated to a step-down program. You have terminated services with them and are now conducting an aftercare appointment to check in. This client shares that they are struggling to build rapport with the therapist in their new program and are seeking to return to your program, fearing they may relapse. What is the MOST appropriate response in this situation?

    a. Refer the client to a new program in order to prevent relapse.

    b. Empathize with the client and process how difficult change can be.

    c. Readmit the client in your program, respecting the client's request.

52. Jake is a school social worker at a high school. He has been meeting with Tyler, a tenth-grade student, for a few weeks. Tyler was referred by his teachers after he began missing classes and skipping school. They have spent the past few sessions building rapport, talking about some of the stressors in Tyler's home life that have been impacting him at school, and Jake has completed his assessment. What should Jake do NEXT?

    a. Work with Tyler to create a treatment plan and goals for their work together.

    b. Create a treatment plan to reduce Tyler's truancy and inform Tyler of this plan in their next session.

    c. Refer Tyler to the school psychologist for academic testing and evaluation.

    d. Contact Tyler's teachers to update them so they can be more understanding.

53. Jonah is a social worker at a substance use treatment facility that uses a harm reduction philosophy. He works with a program that provides individual, group, and family counseling services for people struggling with substance abuse. He is meeting with Cody, who has been struggling to maintain sobriety. What is the MOST appropriate response?

    a. Review the facility's zero tolerance policy and explain that Cody will be referred to a new program if he continues not to comply.

    b. Mandate weekly drug testing to monitor Cody's sobriety and report the results to his treatment team.

    c. Provide Cody with overdose prevention education, safety planning, and overdose reversal medication resources.

    d. Begin the process of involuntary commitment for inpatient detox and substance use treatment.

54. Social work supervisors use a variety of methods to teach supervisees the skills and knowledge they need to practice social work. Which of the following teaching techniques is the MOST effective in supervision?

    a. Visual techniques, such as watching videos or reading journal articles

    b. Hands-on techniques, such as field work or shadowing a mentor

    c. Auditory techniques, such as podcasts and lectures

    d. Depends on the supervisee

55. Drew is a social worker who provides grief counseling services at a hospital. He is having his second session with Hannah, a 40-year-old woman who has been struggling with her grief after losing her husband unexpectedly a few weeks ago. Hannah shares that she has been struggling with appetite changes, being able to sleep, maintaining her normal chores and activities, and feeling intense sadness and loneliness. Hannah tells Drew that she tries to forget that her husband is gone and struggles to believe that this is real. Which intervention would NOT be appropriate?

    a. Refer Hannah to a grief support group for bereaved spouses.

    b. Provide education and normalization on grief and its impact.

    c. Give Hannah a diagnosis of prolonged grief disorder.

    d. Conduct a standard biopsychosocial and risk assessment.

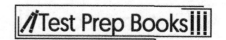

56. Hollis is a social worker supervisor at a hospital. Part of his role is to supervise the graduate social work interns each year. Hollis is supervising a student intern named Nadia this year, and he receives a social media friend request from her. When he addresses this with Nadia in supervision, she explains that using the social media app's messaging feature is the easiest way for her to be in touch about anything urgent that comes up with her schedule or the internship. How should Hollis respond?

    a. Agree to communicate on social media only for this purpose and set boundaries they are both comfortable with.

    b. Explain that this crosses a boundary in their relationship and she will need to communicate by phone or email.

    c. Accept the friend request and offer to connect with all the interns he supervises on social media if this is their preferred communication method.

57. Liza is a social worker at a shelter for people experiencing homelessness. She has been working with Jim, an older man who has been seeking shelter services for many years, to find housing so he can move out of the shelter. In their session, Jim makes a list of the steps needed to obtain an apartment and asks Liza if she can help him apply for state funding during a future session. What stage of change BEST represents where Jim is at?

    a. Precontemplation

    b. Action

    c. Preparation

    d. Maintenance

58. Winnie is a social worker at a counseling center for children. She is meeting with Laurel, the mother of her 7-year-old client named Jack. Laurel shares that she's been struggling to get Jack to listen to her and that he only follows the rules at home when she rewards him for good behavior or yells at him for misbehaving. Laurel tells Winnie that she wants Jack to do the right thing without having to be told and asks Winnie what she thinks is going on. What is the BEST explanation for Jack's behavior?

    a. Jack is displaying developmentally normal behavior for a child with preconventional morality.

    b. Jack is displaying developmentally normal behavior for a child who has just learned to grasp object permanence.

    c. Jack is displaying developmentally normal behavior for a child grappling with the stage of initiative vs guilt.

    d. Jack is displaying developmentally normal behavior for a child who does not yet understand abstract thought.

59. Jenna is a social worker working as a therapist in a local community mental health center. Her 38-year-old client, Betty, has been coming in for sessions with Jenna for about four months. Betty is now going through a contentious divorce that involves a custody battle for the couple's young children. The judge overseeing the case has subpoenaed Jenna to testify regarding Betty's mental health. Betty is greatly upset by this and asks Jenna not to testify. Which option reflects the BEST strategy moving forward?

    a. Jenna should consult with her organization's legal team.

    b. Jenna should not reply to the subpoena per HIPAA guidelines.

    c. Jenna should immediately submit treatment plans and therapy notes to the court.

    d. Jenna should be intentional about what she shares so that she doesn't damage rapport with Betty.

60. If a client needs a social worker to discuss their situation with another agency or professional, they need to sign which of the following?

    a. Release of conditions

    b. Developmental disability waiver

    c. Contract

    d. Release of information

61. Dee is a 25-year-old in therapy for traumatic grief following a car crash in which they survived and their partner died. They have experienced intermittent symptoms of detachment, intense sadness, and anxiety. Dee's social worker has been working with them for a few weeks on feeling comfortable to share about their experience that night. They sit down for their latest session and the therapist opens with, "Hey there, Dee. I'm so glad you're here. Talk to me about what's been going on for you this week." In psychoanalysis, this method can BEST be described as what?

    a. Guided discovery
    b. Mindfulness
    c. Validation
    d. Free association

62. Marie is a social worker at an agency that provides in-home care for seniors in a small rural community. She is working on improving the agency's policy on home visiting safety for the staff after receiving a few complaints by staff members that they felt unsafe or uncomfortable. What should she do FIRST?

    a. Implement the policy utilized at a different branch of the agency located in a nearby city.
    b. Create a policy for all home visits to be done in pairs to promote worker safety.
    c. Meet with staff to hear their perspective on the areas of concern as well as what is working.
    d. Work with the staff to understand the importance of home visiting and how it benefits clients.

63. Johanna is a social worker who works in a clinic for immigrant and refugee families. She is meeting with an elderly Chinese couple who speak Cantonese as their primary language. This is their first session, and Johanna plans to conduct an intake assessment. When she meets them in the waiting room, their niece Lin is also present, who says she is there to translate the session. She explains this is what her aunt and uncle are most comfortable with, and they requested she join them. How should Johanna respond?

    a. Allow Lin to translate the session if her aunt and uncle consent and sign a release of information.
    b. Explain that all translation services must be done by a certified third-party interpreter.
    c. Inform the family that only the identified clients are allowed in the meeting space due to confidentiality protocols.

64. Howard supervises the social work student interns at a community mental health clinic. He is meeting with Jody, a social work student intern whom he supervises. Jody states that she is struggling with where to begin with her new client because they have so many challenges. Jody explains that her client is dealing with chronic homelessness, anxiety, and loneliness, among other issues. She asks for Howard's input on what she should work on first with her client. What is the BEST suggestion?

    a. Application for housing and food assistance
    b. Cognitive behavioral therapy for anxiety
    c. Referral to a support group to build skills of interpersonal effectiveness
    d. Education on financial literacy and employment

65. According to Kohlberg's theory, at which level of moral development do people conform to established rules and laws of society?

    a. Preconventional
    b. Conventional
    c. Postconventional
    d. Adult

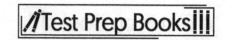

66. Margot is a social worker at a college counseling center. She is meeting with Will, a freshman college student who has been having trouble adjusting. Will shares that he has been having a lot of anxiety and feels easily overwhelmed since coming to college. He reports that this has caused him to miss some classes and avoid socializing. Will tells Margot that when he felt anxiety at home, he would spend time with his parents, but now that he's living on campus, he does not know what to do when he feels this way. What would be the MOST relevant treatment goal for Will?
    a. Transfer to a community college program to be able to live at home with his parents.
    b. Develop and practice coping skills to use when he is anxious and overwhelmed.
    c. Join a campus club based on his interests to meet new people.

67. Justin is a social worker at a psychiatric hospital. He receives a subpoena to release the full record for a former patient as part of a court case. He consults his supervisor and the hospital's legal department to confirm that it's legitimate. What should he do NEXT?
    a. Contact the client and obtain his written consent before releasing the record.
    b. Immediately submit the full records to the court as is required by law.
    c. Submit the record but ask for the records to be sealed from public view after the trial concludes.
    d. Request that the court withdraw the request or limit the request to specific parts of the record.

68. Carrie is a social worker at a hospital. She is meeting with Tim, a 40-year-old man who has recently been diagnosed with a terminal illness. Carrie is providing social work services to support Tim with processing and coping with this difficult diagnosis, and she is working to connect him to the appropriate resources. During their meeting, Tim has a hard time controlling his anger, and he takes a lot of anger and frustration out on Carrie. What is the BEST response?
    a. Carrie should provide validation, normalization, and education on the stages of grief.
    b. Carrie should connect Tim with an anger management support group.
    c. Carrie should request a medical consult to ensure that this personality change does not have an organic cause.
    d. Carrie should wait to meet with Tim until he feels less angry and is ready to work together.

69. Margo is a 54-year-old who is working with a social worker to help navigate her own depression amidst a challenging separation with her wife, who recently disclosed that she had an affair. Margo and her wife share three teenage children. Margo's wife is currently living separately from the family amidst the separation. During their second session, Margo shares with the social worker that she is considering allowing her wife to move back in. What is the BEST approach for the social worker to take?
    a. Advise that this will make things more complicated and that she probably should not do that.
    b. Acknowledge that Margo knows best what will work for her and her family.
    c. Encourage Margo to bring her wife in for couple's therapy.

70. If a person experiences major depression and alcohol use disorder at the same time, the two conditions are said to be _____.
    a. comorbid
    b. postmorbid
    c. contraindicated
    d. aggravated

71. Minh is a social worker who is the owner of an outpatient counseling center for adults. Recently, many clients have requested that the agency and clinicians communicate electronically for easier communication. What should Minh do NEXT?
   a. Allow clients to communicate with their clinician by text or email if they sign a waiver indicating informed consent of the associated risks.
   b. Explain to the clients that this is not possible because social workers are legally prohibited from electronically sharing anything considered to be personal health information.
   c. Implement a system that allows for encrypted and password-protected electronic communication.
   d. Consult the insurance payors who are paneled with the agency to determine if electronic communication would be billable.

72. Jim is a social worker at a community health center. He is meeting with a new patient named Mary, a young woman who is deaf and uses American Sign Language as her primary method of communication. Jim has never worked with a deaf patient before and wants to be sure that he provides adequate support. Which response displays cultural competence the LEAST?
   a. Utilizing a certified ASL translator for all sessions and services
   b. Making referrals to other agencies that provide accessible services for deaf patients
   c. Researching deaf culture prior to meeting with Mary to better educate himself
   d. Asking Mary to educate him on deaf culture and resources in the area

73. Deanna is a social worker who runs a grief support group for community members. One of the members is Jonas, a 70-year-old man who lost his wife last year in a car accident. Jonas has been coming to the group for several months and almost always shares about his journey with grief. Deanna is often struck by how he has been able to cope with his grief in healthy ways and maintain his sense of identity even when faced with tragedy. What does this demonstrate?
   a. Jonah has well-developed ego strength.
   b. Jonah does not have any diagnosable mental illnesses.
   c. Jonah has ego-dystonic coping strategies.
   d. Jonah has a healthy attachment style.

74. You are a social worker in a college counseling center. You have been working with Ashley, a student seeking support for anxiety and school-related stressors, for several months. During your session one day, Ashley is talking about some dental work she has to get done, finally disclosing that she has engaged in binging and purging behaviors regularly for the last few years. She shares that she is ready to start addressing these behaviors in treatment. Your experience with disordered eating is very minimal. What is the MOST appropriate course of action to take?
   a. Refer Ashley to a treatment program that specializes in eating disorders.
   b. Increase your knowledge around eating disorders, as you already have a strong rapport with Ashley.
   c. Recommend a support group for Ashley.

75. A social worker is conducting research to determine the effectiveness of a new tool for measuring symptoms of depression. The tool asks a series of questions and assigns each participant a number from 0 to 10, with 10 indicating the highest level of depression and 0 indicating no evidence of depression. The tool is used multiple times for each participant and produces consistent results; however, the results do not accurately reflect each participant's depressive symptoms. What can be said about this tool?
   a. It lacks reliability.
   b. It lacks validity.
   c. It has internal validity but not external validity.
   d. It has external validity but not internal validity.

76. Kate is a social worker at a college counseling center. She is meeting with May, a 19-year-old student of Asian American descent. May is processing a recent incident during which she experienced racial discrimination from other students, and she is telling Kate about how this impacted her. She shares that it led her to get connected to other groups of students with similar cultural identities and to strengthen her own cultural identity. What is the BEST explanation for what May is experiencing?
    a. May is exploring and learning about intersectionality.
    b. May is experiencing the immersion-emersion stage of identity development.
    c. May is learning to develop cultural competence for interpersonal relationships.
    d. May is navigating the psychosocial developmental stage of identity vs. role confusion.

77. Linda is a social worker at a residential program for young adults. She is working with Mindy, a 24-year-old woman who moved into the program following a psychiatric hospitalization prompted by thoughts of a suicide. Mindy has a history of multiple hospitalizations and of mood instability, impulsive behavior, feelings of emptiness, and difficulty maintaining stable relationships. Linda and Mindy are working on treatment goals that include increasing Mindy's ability to regulate her emotions and tolerate distress. Mindy has also been attending a weekly group for dialectical behavioral therapy that she reports is helpful. What is the MOST likely diagnosis?
    a. Schizoid personality disorder
    b. Borderline personality disorder
    c. Antisocial personality disorder
    d. Histrionic personality disorder

78. Farrah is a 29-year-old in therapy to support and encourage positive parenting skills. This week, she is discussing feeling overwhelmed with establishing a seamless bedtime routine with her 4-year-old daughter. Farrah shares that her daughter becomes tearful and throws her toys when Farrah asks her to brush her teeth. Utilizing the ACT model, how might Farrah's social worker suggest that Farrah approach limit setting with her daughter?
    a. Establish clear, reasonable consequences for her daughter's behavior and remain firm in her decision to discipline her.
    b. Validate her daughter's sadness, affirm that throwing is not safe, and offer alternative behavior options for her choose from.
    c. Empathize with her daughter's sadness and offer her space to cool down.
    d. When her daughter begins throwing things, redirect her to a safe location where she cannot do harm.

79. Ginny is a social worker at an elementary school. She's been working with Olivia, a second-grade student who has been struggling academically and appears to have withdrawn socially. Ginny observes that Olivia has repeatedly come to school with bruises. When she asked Olivia about the injuries, Olivia became quiet and tearful, then said they were from playing outside. Ginny has been unable to reach her parents, and they haven't responded to her outreach. She is concerned that Olivia is being physically abused but does not have definite proof. What should Ginny do NEXT?
    a. File a Child Protective Services report citing the concerns of physical abuse due to her obligation as a mandated reporter.
    b. Speak to Olivia's teachers to see if anyone else has similar concerns and ask them to notify her if they see further injuries.
    c. Continue to talk to Olivia about the situation until she can gather enough evidence of physical abuse to warrant a Child Protective Services report.
    d. Consult the school principal and legal team before filing a report to ensure that Ginny or the school will not be legally liable if the allegations are incorrect.

80. A social worker is meeting a new client with a previous diagnosis of schizophrenia. When asked about their diagnosis, the client states that they don't know much about the disorder except that it is caused by demons and bad spirits. The social worker explains what schizophrenia is, what causes it, how it affects people, what symptoms they might experience, how it's treated, and what community resources are available. What is this type of explanation called?
- a. Partializing
- b. Psychotherapy
- c. Psychoeducation
- d. Assessment

81. What is an example of an invisible disability?
- a. Down's syndrome
- b. Tourette's syndrome
- c. Chronic fatigue syndrome
- d. Paraplegia

82. Kurt is a social worker at an outpatient clinic in an urban area. His client is a 22-year-old man who is struggling with intrusive thoughts and anxiety, and he just started therapy with Kurt last week. Kurt is curious about the efficacy of asking the client to utilize a journal to record thought and mood patterns. How should he incorporate this into treatment?
- a. Kurt should wait until this client has been in treatment for at least two months.
- b. Kurt should not, as self-monitoring is not a recommended intervention for anxiety.
- c. Kurt should make it optional so that the client doesn't feel unnecessary pressure.
- d. Kurt should introduce the concept as soon as possible.

83. Olivia is a social worker at an outpatient counseling center. She has been working with Lucas, a middle-aged man, for several months. Lucas began seeking therapy for anxiety after his anxiety led to him quitting his job and avoiding social settings. Lucas has made significant progress over the past few months and met his treatment goals. Lucas and Olivia have decided together that he is ready to terminate services. What should Olivia do NEXT?
- a. Submit a referral to a psychiatrist to assess for medication management needs.
- b. Contact Lucas's primary care provider to give an update on their treatment and the services provided.
- c. Work with Lucas to create an aftercare plan that includes how to contact other resources as needed.
- d. Provide Lucas with her personal contact information and tell him he can reach out to her anytime.

84. Raven is a social worker in private practice. One of her clients, Sam, owns a local restaurant. During a session, Sam explains that he is temporarily low on money because he is expanding his business. He proposes a deal where he will pay Raven half of her usual fee and make up the rest in gift certificates to his restaurant. Otherwise, Sam will have to reduce the frequency of his sessions. Raven is tempted because she hates cooking and does not want Sam to reduce the frequency of his sessions. It would be unethical for Raven to accept Sam's offer because it is an example of which of the following?
- a. Dual relationship
- b. Bartering
- c. Personal gain
- d. Altruistic instinct

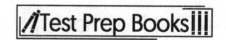

85. Jada is a social worker at a counseling center for children and adolescents. She is working with an 8-year-old client named Savannah who has been in therapy since her parents' recent divorce. Savannah's parents are concerned because she has started wetting the bed again, crying uncontrollably when her mother drops her off at school, and having trouble sleeping. What is the BEST explanation for Savannah's change in behavior?
    a. Savannah is experiencing a behavioral regression.
    b. Savannah is projecting her feelings about the divorce.
    c. Savannah is showing signs of an insecure attachment to her parents.
    d. Savannah is showing delays in her cognitive development.

86. Jeremy is a social worker conducting an evaluation of a pilot program run by a local hospital. The program was designed to provide education to parents of teenagers on the topic of mental health. Jeremy is reviewing the results to identify if the program was successful. Which statement provides objective evidence that the program met its goal of educating parents on adolescent mental health?
    a. The facilitators of the program felt as though parents were engaging with the material, asking questions, and sharing their own stories.
    b. Most of the parents enrolled came to every class offered, and three-quarters of the parents signed up for a second session.
    c. The majority of parents who attended were able to correctly identify adolescent mental health concerns and community resources on the post-test.
    d. None of the children of the parents in the course required psychiatric hospitalization during the time the evaluation was conducted.

87. Which of the following alterations in self-image is NOT associated with trauma?
    a. Feeling like a bad person
    b. Developing gender dysphoria
    c. Feeling like the world is unsafe
    d. Having difficulty trusting others

88. Matt is a social worker at a clinic that provides mental health services to veterans. Matt is a veteran himself, a fact he is open about with his clients. Matt is working with Jacob, a 30-year-old veteran, to provide trauma treatment. Jacob recently returned home and is struggling to find employment. Matt finds himself wanting to help Jacob with this because he remembers how difficult the reintegration process can be. During a recent session, Jacob asks Matt if he can list him as a professional reference. How should Jacob respond?
    a. Agree to be listed as a reference to support the client's self-determination, but ask him to use his personal email rather than his agency one to avoid breaching confidentiality.
    b. Explain that he is not able to provide a job reference due to the nature of their relationship, but offer to refer him to a vocational program for veterans.
    c. Refuse to provide a reference to avoid a dual relationship, but offer to get him an interview at a friend's company who likes to hire fellow veterans.
    d. Discuss the pros and cons of Matt providing a professional reference and agree to do so if Jacob is comfortable with the risks.

89. Social workers help clients recognize stressors and problems in their lives, make plans for how to address them, and put the plan into action. What theoretical model describes this process?
    a. The cognitive behavioral model
    b. The problem-solving therapeutic model
    c. The psychoanalytic model
    d. The person-in-environment model

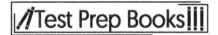
90. Maura is a social worker at a program for adults with developmental disabilities. She runs a weekly group on independent living skills. She often leads activities in which clients have opportunities to teach each other new skills by modeling them for the group. What framework is guiding this group?
   a.   Strengths-based approach
   b.   Humanistic theory
   c.   Social learning theory
   d.   Cognitive learning theory

91. You facilitate a weekly group therapy session and are several weeks into the group. One week, two of the group members get into an intense conversation about religion, which eventually devolves into an argument. The other group members remain quiet and are visibly uncomfortable. What is the BEST way to intervene?
   a.   Intervene and bring the focus back to the group's ground rules.
   b.   Ask the members who are arguing to finish the argument outside of the room.
   c.   Interrupt and take the opportunity to set ground rules for the group.

92. Tammy is a social worker at a high school. One of the students on her caseload is Kayla, a 19-year-old student receiving special education services due to her developmental delays. Kayla's mother is her guardian and is very involved. Kayla is graduating this year, and the plan is for her to attend college while continuing to live with her mother. However, Kayla tells Tammy that her goal is to work on her independent living skills so she is able to move into her own apartment. What should Tammy do NEXT?
   a.   Talk to Kayla's mother and share Kayla's goal of independent living, and advocate for her mother to respect her daughter's self-determination.
   b.   Tell Kayla she needs to accept her mother's decision for her to continue living at home because her mother makes the financial decisions as her guardian.
   c.   Advocate for Kayla to be included in the upcoming family meeting with the special education team and support her in voicing her thoughts and goals.
   d.   Advocate for the guardianship terms to be reviewed because Kayla's mother isn't acting in Kayla's best interest or in alignment with her wishes.

93. Jan is a social worker at an intensive outpatient program for adolescents. She is having her first session today with Tom, a 16-year-old male who just completed a year-long residential program for depression treatment. Prior to starting outpatient care, Tom's mother signed a release for Jan to talk to the residential social worker. Jan spoke to the previous counselor and received Tom's records that provided detailed background on his history. In the first session, Tom states he knows she already talked to his last counselor, and he doesn't feel like retelling his story to someone new. Why is it still necessary for Jan to conduct a biopsychosocial assessment with Tom?
   a.   It will not be possible to bill for insurance coverage unless the first visit is an assessment.
   b.   Social workers need to conduct their own assessment to build rapport and inform treatment planning.
   c.   It is required that a new biopsychosocial assessment be conducted every two months and documented in the record.

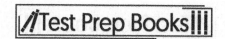

94. Ben is a social worker at a child welfare agency. He provides individual and group-based parenting support to parents who have had child welfare involvement. He is meeting with Maggie, a young mother who is new to his caseload. Maggie has an 8-year-old son who has been struggling at school and has been disciplined frequently. She tells Ben that her son never listens to her, despite how much she tries to get him to like her. She says that she tries not to ask too much of her son at home and always tries to talk to him instead of punishing him. Maggie asks for advice. What should Ben do NEXT?
    a. Explain that the child is exhibiting developmentally normal and age-appropriate behavior and should be supported.
    b. Educate Maggie that her behavior is a form of permissive parenting, which can often lead to challenges for children, such as behavioral issues and conflict with authority.
    c. Encourage Maggie to spend more time with the child so that he doesn't need to seek her attention through negative behavior.

95. A social worker is providing therapy to a 10-year-old boy whose parents are going through a divorce. He recently had a doctor's appointment at the suggestion of the school nurse who said the boy was coming to her office several times a week complaining about a sore tummy. The doctor did a full evaluation and determined that the boy is healthy and has no signs of gastrointestinal illness. The boy continues to complain about tummy aches frequently, and the social worker has observed that these episodes appear genuinely painful. The social worker does not believe that the boy is faking his symptoms. What is the MOST likely explanation for the tummy aches?
    a. A medical condition missed by the doctor
    b. Factitious disorder
    c. Hypochondria
    d. Somatization

96. Kara is a social worker in a hospital. She's asked to meet with Ivan, a 90-year-old man who was recently diagnosed with a chronic health condition. Ivan lives alone and has refused the recommendation for in-home support services or moving to a skilled nursing facility. Ivan states that he has lived alone for a long time and that will not be changing. His doctor confirms that he is competent and decisional. What should Kara do NEXT?
    a. Talk about the risks of living alone without assistance, provide resources, and allow Ivan to make his own decision.
    b. Set up a family team meeting with Ivan's children and medical team to discuss the severity of his health condition and the potential safety concerns with living alone.
    c. Explain to Ivan that if he declines the assistance being recommended, it will be documented in his chart and may impact his ability to receive treatment at the hospital in the future.
    d. Accept his refusal, end the meeting, and document his decision in his medical chart.

97. Lorraine is a social worker at a hospital-based mental health center. She is meeting with Joel, a 20-year-old young man referred for treatment for mild depression. Joel is also receiving medication management at the clinic. Joel's insurance has approved 12 sessions of therapy. He reports that his goals for treatment include gaining more control over his depressive thoughts, changing his response to these thoughts, and increasing healthy coping skills. What treatment modality would be MOST appropriate?
    a. Prolonged exposure therapy
    b. Cognitive behavioral therapy
    c. Structural therapy
    d. Play therapy

98. Dan is seeing a social worker about his depression. They have met for a couple of sessions during which the social worker asked a lot of questions and had Dan complete the Beck Depression Inventory. Together they have come up with goals for Dan, and now they are talking about different ways they could accomplish those goals. The social worker has suggested some evidence-based interventions, and they are determining which one would work best for Dan's situation. Which phase of treatment is Dan in?
   a. Engagement
   b. Evaluation
   c. Planning
   d. Implementation

99. Jerry is a social worker at an assisted living facility for elders. He is facilitating a family meeting for a 70-year-old resident named Michael and his three adult children. Michael has been declining physically, and his children want him to move along the continuum of care to a skilled nursing facility. Michael says that he is not ready for that; he would like to remain as independent as possible for as long as he can. Michael's children become upset and frustrated, and they ask Jerry to convince their father to move. What should be Jerry's FIRST response?
   a. Validate everyone's emotions and facilitate a discussion around the pros and cons of all possible choices.
   b. Explain to Michael the risks of remaining independent and the possible consequences of remaining in the assisted living facility.
   c. Require Michael to consult with his primary care provider to assess if he has decision-making capacity.
   d. Tell the children that it is not their decision because they do not hold the role of financial power of attorney.

100. Jim is a social worker supporting a client, Nat, who has been married for 22 years. Her husband has struggled with alcoholism for several years, which can manifest as not being well enough to support Nat with taking care of the children, pets, and home in general. Nat finds that she is overwhelmed and near her breaking point. What is the BEST response for Jim to use to support Nat in setting boundaries?
   a. "I hear how stressful this is for you. It makes sense to me that you should ask him to move out until he is willing to get sober."
   b. "You've been dealing with this for so long. How are you taking care of yourself?"
   c. "You have been managing so much on your own. I wonder, how is your husband is being held accountable for his share?"
   d. "In these situations, it can make sense to ask for a divorce in order to maintain your own well-being."

101. Wanda is a social worker in an emergency department at a hospital. She is meeting with Jorge, an elderly man who was admitted to the hospital earlier in the evening for treatment of a respiratory illness. His medical team requested a social work consult because he was unable to provide information about next of kin and appeared confused and combative. His medical team determined that there was no organic or medical reason for his behavior. Wanda notices that Jorge is struggling to follow the conversation and appears forgetful. What should she do FIRST?
   a. Conduct a mental status exam.
   b. Initiate treatment for psychosis symptoms.
   c. Refer Jorge to a neuropsychologist for further testing.
   d. Ask Jorge to sign a release of information so she can contact his primary care provider.

102. Jeanne is a social worker at an outpatient counseling center. She has been working with her client Dee, a 50-year-old woman, for six months, and they have a good rapport. Dee recently shared with Jeanne that she's considering asking her spouse for a divorce and that this decision is causing a lot of stress. Jeanne belongs to a religion that does not condone divorce, and this belief is impacting her work with Dee. What should Jeanne do NEXT?
   a. Be transparent with Dee about her religious beliefs so they can work through the problem collaboratively.
   b. Transfer Dee to a different social worker at the clinic to avoid Jeanne's bias impacting Dee's treatment.
   c. Seek supervision to discuss and process the bias and countertransference she's experiencing.
   d. Ignore her personal feelings and be professional towards Dee so her treatment is not disrupted.

103. According to Elizabeth Kubler-Ross, there are five stages of grief. They occur in what order?
   a. Denial, anger, bargaining, acceptance, depression
   b. Anger, depression, denial, isolation, bargaining
   c. Refusal, denial, isolation, anger, acceptance
   d. Denial, anger, bargaining, depression, acceptance

104. In an initial session with a social worker, John, who is a new father, tells a funny story about his baby. The social worker tells him that almost the exact same thing happened when his first child was a baby and quickly relays the anecdote. What is this an example of?
   a. Dual relationship
   b. Self-disclosure
   c. Boundary violation
   d. Empathic communication

105. Mary is a school social worker. Recently, school officials made policy changes that Mary believes will negatively impact students' long-term emotional well-being. What should Mary do FIRST to respond to this situation?
   a. Form a coalition of students and teachers to present their concerns.
   b. Start a regular parent support group to increase advocacy skills.
   c. Speak directly to the school officials to voice her concerns.

106. Kim is a social worker at a community mental health clinic. She is providing family therapy to the Johnson family, which consists of two parents, a 16-year-old daughter, and a 14-year-old son. The family has been struggling with conflict and communication challenges that have led them to seek family therapy. Kim has observed that the family members tend to escalate quickly into verbal conflict, say hurtful comments, and then quickly apologize when someone becomes upset without addressing the root of the issue. When Kim addresses this, the family members become defensive and state that they don't want to "cause problems," but they also can't help how they feel. What is the BEST explanation for this family dynamic?
   a. The family members are using the strategy of equifinality in their communication.
   b. The children are triangulating the parents, which leads to conflict.
   c. The family members are stuck in a negative feedback loop.

107. Which of the following is NOT a collateral source?
   a. Family members
   b. Police officers
   c. Client
   d. Other medical providers

108. Derek is a social worker at a hospital. He is participating in a multidisciplinary case review meeting. The patient being discussed is Brad, a 50-year-old male patient with a substance use disorder who is requiring treatment for liver failure. During the meeting, Derek notices that one physician is using judgmental and blaming language regarding the substance use. What is the BEST response?
   a. Discuss the situation in the upcoming peer supervision meeting for the hospital social workers.
   b. Provide education on the nature of substance use disorder and the appropriate language to utilize and advocate for the patient's best interest.
   c. Report the physician to the ethics review board at the hospital.
   d. Give feedback on the social work needs but do not acknowledge the physician's comments because it could be out of scope of practice.

109. Controlled observation can be BEST defined as which of the following?
   a. Picking up on non-verbal cues in the surrounding environment for a holistic assessment
   b. Recalling interactions with the client to fill in gaps of information
   c. Purposely targeting a client's behaviors in a pre-determined setting
   d. Looking at facial expressions and mannerisms to gain insight on communicative deficits

110. Dave is a social worker at a community center in a large, diverse town. He runs a family life education program that offers multiple different services, but he has been tasked with cutting one of their programs due to a loss of funding. He is working with his team to determine what options would best support all families in the area. Which is the LEAST appropriate program?
   a. A financial planning workshop for families run by a local accounting agency
   b. A workshop for caregivers on the topic of attachment run by a social worker
   c. A course for new parents on newborn safety facilitated by the local hospital
   d. A Christian premarital education course for couples led by a local church

111. Hector is a school social worker at a middle school. He is attending the annual IEP meeting for Ramona, a seventh-grade student who has been struggling in her classes. Ramona recently had educational testing completed by the school psychologist to determine her educational needs. The purpose of the meeting is to set goals for her IEP. During the meeting, it is shared that Ramona scored low on the WISC-V. What intervention would be MOST appropriate?
   a. Ramona will receive weekly counseling with Hector to treat social anxiety to help her do better in school.
   b. Ramona will join a female empowerment group run by school staff designed to help build self-esteem.
   c. Ramona will be given academic support designed to benefit students with intellectual disabilities.

112. Phoebe is a social worker who is meeting for individual sessions with a 13-year-old client. During their session, the client shares that they've been struggling with suicidal ideation. Not only that, but they have considered a specific plan and know how to gain access to means to implementing this plan. They have not shared this with their parents. The social worker provides empathy and validation for client. What should the social worker do NEXT?
   a. Talk to the client about their limits of confidentiality when it relates to imminent risk of harm to self.
   b. Engage in the session as usual and then call the client's parents afterwards to express her concerns.
   c. Dispatch emergency services to transport the client to the hospital for evaluation.

113. Judy is a social worker at an eating disorder treatment facility. She is working with a new client named Ella, a 20-year-old young woman. Ella reminds Judy of her daughter, and she finds herself feeling protective of her and looking forward to their sessions. Judy feels very motivated to help Ella in her treatment. What should Judy do about these feelings?
    a. Seek clinical supervision to process her feelings of countertransference.
    b. Transfer Ella to a different social worker because it's not possible to remain objective when there is transference.
    c. There is no need to change anything because her feelings are positively impacting their rapport and work together.

114. According to Sue & Sue's stages of racial/cultural identity development, which stage is characterized by a period of rethinking or challenging one's beliefs where the individual examines and appreciates positive aspects of their own racial/cultural group for the first time?
    a. Dissonance
    b. Conformity
    c. Introspection
    d. Resistance and immersion

115. Juliet is a social worker with a child welfare agency. She is meeting with Bryan, a 6-year-old boy on her caseload. Bryan was recently placed in foster care due to experiencing neglect and physical abuse at home and is living with a new foster family. During Juliet's monthly visit with Bryan and his foster parents, they share that Bryan has been misbehaving, is not getting along with the other child in the home, and has frequent emotional outbursts. When Juliet contacts Bryan's school counselor to gather more information, she learns that this behavior at home started recently. What is the MOST likely cause of Bryan's behavior?
    a. Bryan is showing signs of bipolar disorder that has gone untreated.
    b. Bryan has experienced adverse childhood experiences and traumatic stress.
    c. Bryan has an autism spectrum disorder.
    d. Bryan is not being treated well by his foster parents and foster sibling.

116. When should a licensed clinical social worker ask about a client's sexual history?
    a. Only when the information is necessary for treatment
    b. During the initial meeting with the client
    c. Early in the therapeutic process, once rapport has been established
    d. On the standard intake form for all clients

117. Ingrid is a 34-year-old mother of two who is coming to therapy to address ongoing depression. During her first session with her social worker Jack, Ingrid shares that she has been struggling with fatigue and shortness of breath and feels cold constantly. What should Jack do NEXT?
    a. Establish treatment goals to improve these symptoms.
    b. Ask Ingrid to get a medical assessment.
    c. Initiate a substance use assessment.
    d. Gather a complete social history for Ingrid.

118. Lucas is a social work supervisor at a community health center. Part of his role is to provide weekly clinical supervision to the master's level social workers on his team. He's been meeting with a new social worker named Lori for the past few months. Lori has been using her supervision time to process some personal challenges and how they could impact her work. Lately, Lucas has noticed that Lori uses the majority of her supervision time to discuss her own mental health challenges. When he addressed this, she said that Lucas is a good listener and this was where she felt most comfortable to discuss these issues. What should Lucas do NEXT?

a. Continue providing emotional support for Lori during supervision because this is part of his role as clinical supervisor.

b. Address the concerns, discuss boundaries in the supervisor role, and direct Lori to resources such as EAP to help her find other options for personal therapeutic support.

c. Tell Lori he is no longer comfortable providing her clinical supervision hours because she is not adhering to appropriate boundaries in the supervisor/supervisee relationship.

d. Require Lori take a medical leave of absence to receive mental health treatment and request a physician letter before she returns to her role.

119. Mistrust of others, fear of going home, presence of marks, and frequent vomiting are indicators of what?

a. Physical neglect

b. Physical abuse

c. Sexual abuse

d. Psychological abuse

120. You are a supervisor within an in-demand intensive treatment program for eating disorders. You hold a weekly meeting with your team to review new applicants and establish whether or not they would be a good fit for the program. Team members have begun to voice frustration about these meetings, citing that much of the time is taken up by unrelated discussion of other team members processing current patient situations. What is the BEST way to manage this situation?

a. Review fewer applicants during the meeting so that there is time to process current concerns.

b. Set firmer time limits for this meeting.

c. Meet with problem staff members individually.

d. Establish a separate meeting for current case consultations.

121. Lula is a social worker at a primary care office that uses a trauma-informed care model. She received a referral to meet with Nadia, a young woman who was referred by her primary care provider due to stress and anxiety. During the intake, Lula asks Nadia to fill out a trauma screening questionnaire. Nadia asks why this is necessary, as she did not report experiencing any trauma to her doctor. How should Lula respond?

a. Tell Nadia that it must have been a mistake, and this form is only for patients who have reported a traumatic experience.

b. Explain that this questionnaire is given to all patients during the first session, but it's her choice to not complete this if she isn't comfortable.

c. Tell Nadia that she has to complete this form in order to receive therapy services through this program.

d. Explain that completing this questionnaire is required for insurance reimbursement and billing.

122. Kelly is heading a board of social workers who are developing a local program to help recently incarcerated individuals reintegrate into society. When considering how their team will implement successful service delivery, what is the MOST important thing to consider?

a. Establish ethical employment practices that support diverse staffing.

b. Mandate participation for all involved members to set an example for future clients.

c. Consider the needs of the former inmates to be at the forefront of creating policies.

d. Ensure that all staff members are receiving annual ethics training.

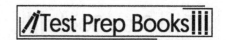

123. A social worker has been meeting with Sam for weekly therapy sessions to address his alcohol use. Sam has a history of severe alcohol use disorder resulting in decreased liver function, relationship problems, and a DUI. His doctor has informed him that if he drinks again, he could be at risk of exacerbating his liver problems, which could eventually cause more serious illness or even death. With the help of therapy, he stopped drinking two months ago and has been making great progress. One day, he arrives to therapy and states that he has decided to start drinking again. The therapist is contemplating putting Sam on an involuntary psychiatric hold. Would this be ethical?
   a. Yes, because drinking could cause Sam's death.
   b. Yes, because the DUI proves that Sam's drinking is a threat to other people.
   c. No, because alcohol use disorder is a medical issue, not a psychological issue.
   d. No, because Sam has the right to make this decision for himself.

124. Hypervigilance, disturbing dreams, and eruptions of anger are symptoms of what psychiatric disorder?
   a. Claustrophobia
   b. PTSD
   c. Borderline personality disorder
   d. Severe anxiety with panic attacks

125. Leanne is a social worker at a college counseling center. She is meeting with Amanda, a college student who was referred by her primary care provider for counseling. Amanda discloses that she went through a difficult breakup that caused her symptoms of anxiety to increase, she has been withdrawing socially, and she feels ashamed about her looks. Amanda states that she constantly compares her body to those around her, and she believes that her breakup was related to weight gain. What should Leanne do NEXT?
   a. Provide emotional support, validate that body image struggles are normal at this age, and provide education on healthy vs. unhealthy relationship dynamics.
   b. Listen empathetically, educate Amanda that she is showing signs of an eating disorder, and suggest inpatient treatment as the best way to improve her symptoms.
   c. Provide validation, provide education around the impact of body image struggles, and engage in interventions to treat body image issues and increase self-esteem.

126. Emily is a social worker in an early intervention program. She is doing a home visit to conduct a biopsychosocial assessment with a new family that was referred by their child welfare case worker. The clients are a 1-year-old infant named Maggie and her mother Joanna. Emily asks about the problems that prompted the referral, family history, Maggie's medical history and developmental milestones, and family dynamics. Emily then asks Joanna to complete an ecomap together. What is the MOST likely reason Emily utilized this intervention?
   a. Ecomaps are required in all assessments with the birth-to-three population.
   b. Emily is assessing the family's current support systems, resources, and potential gaps in support.
   c. Emily needs to obtain history on Maggie's father, who is not a part of their life.
   d. Insurance and billing require an ecomap as part of the biopsychosocial assessment documentation.

127. Mickey is a social worker who runs an anger management group for adolescent boys at a local community center. During this week's group, Aaron, a 13-year-old participant, says that sometimes he gets so mad at another student at his school that he wants to hurt him. How should Mickey respond?
   a. Conduct a thorough risk assessment to determine the severity of the threat.
   b. Contact the school guidance counselor and ask them to move Aaron out of the student's class.
   c. Immediately call the police to file a report based on what Aaron shared in the group.
   d. Normalize this feeling and help Aaron identify coping skills to use when he feels angry.

235

128. Cecilia is a social worker who often works with families of migrant workers. A large part of her responsibility to these families is supporting them in accessing public assistance. Cecilia works in a state near an international border, and the political atmosphere is often wrought with opposing views. What is MOST important for Cecilia to be aware of?
    a. Public assistance eligibility varies depending on the jurisdiction and the program.
    b. The families must be of refugee status to be considered for public assistance.
    c. Immigrant families are not permitted to apply for most types of public assistance.
    d. Citizenship is required for immigrants to be considered for public assistance.

129. Leo is a social worker at a homeless shelter. He has been working with Maggie, another social worker, for many years. Recently, Leo has noticed that Maggie has often been late to work and is not acting like herself. During their recent peer consultation, Leo noticed the smell of alcohol on her breath. Leo is concerned, both for Maggie's well-being and the impact this could have on her work with clients. What should Leo do FIRST?
    a. Report Maggie to the human resources department of the agency due to her behavior.
    b. Continue to monitor her behavior to determine if this is a pattern before intervening.
    c. Talk to Maggie directly to address his concerns and offer assistance for her to get help.
    d. He should not get involved because Leo is not in a supervisory capacity.

130. The process of social development as defined by Lev Vygotsky suggests that one's development in life is deeply impacted by:
    a. Income status
    b. Birth order and gender
    c. The variety of social institutions, such as family, school, or church, to which someone is exposed throughout life
    d. Physical stamina and overall health

131. Perception of family relationships, mental functioning, occupation, and social class are elements that help guide which of the following?
    a. The assessment process
    b. Formal observation
    c. Diagnosis
    d. Life span development

132. You are supervising staff within a program that provides career advancement and resume writing support for first-generation college students. This program attracts clients from a variety of ethnic backgrounds. Recently, you have fielded complaints regarding a staff member's lack of sensitivity. What should you do FIRST?
    a. Remove this staff person from the program to prevent further concerns.
    b. Assess this staff person's cultural competency.
    c. Provide suggestions for workshops to the staff person to increase their knowledge.

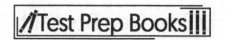

133. Pat is a social worker in private practice. She's conducting an intake session with Amelia, a 16-year-old female. Amelia's mother is also present for the intake, which Amelia agreed to. The mother states that they are here because Amelia has an eating disorder. She says that Amelia has recently lost 40 pounds, has passed out on multiple occasions, and her eating habits have changed over the past few months. The mother says that she is very worried and is hoping that Amelia will be able to begin treatment for this. Amelia states that she does not have an eating disorder, and she "just hasn't really been hungry." What should Pat do FIRST?
   a. Provide education on the different types of eating disorders and the impact they can have.
   b. Create a treatment plan to provide treatment for anorexia nervosa and connect the mother with a support group for parents of children with eating disorders.
   c. Connect Amelia with a medical provider to assess if she is medically stable and rule out a medical cause for her symptoms.
   d. Explain that eating disorders cannot be treated in an outpatient setting and refer Amelia to a residential treatment program.

134. Grace is a social worker at a family therapy clinic. She is meeting with the Logan family, which consists of two parents, an 11-year-old child, a 10-year-old child, and a newborn baby. The parents state that the older children have had many behavioral problems since the baby's birth, and the children express frustration that they don't have the same amount of time with their parents anymore. The youngest child begins to cry and says he just wishes that everything could "go back to normal," and the parents become upset with this statement. What should Grace do NEXT?
   a. Talk to the parents about setting up individual therapy for each of the children instead of family therapy so that the children can process their feelings of abandonment.
   b. Validate everyone's feelings, normalize the children's responses, and help the family find ways to achieve homeostasis despite the changes.
   c. Validate everyone's feelings, inform the family that they appear to be struggling with enmeshment, and provide treatment to remedy the issue.

135. Maya is a social worker at a nursing home. She has a large caseload and often struggles to find time to meet with all her patients, which often causes her to have to work overtime. She is expected to meet with each patient for at least 30 minutes a week due to insurance billing requirements. Maya is talking about this problem with a colleague, who tells her to just document that some patients refused to meet for the whole time. Her colleague says many staff members do this, otherwise they would never get their work completed. Maya is unsure about this. Which professional value is MOST at conflict here?
   a. The importance of human relationships
   b. Integrity
   c. Social justice
   d. Competence

136. Interventions matched to client problems are based on _____ and empirical data gathered by the social worker.
   a. biopsychosocial assessment information
   b. behavioral approach
   c. problem causation
   d. solution identification

137. Liza is a social worker at a shelter for survivors of intimate partner violence. She is meeting with Mary, an adult woman seeking counseling. Mary has been married to her husband for 10 years, and they do not have any children. Mary shares that she left her home and husband after an episode of physical violence. She states that nothing similar has happened before, and it was a difficult choice to leave. She tells Liza that he has since apologized and told her that it will not happen again if she returns. What is the BEST response?

    a. Offer emotional support and suggest setting up couples counseling for Mary and her husband before she moves back in with him.

    b. Engage in safety planning and provide education that violence rarely escalates after a first incident; however, Mary should still be aware of the warning signs to maintain her safety in the future.

    c. Provide emotional support, support Mary's decision making, and provide education on the dynamics of the power and control cycle and patterns of intimate partner violence.

    d. Provide trauma-specific counseling, tell Mary that she cannot return home, and contact the local police department to file a mandated report against her husband.

138. A social worker is acting as a mediator in a family conflict. She wants to bring attention to how the way the family communicates might contribute to the conflict. She asks them to talk about how they communicate with and react to each other both verbally and nonverbally. What is the term for this type of communicating about communication?

    a. Metacommunication

    b. Empathic communication

    c. Miscommunication

    d. Structured communication

139. Bethany is a social worker within a local community mental health organization. She is preparing a case presentation for one of her clients, Jeremy, a 32-year-old formerly incarcerated person who is currently combatting a relapse into alcohol use, relationship issues, and post-traumatic stress disorder related to his imprisonment. In order to provide a comprehensive presentation that will yield helpful discussion, what should Bethany prioritize?

    a. Focus primarily on Jeremy's alcohol use, given the risk associated with relapse.

    b. Emphasize discussion surrounding Jeremy's imprisonment to understand the root of his diagnosis.

    c. Give an overview of Jeremy's current issues, important biopsychosocial history, and potential interventions.

    d. Offer a detailed timeline of Jeremy's life events to offer context.

140. When the social work practitioner uses information and asks finding questions to better understand where the client is emotionally while distinguishing the facts related to the situation, he or she is using what?

    a. Controlled data

    b. Objective data

    c. Subjective data

    d. Qualitative data

141. Jill is a social work graduate student completing her internship at a community health center. She is meeting with her field instructor for weekly supervision. Jill is working on becoming more comfortable with the diagnostic criteria in the *DSM-5* and when to use this resource. Jill asks her supervisor why the *DSM-5* is used by social workers. Which of these responses would NOT be correct?

    a. The *DSM-5* provides diagnostic criteria and billing codes that are utilized in the insurance and billing process to provide care coverage.

    b. The *DSM-5* provides a common language for providers across different disciplines when discussing mental health conditions.

    c. Standardized diagnostic criteria decreases provider bias or inexperience when making a diagnosis of a mental health disorder.

    d. Psychiatric diagnosis is required for every patient to be able to receive effective services and treatment.

142. Trey is a social worker working with a couple who is struggling with communicating effectively to get their needs met. Trey has completed assessment for the couple, and goals have been established. How can Trey BEST intervene to support this couple?
    a. Utilize role-play in sessions.
    b. Offer homework for the couple to complete at home.
    c. Discuss ways to increase self-sufficiency in order to lift each person's demands on their partner.

143. Social workers typically examine a client's personal history holistically through what kind of lens?
    a. Clinical
    b. Biopsychosocial
    c. Psychosomatic
    d. Environmental

144. Micah is a social worker in a hospital emergency department. He is asked to meet with Carlos, an elderly man who has been repeatedly hospitalized after failing to proper care for a chronic health condition. He arrived at the emergency department with unmanaged symptoms, and his medical team is concerned that he is not taking his condition seriously. Carlos has been experiencing homelessness for many years, and he does not have any family available to help him. What should Micah do NEXT?
    a. Tell the medical team that denial is a normal and expected stage of grief associated with a life-limiting medical diagnosis and encourage them to be more understanding.
    b. Meet with Carlos and his medical team to explain that his behavior is the reason why his symptoms continue to worsen and encourage Carlos to take more responsibility for his care.
    c. Conduct a risk assessment for thoughts of suicide and/or self-harm and require psychiatric care since it appears that Carlos is not concerned with his own well-being.
    d. Talk to Carlos about the barriers to caring for his health, connect him to resources to address his housing and basic needs concerns, and advocate with his medical team regarding the impact of homelessness on his health.

145. Theo is a social work supervisor at a counseling center. He is meeting with Jen, a social work graduate student intern he supervises. Jen reports that she has been meeting with her client for several months for depression treatment and that they did an assessment and made a treatment plan that the client has worked on. Jen asks Theo how she will know it's time for termination. What is the BEST response?
    a. When the allotted 12 sessions have been completed as indicated by insurance constraints
    b. When Jen feels the client is no longer depressed and has been taking their antidepressant medication
    c. When Jen and the client have evaluated if treatment was successful, and goals were met

146. A young man who recently graduated from college and moved home to his parents' house is seeking treatment from a social worker to address his anxieties about starting his career. During the conversation, the social worker notices that the client views his situation in "all-or-nothing" terms, fixates on minor details, and tends to catastrophize. What type of treatment would be MOST helpful for this client?
    a. Eye movement desensitization and reprocessing (EMDR)
    b. Psychodynamic therapy
    c. Cognitive behavioral therapy
    d. Family therapy

147. Tony is a social worker at a psychiatric treatment facility for children. He is meeting with Lina, a 7-year-old female child. He is working on an assessment for diagnostic clarity. Lina has symptoms of anger, irritability, and emotional instability. Her parents report regular episodes of this behavior, and it has caused problems at school and at home. They said that she has gotten disciplined at school for being oppositional with her teachers and these other behaviors. When he asked Lina about her behavior, she acknowledged feeling sorry for upsetting other people at school, but it was hard to control. Her parents also shared this has been happening since Lina started school almost two years ago. What diagnosis is MOST appropriate?
   a. Disruptive mood dysregulation disorder
   b. Antisocial personality disorder
   c. Schizoaffective disorder
   d. Bipolar disorder

148. According to cognitive behavioral approaches, what causes negative feelings and problematic behaviors?
   a. Chemical imbalances in the brain
   b. Thoughts, assumptions, and beliefs
   c. Unprocessed trauma
   d. Early childhood experiences

149. A client tells a social worker that he has persistent and intense fantasies about watching an unsuspecting woman take off her clothes. He and his wife sometimes role play this scenario for fun. The fantasy started after an incident that occurred when he was 16. He was walking by a neighbor's house, saw her undressing through the window, ducked behind a tree, and watched until she got in the shower. He says his teenage curiosity got the better of him that time, but he never did anything like it again. He states that he would never actually attempt to watch another person undress because it would be illegal and immoral. What is the MOST accurate description of the client's sexual fantasies and behaviors?
   a. Paraphilia
   b. Paraphilic disorder
   c. Voyeuristic disorder
   d. Exhibitionistic disorder

150. Jayla is a social worker with a child welfare agency. She is working with Angie, a young mother who recently lost custody of her children due to physical abuse. Angie shares that she also experienced physical discipline as a child; she does not want to continue the cycle, but she gets overwhelmed when her children aren't listening. Angie also shares that she has been stressed lately due to a reduction of hours at work, and she's concerned that they could lose their apartment. Jayla is working with Angie to develop a parenting plan as she works towards the goal of reunification. Which activity would be the LEAST effective?
   a. Offering parenting education courses on effective and safe conflict resolution and communication
   b. Building up Angie's and her children's support system of safe and reliable adults
   c. Increasing case management supports to meet Angie's financial, housing, and childcare needs
   d. Suggesting psychiatric treatment and medication management for Angie to assess for a psychiatric cause of violence and to treat her symptoms of anger

151. A social worker is working with a child to increase pro-social behaviors. At the end of each session, the social worker reads the child a story that involves characters engaging in the behavior they talked about that day. What type of modeling is this considered?
   a. Live modeling
   b. Participant modeling
   c. Covert modeling
   d. Symbolic modeling

152. A client has a long list of goals they want to work on. The social worker is using partializing techniques to help the client decide which ones to pursue first. Which theoretical construct would be MOST helpful in this situation?
    a. Maslow's hierarchy of needs
    b. Erikson's stages of psychosocial development
    c. Freud's stages of psychosexual development
    d. Systems theory

153. Naomi is a social worker in a private practice setting. She is providing couples counseling to Alex and Morgan, a couple in their thirties who have been dating for two years. They are in couples therapy to address relational conflict before determining if they want to get engaged. Alex and Morgan share that lately they have been arguing more, wanting different things, and missing how easy their relationship was in the beginning. They express frustration that the other doesn't always want to engage in the same hobbies, and it can be difficult to meld their different social groups at times. What is the BEST response?
    a. Naomi should suggest that they pick a shared hobby to engage in weekly to spend more time together and recreate the closeness and harmony they felt at the start of the relationship.
    b. Naomi should provide education that differentiation is a normal stage of couple development, and the way forward is to determine if they can acknowledge and accept these differences and find ways to work through the conflict.
    c. Naomi should provide supportive listening, explain that this conflict appears to be rooted in their incompatible attachment styles, and suggest individual therapy to work through this.
    d. Naomi should offer emotional support, provide education on healthy and unhealthy relationship dynamics, and set them up with a support group.

154. Fred is taking on a new client, 9-year-old Tim, who has been struggling to manage his emotions at home. Fred met with Tim's parents separately to get a better idea about how Tim's behaviors have been impacting the family. Tim's dad remarks, "He seems to get the most triggered when he gets home from school. We ask him to take out the trash, and it almost always turns into an outburst." In Fred's next meeting with Tim, what would be the BEST topic to explore initially?
    a. Explore how Tim feels emotionally and physically when school releases for the day.
    b. Suggest a reward chart for completion of taking out the trash without argument.
    c. Share Tim's dad's statement with Tim to get his perspective.

155. Julie is a social worker with a home health agency. She is meeting with Lewis, an 80-year-old male patient with dementia. Lewis is declining quickly, and his doctor has determined that he needs full-time care to manage his basic medical and personal needs and that he is no longer competent to make decisions. Lewis lives with a paid caregiver through the state adult foster care program. When Julie arrives for the visit, she finds Lewis home alone and having fallen. Lewis tells Julie his caregiver is out for the day, and he fell trying to get his medication from the bathroom. Julie attempts to call the caregiver but is unable to reach her. She then notifies her supervisor of the situation. What should Julie do NEXT?
    a. Call Lewis's daughter, explain the situation, and ask if she can come stay with her father.
    b. Obtain medical care for Lewis and file an urgent elder protective services report.
    c. Stay with Lewis until the caregiver comes home and then conduct a care plan meeting with her.
    d. Gather resources for the caregiver on caring for people with dementia and refer her to a local caregiver support group.

156. Group therapy is NOT recommended for which type of client?
    a. Children
    b. People with substance use disorders
    c. People with histories of trauma
    d. People who are suicidal

157. Brad is a social worker at a children's counseling center. He is meeting with a 13-year-old patient, Carter, and Carter's mother, Shawna. Shawna is a single mother to Carter and his 2-year-old brother, and she has a history of depression and mood disorders. Carter was referred for counseling after his school staff noticed signs of anxiety, decreasing academic performance, and being late to school. Carter told Brad that he's had to help out more at home since his mom has been having a difficult time again. What should Brad do NEXT?
   a. Contact Child Protective Services and file a mandated report with concerns of neglect because Carter's home responsibilities are impacting his academics.
   b. Educate Shawna on the signs of anxiety disorders in adolescents, the potential impact of such disorders, and psychiatric treatment options available for Carter.
   c. Offer emotional support and discuss the options to increase support for the entire family, including individual and family therapy, parenting resources, and case management.

158. Jon is a social worker in a critical care unit at a hospital. He is asked to join a family meeting for a patient named Kevin. Kevin's family just received difficult news about his medical condition. Kevin is no longer able to make his own medical decisions, and the family members are arguing about next steps. The doctor asks Jon to assist, as this is time sensitive. What should Jon do FIRST?
   a. Identify who is Kevin's medical power of attorney and support them in their role.
   b. Educate the entire family on Kevin's medical condition and their options.
   c. Connect the family members with grief support and chaplaincy resources.
   d. Facilitate a family meeting for everyone to process their emotions.

159. You are a social worker working with a client who is in treatment to address achieving sobriety. They are typically engaged in recovery-focused discussions with you. During your current session with them, they appear irritated and disengaged when you ask about their steps towards recovery. After several failed attempts at engaging them in discussion, you say, "You tell me that recovery is the most important thing for you. This is what led you to start treatment. I'm wondering what has changed for you that I'm not seeing." What BEST describes this approach?
   a. Empathy
   b. Confrontation
   c. Clarification
   d. Reflective listening

160. Kyle is a social worker with a substance use prevention agency. He recently received a federal grant to develop a program for local middle-school-aged youth and families. Kyle plans to gather information on what programs already exist as well as the gaps in resources. Kyle also wants to work with community members and local providers to get input on what services would be most beneficial. What tool would be MOST helpful for this process?
   a. Genogram
   b. Risk assessment
   c. Collateral contact
   d. Needs assessment

161. You are a social worker working in a college counseling center. Your center specializes in brief and task-centered support, as students are only eligible for five total sessions. You are completing the intake for a student who has shared that they were referred to the counseling center by a professor because of test-taking anxiety. What should be your NEXT step with this client?
   a. Collect a complete biopsychosocial history.
   b. Formulate specific tasks to complete.
   c. Establish SMART goals.
   d. Briefly explore the context surrounding the presenting concern.

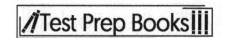

162. Jose is a worker at a community health center. He is meeting with the parents of Nick, a 16-year-old boy who has been in treatment for a mood disorder. Nick recently got into trouble at school for marijuana use and has since confided in his parents and Jose that he is struggling with a substance use disorder. Nick says the substances are a coping strategy for some of his difficult mood symptoms. Nick's parents are angry and tell Jose that they feel Nick like is just causing more problems, and it's been one thing after another with his behavior. What is the BEST response from Jose?

   a. Provide psychoeducation that substance use and rebellious behavior are developmentally expected aspects of adolescence and support the parents in finding strategies to respond to their child during this stage.
   b. Inform the parents that they are demonstrating signs of authoritarian parenting styles that can be detrimental to children and that they should not be disciplining a child this age.
   c. Provide support and psychoeducation around the dynamics of co-occurring disorders and discuss treatment options and available support options for the whole family.

163. Whitney is in the treatment-planning stage with her client, Eliza, a 23-year-old who is seeking treatment for anxiety related to performance at her new job. One of Eliza's self-identified goals is to share her ideas more often during meetings. What would be the BEST way for Whitney to write this goal?

   a. Eliza will practice speaking up during meetings.
   b. Eliza will engage in self-confidence exercises for five minutes before each meeting.
   c. Eliza will engage in dialogue regarding at least one agenda item per meeting.

164. Nina is a social worker at a community mental health center. She has been working with her patient Sheila for three months. Sheila is receiving treatment for anxiety and has treatment goals of utilizing healthy coping skills and practicing mindfulness. After trying different interventions, Nina is curious if the treatment plan is effective. What should she do NEXT?

   a. Seek supervision to get input from a more experienced colleague.
   b. Read case notes from earlier sessions to see if there's been behavioral changes.
   c. Work with Sheila to make a plan to monitor and evaluate treatment efficacy.
   d. Inform Sheila to keep a journal of any changes she notices and bring it to the next session.

165. Crystal is a social worker in an acute inpatient unit at a psychiatric hospital. She is meeting with a new patient named Cody, a 30-year-old man who was admitted one week ago after presenting to a local hospital with acute and unmanaged psychiatric symptoms. Cody has been experiencing chronic homelessness and employment challenges for the past decade, he suddenly stopped taking his psychiatric medications, and he had thoughts of suicide that contributed to the hospitalization. According to his report, he has limited social support and has been inconsistent in following through with treatment and services. Crystal has conducted a risk assessment and determines that Cody is no longer at risk of harming himself or anyone else. What should Crystal do NEXT?

   a. Provide support, address the discontinuation of psychiatric medications and the acute safety concerns that led to the hospitalization, and work with Cody towards stabilization.
   b. Discuss the impact of chronic homelessness and how difficult this has been for Cody and help connect him to services for housing, employment, and financial literacy programming.
   c. Work with Cody to identify why he has chosen not to engage with service providers in the past and provide psychotherapy and communication skill building to address this chronic concern.

166. Jesiah is a social worker working in a private practice setting. His client, Karen, started services with him a few months ago to address social anxiety. She has met all of her treatment goals and has been maintaining progress for some time. When Jesiah brings up the topic of termination with Karen, she becomes tearful. She is insistent that if she ends treatment, all of her concerns with social anxiety will return. What is the BEST way for Jesiah to respond?

   a. Normalize Karen's feelings and collaborate on a date for a final session.
   b. Normalize Karen's feelings and start with a gradual reduction in sessions.
   c. Validate Karen's concerns and continue treatment.
   d. Validate Karen's concerns and establish new treatment goals.

243

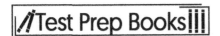
167. Heather is a social worker at a substance use treatment program that offers services for people struggling with addiction and their families. She is meeting with Courtney, a woman whose husband is currently in treatment for an opioid use disorder. She and her husband have two young children. Courtney explains that she feels guilty about how hard this has been on her, but she doesn't have time to worry about herself right now when her children and husband need her. What is the BEST way for Heather to respond?

    a. Acknowledge that her feelings are understandable, provide education on the impact of parental substance use on kids, and work on setting up therapy services for the children.

    b. Validate her experience, then gently explain the impact of substance use disorders on the whole family system and the importance of seeking her own support at this time.

    c. Explain that if she does not take care of herself, then she won't be able to support her family; therefore, family treatment is a mandatory aspect of her husband's recovery.

    d. Highlight the strength and resiliency she is displaying by setting her needs aside to focus on her family.

168. Maureen is a social worker who provides virtual counseling services via a telehealth platform. She is conducting a virtual session with Leon, a 50-year-old man whom she has been seeing for several months. Leon has a history of depression and a suicide attempt and began services with Maureen after his recent hospitalization. Leon lives alone. During their session, Leon tells Maureen he has a plan to attempt suicide and has access to a weapon in his home. When Maureen asks follow-up questions, Leon becomes upset and disconnects the call. When Maureen attempts to call back, there is no response. How should Maureen proceed?

    a. Document her concerns and that she attempted to follow up but there was no answer.

    b. Go to Leon's home unannounced to conduct a risk assessment in person since he is unreachable by phone.

    c. Call Leon's psychiatrist for collateral contact to assess risk to better inform decision making.

    d. Contact emergency services, explain the situation, and request an immediate wellness check.

169. You are a children's therapist at an outpatient clinic. You recently accepted a client who is 7 years old and is struggling to process and express his grief surrounding the loss of his father. Based on your knowledge of developmental stages, what can you MOST likely expect to navigate as you are building rapport with this client?

    a. Deflection through humor, minimizing their loss, or taking on the role of the adult

    b. Crying, clinginess, and changes in eating and sleeping habits

    c. Blaming themselves for the death, somatic symptoms, and embarrassment

170. Jared is a social worker at a community health center. He is meeting with Monica, a new patient, for their second session. Jared is providing time-limited treatment with a goal of eight total sessions. Today they are working on treatment goals. Jared asks Monica, "If a miracle happened and the problem was gone tomorrow, how would you know?" What approach is Jared using to guide treatment and treatment planning?

    a. Solution-focused therapy

    b. Narrative therapy

    c. Cognitive behavioral therapy

    d. Psychodynamic therapy

Answer Explanations #2

1. A: The correct answer is Choice *A*, validate how difficult that was to share and tell Kat she gets to choose what she's comfortable discussing. Social workers often have to discuss sensitive topics with their clients, such as a history of violence, and need to always respond in a way that is compassionate, sensitive, and non-judgmental. Social workers also let their clients dictate what they are comfortable sharing unless there is an imminent safety concern, which is not the case here. Tanya's role is to provide support and a safe space and follow Kat's lead. There is no obligation to file a mandated report because Kat is an adult. It would not be appropriate to discuss this further during the intake, as Kat has said she does not want to. While it could be relevant to the presenting problem, building the relationship is more important at this time.

2. D: Sam was the scapegoat in his family of origin. The scapegoat is a common role produced by certain kinds of family dynamics. The scapegoat is the person who takes the blame for the family's problems. The rest of the family is seen as good, while the scapegoat is seen as bad. In the example, instead of recognizing and addressing their own shortcomings, Sam's parents attribute all their problems to Sam. A social worker could help Sam recognize and challenge his internalized feelings of being bad. Choice *A* is incorrect because the peacekeeper is the person who smooths over conflict and maintains communication in a family. Choice *B* is incorrect because the lost child is the child who is ignored and not given much in the way of attention or expectations. Choice *C* is incorrect because the problem child is the child whose behavior becomes the focus of the family's concern often as a way to avoid paying attention to deeper issues.

3. B: Amy's course of action should be to make a report to adult protective services. Amy's job is not to prove or disprove that abuse or neglect is occurring; that is the job of adult protective services. Amy has enough information to be concerned that something is not right about the situation and that Sofia may not be safe. A report should be made. Recall that mandatory reporting laws require social workers, and other professionals, to report any suspected abuse or neglect. This means that any professional who has a suspicion of abuse or neglect of a child or a vulnerable adult must legally make a report to either child protective services or adult protective services.

4. C: When clients decide to terminate before completing their treatment plan, the social worker must explain the risks of terminating and document the interaction. Documentation is important to show that the client initiated the termination and to protect the social worker against claims of abandonment, which is malpractice. The social worker should remain objective and avoid taking the termination personally.

5. C: Mr. M is dependent on Prozac and is experiencing discontinuation symptoms. Over time, the body adjusts to psychotropic medication and stopping it suddenly can cause adverse effects. This can happen with Prozac and other SSRIs after about a month of daily use, and Mr. M has been taking the drug for 10 years. People vary in whether and to what extent they experience discontinuation symptoms, but it is generally unpleasant and can last for weeks or months. To reduce these symptoms, it is recommended that people who want to stop taking a psychotropic medication work with a psychiatrist to slowly taper their dose down over time. Choice *B* is incorrect because there is a difference between being dependent on a drug and being addicted to it. Mr. M is not experiencing negative life consequences or drug cravings, which are hallmarks of addiction. Just as people with diabetes are not addicted to insulin, Mr. M is not addicted to Prozac. Choice *D* is incorrect because antidepressant discontinuation syndrome is a documented physical phenomenon; it is not psychological or psychosomatic.

6. D: June's change in behavior is concerning because it is clearly associated with going to the day center. People with intellectual disabilities are vulnerable to abuse, and June is especially vulnerable since she is nonverbal. The fact that the behavior change coincided with a urinary tract infection indicates that she may be experiencing sexual abuse. Urinary tract infections can cause psychiatric symptoms; however, in the context of June's sudden fear of the day center, abuse is the more likely explanation. Although moodiness, changes in preferences, and withdrawal from parents is typical adolescent behavior, a sudden change in behavior like June's indicates that something more is

245

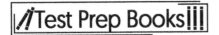

going on. June is experiencing a sudden, acute change in symptoms related to one specific activity, not a global decline in functioning.

7. B: The client meets the full criteria for a manic episode (manic symptoms affecting functioning and lasting for at least one week), which means her diagnosis should be changed to bipolar I disorder. Choice *A* is incorrect because her psychotic symptoms are accompanied by an elevated, expansive mood indicating mania rather than depression. Choice *C* is incorrect because the severity and duration of the manic symptoms meet the criteria for mania, not hypomania. If the symptoms were less severe and lasted only four days, bipolar II would be an appropriate diagnosis. Choice *D* is incorrect because the client's psychotic symptoms occur in the context of a mood disturbance. If the client were experiencing hallucinations, delusions, and negative symptoms even when her mood was not disturbed, schizoaffective disorder could be considered.

8. D: There are three main steps to take when helping a client manage stress: identify triggers, identify which parts of the situation the client can control, and teach techniques to manage the stress from things that are outside the client's control. The client in the example has already identified their stress triggers. The next step is to determine what the client can control. In this example, the client can control their uncertainty about how their work is perceived by having a conversation with their boss or requesting a performance review. The client can control their time management issues by developing new skills in that area. The client cannot control whether their colleague receives a promotion. Choice *A* is incorrect because any needed stress management techniques should be taught after identifying and working on the parts of the situation the client can control. Choice *B* is incorrect because encouraging the client to speculate about their coworker shifts attention away from the parts of the situation that are within the client's power to change. Choice *C* is incorrect because reassuring the client that everyone gets stressed at work minimizes the client's problem without offering any solutions.

9. D: Alan should terminate with Mr. S because it is unethical to continue providing services when a client is no longer benefitting from them. Meeting with a client just to have enjoyable conversations would be a breach of the social worker-client relationship.

10. D: Community development theory describes how community members come together and organize to advocate for the changes they want to see. Communities can be based on geographic location (like in the example), interests, identities, and many other factors. Social workers can help by taking on an organizing role. They can help community members come together, build power, identify issues, define problems, explore potential solutions, and build the capacity of community leaders. A well-organized community with a clearly identified problem and an achievable solution is powerful enough to hold decision makers accountable. The goal of community development is community-level change that benefits individuals and the whole group. Community development theory does not blame individuals for community-level problems; instead of viewing them as issues of individual failure, they are framed as problems of injustice. Choice *A* is incorrect because social workers doing community development do not speak for a community; they work alongside it. Choice *B* is incorrect because community development generates collective solutions, not individual ones. Choice *C* is incorrect because helping families find other resources does not solve the community's problems with the school.

11. C: The first goal of the child welfare system is family reunification. This is called the permanency planning approach, and it is based on the idea that children require a permanent home to thrive, ideally with their original family. In this example, the social worker should assist the family in addressing the issues that led to the child's removal in order to create a safe and stable environment for the child to return to. Choice *A* is incorrect because a group home is considered less beneficial for a child than a permanent family home. A group home should only be considered when other options have failed. Choice *B* is incorrect because the first goal should be family reunification. A foster family should be considered when family reunification is not possible. Choice *D* is incorrect because the child should be placed with a relative only if family reunification is not possible.

12. C: Solution-focused brief therapy includes the miracle question, scaling questions, exception questions, and past success questions. Solution-focused brief therapy is often used because it is time sensitive and allows clients access to self-direction.

13. D: The zone of proximal development describes the range of tasks a developing child can do with assistance from an adult but can't yet do on their own. For example, if a child can tie their shoes with their mother's help, shoe-tying would be a task in the child's zone of proximal development. These tasks present the right level of challenge—hard enough to require the child to stretch themselves but not so hard that they are impossible and frustrating. Encouraging children by providing ample opportunities for them to practice things within the zone of proximal development can help children learn faster. Choices *A*, *B*, and *C* are incorrect because they are unrelated to the concept of the zone of proximal development. The zone of proximal development does not describe a child's immediate environment, neighborhood, or developmental level as compared to their peers.

14. C: The client meets the criteria for bulimia nervosa because he binges on junk food then engages in compensatory behaviors (skipping breakfast and overexercising) at least once a week. He is also preoccupied with body image, and his symptoms are causing distress and difficulty functioning. Choice *A* (anorexia nervosa) is incorrect because the client is a normal weight. Choice *B* (binge-eating disorder) is incorrect because the client attempts to compensate for the binges by skipping meals and overexercising. Binge-eating disorder involves binges only, without these types of compensatory behaviors. Choice *D* (unspecified feeding and eating disorder) is incorrect because this diagnosis is given when a client exhibits disordered eating behavior but does not meet the full criteria for another eating disorder.

15. D: The social worker should terminate couples therapy and refer Mark and Breanne to individual therapists because their relationship is abusive. Couples therapy is contraindicated for couples who are experiencing domestic abuse; research has shown that couples therapy can make the abuse worse and increase the risk of harm to the victim. It is important for social workers to understand that abuse can happen in any type of relationship and can take many forms. Social workers must be able to recognize domestic abuse whether there is physical violence or not. For example, Breanne is the victim of financial abuse, and Mark's behavior is coercive and controlling. Choice *A* is incorrect because if Breanne brings up the abuse in the next session, Mark is likely to become angry, worsening the already abusive dynamic. Choice *B* is incorrect because Breanne has disclosed that she is being abused. Keeping the abuse secret and continuing couples therapy with her abuser would be harmful and unethical. Choice *C* is incorrect because when a client discloses that they are being abused, it is not appropriate, ethical, or helpful to get the abuser's perspective.

16. D: The social worker should reassure the woman that her son's behavior is normal for his age and developmental level. Many children develop imaginary friends around this time, and it does not indicate the presence of a disorder or problem. Although children talk to and play with their imaginary friends, they usually understand that they are not actually real people. The behavior can be distressing for parents, and social workers can help by providing empathy and psychoeducation. In the absence of other concerning symptoms, a 7-year-old having an imaginary friend is not an indicator of abuse/neglect, Choice *A*; psychosis, Choice *B*; or abnormal development, Choice *C*.

17. A: When a social worker receives a subpoena, they should try to protect the client's confidentiality by claiming privilege on behalf of the client. The social worker should refuse to release the records unless the client provides written permission to do so. The social worker may eventually be legally required to release the records if they receive a second request accompanied by a court order.

18. A: Sandra is experiencing compassion fatigue, which includes a combination of the symptoms of burnout and secondary trauma. Burnout involves total exhaustion and feelings of professional inadequacy and hopelessness. Secondary trauma involves experiencing the same symptoms as one's clients who have been exposed to trauma, such as nightmares and hypervigilance. Both burnout and compassion fatigue tend to develop slowly over time,

while secondary trauma is more likely to develop quickly in response to a specific trauma experienced by a client. Stress is a more general term and can be either helpful or harmful depending on the circumstances. Stress is certainly a part of what Sandra is feeling, but compassion fatigue is more accurate.

19. B: The social worker should make a report to child protective services because Amanda's behavior is very concerning. She shows red flags that indicate sexual abuse. It is not normal for a 6-year-old to know sexually explicit language, Choice *C*. Children who have been sexually abused often fixate on the experience and act it out through play, as Amanda did with the dolls. The fact that Amanda asked the adult male social worker if he wanted to engage in sexual activity with her is particularly concerning because it indicates that she expects this behavior with adult men. Engaging much older or younger children in sexualized play is another red flag for sexual abuse.

The fact that the child recently moved to town does not affect the decision to make a report (the report should be made regardless), but it does mean that Amanda could be in even more danger due to not being socially integrated. The fact that the incident happened at the social worker's home, outside of his social work practice, is irrelevant, Choice *A*. Social workers are mandated reporters, which means that they are legally and ethically required to report suspected abuse any time they encounter it, regardless of whether they are working at the time. Choice *D* is incorrect because the social worker should not talk to Amanda's parents before making the report. He has no way of knowing whether the abuse is ongoing or who the perpetrator(s) is/are. If family members are involved, the social worker could be putting Amanda in more danger by talking to the parents about his suspicions.

20. D: The shift in tone of the sessions, the fact that no new issues are arising, and the fact that the client has made significant progress on his goals all indicate that he is ready for termination. Termination should start occurring when the sessions are no longer benefitting the client, meaning that the client is no longer actively working on change. Choice *A* is incorrect because the client is still attending and participating, which shows motivation. He simply no longer has urgent issues to work on. Choice *B* is incorrect because there is no indication that there is a problem in the therapeutic relationship. The client is still happily engaging with the social worker. Choice *C* is incorrect because countertransference is when a social worker projects their feelings onto a client. There is no indication that the social worker is struggling with strong feelings in response to the client.

21. D: Even though Mike signed a release allowing the social worker to discuss his care with the case manager, it would be best to discuss the case manager's request with Mike before responding to it. Choices *A* and *B* are incorrect because it would be better to give Mike the choice about how to respond and what to disclose. Choice *C* is incorrect because Mike signed a release to share the information, so it would not be a HIPAA violation.

22. C: The correct answer is Choice *C*, contact local police and contact Lewis's doctor to inform them of the threat. Duty to warn is a social work ethical and legal obligation informed by the Tarasoff decision. This requires social workers to warn a potential victim of a threat made by a patient and allows them to break confidentiality if they assess that there is a real threat to safety being made. In this case, Mike has enough information that he needs to act on duty to warn and would not be in trouble for breaking confidentiality. While the other steps may be necessary to secure both Lewis's and others' safety, they are not the obligation of duty to warn.

23. B: This is not a SMART goal because it is not realistic. When assisting clients in setting goals, social workers must ensure that each goal is specific, measurable, achievable, realistic, and time limited. They also must ensure that the goals are directly related to problems the client wants to solve. Choice *A* is incorrect because although the goal is technically achievable, Choice *C*, it is not realistic. The client would have to engage in unhealthy behaviors to lose that much weight that quickly. Choice *D* is incorrect because the goal is time limited (one month). In this situation, the social worker could encourage the client to think of losing weight as a longer-term goal and assist him in developing a series of smaller, short-term goals to move in that direction. For example, a short-term SMART goal could be to bring a healthy lunch to work every day for the next two weeks instead of eating out.

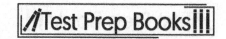

24. D: The mother expressed a common misconception about gender identity and sexual orientation. They are distinct and unrelated concepts. The child identifying as transgender does not say anything about their sexuality. Transgender people can have any sexual orientation, just like cisgender people. Choice *A* is incorrect because although it is typical for teenagers to explore their sexuality, it does not mean that they are going through a phase that they will eventually snap out of. It can be harmful for parents to assume that their child is heterosexual and cisgender and dismiss anything else as a "phase." Choice *B* is incorrect because gender identity and sexuality are unrelated. People do not decide to change their gender to avoid being homosexual. Choice *C* is incorrect because expressing one's gender identity is normal behavior and not an indication of dysfunction or attention-seeking.

25. A: The social worker should continue treating the client as usual. It would be appropriate to explore how the relationship is going and monitor for red flags that violence might occur, but simply feeling uncomfortable is not enough to justify limiting the client's self-determination and privacy in any way. Therefore, it would not be ethical to contact the girlfriend, suggest ending the relationship, or conduct an internet search on the client without his permission.

26. A: The correct answer is Choice *A,* an intensive outpatient program. An intensive outpatient program is a lower level of care than a residential setting, as it provides treatment multiple days a week, but individuals live independently in the community. An inpatient facility would be a higher level of care than Owen currently receives. A dual diagnosis program is not appropriate, as nothing here suggests that Owen has a comorbid substance use disorder.

27. B: The correct answer is Choice *B*. You are reframing Claudette's experience with this class to emphasize the hard work and survival aspect. Choice *A* is incorrect, as this is an example of clarifying. Choice *C* is incorrect, as this is an example of confrontation. Choice *D* is incorrect, as this is an example of validation and universalization.

28. D: Delusions are a positive symptom of schizophrenia. Schizophrenia involves positive and negative symptoms. In this context, positive means that symptoms are distortions of or additions to normal functioning, like hallucinations and delusions. Negative symptoms are reductions in or subtractions from normal functioning, like poverty of speech, Choice *A*; reduced emotional expression, Choice *B*; and lack of motivation, Choice *C*.

29. C: Follow-up meetings can be an important part of the treatment process. They give the client a chance to celebrate post-treatment progress and request additional support if needed. They provide the social worker with valuable information about treatment effectiveness over time. Scheduling an additional follow-up meeting would be okay if the client needed it, but this client does not. The client has achieved his goals, completed treatment, and continued symptom-free. The client's continual desire to chat indicates that he didn't even need the original follow-up. The client chatting is not inappropriate behavior, Choice *D*, but it would be inappropriate for the social worker to allow the client to continue scheduling meetings just to chat. This client is showing signs of becoming dependent on the social worker; he struggled with termination and wants to continue the relationship even though he has not identified any need for additional support. The social worker might feel bad about refusing the client, but it is unethical to continue treatment with a client who no longer needs it, Choice *B*, even if the client states that he feels he needs another session, Choice *A*.

30. B: The correct answer is Choice *B*, literature review. The common research process in the social work field includes topic selection, problem formation, literature review, hypothesis, research methodology selection, data collection, data analysis, and dissemination of results. In this example, Lee is conducting a literature review to understand and review the current journal articles and data that exist on this topic. This is vital in research to understand current trends and information in the field, ensure your research will be relevant, and avoid duplication of existing work.

31. A: The correct answer is Choice *A*. This is utilizing a motivational interviewing framework, as you are using reflection, affirming Justina's choices, and emphasizing her autonomy. This framework is especially important to

take with involuntary clients. Choice *B* is incorrect, as the conversation regarding limits of confidentiality would be better suited for later in the conversation, as this is a better opportunity to build rapport. Choice *C* is incorrect, as it is not the social worker's responsibility to determine what the client's motivation for treatment is.

32. B: The correct answer is Choice *B*, schizophrenia. The *DSM-5* criteria for schizophrenia includes symptoms of disorganized speech, paranoia, delusions, and hallucinations. The initial onset of schizophrenia is commonly in late adolescence or early adulthood, and the symptoms typically impact the individual's functioning in relationships, work, and school.

33. B: Erikson's stages of psychosocial development assign different tasks to each age-based stage. Adolescents are in the stage of identity vs role confusion; self-exploration and identity development are critical activities for the healthy completion of this stage. Choice *A* is incorrect because while bullying can be a challenge for adolescents, bullying prevention is not connected to the needs of the psychosocial stage. Choice *C* is incorrect because the purpose of the group is psychosocial development, not prevention of substance use. While avoiding bullying and not using substances could be considered an aspect of healthy adolescent development, they are not as relevant as Choice *B*. Choice *D* is incorrect because exploring one's family of origin is not connected to the developmental needs of adolescents, a stage in which it's developmentally normal to explore relationships outside of the family.

34. C: Minor clients do not have the ability to provide informed consent unless they are legally emancipated. Unemancipated minors require consent from their parent or guardian to access services. The age at which a minor can access services without parental involvement varies by state. Even though the child is the client, the parent is legally allowed access to the child's records, and they decide who the records will be shared with because they are the one providing informed consent. It is considered best practice for social workers to seek a minor's assent to treatment and to make sure they understand the limits to their confidentiality. When parents request their child's treatment information, social workers should let the child know before sharing with the parents if possible. Choices *A*, *B*, and *D* are incorrect because social workers must get written permission from a client to share their information with insurance companies or other payers; consultants, colleagues, and supervisors; interdisciplinary teams; and any other third party requesting the client's information.

35. B: The correct answer is Choice *B*, the Columbia-Suicide Severity Rating Scale. This risk assessment tool is one of the most commonly used metrics to assess suicidality and risk related to thoughts of suicide. This assessment will allow Heidi to decide on the appropriate next steps based on the outcome. None of the other assessments focus specifically on risk assessment for suicide.

36. D: Zach's anger and frustration at his removal from his home are normal and appropriate given the situation, so validation is appropriate. Validation and offering choices to a child who feels as though everything else is out of their control are the most appropriate responses given the dynamics of out-of-home placement and foster care. Choice *A* is incorrect because although validation is appropriate, Roland should not make promises that are outside his control. Choice *B* is incorrect because children in foster care should maintain visitation with their biological family unless there is a safety concern, which is not the case here. Choice *C* is incorrect because further change should be avoided unless absolutely necessary, as consistency and routine are important for children who have experienced other major changes in their lives.

37. A: When there is a conflict between a social worker's values and their client's values, the social worker should first engage in self-reflection about her values and whether she is able to put them aside to remain professionally objective. Choice *B* is incorrect because a trusted friend is not qualified to advise on social work ethics, and discussing the client would be a violation of his privacy. Choice *C* is incorrect because referring the client to another social worker should only be done in extreme cases where the social worker has already engaged in self-reflection, consulted with a supervisor, and still cannot remain objective. Choice *D* is incorrect because asking clients about their values on an intake form is unethical unless this information is required for treatment. Additionally, screening clients based on their values is discrimination, which is unethical.

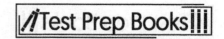

38. D: The correct answer is Choice *D*. An effective approach to resolving an issue that is identified in a program evaluation is to organize a committee of members who have intimate knowledge of the issue as well as the power to implement effective change. Choices *A* and *B* are incorrect, as these both jump to a solution without first engaging members and staff in ongoing discussion to ensure that an effective solution is chosen. Choice *C* is incorrect, as there is not enough information about this issue to jump straight to the dissolution of the program.

39. C: Defense mechanisms protect the ego from absorbing information it does not want to see, feel, or experience. This protective shield—which comes in many forms, such as rationalization, sublimation, or projection—helps reduce anxiety and guards against unwanted emotions like shame or guilt. Defense mechanisms can be helpful in reducing anxiety or can sometimes help one become immune to reality. Choices *A* and *B* imply that defense mechanisms are used to protect others from the truth about themselves, but this is not entirely accurate. Choice *D* suggests that defense mechanisms better allow one to exploit others. In some instances, this could apply, but for the most part, these mechanisms are acts of self-defense that keep the ego from accepting an unwanted truth.

40. C: The correct answer is Choice *C*. Given Sienna's newness to the field, supervision is vital to support her in processing her overwhelmed feelings and identifying best practices for organizing and prioritizing her responsibilities. Choice *A* is incorrect, as there is no indication that Sienna's caseload is too large. Choice *B* is incorrect, as the focus should be to support Sienna's inexperience with managing a caseload. Choice *D* is incorrect, as this skill is better explored and developed within individual supervision.

41. B: Cultural competence is critical for social workers. It refers to the ability to respect/understand cultural differences and to respond and engage appropriately with individuals from different cultures. Social workers provide services to diverse populations, so this is a critical skill. Cultural competence involves educating oneself on different cultures while treating the client as the expert on their own experience. Therefore, asking respectful questions while also doing her own research is the best choice. Choice *A* is incorrect because religion is an important part of the client's identity, so it would not make sense to avoid discussing it. Choice *C* is incorrect because although asking respectful questions is appropriate, social workers should not expect clients of minority cultures to educate them. Choice *D* is incorrect because social workers should be able to work with people of any background, not just those who share the same culture, race, ethnicity, or religion as themselves.

42. D: According to the NASW Code of Ethics, it is unethical for social workers to ask current clients for testimonials. This would be a misuse of social workers' power and influence over their clients. Even though she plans to tell them that refusing will not affect their treatment, her clients could still feel pressured to participate. To avoid the potential for manipulation, coercion, and undue influence, the Code of Ethics instructs social workers to avoid soliciting testimonials in general and especially from current clients.

43. B: The correct answer is Choice *B*, state that she is not able to confirm or deny if he is a patient and that she cannot give out patient information. Social workers are obligated to keep client information confidential except in designated circumstances where there is a serious risk of harm, and this would not qualify. Since the patient is an adult, the social worker cannot give out information to his parents unless he signed a release of information, which is not indicated here. Therefore, the social worker is unable to engage with the mother at all and is not even able to tell her whether or not she is working with Dominic.

44. A: A cost-effectiveness evaluation would help the organization determine which program model would allow them to prevent the most overdoses using the money they have. A cost-effectiveness evaluation is similar to a cost-benefit evaluation, Choice *B*, but instead of money spent vs. money earned or saved, it considers money spent vs. non-monetary benefit gained (in this case, number of overdoses prevented). This type of evaluation can identify what the cost of achieving a certain non-monetary benefit will be, as well as the most cost-effective way of ensuring the desired outcome. Choice *C* is incorrect because an outcome assessment looks at whether and to what extent a program has achieved its intended goals. Choice *D* is incorrect because a process evaluation looks at how a program is actually implemented vs. how it was intended to be implemented.

251

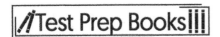

45. D: A systems-based approach considers the macro level and societal systems that impact people and their behavior. This approach is rooted in the idea that people do not exist in a vacuum, and their behavior is constantly impacted by their environment. Choice *D* is the best option because it is the only one that helps Jackson navigate other systems in his life (such as housing and employment) that are known to be directly linked to incarceration risk. Choices *A*, *B*, and *C* are all reasonable interventions for the setting, but they all focus on Jackson as an individual rather than focusing on systems.

46. A: The correct answer is Choice *A*, meet Ruby where she is at by exploring the resistance she is experiencing. It is essential that social workers meet clients where they are at in the change process rather than pushing them to enact changes they aren't ready for. Exploring resistance with the client can be a useful tool in this process. Ruby appears to be in the contemplation stage of the change process; creating a treatment plan to stop her substance use would be premature. There is also no indication yet that services should be terminated, as contemplation and resistance are normal aspects of the change process.

47. C: The correct answer is Choice *C*. Martha should incorporate assertiveness training in their supervisions, which includes using educational activities to improve Bart's communication, body language, and conflict resolution. Choice *A* is incorrect, as this is a more invasive approach that may not be appropriate in this setting. Choice *B* is incorrect, as this is an overcorrection to a situation which could be resolved through assertiveness training.

48. B: The social worker should bring up her concerns and frustrations with the supervisor directly during their next session. Effective supervision, just like social work treatment with clients, requires a strong relationship as a foundation. Both the supervisor and supervisee play roles in building and maintaining that relationship. Addressing concerns openly when they arise is one way to strengthen the relationship and ensure that the supervisee is getting what they need. Choice *A* is incorrect because the social worker should at least bring up her concerns with her current supervisor before finding a new one. It could be that this supervisor is a better fit for recent graduates than mature professionals, but it could just as easily be the case that the supervisor is not aware that this supervisee needs a different approach.

There is also no guarantee that things would be any better with a different supervisor. Instead of ending supervision any time there is a problem, the social worker should see this as an opportunity to work through the problem and get her needs met. Choice *C* is incorrect because the social worker's problem is not primarily that she is having a strong emotional reaction; it is that she is not getting what she needs from supervision. It's not that she wants the supervisor to acknowledge her experience; it's that she wants to work on new skills rather than reviewing things she already knows. Self-reflection is a vital skill for social workers, but in this case, self-reflection would not solve her problem. Choice *D* is incorrect because the supervisor has not done anything harmful or unethical that would require notifying the board. The problem is related to poor communication between the supervisee and supervisor, not the supervisor's incompetence.

49. D: A genogram is most useful for understanding life events and familial patterns. A genogram is not useful for Choice *A*, determining the occurrence of behaviors. While the genogram can provide insight into the perceived relationship between the client and family and existing support systems, it does not establish peer support systems, as in Choice *B*, nor does it pinpoint significant life events, as in Choice *C*—it is only useful for understanding them.

50. C: Many social workers choose to participate in research, and ethical practice is just as important in research settings as it is in clinical care. When working with human subjects, approval from the institutional review board (IRB) is required before beginning the study, making Choice *C* the correct choice. The actions outlined in Choices *A*, *B*, and *D* are all parts of ethical research practice but occur later in the process and after IRB approval.

51. B: The correct answer is Choice *B*. Oftentimes, clients use follow-up or aftercare appointments to prolong the client-worker relationship. In this case, the client has met their goals and is likely struggling to adjust to this change. Acknowledging the client's feelings is the best initial response. Choice *A* is incorrect, as it is not the social worker's

252

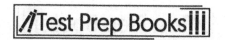

responsibility to prevent relapse and, additionally, the new referral would come from their new program. Choice *C* is incorrect, as they have already graduated to a step-down program, so readmitting them to a more restrictive program would be inappropriate.

52. A: The correct answer is Choice *A*, work with Tyler to create a treatment plan and goals for their work together. In the social work process, treatment planning is the next step after the assessment phase. Treatment planning should be collaborative and client centered, so it would not be appropriate for Jake to create the treatment plan without working together with Tyler. There is no indication here that Tyler is in need of academic testing. While Jake may choose to include Tyler's teachers in the support plan if Tyler agrees, this would not be the next step and would not be done without Tyler's consent.

53. C: Providing Cody with overdose prevention resources is the option that is most aligned with a harm reduction approach, a common framework in substance use care. Harm reduction is a public health and treatment approach that does not require total abstinence from substance use; instead, it focuses on mitigating negative consequences, such as overdose. Choice *A* is incorrect because a facility with a zero-tolerance policy would not be considered harm reduction. Choice *B* is incorrect because a harm reduction approach would not involve monitoring of substance use in a punitive manner. Choice *D* is incorrect because a harm reduction model would typically only utilize hospitalization if this was the patient's choice, not as a mandated or punitive intervention.

54. D: The most effective teaching technique is the one that fits best with the learning style of the supervisee. Some supervisees will have a strong preference for either visual (Choice *A*), hands-on (Choice *B*), or auditory (Choice *C*) techniques, while others will learn best from a combination of all three. It is the supervisor's responsibility to assess the learning needs and styles of their supervisees at the beginning of supervision and periodically thereafter. The supervisor should regularly encourage feedback from the supervisee and adjust their teaching style accordingly. The supervisee also has a role to play by being cooperative, following the supervisor's directions, being willing to try new things, taking initiative, looking for opportunities to practice new skills, and being clear and honest with feedback when things are not going as well as they could. Just like in sessions with clients, supervision is most successful when the supervisor and supervisee are engaged and attuned to each other.

55. C: The correct answer is Choice *C*, give Hannah a diagnosis of prolonged grief disorder. Hannah lost her husband a few weeks ago, and the *DSM-5* criteria for prolonged grief disorder states that the death had to have occurred at least a year ago. Therefore, this would not be an appropriate diagnosis even if she demonstrated some of the symptoms. The other interventions of risk assessment, referral to a grief group, and education on grief would all be appropriate in this situation.

56. B: Social workers in a supervisory role need to maintain appropriate boundaries and avoid dual relationships and unnecessary self-disclosure with those they supervise, just as they would do with their clients. The best response is Choice *B* because it's almost impossible to avoid self-disclosure and a possible dual relationship with social media connection. Choice *A* is incorrect because it allows the social media connection when there's other reasonable communication options, such as phone or email. Choice *C* is incorrect because the primary ethical conflict here is the boundary crossed by social media connection, not a particular supervisee being treated differently.

57. C: The correct answer is Choice *C*, preparation. This question is looking at the stages of change model typically used in a motivational interviewing framework. The stages include precontemplation, contemplation, preparation, action, and maintenance. Jim is working on steps that will lead to him actually making the identified change, which puts him in the preparation stage at this time.

58. A: Jack's behavior is normal and expected for a child his age, according to Kohlberg's stages of moral development. The preconventional stage of moral development lasts from birth to age eight or nine, and it is the first stage of moral development. It is characterized by an understanding of morality rooted in concrete thinking and right and wrong. Children typically accept the rules set by others in positions of authority, and they follow the rules

to avoid getting in trouble. They do not think about morality in a more nuanced way at this stage. The characteristics of this stage are displayed by Jack's ability to follow only set rules and his reliance upon a reward system to continue following them. This is not behavior that needs treatment or modification because it's age appropriate.

59. A: The correct answer is Choice *A*. Therapists often have a legal and ethical duty to respond and provide impartial testimony if a judge orders their appearance. However, consulting first with her organization's legal team can guide her choice in response, as there is sometimes an option to claim therapist-patient privilege in lieu of testifying. Choice *B* is incorrect; a subpoena should never be ignored, as the therapist could be held in contempt of court. Choice *C* is incorrect, as there is typically patient privilege surrounding therapy notes and, additionally, required documentation varies depending on the subpoena type. Choice *D* is incorrect, as if Jenna is called to testify, her responsibility is to provide impartial testimony, despite her rapport with Betty.

60. D: Clients need to sign a release of information waiver for each agency or professional the social worker will speak to on behalf of the client. A release of information waiver is also required for family members and friends of the client that the social worker may speak to.

61. D: The correct answer is Choice *D*. Free association is a psychoanalytic technique that encourages stream-of-consciousness sharing by the client. It is based on the belief that stream of consciousness allows for increased openness and a greater chance of gleaning deeper feelings. Choice *A* is incorrect, as this is a cognitive behavioral technique that takes an open, inquisitive approach to questions while also intentionally probing to uncover specific thought and behavior patterns and growth. Choice *B* is incorrect, as this is a dialectical behavioral approach that focuses on encouraging clients to be present in each moment. Choice *C* is incorrect, as this is a standard therapy technique that acknowledges to the client that their thoughts and feelings are valid and understandable.

62. C: Social work supervisors and agency leadership need to value and promote social worker safety. Policies and protocols are how this is often done. The best option here is Choice *C* because the supervisor needs to hear directly from the staff doing the home visits about their perspectives and the areas of concern before creating a new policy. Choice *A* is incorrect because it does not make sense to assume that a policy from a large urban agency will automatically meet the needs of a small rural program, and it doesn't include input from the social workers doing the home visiting. Choice *B* is incorrect because while this may be a good policy, the first step is to gather information. Choice *D* is incorrect because it does not address the concerns of worker safety.

63. B: The correct answer is Choice *B*, explain that all translation services must be done by a certified third-party interpreter. Social workers are ethically obligated to utilize a professional interpreter, not a family member or friend, for any stage of social work services including an intake assessment. Even if the client states they are comfortable with family interpreting or that is even their preference, the social worker would be obligated to obtain a qualified interpreter and explain that this is a required protocol.

64. A: When a client has multiple areas of need, the most basic human needs should be addressed first; in this case, those would be housing and food assistance. Maslow's hierarchy of human needs illustrates this concept; it posits that basic human needs for safety, shelter, and security must be addressed before anything else. While anxiety therapy, interpersonal skill development, and financial literacy may also benefit this client, basic needs must be addressed first. This model is often used by social workers to determine where to begin when working with a client who presents with multiple concerns and needs.

65. B: Kohlberg theorized that people go through three main levels of moral development, subdivided into six stages. The second level (stages three and four) is conventional morality. At this level of moral development, people conform to the rules of society. They follow the rules both to be seen as a good person by others and because they believe that rules are important to society. Choice *A* is incorrect because the preconventional level is the first level of moral development and lasts until age nine. At this level, children are focused on avoiding punishment and

seeking rewards. Choice *C* is incorrect because the final level of moral development is postconventional. At this level, people are motivated by concern for the general welfare of others and develop their own set of principles based on a broad understanding of ethics. Choice *D* is incorrect because adults can be at either the conventional or postconventional level; many adults do not make it past conventional morality.

66. B: The correct answer is Choice *B,* develop and practice coping skills to use when he is anxious and overwhelmed. In the assessment phase, one of the areas that social workers assess is whether clients have healthy coping skills. Identifying, improving, or practicing coping skills is a common treatment goal for many clients. In Margot's assessment, she was able to learn that Will is experiencing anxiety, and the coping skills he was using before the transition to college no longer apply. There is no indication that Will should leave the college setting at this time. Joining a club would not be an appropriate goal at this time, as this would not address the anxiety Will reports feeling around socializing.

67. D: Social workers will occasionally receive a request for client records to be shared as a part of a court case through a subpoena. While this can be one of the times that social workers are obligated to break confidentiality, there are steps the social worker should try before releasing the record. This should typically be done in consultation with a supervisor and in accordance with agency policy, as indicated in the example. Choice *D* is the correct answer here because the first step out of the choices listed is for the social worker to request that the court either withdraw or limit the record request. Choice *A* is incorrect because client consent may not be required in the event of a subpoena. Choice *B* is incorrect because there are steps to mitigate harm, such as requesting that the records be withdrawn or limited in scope, that the social worker should attempt before releasing the entire client record. Choice *C* is incorrect because the social worker should first ask for the court to withdraw the request; if that were denied, then requesting them to be sealed would be the next appropriate step.

68. A: Anger is a common reaction to the grief associated with a terminal diagnosis, and it is an expected reaction. This is rooted in the stages of grief model developed by Elizabeth Kubler Ross, which includes denial, anger, bargaining, depression, and acceptance. These stages are fluid rather than non-linear, and social workers should support their clients wherever they are and provide validation and normalization of these feelings. Choice *B* is incorrect because Tim's anger is warranted in this context, and there's no indication that it's chronic or detrimental to his functioning. Choice *C* is incorrect because anger is an expected reaction to a terminal prognosis, and there's no reason to suspect that it's due to a medical condition. Choice *D* is incorrect because the social worker's role with grieving patients is to meet them where they are and navigate the stages alongside them; therefore, it would not make sense to wait until he is less angry.

69. B: The correct answer is Choice *B*. In order to continue building the helping relationship with Margo, it's important that Margo's autonomy is respected and encouraged. Choice *A* is incorrect, as advice giving is not recommended and is a barrier to developing an effective helping relationship. Choice *C* is incorrect, as there is nothing to indicate that Margo is seeking therapeutic support within her relationship; she is in treatment to address her own depression.

70. A: Comorbid disorders are disorders that occur at the same time. Choice *B* is incorrect because postmorbid means happening after an illness began. If someone develops depression and then later develops alcohol use disorder (AUD), the AUD would be postmorbid. Choice *C* is incorrect because contraindicated means not indicated. For example, taking Tylenol is contraindicated for people with AUD because both alcohol and Tylenol can damage the liver. Choice *D* is incorrect because aggravated means made worse. For example, if someone is depressed and drinking makes their symptoms worse, drinking aggravates their depression.

71. C: Social workers who utilize electronic communication need to be aware of the rules surrounding its use and be sure that confidentiality is maintained. Best practice for electronic communication is to use a system that employs tools such as encryption and password protection as forms of information security, especially when sharing private health information. Therefore, Choice *C* is the best option. Choice *A* is incorrect because the social worker should

first ensure that there is a system for secure electronic communication; once that is in place, then a consent form may be appropriate. Choice *B* is incorrect because social workers can utilize electronic communication when they follow the appropriate protocols and maintain confidentiality. Choice *D* is incorrect because this decision would not be made by the insurance payors.

72. D: Cultural competence is a key value in social workers. It's the ability to understand and respect all cultures and to respectfully work with clients of different cultural backgrounds than oneself. Social workers are expected to educate themselves in areas of identity and to provide proficient services to all. The social worker should not ask the client to educate him on deaf culture; this is research he should have done himself to be able to provide appropriate care. Choices *A*, *B*, and *C* would all be examples of displaying cultural competence and providing effective service for a deaf patient.

73. A: The correct answer is Choice *A*. Jonah has well-developed ego strength. Ego strength is a psychoanalytic concept that involves resiliency and the ability to bounce back and maintain a strong sense of self even through adversity. Jonah is demonstrating this by his reaction to his grief and the loss of his wife.

74. A: The correct answer is Choice *A*. Your ethical duty as a social worker restricts you from providing treatment outside your scope of knowledge. As a social worker, you should be transparent in your limitation as a provider. Choice *B* is incorrect, as although it is always a great idea to increase your knowledge base in general, it is *more* appropriate here to get Ashley referred to someone who can begin treating her now. Choice *C* is incorrect, as Ashley's symptoms are such that she is experiencing medical concerns as a result of her disordered eating, meaning that a support group would not be a high enough level of care in this case.

75. B: The tool lacks validity, meaning that it is not measuring what it intends to measure. The fact that the tool produces consistent results means that it is measuring something, just not depressive symptoms. Choice *A* is incorrect because *reliability* means producing consistent results. The tool has reliability, but not validity. Choices *C* and *D* are incorrect because *external validity* means that the results from the study participants can be applied to the general population. *Internal validity* means that participant results are caused by the intervention and not by some other factor.

76. B: May is demonstrating signs of the immersion-emersion stage of cultural, racial, and ethnic identity development. These stages are not necessarily linear, but they represent the progression of one's identity. This stage is typically prompted by an encounter that makes the individual reflect on their own cultural, racial, or ethnic identity and leads to identity exploration and the desire to surround oneself with those of similar backgrounds. This is the behavior demonstrated by May in the question. None of the other choices specifically address racial and cultural identity development, making Choice *B* the only correct answer.

77. B: The correct answer is Choice *B*, borderline personality disorder. To meet the *DSM-5* criteria for borderline personality disorder, patients must present with at least five of the nine criteria, which are chronic feelings of emptiness, emotional instability, efforts to avoid abandonment, identity disturbance, impulsive behavior, anger, a pattern of unstable relationships, suicidal or self-harming behavior, and paranoid ideation. Common treatment goals include emotional regulation and distress tolerance skills, as these are known interventions to reduce the symptoms of BPD. Many patients with BPD also benefit from DBT treatment, like Mindy. Based on this information, BPD is the most likely diagnosis.

78. B: The correct answer is Choice *B*. The ACT model involves acknowledging the emotion (sadness), communicating the limit (no throwing allowed), and targeting an acceptable behavior (giving choices for different behaviors to choose from). Choice *A* is incorrect, as this tactic only focuses on discipline and the "communicating the limit" step of the ACT model. Choice *C* is incorrect, as this only incorporates the "acknowledging emotions" step of the ACT model. Choice *D* is incorrect, as this only focuses on the "targeting acceptable behaviors" step of the ACT model.

256

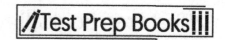

79. A: Social workers are mandated reporters, which means that they are required to break client confidentiality if there is risk of harm to the client or someone else. Suspected physical abuse of a minor falls into this category, making the correct answer Choice *A*, file a mandated report with the appropriate Child Protective Services agency. Choice *B* is incorrect because it does not immediately protect the child, and it involves the social worker conducting an investigation themselves, which is not their role. Choice *C* is incorrect because it does not protect the child, and social workers are obligated to file on suspicions of neglect or abuse, not just when there's definitive evidence. Choice *D* is incorrect because the social worker with the concerns is ethically obligated to file themselves, and they would not be liable. If a report is made in good faith, social workers are not liable in the event that the concern turns out to be false or unsubstantiated. The priority here is getting a report filed with protective services so they can investigate the potential abuse and intervene as needed.

80. C: This type of explanation is called psychoeducation, and it is an important component of social work. Psychoeducation involves providing clients with information about their problems and disorders. When clients understand the nature of their problem, its causes and effects, and the treatment options available, it helps them feel more in control and make better decisions. In the example, the client believes their schizophrenia is caused by demons, so logically the way to get better would be to remove the demons. To solve a problem effectively, a client must understand it.

Once the client understands that schizophrenia is caused by biological, psychological, and social factors, they will be more likely to pursue appropriate treatments. Choice *A* is incorrect because partializing is the process of breaking complex issues into smaller, more manageable components. Choice *B* is incorrect because psychotherapy is the general term for treatments that involve talking and listening to a client about their problems. Psychoeducation can happen during psychotherapy. Choice *D* is incorrect because assessment is the process of gathering information about a client to inform their treatment plan. In the example, the social worker is in the process of assessing the client when they provide the psychoeducational explanation about schizophrenia. Assessment is about collecting information, while psychoeducation is about providing information.

81. C: Chronic fatigue syndrome (CFS) is an example of an invisible disability. Invisible disabilities are conditions that cause problems with everyday functioning even though they are not immediately obvious to others. Invisible disabilities are common, and their impact can be devastating. People with invisible disabilities must deal with their symptoms while also dealing with reactions of confusion, anger, and disbelief from others. For example, many people with chronic pain or limited mobility need to park in a handicapped parking spot. When they exit their vehicle without a cane, crutch, or wheelchair, other people may react with anger and aggression.

Even health professionals are not always trained in identifying and understanding the impact of invisible disabilities. It is important for social workers to know how to support people with these conditions and assist them in educating their loved ones and the rest of their care team about their condition and needs. Social workers must also remember not to make assumptions about anyone's abilities, including their clients. Choice *A* is incorrect because Down's syndrome is associated with specific facial features that make it readily apparent to others. Choice *B* is incorrect because Tourette's syndrome involves vocal and/or motor tics that are apparent to others. Choice *D* is incorrect because paraplegia means that a person's lower body is paralyzed. People with paraplegia need assistive mobility devices, making their disability visible to others.

82. D: The correct answer is Choice *D*. It is advised to incorporate self-monitoring techniques earlier rather than later in treatment so as to increase the quantity of empirical data and the likelihood that the client will engage in the intervention. Choice *A* is incorrect, as waiting later to introduce this intervention could run the risk of decreasing the client's likelihood of engagement. Choice *B* is incorrect, as self-monitoring is an evidence-based intervention for anxiety. Choice *C* is incorrect, as although Kurt doesn't want the client to feel unnecessary pressure, if he wants to incorporate an intervention effectively, it's okay to set the expectation that the client should complete the homework as a therapeutic activity.

83. C: The correct answer is Choice *C*, work with Lucas to create an aftercare plan that includes how to contact other resources as needed. Termination is the final stage of social work practice. Aftercare planning is a critical part of the termination stage and includes working collaboratively with the client to create a plan that makes them feel supported after services conclude. A good aftercare plan includes information on how to reach out to additional resources if needed. Olivia cannot contact Lucas's primary care provider without a release and reason to do so, which is not indicated here. There is no indication of medication management needs at this time, as it states that Lucas has met his treatment goals. Olivia should also not provide her personal contact information, as this would not be appropriate for the client-social worker relationship, even if services are ending.

84. B: Bartering is exchanging goods or services instead of money to pay for something. It is considered unethical except in extremely limited circumstances. To justify bartering, the social worker must demonstrate that it is common practice in the community, that there is no other way to pay for services, that the client initiated the barter, and that the client will not be harmed by the arrangement. Typically, this would only occur in small, isolated communities. Choice *A* is incorrect because a dual relationship is when a social worker provides treatment to a client with whom they have another relationship, such as a friend or business partner. Choice *C* is incorrect because personal gain is when a social worker does something with a client in order to gain something for themselves. An example of personal gain would be a social worker selling a book they wrote to their clients. Choice *D* is incorrect because altruistic instinct refers to a social worker's good intentions leading them to overstep a boundary with a client, such as attending the client's birthday party.

85. A: Savannah is demonstrating signs of a behavioral regression, which is a psychological defense mechanism in which one displays behavior associated with an earlier stage of development. Savannah's behaviors of bed wetting, separation anxiety, and not sleeping through the night are typical of a child much younger than eight, but this type of regression can occur in response to a stressor. The most likely explanation is that Savannah is experiencing a regression in her behavior due to her parents' divorce.

86. C: The correct answer is Choice *C*, the majority of parents who attended were able to correctly identify adolescent mental health concerns and community resources on the post-test. Objective evidence means information that is based on facts and data, whereas subjective evidence would be rooted in emotions and opinion. A post-test is an objective method to assess how much information was learned during the program, as it implies that the parents' knowledge was tested before and after the course. The facilitator's perception is a subjective measure, parent attendance does not indicate anything about how much they are learning, and it's impossible to draw a conclusion about the impact of the course by looking at hospitalization rates of the children.

87. B: Gender dysphoria means feeling like one's gender does not match the sex they were assigned at birth. Gender dysphoria does not develop as a response to trauma; this is a pernicious myth about which social workers should be informed. The myth assumes that trauma, especially sexual trauma, causes people to develop gender dysphoria, but this is not true. On the other hand, transgender people are at a much higher risk of experiencing trauma due to stigma and discrimination. Although trauma does not change someone's gender, it does have profound effects on other aspects of their sense of self.

People who have been through traumatic events often feel unsafe in their bodies and environments. They come to view the world as being a fundamentally dangerous place. Particularly for survivors of interpersonal trauma, there may be a deep sense of betrayal. Survivors may feel like other people cannot be trusted. They may also develop a belief that they are bad or otherwise deserving of the trauma they suffered. They may feel broken, damaged, or fundamentally different from other people. It is common for trauma survivors to engage in self-harming and self-destructive behaviors in response to these alterations in self-esteem. Social workers can help trauma survivors heal their self-image by processing their trauma and challenging the maladaptive self-beliefs that came from it.

88. B: Social workers need to remain objective and professional in their relationship with clients. The client/social worker relationship is not the same as an employer relationship; therefore, the social worker should not provide a

258

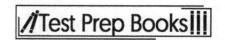

job reference for a client even if it supports a client goal. The best option here is Choice *B*, to not provide the job reference, as that is not acting in accordance with the value of integrity, but to support the client in working towards employment in a way that's appropriate. Choice *A* is incorrect because it's not ethical or appropriate to act as the client's job reference, and there are other ways to promote self-determination in this situation. Choice *C* is incorrect because getting the client a job through the social worker's friend creates a dual relationship and could cause future harm or exploitation to the client or impact the working relationship. Choice *D* is incorrect because regardless of the client's comfort with the risks, this is still an unethical choice.

89. B: The problem-solving therapeutic model describes the role of the social worker in the problem-solving process. The goal is to help clients learn how to manage problems effectively and healthily. The client must learn how to identify a problem, stressor, or negative situation; understand and manage their reactions; plan how to respond; and carry out the plan. The social worker helps by guiding the client through these steps, modeling the process, and teaching the client skills they need to solve problems on their own.

90. C: Social learning theory states that learning is the result of observation, imitation, and modeling. It views learning as an interactive and interpersonal process, which is being demonstrated by the group described in the question. Choice *A* is incorrect because this framework focuses on highlighting individual strengths and resilience as part of the change process, not learning from others. Choice *B* is incorrect because humanistic theory is rooted in individual fulfillment, not social learning. Choice *D* is incorrect because cognitive learning theory views learning as an internal process and would not focus on learning from others.

91. A: The correct answer is Choice *A*. Given that this group is several weeks in, there would have been ground rules established in the beginning of treatment surrounding acceptable behavior and conversations. Choice *B* is incorrect, as this is an overcorrection that misses the opportunity to model conflict resolution within the group setting. Choice *C* is incorrect, as ground rules would have already been established.

92. C: Social workers strive to promote client self-determination and autonomy. That should still be the case with clients who have a guardian, although it can be a bit more complicated to navigate. While it's true that the client's mother is her guardian and has decision-making authority, the role of the social worker in this situation should still be to advocate for the client's wishes, advocate for the client's voice to be heard, and promote self-advocacy. This makes Choice *C* the best response. Choice *A* is incorrect because it does not promote self-advocacy and continues to exclude the client from the decision-making process. Choice *B* is incorrect because it does not promote self-determination, even within the reality of guardianship. Choice *D* is incorrect because nothing in the example indicates that her mother is an unfit guardian requiring legal intervention; guardians act in the best interest of the client, but that does not always align with their wishes. More information would be needed before that action would be indicated.

93. B: The correct answer is Choice *B*. Social workers need to conduct their own assessment to build rapport and inform treatment planning. While collateral contact can be helpful during the assessment phase, social workers need to conduct their own assessment of each client. While Tom's response is understandable, it is important for Jan to still conduct her own assessment rather than base her treatment planning on what she has heard from others. There is no universal requirement for assessments to be conducted every two months, although it is good practice to regularly reassess. It is also not a requirement for insurance coverage.

94. B: Permissive parenting is a parenting style characterized by acting as a friend or peer rather than a parent. Permissive parents do not discipline the child, do not demand much from the child, and respond to them frequently. It is known to result in children who struggle with authority and have behavioral issues at school, as demonstrated by the child in this example. Choice *A* is incorrect because struggles with authority figures are not developmentally expected in an 8-year-old child. Choice *C* is incorrect because there is no indication that Maggie is not spending time with her child or that lack of time spent with his mother is the reason for his behavior.

95. D: Somatization is when a person's psychological distress manifests as physical symptoms. People experiencing somatization are not aware that their symptoms have a psychological origin and often seek medical treatment, only to be told that there is nothing wrong with them. The stomach aches are most likely a manifestation of the boy's distress about his parents' divorce. Choice *A* is unlikely because the doctor did a full workup to rule out gastrointestinal issues and the symptoms occurred in conjunction with the divorce. Choice *B* is unlikely because a factitious disorder involves faking symptoms or intentionally making oneself sick out of a desire for attention. The social worker believes that the boy is genuinely experiencing stomach pain, and there is no evidence that he is causing or faking his symptoms. Choice *C* is unlikely because there is no indication that the boy is experiencing health anxiety or excessive worry about his symptoms.

96. A: One of the important professional values of social workers is promoting client self-determination. If clients are competent to make their own decisions and there's not an acute risk of harm to themselves or others, social workers strive to support clients' goals and decision-making even if they do not agree. Choice *A* is the best option because the social worker talks about the risks of the client's choice and offers supportive resources but allows him to make his own decision about his care and living situation. Choice *B* is incorrect because it would breach confidentiality to contact the client's family and does not respect his choice. Choice *C* is incorrect because it may be perceived as threatening or coercive and does not promote self-determination. Choice *D* is incorrect because although those actions support the client's decision-making, social workers should be transparent about their concerns and risks and offer resources in this type of situation.

97. B: The correct answer is Choice *B*, cognitive behavioral therapy. Cognitive behavioral therapy is a common treatment for depression and anxiety and is an evidence-based approach that examines the connection between thoughts, feelings, and behavior. Prolonged exposure therapy would be incorrect, as this is a trauma treatment. Structural therapy is a family therapy model, not individual, and play therapy would be an intervention typically used for pediatric clients.

98. C: Dan is in the planning phase of treatment. Different sources provide different labels for the phases of treatment in social work (for example, planning is also referred to as goal identification and intervention planning), but there is general agreement on how the treatment process progresses. It starts with engagement, Choice *A*, which involves rapport-building, then moves to assessment, where strengths, needs, barriers, and problems are identified. Based on information gathered during engagement and assessment, a treatment plan with goals and an intervention is created. Next is implementation, also called intervention, Choice *D*, in which the intervention is used to achieve the client's goals. In the final phases, the client's progress is evaluated, Choice *B*, and the process of termination and preparing the client for life post-treatment is completed.

99. A: Navigating the needs of both elderly clients and their adult children can be a complicated balancing act for social workers in geriatric settings. They often have to play multiple roles, including carefully facilitating family meetings to respect the needs and experiences of all family members. Both Michael's desire for independence and his children's worry/frustration are normal responses to this situation, so validation is appropriate. The social worker's role is to provide support and transparency about options for his client while understanding that many elders are worried about losing their independence. Ultimately though, the decision is Michael's. There is no indication that Michael does not have decision-making capacity, and it's critical for social workers to understand that aging does not make a client incapacitated or in need of medical intervention. Financial power of attorney is not relevant to decisions about care and housing.

100. C: The correct answer is Choice *C*. Engaging Nat in a conversation about accountability can lead to a more specific conversation surrounding ways in which her husband can accept accountability and face potential consequences that Nat might be shouldering on his behalf. A great deal of the work that social workers do with the loved one of a person with addiction issues is surrounding codependency and maintaining boundaries. Empowering Nat to hold her husband accountable for his own recovery is the best intervention here. Choice *A* is incorrect, as this is advice giving and should be avoided within the client relationship. Choice *B* is incorrect, as this question concerns

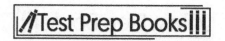

self-care, not boundary setting. Choice *D* is incorrect, as this is a presumptive statement, as Nat has not mentioned seeking divorce.

101. A: A mental status exam is a commonly used tool in social work assessment that can provide valuable insight into domains such as cognition, thought process, mood, level of insight, and risk level. This is the first step in most assessments, and it is the most appropriate first step in this scenario because Wanda needs more information about Jorge's condition to determine how to proceed. Contacting his primary care provider and making referrals for further services may be appropriate future steps, but a mental status exam must take priority for both treatment planning and safety.

102. C: Social workers need to remain aware of their personal biases and how they may impact care. It's the professional responsibility of the social worker to work through these types of issues to avoid causing harm to their clients. Choice *C* is the best option because this would be a topic that requires seeking supervision to address. Choice *A* is incorrect because it would be inappropriate and damaging to the therapeutic relationship for the social worker to share her religious bias with the client. Choice *B* is incorrect because this should be a last resort and not occur prior to seeking supervision; social workers should strive to work with all clients fairly and respectfully. Choice *D* is incorrect because the social worker needs to seek supervision and address these biases or she risks them inadvertently impacting her treatment of the client.

103. D: Denial is first so that the person has a moment to process the loss, followed by anger at others or themself for causing the loss to occur. The grieving person in desperation tries to bargain with their God or others in hopes of bringing back that which was lost. As reality sets in, the person grieves the loss and experiences sadness and depression. Resolution occurs when the person accepts the loss and is ready to move on, with an understanding that in spite of that which is gone, they will be fine in the long run. The other responses do not outline the order correctly.

104. B: Telling the story is an example of self-disclosure. Though inappropriate self-disclosure can be harmful to clients and lead to boundary violations, self-disclosure can be helpful when used correctly. This scenario describes an initial session, and the anecdote probably helped the social worker build rapport with John. Generally, self-disclosure is rarely required to achieve a treatment goal, and it should be used judiciously, if at all.

105. C: The correct answer is Choice *C*. Attempting direct professional discourse is the best first step, as Mary can directly advocate for her students' needs. Choice *A* is incorrect, as involving students and parents to support Mary's attempts to advocate is better reserved for a situation in which Mary is finding barriers to direct communication with school officials. Choice *B* is incorrect, as this would be a resolution better suited for a situation in which Mary identified this need among parents, which is not noted in this question.

106. C: The members of the Johnson family are demonstrating signs of a negative feedback loop, which is an unproductive communication pattern that maintains homeostasis and the status quo but does not foster necessary changes in family dynamics. This type of communication pattern is something that family therapists identify so they can highlight it and provide feedback to the family that will promote changes in the family system. Choice *A* is incorrect because equifinality is a concept in family systems theory that refers to the fact that multiple events can lead to the same outcome. Choice *B* is incorrect because triangulating is a behavioral pattern in family systems theory that involves avoidance and manipulation.

107. C: The question asks which of the answer choices is not a collateral source. Let's look at the answers that do qualify as collateral sources:

Collateral sources are persons outside of the client like family members, Choice *A*; police officers, Choice *B*; friends; or other medical providers, Choice *D*, who can provide information related to the client's levels of functioning, life

261

events, and other potential areas of significance in the client's treatment. Choice C is the only answer choice that is not considered a collateral source.

108. B: Social workers have a responsibility to promote ethical practice, even while working in multidisciplinary settings. Choice B is the best response because the most ethical choice is to provide education, advocate for the client, and address the bias being displayed by another provider. Choice A is incorrect because it avoids addressing the problem and does not help the client. Choice C is incorrect because the social worker should first address this situation with the provider making the inappropriate comments, and the actions in the example do not appear to meet the criteria for a report. Choice D is incorrect because client advocacy is not out of scope in this situation, and the social work values of social justice and integrity should be upheld by speaking up.

109. C: Controlled observation can best be defined as purposely targeting a client's behaviors in a pre-determined setting. A client may be observed in a setting such as a school environment or home to allow the social work practitioner to get a better understanding of how the client functions in their natural environment.

110. D: Family life education is an essential social work skill and area of practice, and it includes programs and initiatives focused on supporting and improving families. An important component of family life education is ensuring that programs are accessible and not led by the values, views, and biases of the social worker facilitating the program. Since Dave's goal is to provide services to a diverse array of families, Choice D is the least appropriate because it's specific to families who observe a particular religion and would not feel inclusive to all. While couples counseling, financial education, and parenting/caregiving courses are all examples of activities in family life education, a course with a focus on religion is the least appropriate choice here.

111. C: The correct answer is Choice C. Ramona will be given academic support designed to benefit students with intellectual disabilities. This question is testing knowledge of academic and psychological testing measures in educational settings. The WISC-V stands for the Wechsler Intelligence Scale for Children Fifth Edition, and it measures cognitive and intellectual abilities in children. Based on the information shared about Ramona's test scores, academic support would be most appropriate. While joining a group or receiving counseling may be helpful, nothing here indicates that Ramona is struggling with social anxiety or self-esteem.

112. A: The correct answer is Choice A. Although this should be touched on at the beginning of treatment, it bears exploring again with the client that matters of imminent risk require a breach of confidentiality. Choice B is incorrect, as although you'll likely need to involve the parents in mitigating risk and safety planning, not exploring this in the session with the client lacks transparency and could damage rapport. Choice C is incorrect, as this approach is more invasive than necessary, lacking consent and respect for autonomy.

113. A: This question is referring to the issue of countertransference, which is when the social worker becomes attached to their patient or engages in actions that blur the professional boundary. The social worker here is experiencing countertransference prompted by the client reminding her of her daughter. Choice A is the correct option because social workers need to be aware of this occurrence and address it in supervision to mitigate harm to their client as a result. Choice B is incorrect for two reasons: this example is discussing countertransference, not transference, and this is something that's possible to work through while maintaining the therapeutic relationship. Choice C is incorrect because countertransference is problematic regardless of whether or not it's having a positive impact on the relationship; it creates boundary issues and can cause the social worker to lose their professional objectivity, so it must always be addressed by the social worker.

114. A: Sue & Sue's stages of racial/cultural identity development include the following: conformity, dissonance, resistance and immersion, introspection, and integrative awareness. In the conformity stage, individuals hold a strong preference for the dominant culture and display negative views, shame, or embarrassment regarding their own racial and/or cultural groups. In the dissonance stage, individuals reconsider or challenge their beliefs. For the first time, they appreciate positive aspects of their own racial/cultural group. During the resistance and immersion

stage, individuals have pride in their racial and cultural group along with a preference for minority views and actively reject the views of the dominant culture. In the introspection stage, individuals become aware of the negative impact of the earlier resistance and immersion stage. At this point, they may realize that they do not actually disagree with all majority views or endorse all minority views, and they find some sort of balance. Lastly, in the integrative awareness stage, individuals are able to appreciate both their own culture and differing cultures.

115. B: The correct answer is Choice *B*. Bryan has experienced adverse childhood experiences and traumatic stress. Because of that, Bryan's behavior makes sense as a response. While it's possible Bryan is being mistreated by his foster family, nothing here suggests that. While it's possible to diagnose bipolar disorder in a young child, it's very unlikely, and Bryan's symptoms do not meet the *DSM-5* diagnostic criteria. It is unlikely to be autism spectrum disorder, as it appears that this behavior began recently, which would mean this is most likely not caused by a neurodevelopmental disorder.

116. A: Clients have a right to privacy. Social workers should only ask clients for personal information that is required for treatment. It is not appropriate to have a policy of asking all clients about their sexual history, so that should not be included in a standard intake form or first session assessment. If a social worker does require information about sexual history to provide services to a client, the social worker should use their professional judgment about when and how to solicit the information.

117. B: The correct answer is Choice *B*. It is important for Ingrid to follow up with a medical professional, given the significant physical symptoms she is sharing. Consulting with a medical professional ensures that Ingrid is getting holistic care. Choice *A* is incorrect, as the treatment goals need to be first informed by gaining complete information about the issue. Choice *C* is incorrect, as these symptoms are not indicative of a substance use issue and, furthermore, medical issues need to be ruled out. Choice *D* is incorrect, as although completing a social history may be relevant later in the assessment phase, it is not a relevant response to this situation.

118. B: This question is dealing with appropriate boundaries and the supervisor role. It is the responsibility of the social work supervisor to set boundaries and keep the supervisor role clear. The intern here appears to be using her supervisor as a therapist rather than utilizing the space to process her work with clients. The best response at this stage is for the supervisor to be clear about his concerns, set boundaries, and assist her in finding other resources to meet this need. Choice *A* is incorrect because the support being provided here is falling outside the role of a supervisor. Choice *C* is incorrect because the supervisor needs to set boundaries and expectations before considering terminating the relationship. Choice *D* is incorrect because it's not the supervisor's role to mandate mental health treatment, especially when there's no indication that her work with clients is being significantly impacted. This would not be an appropriate next step.

119. B: Mistrust of others, fear of going home, presence of marks, and frequent vomiting are indicators of physical abuse. Indicators of Choice *A*, physical neglect, may be the appearance of being malnourished, excessive sleepiness, or untreated medical problems. Victims experiencing Choice *C*, sexual abuse, may have mistrust or fear of those who bear resemblance to the abuser or may have severe alterations in behavior such as depression, anxiety, or fearfulness. Choice *D*, psychological abuse, is indicated by extreme fluctuations between aggression and passiveness, manifestation of emotional stress, people-pleasing, or developmental delays.

120. D: The correct answer is Choice *D*. You have identified that there needs to be dedicated space to process current case concerns and are establishing that this should be outside of this particular meeting. Choice *A* is incorrect, as this program is stated to be in demand; thus, there needs to be continued space to review potential new clients. Choice *B* is incorrect, as going over on time is not identified as the concern here. Choice *C* is incorrect, as given the prevalence of this concern, this issue is more systemic than individualized.

121. B: The correct answer is Choice *B*, explain that this questionnaire is given to all patients during the first session, but it's her choice to not complete this if she is not comfortable. The trauma-informed care model recommends that

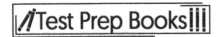

universal trauma screening be done for all patients, not just those who have reported a traumatic experience. This is to avoid clinician bias in who is screened and to acknowledge that not everyone has the words or definitions for stressors they have experienced. However, patient choice is another key component of trauma-informed care, so the correct response is for Lula to be clear and transparent about this practice and then allow Nadia to make her own decision around what she is comfortable with.

122. C: The correct answer is Choice *C*. Taking a client-centered approach to service delivery is crucial for any other positive policies and practices to work. Choices *A* and *D* are incorrect, as although these might be beneficial approaches for the program to take, it is more crucial to ensure a client-centered approach. Choice *B* is incorrect, as focusing on mandated participation is not a person-centered approach.

123. D: It would be unethical to limit Sam's right to self-determination in this case, even though the therapist may strongly disagree with his choice. According to the NASW Code of Ethics, it is only ethical to limit a client's self-determination when they "pose a serious, foreseeable, and imminent risk to themselves or others." Sam's behavior, though alarming, does not rise to this level, especially with regard to the "foreseeable and imminent risk" standard. Engaging in unhealthy behavior that is likely to have negative consequences at some point is not the same as having a suicide plan and the means to carry it out. Sam's situation is more comparable to a diabetic who continues to eat sweets.

Their behavior is damaging and unhealthy, but the social worker can't say that it will definitely and immediately cause serious harm. Choice *A* is incorrect because although drinking will almost definitely have a negative effect on Sam's health, it does not rise to the level of immediate danger required for a psychiatric hold. Similarly, Choice *B* is incorrect because a DUI in the past does not guarantee that Sam's drinking will put others at an immediate risk of harm. Choice *C* is incorrect because alcohol use disorder is both a medical and a psychological issue.

124. B: The three symptoms noted are common experiences for persons diagnosed with post-traumatic stress disorder (PTSD). Along with these, PTSD survivors can be triggered into a state of anxiety or panic when exposed to stimuli associated with the trauma, such as smells, sensations, or sights. Those diagnosed with PTSD may be easily startled, and they can even have periods in which they feel they are re-experiencing the traumatic event. Choice *A*, claustrophobia, is a fear of small spaces. Choice *C* is incorrect; although persons with borderline personality disorder (BPD) may have a history of PTSD, the common symptoms of BPD don't align with the ones provided. Choice *D* can be a symptom of PTSD, but it is generally seen as a completely different diagnosis with a different set of criteria.

125. C: Amanda is demonstrating signs of unhealthy body image, which can lead to challenges such as social withdrawal, low self-esteem, and comparison to others. It can have a negative impact on many aspects of one's life; therefore, Choice *C* is correct because the social worker should recognize the impact of body image issues and make this the focus of treatment. Choice *A* is incorrect because while body image issues can be common in young adults, they are distressing and requires attention; they are not part of a normal stage of development that resolves on its own. Choice *B* is incorrect because while body image issues can be a risk factor for an eating disorder, they do not always occur simultaneously. The issues described in the example do not describe an eating disorder; therefore, this would be an inappropriate escalation of care by the social worker.

126. B: The correct answer is Choice *B*, Emily is assessing the family's current support systems, resources, and potential gaps in support. An ecomap is a social work assessment tool that gathers information on an individual or family's connections and resources, as well as the strengths and weaknesses of those connections. It is useful for any assessment but would be especially helpful here, as building connections is important for new mothers and young children. Ecomaps are not required for assessment for this population or for insurance purposes. If Joanna is not sharing information on Maggie's father, and he is not a part of the family system she is meeting with, it would not be appropriate for Emily to push for more information at this time.

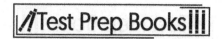

127. A: The correct answer is Choice *A,* conduct a thorough risk assessment to determine the severity of the threat. Social workers are obligated to assess the risk of threats made by clients to harm others and respond accordingly. If there is a threat that is determined to be serious and valid, social workers are obligated to break confidentiality to warn the potential victims or contact law enforcement. While that may be the case here, Mickey first needs to conduct a risk assessment to determine next steps and interventions. It would not be appropriate to contact the school guidance counselor at this time, as there is no release of information, and asking them to move classes would not be included under the duty to warn act that allows for confidentiality to be broken in this circumstance.

128. A: The correct answer is Choice *A.* There is a great variance in eligibility for public assistance for immigrant families depending on the jurisdiction, particularly given that the political climate can influence policy and lawmakers to make changes regularly. Choice *B* is incorrect, as refugee status does not determine public assistance eligibility. Choices *C* and *D* are incorrect because they are dependent on jurisdiction.

129. C: Social workers are obligated to promote safe workplaces and intervene when they become aware of colleagues' unsafe or concerning behavior. Choice *C* is correct because the Code of Ethics mandates that social workers in this situation should first attempt to address the situation with their colleague directly if at all possible. Choice *A* is incorrect because the social worker should try to speak to the colleague prior to escalating the intervention. Choice *B* is incorrect because the social worker needs to respond to this unethical and concerning behavior regardless of whether it's a pattern or an isolated incident. Choice *D* is incorrect because social workers are ethically obligated to intervene regardless of their role as supervisors or colleagues in this type of scenario.

130. C: Vygotsky believed individuals are significantly shaped by the formal and informal social groups in which they interact. These institutions teach values, how to behave in relationships, how closely one must follow rules and laws, and, in general, what is important in life. A child growing up hungry and neglected will have a very different view of life than one who is cherished and provided with love, support, and material needs. Choices *A, B,* and *D* all impact the quality of one's life, but Vygotsky leaned toward a more global explanation of social development that encompasses multiple social factors.

131. C: Perception of family relationships, mental functioning, occupation, and social class are elements that help guide diagnosis. Finding questions about what is going on in the client's life and desired outcomes from therapy may help guide the diagnostic process. Choice *A,* the assessment process, focuses on the person-in-environment (PIE) and is an ongoing part of client treatment that involves review of the client's situation. Choice *B,* formal observation, is where specific data is collected on the client in a predetermined setting. Choice *D,* life span development, refers to physical and cognitive alterations throughout a client's lifespan.

132. B: The correct answer is Choice *B.* Conducting an assessment to first establish a baseline for cultural competency is important to help consider next steps. Choice *A* is incorrect, as this is an overcorrection that does not attempt to engage the staff person in conflict resolution first. Choice *C* is incorrect, as this circumvents conducting an assessment to first ascertain the level of competency for this individual. Intervention cannot come before assessment.

133. C: The correct answer is Choice *C,* connect Amelia with a medical provider to assess if she is medically stable and rule out a medical cause for her symptoms. Regardless of the cause, a medical doctor needs to first assess Amelia due to the reports of significant weight loss and losing consciousness. Social workers need to be able to identify when a medical need must be addressed before other types of care can begin, as is the case here. A medical provider will be able to assess if there is a medical reason for these symptoms as well as if Amelia is medically stable enough for treatment. Treatment for eating disorders can be provided in either an outpatient or inpatient setting, but it will depend on if the patient is medically stable and the level of risk. Creating a treatment plan for eating disorder treatment or providing psychoeducation may be necessary in the future, but the medical concerns need to take precedence before further assessment and treatment planning can occur.

134. B: The goal of family therapy is typically to help families return to a state of homeostasis or equilibrium. Families are a system, and they can engage in behavior to return the system to its equilibrium after a change. It is normal for a new baby to upset the family dynamic, especially when there are older siblings whose routines and parental interactions change as a result of the addition to the family. The best response for the social worker is to validate these normal feelings and assist the family in finding stability again. Choice *A* is incorrect because family therapy views the family as a system that should be treated together, not in individual therapy. Choice *C* is incorrect because the children's responses are normal given the circumstances and do not suggest enmeshment.

135. B: Social workers follow many professional values as outlined in the Code of Ethics, including the importance of human relationships, competence, integrity, social justice, and the dignity and worth of the person. Choice *B* is correct because this situation challenges the social work value of integrity; the social worker is faced with a choice to behave in a way that's not aligned with ethical practice. Social workers are expected to maintain integrity in their work with clients, their interactions with colleagues, and their general behavior.

136. A: The components of the biopsychosocial assessment drive the data pertinent to designing interventions that match the client's problems, such as client strengths and risk factors. In turn, these strengths and risk factors help guide the practitioner in the selection of a theoretical model to apply (in an effort to enhance client functioning and improve the client's overall well-being).

137. C: Social workers must understand the dynamics of violence, power, and control and how these impact their clients who have experienced abuse. Choice *C* is correct because it includes providing emotional support, allowing the client to make their own decisions, and providing accurate safety information regarding the dynamics of violence. This is the social worker's best response in this situation. It is common in intimate partner violence for the perpetrator to be apologetic and promise that it will never happen again following an episode of violence. However, previous violent behavior is one of the biggest indicators for future violence. Choice *A* is incorrect because couples therapy is not indicated when there is intimate partner violence. Choice *B* is incorrect because it includes the incorrect statement that violence rarely escalates after a first offense. While the social worker cannot tell their client what to do, she should provide appropriate support and education around the dynamics and patterns of violence. Choice *D* is incorrect because the social worker should not tell her adult client what to do, and this is not a situation that calls for mandated reporting based on the information provided.

138. A: Metacommunication means communicating about communication. It involves bringing awareness to the way we communicate rather than the information we are communicating. Developing this skill can help clients express themselves more effectively, understand other peoples' reactions, and reduce or prevent misunderstanding and miscommunication. Metacommunication is particularly helpful in conflict resolution situations because often the conflict has as much to do about how something is said as what is actually said. Choice *B* is incorrect because empathic communication is about being accepting, genuine, and offering unconditional positive regard. Choice *D* is incorrect because structured communication refers to planned communication, such as a formal interview with preplanned questions.

139. C: The correct answer is Choice *C*. Bethany should prioritize giving an overview of what Jeremy is currently dealing with and relevant historical data, coupled with ideas for how to intervene with him. Choices *A* and *B* are incorrect, as overemphasis on one topic or another can skew the case presentation toward Bethany's own biases or oversights. Choice *D* is incorrect, as the nature of case presentations are not to be overly detailed but to offer an overview and explore interventions.

140. B: Objective data is correct. The social worker collects objective data to determine the facts in a client's situation. Subjective data, Choice *C*, is when the client provides their perspective on what happened and the experiences felt. Controlled data, Choice *A*, and qualitative data, Choice *D*, are not relevant to the context of the question.

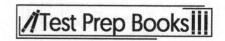

141. D: The correct answer is Choice *D*. Psychiatric diagnosis is not required for every patient to be able to receive effective services and treatment. Social workers utilize the *DSM-5* for many purposes, including accurate diagnostic assessments, having shared language and diagnostic criteria across different disciplines, and billing code purposes. However, social workers also advocate to not over-pathologize patients and their behavior and take a person-in-environment approach. Not every situation or patient requires a psychiatric diagnosis to be in need of social work services.

142. A: The correct answer is Choice *A*. Given the couple's admittance that they are struggling with how to communicate effectively, one of the best tools at Trey's disposal is to engage in role-play scenarios in sessions to model ways of effective communication. Choice *B* is an intervention best utilized later in treatment when it has been established that the couple has been able to identify methods for effective communication. Choice *C* is incorrect, as this deflects from the original issue established: ineffective communication within the partnership.

143. B: While social workers look at an individual's clinical, psychosomatic, and environmental history, these are small components that make up a full spectrum of influences in the individual's history. The biopsychosocial lens allows the social worker to look at biological, psychological, and social factors together to make reliable diagnoses and plan treatments.

144. D: When people are experiencing chronic poverty and housing insecurity that makes them unable to meet their basic needs, it can be very difficult for them to maintain other aspects of their life such as healthcare. Social workers must be able to recognize the impact of poverty and homelessness and intervene accordingly. In this example, the best choice is to help the client address his basic needs and help the medical team understand Carlos's barriers to engaging in his healthcare treatment; hopefully this will help them understand how to provide more accessible care. While denial is an expected response to a serious diagnosis, Choice *A* is incorrect because the social worker should address the needs identified. Choice *B* highlights activities that may be appropriate in the future but should not be the next step. Choice *C* is incorrect because although there are some risk factors present, Carlos is not demonstrating any acute symptoms; therefore, a risk assessment would not be the next step. Furthermore, he does not appear to warrant mandated care.

145. C: The correct answer is Choice *C*, when Jen and the client have evaluated if treatment was successful, and the goals were met. Evaluation and monitoring of treatment goals is a critical step in the social work treatment process. Social workers need to work collaboratively with their clients to create a system to measure if the interventions are effective and if both parties agree the treatment goals are being met.

146. C: The young man would benefit most from cognitive behavioral therapy (CBT). CBT teaches clients how their thoughts, feelings, and behaviors influence each other. Specifically, CBT teaches clients how changing their thoughts by challenging cognitive distortions can help them feel better and act the way they intend to. The young man in the example is experiencing distress and exhibiting multiple cognitive distortions (all-or-nothing thinking, overgeneralizing, and catastrophizing). CBT would help him reframe the cognitive distortions into more realistic and accurate thoughts, which should reduce his anxiety. For example, the man might think, "if I don't get this job, I'll never succeed in life, and I should just give up."

CBT would help him consider the evidence and reframe this thought to something like, "if I don't get this job, I will be disappointed, but there will be many other opportunities for me to pursue, and eventually I will probably find something that is a good fit." Choice *A* is incorrect because EMDR therapy is used to process traumatic events and reduce the accompanying trauma symptoms. Choice *B* is incorrect because psychodynamic therapy explores childhood experiences and unconscious motivations and drives. Choice *D* is incorrect because although the client is living with his parents, there is no indication that family dynamics are contributing to his difficulties.

147. A: The correct answer is Choice *A*, disruptive mood dysregulation disorder. This diagnosis is most appropriate based on the *DSM-5* criteria. Disruptive mood dysregulation disorder was added in the latest edition of the DSM and

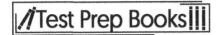

includes diagnostic criteria of inappropriate anger outbursts, opposition, and chronic irritability. Children must be at least 6 years old to be diagnosed, but their symptoms have to have started prior to age 10 and be present for at least one year. This criteria has been met by the information provided in the vignette, making this the most likely diagnosis. While some of these symptoms overlap with a diagnosis of bipolar disorder, disruptive mood dysregulation disorder is more likely based on the child's age. It would not be schizoaffective disorder because there would need to be symptoms of psychosis present along with the mood symptoms, such as paranoia, delusions, hallucinations, disorganized speech or behavior, or negative symptoms. Lina would also not meet criteria for antisocial personality disorder because it cannot be diagnosed in a child as young as she is and because she does demonstrate some remorse for her behavior.

148. B: Cognitive behavioral approaches conceptualize a relationship among thoughts, feelings, and behaviors such that unwanted feelings and behaviors are caused by distorted, inaccurate, and overly negative thoughts, assumptions, and beliefs. The goal of cognitive behavioral therapy (CBT) is to teach clients to change the thought patterns that drive how they feel and behave. People are often not aware of their own limiting beliefs and habits of thinking. CBT first teaches clients to become aware of their thought patterns through self-monitoring, often including homework. Then, the therapist works with the client to practice challenging unhelpful thoughts, assumptions, and beliefs and replacing them with statements that are more accurate and helpful. Choice *A* is incorrect because psychiatry, not psychotherapy, conceptualizes problems as resulting from chemical imbalances in the brain. Choice *C* is incorrect because although CBT can be used to treat trauma, it focuses on the thoughts, assumptions, and beliefs related to the trauma. This is different from psychotherapies like EMDR, which see the trauma itself as the source of the problem and processing the trauma as the solution. Choice *D* is incorrect because CBT focuses on solving problems in the present without going deeply into past experiences.

149. A: The client can be said to have a paraphilia, which is a strong sexual interest in anything other than sex with a mature, consenting partner. Paraphilias are common, and if they do not distress or harm, then they are not considered disordered in any way. If the sexual interest causes harm or distress to the client or others, it would be considered a paraphilic disorder, Choice *B*. Voyeuristic disorder, Choice *C*, is an example of a paraphilic disorder that involves secretly watching a person take off their clothes or engage in sexual behavior. It can also involve secretly filming or photographing an unsuspecting person, which is illegal in many places. Voyeuristic disorder is harmful because the person being watched or photographed has not given consent. It is only diagnosed in people over the age of 18 to differentiate a serious disorder from age-appropriate curiosity typical of puberty. Choice *D* is incorrect because exhibitionistic disorder involves sexual interest in exposing oneself to unsuspecting others.

150. D: Family violence is known to be cyclical and repeat across family generations. It is not uncommon for people who experienced violence as children to engage in those behaviors as adults, especially if they did not receive adequate treatment. Overwhelm, limited support, lack of conflict management skills, and financial stressors all further increase the risk of physical abuse towards children; therefore, addressing these concerns would be the primary goal of a child welfare social worker in this scenario. While psychiatric treatment may or may not benefit Angie, the information provided suggests that the reasons for the violence are due to her own history and lack of healthy coping and communication skills, not a psychiatric diagnosis. Therefore, Choice *D* would be the least effective strategy to reduce the risk of continued violence.

151. D: The correct answer is Choice *D*. Reading these stories is an example of symbolic modeling, as it involves using pictures and words to model the desired behavior for the child. Choice *A* is incorrect, as live modeling would entail a live person, such as the social worker, modeling the pro-social behavior in real life. Choice *B* is incorrect, as participant modeling would involve first the social worker modeling the behavior and then encouraging the child to do the same. Choice *C* is incorrect, as covert modeling would involve the social worker prompting the child to use their imagination to create a situation in which this pro-social behavior is enacted.

152. A: When using partializing techniques to help clients prioritize their treatment goals, Maslow's hierarchy of needs is a useful theoretical construct. Maslow's hierarchy conceptualizes human needs in the form of a pyramid

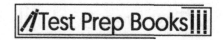

with the most basic on the bottom and the most complex at the top. To build a strong and stable pyramid, you start at the foundation and move up as each level is completed. The base of the pyramid includes physiological needs like food, air, and water. The next level is safety, then love and belonging, followed by esteem. At the top of the pyramid is self-actualization. If a client is facing food insecurity and wants to make new friends, then food insecurity should be the priority. Choice *B* is incorrect because Erikson's stages of psychosocial development describe human development in terms of eight life stages, each defined by a specific conflict that needs to be resolved to progress to the next stage successfully. The theory can help social workers understand what concerns a client is likely to have based on their life stage, as well as identify areas where a client is more or less advanced than expected. However, the theory has been criticized for cultural and gender bias and would not be particularly helpful in prioritizing the goals of an individual client. Choice *C* is incorrect because Freud's stages of psychosexual development describe human personality development in terms of five stages of sexual maturation. The theory has always been controversial and would not be helpful in prioritizing client goals. Choice *D* is incorrect because systems theory describes how systems function and interact. It can help in understanding how changes in one part of a system can affect the rest of the system; for example, when a child develops a serious illness, the rest of the family will be affected. Systems theory is very important in social work, but it does not directly address how goals should be prioritized.

153. B: Couple development theory indicates that this couple is in a normal stage of couple development known as differentiation. This stage follows the bonding or honeymoon period. The couple realizes that they are separate people, which creates conflict. In order to continue to develop a healthy relationship, the couple must find a way to accept each other and navigate the conflict. Normalizing this experience and providing support to help them move through this relationship stage is the most appropriate social work intervention.

154. A: The correct answer is Choice *A*. An important technique for anger management is awareness of one's emotional and physical feelings at the times that anger is most often getting triggered. Often, feelings of exhaustion can place a person at a higher vulnerability for emotional triggers. Choice *B* is incorrect, as moving into intervention without exploration of the situation with Tim would be premature. Choice *C* is incorrect, as this is non-person centered and is likely to be a triggering and ineffective approach.

155. B: The correct answer is Choice *B*, obtain medical care for Lewis and file an urgent elder protective services report. Social workers must be able to assess risk and prioritize needs appropriately during a crisis situation. The first step is for Julie to obtain urgent medical care for Lewis, as he has had a fall, and she is unable to assess his medical status as a social worker. This situation also warrants an elder protective services report, as Lewis is considered a vulnerable person based on his age and dementia diagnosis. Therefore, Julie is obligated to report the neglect and safety concerns she has observed to the appropriate protective services agency. This is a situation in which social workers can break confidentiality because there is risk of harm to the client. While calling Lewis's daughter may be a part of future safety planning, there is not enough information to know if this would be appropriate and would not be the first step. Julie needs to obtain medical care and file a protective report regardless of whether or not she can get in contact with the caregiver. It would not be appropriate to simply increase support and resources to the caregiver in this situation, as Julie has an obligation as a mandated reporter to file an elder protective report regarding the observed neglect.

156. D: Group therapy is beneficial for a wide range of clients and issues. It is effective for people of all ages, including children, Choice *A*, and many types of disorders and difficulties. Substance use disorder treatment often includes a group therapy component, Choice *B*. Group therapy has been shown to be extremely effective for trauma, Choice *C*. Different groups will be appropriate for different people. In general, group therapy is contraindicated for certain types of clients and situations. It is not recommended for clients in crisis or those experiencing suicidality because these clients require a higher level of care. Group therapy requires active participation, which certain disorders can make difficult. For example, group therapy is not generally beneficial for people with active psychosis, paranoia, or severe personality disorders that make interaction difficult.

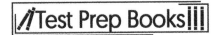

157. C: A parent's mental health condition can impact the entire family system, especially if symptoms are not managed. Children in this situation often display their own behavior or mood changes, and often there is an impact on their school performance or relationships. The best way to support the family is to provide services for the whole family and increase the number of resources available. The parent's needs must be addressed to allow for sustainable changes that will benefit the children; therefore, only treating the child's anxiety is not the best choice. Choice A is incorrect because although a mandated report could be warranted, further assessment is needed first, and a report for neglect would not be the next step. The social worker should support this family, explore the situation further, and provide the necessary resources before taking that type of action because there is no definite evidence of neglect.

158. A: The correct answer is Choice A, identify who is Kevin's medical power of attorney and support them in their role. Social workers need to understand who they are legally able to talk to in a situation such as this. Since the patient is no longer able to speak for himself or make decisions, the social worker needs to identify which family member is the legal decision maker. It will be that person's decision whom to include moving forward, so identifying this person is the first step. While supporting other family members and providing education may be useful in the future, the social worker first needs to identify who can be included in the decision-making and information-sharing process in this highly sensitive situation.

159. B: The correct answer is Choice B. Your role as a social worker is to utilize confrontation when you notice a significant change in the client that deviates from their established goals. By confronting, you are encouraging the client to be vocal about the source of their irritation. Choice A is incorrect, as empathy would be noticing and acknowledging out loud how the client was feeling. Choice C is incorrect, as clarification would be asking the client to reword or explain what they were saying to you. Choice D is incorrect, as reflective listening would be reflecting back what a client was communicating to you in a nonjudgmental way.

160. D: The correct answer is Choice D, needs assessment. A needs assessment is a tool utilized in program development and is a way to identify the strengths and resources of a community as well as the gaps and areas of need. Conducting a needs assessment would allow Kyle to learn more about this community, identify strengths, and highlight areas of need prior to designing a program. This is done so that the program actually meets the community's needs and does not duplicate what already exists. None of the other options would be relevant here, as a genogram is a tool to examine an individual's family relationships, collateral contact is the process of contacting other providers or systems in a client's life, and a risk assessment is a tool to measure risk factors demonstrated by a client.

161. D: The correct answer is Choice D. In order to move forward to establishing goals and breaking the goals up into tasks, you need to explore the context surrounding the student's concerns. Choice A is incorrect, as this is unnecessary when using a task-centered approach. Choice C is incorrect, as you need more information surrounding the presenting problem first. Choice B is incorrect, as the formulation of tasks comes after goals are established.

162. C: Co-occurring disorders occur when there is a dual diagnosis of both a mental health condition and a substance use disorder. This is a very common pattern, and it can be difficult to treat. It also tends to create distress for the patient experiencing both sets of symptoms. Nick needs the support and understanding of his parents regarding this diagnosis, so the best response is for the social worker to provide education about it. Co-occurring disorders can impact the entire family system, so it's also appropriate to recommend services for the whole family. Choice A is incorrect because although some rebellious behavior is characteristic of adolescence, Nick's symptoms and the presence of co-occurring disorders are not a normal aspect of development. Choice B is incorrect because the parenting style is not the presenting problem here, and the stress of the parents is understandable in this instance.

163. C: The correct answer is Choice C. This goal meets SMART criteria in that it is specific, measurable, attainable, relevant, and time-bound. Choice A is incorrect, as this goal lacks both specific and measurable components. Choice

270

B is incorrect, as this is not relevant to the specific activity that Eliza has identified that she is looking to increase. Self-confidence is not noted as a concern in this example.

164. C: The correct answer is Choice *C*, work with Sheila to make a plan to monitor and evaluate treatment efficacy. Social workers need to work collaboratively with their clients to determine if the treatment goals and interventions are being addressed adequately. Social workers need to work together with their client to design a system to evaluate and monitor efficacy. A supervisor may be helpful, but they can't tell Nina whether or not treatment is effective. Reading case notes will also not necessarily provide this information. While having Sheila keep a journal of her behavior may be a helpful tool in this process, evaluation should be collaborative, and Nina should not tell her client what she has to do.

165. A: This question is discussing the dynamics of crisis intervention theory in social work practice. The correct answer is Choice *A* because it focuses on stabilization and addresses the acute symptoms of crisis, which are the core of a crisis intervention approach. Social workers implementing crisis intervention care need to focus on effective and concrete steps that return the client to their previous state of functioning. While the actions described in Choices *B* and *C* may help this client, they are not considered to be a part of a crisis intervention approach because they are targeting chronic and longstanding issues.

166. B: The correct answer is Choice *B*. It is normal for clients to feel worried about a relapse in symptoms. Jesiah can help ease the discomfort by starting with a reduction in therapy sessions to see how Karen tolerates this. If she continues to maintain progress, this is a good sign that she is ready for termination. Choice *A* is incorrect, as Karen's strong emotional reaction to the idea of termination suggests that a gradual reduction is more appropriate. Choice *C* is incorrect, as movement forward should still be explored, given Karen's completion of treatment goals and maintained progress. Choice *D* is incorrect, as there is no indication in this example that there are new concerns to address through treatment.

167. B: Substance use disorders create challenging family dynamics that impact the entire family system, not just the individual with the addiction. It is critical to provide services and support to the entire family system as a part of the recovery process. Courtney is also a caregiver; therefore, the social worker should educate her on the importance of taking care of her own needs as part of caring for others. The best response for the social worker here is to provide validation but also education on why services for Courtney are necessary. Choice *A* is incorrect because the entire family needs support, not just the children. Choice *C* is incorrect because this approach is blaming, not supportive, and it's not true that family therapy would be mandated. Choice *D* is incorrect because it's an incomplete answer; while highlighting her resiliency makes sense, the answer choice does not address the needs expressed in the example.

168. D: The correct answer is Choice *D*, contact emergency services, explain the situation, and request an immediate wellness check. In cases where there is significant risk of harm to the patient or others, social workers are both allowed to and obligated to break confidentiality to take the appropriate steps to promote safety. There are enough safety concerns shared here to warrant contacting emergency services, as the client has verbalized thoughts of suicide with a plan and access to lethal means. A history of depression and a suicide attempt, as well as a recent hospitalization, are additional red flags. While documentation is always necessary, Maureen needs to take further steps here than just attempting to call Leon back. This situation is too urgent to engage in collateral contact, and it's not necessary, as there is enough risk documented here to involve emergency services. Maureen should not go to the home alone due to the safety concerns and urgency of this situation.

169. C: The correct answer is Choice *C*. Blaming themselves for the death, noting somatic symptoms, and embarrassment are all usual reactions for school-aged children. Choice *A* is incorrect, as this option is more commonly what one might see a teenager exhibit. Choice *B* is incorrect, as this is reflective of a preschooler's typical reaction to grief.

170. A: The correct answer is Choice *A*, solution-focused therapy. The miracle question utilized by Jared is a common technique utilized in solution-focused therapy, which is a concrete and practical model often used for time-limited treatment. It is goal directed and focuses primarily on coming up with solutions that can be implemented rather than spending time examining history and the problems in depth.

ASWB Clinical Practice Test #3

To keep the size of this book manageable, save paper, and provide a digital test-taking experience, the 3rd practice test can be found online. Scan the QR code or go to this link to access it:

testprepbooks.com/bonus/aswbclinical

The first time you access the test, you will need to register as a "new user" and verify your email address.

If you have any issues, please email support@testprepbooks.com

Index

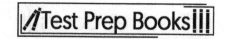

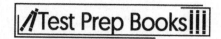

Dear ASWB Clinical Test Taker,

Thank you for purchasing this study guide for your ASWB Clinical exam. We hope that we exceeded your expectations.

Our goal in creating this study guide was to cover all of the topics that you will see on the test. We also strove to make our practice questions as similar as possible to what you will encounter on test day. With that being said, if you found something that you feel was not up to your standards, please send us an email and let us know.

We have study guides in a wide variety of fields. If you're interested in another one of our products, try searching for it on Amazon or send us an email!

Thanks Again and Happy Testing!
Product Development Team
info@studyguideteam.com

FREE Test Taking Tips Video/DVD Offer

To better serve you, we created videos covering test taking tips that we want to give you for FREE. **These videos cover world-class tips that will help you succeed on your test.**

We just ask that you send us feedback about this product. Please let us know what you thought about it—whether good, bad, or indifferent.

To get your **FREE videos**, you can use the QR code below or email freevideos@studyguideteam.com with "Free Videos" in the subject line and the following information in the body of the email:

a. The title of your product

b. Your product rating on a scale of 1-5, with 5 being the highest

c. Your feedback about the product

If you have any questions or concerns, please don't hesitate to contact us at info@studyguideteam.com.

Thank you!

Made in the USA
Middletown, DE
28 July 2024

58109601R00163